THE MATHEMATICS OF PERSONAL FINANCE:

USING CALCULATORS AND COMPUTERS

E. Thomas Garman

&

Jing J. Xiao

DAME
Publications, Inc.

Artist & Proofreader: **Pamela S. Porter**
Computer Graphics: **Amanda Austin**
Cover Design: **Amanda Austin**
Cover Photos: **©Corel Professional Photos**. Images may have been combined and/or modified to produce final cover art.

© **DAME PUBLICATIONS, INC.—1997**
  Houston, TX
  e-mail: dame.publications@worldnet.att.net

ISBN 0-87393-533-0
Library of Congress Catalog No. 97-67118

Printed in the United States of America

Table of Contents at a Glance

Table of Contents

Chapter 7   **Financial Statements and Budgeting**   **119**

Chapter 8   **Using Financial Ratios**   **141**

Chapter 9   **Consumer Credit Mathematics**   **155**

Chapter 10 **The Mathematics of Income and Estate Taxes** **173**

Chapter 11 **Planned Purchasing Math** **197**

PREFACE

The Mathematics of Personal Finance is a book designed primarily to serve college students who have just taken an introductory course in personal finance. It also will help people preparing for professional certification examinations in personal financial planning, insurance, credit counseling, and financial counseling learn to master concepts and formulas that are required on such exams. The book is uniquely focused on personal finance, rather than business, economics, or corporate finance

The purpose of *The Mathematics of Personal Finance* is to emphasize the practice of mathematical concepts used in personal finance. It features mathematical computations to be performed manually using algebraic formulas, employing time value of money tables, manipulating a financial calculator, and utilizing a computer spreadsheet program. In addition, the book introduces the use of Internet sources in personal finance and provides numerous useful web sites on related topics.

GOALS

The goals of *The Mathematics of Personal Finance* are twofold: (1) to enhance a person's mathematical, computer, and information search skills relevant to his or her success in personal finance, and (2) to help develop a person who is confident and proficient when using the mathematics of personal finance.

This is accomplished by providing dozens of math illustrations requiring basic mathematics, algebraic computations, time value of money tables, financial calculators, and computer spreadsheet programs. The book expressly features the use of financial calculators. In addition, *The Mathematics of Personal Finance* offers a number of suggestions regarding utilization of advanced technologies, such as computer software in personal finance and computer network resources.

Each chapter helps the reader answer the following questions:

- What personal finance concepts are involved in a particular subject, such as credit, housing or stocks?
- What math concepts are fundamental to a particular personal finance subject, such as college expenses or mutual funds?
- How are the math calculations performed?
- How should the calculated results be interpreted?

STYLE AND FORMAT

The Mathematics of Personal Finance assumes the reader has some familiarity with the concepts and principles of personal finance. Accordingly, the book is extremely concise in providing narrative text on the traditional topics in personal finance. What the book does quite thoroughly is to offer numerous examples (nearly 200) and exercises (over 400) to help a person develop confidence and proficiency in the mathematics of personal finance. Still, each chapter of the book is relatively short (approximately 20 pages).

Each chapter of the book includes: Overview, Examples of Mathematical Concepts, Information and Computing Resources, Exercise Problems, Endnotes, and Selected References. Also, *The Mathematics of Personal Finance* has two appendices.

Overview

This section provides a concise narrative description of the personal finance and math concepts in a chapter. It offers the fundamental logic that a reader needs to comprehend the subject matter of each personal finance chapter. Typically comprised of two pages of narrative, this overview section features a number of **key definitions** which are highlighted in **bold print**. Concepts that are required on professional certification exams are included.

Examples of Mathematical Concepts

This section is the heart of *The Mathematics of Personal Finance*. It typically includes six to ten carefully selected math examples to display the formulas of the concepts introduced in the chapter.

Each math example section is clearly labeled with a **descriptive heading**. Each example follows the same format: **formula**, **definitions** of terms in the formula, **math example**, **solution**, and **interpretation**. By beginning each math example with the formula, the reader is led directly to and through the mathematics of a concept before confronting any contextual material in personal finance. As a result, the initial emphasis is focused upon the personal finance mathematics. The objective here is for the reader to simply understand the mathematics.

The types of mathematical examples in the chapters include those requiring solutions via (1) performing algebraic formulas, (2) employing time value of money tables, (3) manipulating a financial calculator, and (4) utilizing a computer spreadsheet program.

Four commonly available and inexpensive calculators are featured in the illustrations: (1) Hewlett-Packard's HP-10B, (2) Sharp's EL-733A, (3) Texas Instrument's BA-II PLUS, (4) Hewlett-Packard's HP-12C.

Following the solution to the example is a section on **interpretation**. Here additional **definitions** and **explanations** are offered to place the mathematical concept in **full perspective**. When studying the mathematics of personal finance, it is vital that the reader not only comprehend **"how" to perform** the mathematics, but also to appreciate **"why"** the solution fits the context and perspective of knowledge about personal financial management. To help the reader truly understand both the mathematics and the personal finance concepts involved, some interpretation sections are 15, 20 or even 30 lines in length.

Information and Computing Resources

This section lists useful sources of information related to the subject of the chapter. It includes books, magazine articles, and pamphlets. It also lists **computer software programs** for (1) general personal finance, and (2) computer programs for specific topics in personal finance. In addition, numerous useful **web site addresses** are provided, along with brief introductions, for various topics in personal finance available on the Internet.

Exercise Problems

This section typically presents 20 to 40 math **problems/questions** to allow readers to practice the mathematical concepts in the chapter. Each section of exercise problems is clearly labeled with a **descriptive heading** exactly like the headings within the chapter.

The types of mathematical examples in the chapters parallel the examples in the narrative portion of the chapters, thus, they include questions requiring solutions via (1) performing algebraic formulas, (2) employing time value of money tables, (3) manipulating a financial calculator, and/or (4) utilizing a computer spreadsheet program. Some questions are suitable for **in-class discussion**.

In addition, most chapters have a few questions titled **"out-of-class exercise."** Here the reader is offered the opportunity to personalize his or her learning. Some of these questions ask for **value judgments**, others request an **information search** in the library, and still others invite **exploration on the Internet**.

Endnotes

This section is located at the end of each chapter. Each endnote provides **deeper insights** to the topic being examined. They are omitted from the actual text because inclusion would break the continuous readability and logic of the chapter content. Often the endnotes offer **expansive explanations** of key concepts which should be of particular interest to a serious student of the mathematics of personal finance.

Selected References

The selected references section provides a brief listing of academic research and relevant literature on the personal finance and mathematical topics of each chapter. The sources of papers often are from academic journals, such as *Financial Counseling and Planning* and *Financial Services Review*. Useful articles from the popular literature, such as *Money* and *Kiplinger's Personal Finance Magazine*, are also listed.

Appendix A: Present and Future Value Tables

Because many of the mathematical problems in personal finance involve decisions about money values at varying points in time, four present and future value tables are provided: (1) present value of asset, (2) future value of asset, (3) present value of annuity, and (4) future value of annuity. These tables expand upon the explanations and examples in Chapter 4, The Time Value of Money, as well as explanations in other chapters. This appendix provides more than two dozen illustrations on how to use the present and future value tables.[1]

---

[1]This appendix is copyrighted by the Houghton Mifflin Company. It appears in Garman, E. T., & Forgue, R. E. (1997), *Personal Finance*, Boston: Houghton Mifflin Company, pages A2 - A11. For information, call 1-800-733-1717.

Appendix B: Estimating Social Security Benefits

This appendix allows readers to accurately estimate Social Security benefits, including retirement, survivor's, and disability.[2]

OVERVIEW OF CONTENTS

The contents have been arranged so that as each new topic is introduced, it is fully explained. As a result, its fundamentals are thoroughly examined before commencing further study. The sequence of chapters is developmental. After the first four chapters—which provide all the underlying math in personal finance—the chapters move into the traditional decision making areas of personal finance, such as credit, taxes and investments.

The first four chapters in *The Mathematics of Personal Finance* provide a solid base of understanding of the mathematics of personal finance, and they should be read in sequence. While each chapter follows an overall logical sequence, each also is a complete entity. Therefore, after chapter 4, the chapters can be rearranged to follow any instructor's developmental sequence without losing students' comprehension.

Chapter 1 overviews some of the **basic functions necessary to use a financial calculator** in personal finance, including the function keys, as well as provide details on several fundamental time value of money calculations. More complex personal finance calculations are shown in later chapters.

Chapter 2 gets into **using computers** in personal finance mathematics. It includes several spreadsheet applications (such as Lotus 123) and gives instruction on how to search for information on the Internet. Examples using other spreadsheet programs, such as Excel, are shown in later chapters.

Chapter 3 examines **various important economic factors** in the mathematics of personal finance, including such things as changes in the consumer price index, inflation-adjusted income changes, and using inflation and interest rate estimates to plan for future goals.

Chapter 4 goes into depth on the **time value of money**. It explains and illustrates several types of calculations, including simple and compound interest, annuity, and annuity due.

The remainder of chapters in *The Mathematics of Personal Finance* examine the mathematical aspects within the traditional decision making areas in personal finance. These include planning for college, career planning, financial statements, financial ratios, consumer credit, income and estate taxes, planned purchasing, property and casualty insurance, life insurance, stocks, bonds, mutual funds, options, housing, and retirement planning.

---

[2]The tables in this appendix are copyrighted by William Mercer, Inc. They appear in the *1996 Guide to Social Security and Medicare*, published by William Mercer, Inc., Social Security Division, P.O. Box 35740, Louisville, KY 40202. For information, telephone 502-651-4500.

AN INSTRUCTOR'S TEST BANK IS AVAILABLE

The *Instructor's Test Bank* is comprised of three sections: (1) **answers to chapter exercise questions** (answers are given for all exercises that ask for numerical answers, although discussion and interpretation of case questions and computer spreadsheet exercises do not have answers provided); (2) **additional exercise questions** that could be utilized for in-class work and/or used for testing purposes; and (3) **answers to the additional exercise questions**. All of the questions contained in the *Instructor's Test Bank* also are available on computer disk, so that they may be readily copied, edited if necessary, and used in the classroom.

ACKNOWLEDGMENTS

An instructional book of this scope could not be created without the assistance of many people. Twenty-six professionals around the country—all experts in their fields of specialization—have generously contributed to this book by writing chapters. *The Mathematics of Personal Finance* could not have been completed without the shared vision and dedicated donations of expertise, time, and effort by the authors, who include:

M. J. Alhabeeb, Assistant Professor, Department of Consumer Studies, University of Massachusetts

Joan Gray Anderson, Associate Professor, Consumer Affairs Program, University of Rhode Island

Cathy Faulcon Bowen, Assistant Professor, Consumer Issues Programming, Department of Agricultural and Extension Education, College of Agricultural Sciences, The Pennsylvania State University

Paul Camp, Ph.D. Candidate, Department of Consumer Sciences and Retailing, Purdue University

Regina Chang, Assistant Professor, Department of Consumer and Family Economics, University of Missouri

Sugato Chakravaraty, Assistant Professor, Department of Consumer Sciences and Retailing, Purdue University

Sharon A. DeVaney, Assistant Professor, Department of Consumer Sciences and Retailing, Purdue University

Jessie X. Fan, Assistant Professor, Department of Family and Consumer Studies, University of Utah

Raymond E. Forgue, Department Chair and Associate Professor, Department of Family Studies, University of Kentucky

Jonathan Fox, Assistant Professor, Consumer and Textiles Science Department, The Ohio State University

E. Thomas Garman, Distinguished Fellow, Center for Organizational and Technological Advancement, and Professor of Personal Finance Employee Education, Virginia Tech

Ronald W. Gibbs, Adjunct Instructor, College of Human Resources and Education, Virginia Tech, and Agent and Registered Representative, The Life Insurance Company of Virginia

Vickie L. Hampton, Associate Professor, Human Ecology Department, The University of Texas

Sherman Hanna, Professor, Consumer and Textiles Science Department, The Ohio State University

Celia Ray Hayhoe, Assistant Professor, Department of Family Studies, University of Kentucky

Gong-Soog Hong, Assistant Professor, Department of Consumer Sciences and Retailing, Purdue University

Kenneth Huggins, Professor, Finance Department, Metropolitan State College

Sandra J. Huston, Ph.D. Candidate, Department of Consumer and Family Economics, University of Missouri

Jean M. Lown, Professor, Department of Human Environments, Utah State University

Y. Lakshmi Malroutu, Assistant Professor, Department of Family, Nutrition, and Exercise Science, Queens College

Abraham Mulugetta, Director of the Center for Trade and Analysis of Financial Instruments and Associate Professor, Department of Financial and International Business, School of Business, Ithaca College

Yuko Mulugetta, Director of Research and Planning Analysis for Admissions and Financial Aid, Cornell University

Dorit Samuel, Ph.D. Candidate, Department of Finance, The Ohio State University

Jill Lynn Vihtelic, Associate Professor, Business Administration and Economics, Saint Mary's College

Jing J. Xiao, Associate Professor, Consumer Affairs Program, College of Human Science and Services, University of Rhode Island

Robert O. Weagley, Associate Professor, Department of Consumer and Family Economics, University of Missouri

Some instructors provided a **"favorite example"** of a mathematical concept and example for inclusion in *The Mathematics of Personal Finance*: *Vickie L. Hampton* (Associate Professor, Human Ecology Department, The University of Texas), *Jean M. Lown* (Professor, Department of Human Environments, Utah State University), and *Robert O. Weagley* (Associate Professor, Department of Consumer and Family Economics, University of Missouri). These contributions, which are footnoted in the appropriate chapters, are sincerely appreciated.

Four personal finance instructors and their students were generous enough to field test initial drafts of chapters in *The Mathematics of Personal Finance*. They offered dozens of excellent suggestions which have improved the book. The editors wish to offer a very loud public "thank you" to:

Bruce Brunson, Assistant Professor, Family Financial Management, Virginia Tech

Vicki Fitzsimmons, Associate Professor, Department of Agricultural and Consumer Economics, University of Illinois

Sherman Hanna, Professor, Consumer and Textiles Science Department, The Ohio State University

Jing J. Xiao, Associate Professor, Consumer Affairs Program, College of Human Science and Services, University of Rhode Island

University of Texas graduate student *Michael Ota* was instrumental in developing some supplemental problems. Also deserving appreciation are professors *Sue Greninger* and *Karrol Kitt* in the Department of Human Ecology at the University of Texas. Several graduate students from The Ohio State University provided excellent detailed suggestions during the field testing of *The Mathematics of Personal Finance* and they deserve special thanks: *Peng Chen*, *Yoonkyung Yuh*, *Seonglim Lee*, and *Michael Finke*.

We also wish to thank many students who read the chapter narratives and worked through all of the exercise problems. Many offered suggestions for improvement, which have enhanced the clarity of explanations as well as the accuracy of examples and answers. The editors and the contributing authors remain grateful for the wonderful suggestions of the students.

The editors, of course, accept final responsibility for all errors and omissions. The editors understand that a project of this size usually contains a few mistakes. In addition, the editors made some judgment calls about how much depth to provide in certain explanations, sometimes against the urgings of chapter authors. Accordingly, we invite readers to share with us any corrections and recommendations for improvement.

We invite instructors to submit their **"favorite example"** of a mathematical concept and accompanying example for possible inclusion in the next edition of *The Mathematics of Personal Finance*. Full authorship credit will be given. Do not be shy. Please consider forwarding us your favorite math example.

Over the past two years, dozens of personal finance instructors have been supportive of our interest and effort to develop a personal finance "math book." Many have generously shared their views, in person as well as by letter and e-mail, on what should be included in a high-quality personal finance math book. We have listened and have attempted to meet those needs in every way possible because we share the belief that students need to be able to accurately perform the mathematical calculations in personal finance in order to make effective decisions in their daily living.

The success of *The Mathematics of Personal Finance* is largely dependent upon feedback from instructors, students, and professionals practicing in the real world of personal finance. It must meet your needs. Please share with us your views and suggestions.

E. Thomas Garman
tgarman@vt.edu

Jing J. Xiao
xiao@uriacc.uri.edu

ABOUT THE EDITORS

E. THOMAS GARMAN is a Distinguished Fellow, Center for Organizational and Technological Advancement, and a Professor of Personal Finance Employee Education at Virginia Polytechnic Institute and State University in Blacksburg, Virginia. He received his bachelor's and master's degrees in business administration from the University of Denver and his doctorate in economic education from Texas Tech University. Garman's experience includes work for a United States Senator in Washington, retail sales management in Colorado, economic development project management in West Africa, and teaching for 33 years in 8 states and 3 countries. Garman has taught 15 summer workshops for 10 different universities, and 8 of those were "Consumer Issues in Washington" classes taught on location in the nation's capital. He is a professor who truly enjoys teaching. His work as a COTA Fellow focuses on Personal Finance Employee Education (and he may be reached at his World Wide Web site *http://www.chre.vt.edu/~/pfee/*).

In 1994, Garman received the Stewart E. Lee Consumer Education Award from the American Council on Consumer Interests in recognition of his lifetime achievements in consumer education. In 1995, that same organization elected him a Distinguished Fellow.

Professor Garman has authored or co-authored over 12,000 pages of writing, including 120 refereed articles and proceedings publications, over 60 non-refereed publications, and 18 books, including five currently available titles: ***Ripoffs and Fraud: How to Avoid and How to Get Away*** (winner of the 1996 Association for Financial Counseling and Planning Education's "Journalism Award"), ***Consumer Economic Issues in America***, ***Regulation and Consumer Protection***, and ***The Mathematics of Personal Finance*** (all with Dame Publications), and ***Personal Finance*** (Houghton Mifflin). Garman has been identified by the editor of the journal *Financial Counseling and Planning* as "The Most Cited Author" from 1989 through 1995.

Garman is a past president of two national organizations, the American Council on Consumer Interests and the Association for Financial Counseling and Planning Education, as well as the Consumer Education and Information Association of Virginia. He has made 84 major speeches to professional groups in 23 states and 3 foreign countries. He has appeared on various CBS and NBC affiliate stations as well as The Nashville Network.

Garman has been a consultant to over forty corporations, trade associations and government agencies. He recently completed terms of service for the National Advertising Review Board, Consumer Advisory Council of the Board of Governors of the Federal Reserve System, and National Advisory Council on Financial Planning for the International Board of Standards and Practices for Certified Financial Planners. Garman currently consults as a subject matter specialist for the U.S. Navy and the Department of Defense.

Garman teaches both graduate and undergraduate courses in consumer affairs and family financial management, fields in which his books are widely used. Garman has two grown children, and he lives with his wife in their home located on Gap Mountain near Newport, Virginia.

JING JIAN XIAO is an associate professor of consumer economics at the University of Rhode Island, teaching courses of personal finance, consumer protection, and family and consumer research. He received his bachelor's and master's degree in economics from Zhongnan University of Finance and Economics, in China, and his doctorate in consumer economics from Oregon State University. His dissertation study on the family financial portfolios behavior won the 1992 Dissertation Award of the American Council on Consumer Interests. His research on consumer behavior in household financial asset holdings has been supported by the University of Rhode Island Research Council and the Standards Board of Certified Financial Planners.

Xiao has authored or co-authored over forty refereed journal articles and conference proceedings papers. He is the author of *Modern Family Economics* (Shanghai, 1993), co-editor of *The Mathematics of Personal Finance* (Dame, 1997), and co-author of or contributor to eight other books, including *Personal Finance* (Houghton Mifflin, 1997), *Encyclopedia of Consumer Movement* (Calderlator, 1997), *Regulation and Consumer Protection* (Dame, 1995), *Consumer Economic Issues in America* (Dame, 1996), *Macro Marketing* (Commerce, 1990), *Introduction to Marketing* (Shaanxi, 1988), and *Business Forecasting* (Agriculture, 1987).

Xiao has presented research findings at national conferences of several professional organizations, including the Association of Financial Counseling and Planning Education, American Council on Consumer Interests, American Family and Consumer Science Association, Asian Consumer and Family Economics Association, Chinese Economist Society, and Academy of Financial Services. His research papers and other writings have been published in many academic journals, including the *Journal of Family and Consumer Sciences, Family and Consumer Science Research Journal, Journal of Family and Economic Issues, Advancing the Consumer Interest, Journal of Consumer Affairs, Childhood Education, Journal of Consumer Studies and Home Economics*, and *Financial Counseling and Planning*.

Xiao serves or served the Development Committee and the International Committee of the American Council on Consumer Interests, Student Paper Award Committee of the Association of Financial Counseling and Planning Education, Board of Directors of the Rhode Island Family and Consumer Science Association, and Program Advisory Board of the Center of Financial Education and Information, a joint venture between the Rhode Island Consumer Credit Counseling Service and the University of Rhode Island. He is the proceedings editor for the 1997 conference of Association of Financial Counseling and Planning. Xiao also is on the editorial board of the official journal of the Association for Financial Counseling and Planning Education, *Financial Counseling and Planning*.

Xiao lives with his wife, Sha, and daughter, Ran, in their home located in Wakefield, Rhode Island.

Chapter 1
Personal Finance and the Financial Calculator

▼ **Basic Calculator Functions**

▼ **Time Value of Money Calculations**

▼ **Future Value of a Single Sum**

▼ **Future Value of a Series of Equal Payments**

▼ **Present Value of a Single Sum**

▼ **Present Value of a Series of Equal Payments**

▼ **Solving for the Number of Periods**

▼ **Solving for Rate**

▼ **Solving for an Equal Stream of Payments**

Chapter 1
Personal Finance and the Financial Calculator

Celia Ray Hayhoe[1]

OVERVIEW

The **financial calculator** (or **business calculator**) is one of the most powerful tools in personal financial decision making. Because of its size, it is easier to carry around than a book of tables or a computer. It will perform most of the calculations necessary for personal finance with satisfactory results. Therefore, before you embark on improving your personal finance math skills you need to purchase a financial calculator. These calculators range in price from approximately $15 to $100. A calculator in the $25 to $35 range should be adequate for the needs of most people, including the users of this book.

When purchasing a calculator be sure it offers the following function keys. These keys will allow you to perform the time value of money calculations which are described later in this chapter and in more detail in Chapter 4. Some of the advanced calculations are found in that and later chapters. Below are the keys useful in developing personal finance math skills on a financial calculator.

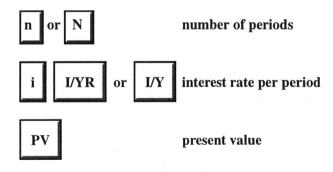

n or N	**number of periods**
i I/YR or I/Y	**interest rate per period**
PV	**present value**

[1]Celia Ray Hayhoe, Ph.D., CFP , Assistant Professor. Department of Family Studies, University of Kentucky, Lexington, KY 40514-0054. crhayh1@ukcc.uky.edu

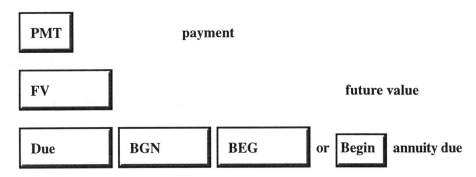

If you are planning on a career in personal finance or seeking a certification designation from some organization, you will also need an [IRR] (internal rate of return) key which is available on some financial calculators. Such calculators will perform regular arithmetic functions as well as some statistical functions.

It would be impossible in the scope of this chapter to cover all types of calculators on the market. For the illustrative purpose, however, this chapter presents the key strokes for three calculators that cost about $25 to $35 (Hewlett-Packard HP-10B, Sharp's EL-733A, and Texas Instruments BA-II PLUS) as well as a more expensive Hewlett-Packard HP-12C. Most other calculators will have keystrokes similar to these. It will be helpful to also have the manufacturer's instruction book handy when you are working on this chapter until you become familiar with your calculator.

This chapter first examines some of the basic functions necessary to use a calculator. Then it describes each of the function keys mentioned above and provides examples that use each key, followed by an interpretation of each solution. The remainder of the chapter provides details on several of the primary uses of the financial calculator in solving personal finance problems. The topics include the following time value of money calculations: future value of a single sum, future value of a series of equal payments, present value of a single sum, present value of a series of equal payments, solving for the number of periods, solving for rate, and solving for an equal stream of payments. A few more complex personal finance calculations are shown in later chapters.

BASIC CALCULATOR FUNCTIONS

If you do not already know how to turn your calculator on/off and how to do arithmetic calculations, you need to first perform some of the practice examples in the manufacturer's instruction book that comes with the calculator. This is especially important if you purchased a Hewlett-Packard HP-12C as it does not use an equal [=] key but an [ENTER] key which takes some practice to become accustomed to its use.

In addition, some of the keys on a financial calculator perform more than one function. Studying the manufacturer's instruction manual will help you understand any **multiple function keys**. These additional functions are printed above or below such keys. For example, the second function for the [PMT] key is [N!] on the EL-733A; [P/YR] on the HP-10B; and [BGN] on the BA-II Plus, and [RND] on the HP-12C. The HP-12C also has a third function of the [PMT] key that is [Cf$_j$]. To reach the second functions on the EL-733A you will need to press the **[2nd F]** key, on the BA-II plus press the **[2nd]** key, and on the HP-10B use the **gold key**□. Use the gold **[f]** key on the HP-12C to reach the second functions which are written above the keys in gold and the blue **[g]** key to reach the third functions written below the key in blue. Practicing the examples in the manufacturer's instruction manual will help you become familiar with these functions. To ensure successful financial calculations performed with financial calculators, the following preparations are needed.

1. Clearing the Register

Purpose	EL-733A	HP-10B	BA-II Plus	HP-12C
Clear all memory registers	0 [X->M]	□ [CLEAR ALL]	[2nd] [MEM] [ENTER] [2nd] [QUIT] [2nd] [CLR Work]	[f] [CLX]
Clear the TVM registers	[2nd F] [CA]	□ [CLEAR ALL]	[2nd] [Reset] [ENTER] [2nd] [QUIT]*	[f] [FIN]

*Using **[2nd]** **[CLR TVM]** only clears the **[N]**,**[I/Y]**, **[PV]**, **[PMT]**, and **[FV]** keys. It does not clear the **[P/Y]** key.*

Before doing any financial calculations and between financial calculations, it is necessary to **clear** the **time value of money (TVM) registers**. Unlike simple arithmetic calculators, financial calculators retain the information in their registers from one problem to the next unless it is replaced. Some will even retain the information when the calculator is turned off! Thus, it is important to get in the habit of clearing TVM registers of your calculator before each problem. You should also read the manual to find out how to clear just the display or previous number so that you do not have to start over every time you make a mistake.

2. Setting Decimal Places

Purpose	EL-733A	HP-10B	BA-II Plus	HP-12C
Display 4 Decimal places	[2nd F] [TAB] 4	□ [DIP] 4	[2nd] [FORMAT] 4 [ENTER] [2nd] [QUIT]	[f]] 4
Floating decimal point	[2nd F] [TAB].	□ [DISP]	[2nd] [FORMAT] 9 [ENTER] [2nd] [QUIT]	[f] 9

You can control the number of decimal places displayed on the register. The above examples set the display to four decimal places which is a good number for interest rates, and to a floating decimal point, respectively. You will want two decimal places when your answer is in dollars and cents. Try to see if you can set the calculator at two decimal places.

3. Setting Number of Periods

Purpose	EL-733A	HP-10B	BA-II Plus	HP-12C
Setting the number of periods—Compounding annually	not necessary	1 ☐ [P/Y]	[2nd] [P/Y] 1 [ENTER]	not necessary
Setting the number of periods—Compounding monthly	not necessary	12 ☐ [P/Y]	[2nd] [P/Y]12 [ENTER]	not necessary

With the HP-10B and the BA-II Plus, it is necessary to set the number of payment periods in a year. The two examples above set the number of payments to one for annual compounding and to 12 for monthly compounding. For quarterly compounding you would change the number to 4, for weekly you would change it to 52, and so forth. It is important that you set the number of payment periods each time you do a problem. Otherwise, the calculator will remember the number from the previous problem.

The EL-733A and HP-12C are set for compounding once per period. For different compounding periods, you adjust the number of periods by multiplying the number of years by the number of periods per year and dividing the annual interest rate by the number of periods per year. For example, 8% interest compounded quarterly for 5 years is 20 periods (5 years X 4 periods per year = 20 periods) and the interest rate is 2% per period (8%/4 periods per year = 2% per period).

The BA-II Plus also allows you to set the number of compounding periods per year. The other calculators set the number of payments equal to the number of compounding periods. If the compounding periods and the payments per month are the same, you only have to set the number of payments. However, if you have quarterly compounding and monthly payments after setting the number of payments to 12, using the steps above, press the [↓] 4 **[ENTER]** for quarterly compounding. Press **[2nd] [QUIT]** to return to calculator mode.

4. Setting Due Mode

Purpose	EL-733A	HP-10B	BA-II Plus	HP-12C
Setting to due mode	**[BGN]**	☐[BEG/END]	**[2nd] [BGN]** **[2nd] [SET]** **[2nd] [QUIT]**	**[g] [BEG]**

When the calculator is set to the due mode, **BEGIN**, **BGN**, or **BEG** will appear in the display. To return to the regular mode, use the same key strokes. When set on the **regular mode** nothing will appear in the display. Always return your calculator to the regular mode after completing a problem using the due mode. See the annuity problems below for when to use due mode; further information is provided in Chapter 4.

5. Changing Signs

Conventionally, all cash outflows or payments carry a **negative sign**, and all cash inflows or receipts carry a **positive sign**. Entering a number with a wrong sign will result in an incorrect answers or an error message. To enter negative numbers on the calculators, except for the HP-12C, use the [+/-] key. Use the [CHS] key to change signs on the HP-12C. You will find it necessary to enter some numbers as negative numbers in order for the calculations to work. There will be times when the solution has an unwanted negative sign in the answer because of the way the calculator works. When this happens, the interpretation of the solution will tell you when to disregard the sign. The [+/-] or [CHS] key can be used with regular arithmetic calculations as well as with time value of money calculations. The signs retain their normal meaning of positive and negative when used in arithmetic calculations. If you change a sign in error, simply press the key again to revert to the original sign.

6. Changing to Financial Mode

Some calculators have two modes of calculation, regular and financial mode. To calculate time values of money, you have to change to the financial mode in this kind of computation. Among the four brands demonstrated in this book, only EL-733A needs this step, and it is performed by pressing [2nd F] followed by [MODE]. The other three brands do not need this step.

EXAMPLES OF CALCULATING THE TIME VALUE OF MONEY

The purpose of this chapter is to show the calculator keystrokes required to execute several types of problems, but not to explain when to use them. A full explanation of when to use these personal finance calculations can be found in Chapter 4.

The basic steps are the same for *all* time value of money problems. There are five basic amounts to every problem: (1) number of periods, (2) interest per period, (3) payment, (4) present value, and (5) future value. In all cases you will enter four of the amounts and solve for the fifth. It does not matter in what order you enter the amounts as long as all four amounts are entered before you solve for the fifth. If you remember to clear your calculator between problems, you do not need to enter zero amounts.

1. Future Value of a Single Sum

A. Using Annual Interest

▼   **Example 1.1.1:** You have $100 today to deposit in a 6-year certificate of deposit (CD)[1] that earns 4% annual interest. How much will you receive when the CD matures? Use the following key strokes.

Purpose	EL-733A	HP-10B	BA-II Plus	HP-12C
setting compounding		1 ☐ [P/Y]	[2nd] [P/Y] 1 [ENTER] [2nd] [QUIT]	
starting amount	100 [+/-] [PV]	100[+/-] [PV]	100[+/-][PV]	100 [CHS][PV]
time period	6 [n]	6 [N]	6 [N]	6 [n]
interest rate	4 [i]	4 [I/YR]	4 [I/Y]	4 [i]
future amount	[COMP][FV]	[FV]	[CPT][FV]	[FV]
answer	126.53	126.53	126.53	126.53

Caution: If you forgot to clear your calculator, enter 0 in **[PMT]** *for all calculators before completing the last step.*

❖ **Interpretation:** It does not matter in what order you enter **[PV]**, **[n]**, **[I]**, and **[PMT]** as long as everything is entered before you complete the **[FV]** step. After entering the starting amount the display should read -100. Either the present or the future value must have a negative sign for the calculator to work. The graphic **time line** below illustrates the concept.

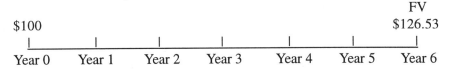

						FV
$100						$126.53

Year 0   Year 1   Year 2   Year 3   Year 4   Year 5   Year 6

You solve for future value whenever you are traveling to the *right* on the time line (e.g., you know the earlier price or the amount of a series of payments and you want to know how much they would be worth at a later date). The answer means that you would receive $126.53 at the end of six years. If you got -126.53, you forgot to change the sign when entering the present value.

B. Using Other Than Annual Interest

▼ **Example 1.1.2:** You have $100 today to deposit in a 6-year certificate of deposit (CD) that earns 4% annual interest compounded quarterly. How much will you receive when the CD matures? Use the following key strokes.

Purpose	EL-733A	HP-10B	BA-II Plus	HP-12C
setting compounding		4 □ [P/Y]	[2nd] [P/Y] 4 [ENTER] [2nd][QUIT]	
starting amount	100[+/-][PV]	100[+/-] [PV]	100[+/-] [PV]	100[CHS] [PV]
time period	6[x]4[=] [n]	6 □ [xP/Y]	6 [2nd] [xP/Y][N]	6[ENTER]4[X] [n]
interest rate	4[÷]4[=] [i]	4 [I/YR]	4 [I/Y]	4[ENTER] 4[÷] [i]
future amount	[COMP][FV]	[FV]	[CPT][FV]	[F]
answer	126.97	126.97	126.97	126.97

Caution: If you forgot to clear your calculator, enter 0 in **[PMT]** *for all calculators before completing the last step.*

❖ **Interpretation:** Each division on the time line above represents one period. Therefore, if interest is compounded quarterly, there are 24 periods in 6 years (6 years times 4 periods per year). This means by having the interest you earn on the CD compounded quarterly rather than annually you earned $126.97 instead of $126.53. Since the interest was compounded quarterly, 4 was used to multiply the number of years. For the same reason, you would use 12 for monthly compounding, 2 for semi-annually compounding, and so forth. Note that with the HP-10B and the BA-II Plus, you set the number of periods per year and the calculator adjusts the interest rate. With the EL-733A and the HP-12C, you have to manually adjust the interest rate. With all of the calculators you have to manually adjust the number of periods. Also note that when entering the time period in HP-10B and BA-II Plus, **[xP/Y]]** is used, which converts the annual periods into quarter periods. The **[xP/Y]** key automatically multiplies the number of years by the amount entered in the **[P/Y]** key.

2. Future Value of a Series of Equal Payments

A. Future Value of an Annuity

▼ **Example 1.2.1:** You deposit $100 at the end of each month into a savings account that pays 3.5% annual interest compounded monthly. How much money will be in the account at the end of 7 years? Use the following key strokes.

Purpose	EL-733A	HP-10B	BA-II Plus	HP-12C
setting compounding		12☐ [P/Y]	[2nd] [P/Y] 12 [ENTER] [2nd][QUIT]	
starting amount	0 [PV]	0 [PV]	0 [PV]	0 [PV]
time period	7 [x]12[=] [n]	7 ☐ [xP/Y]	7 [2nd] [xP/Y]	7[ENTER]12[X] [n]*
interest rate	3.5[÷]12[=] [i]	3.5 [I/YR]	3.5 [I/Y]	3.5[ENTER]12[÷][i]*
payments	100 [PMT]	100 [PMT]	100 [PMT]	100 [PMT]
future amount	[COMP][FV]	[FV]	[CPT][FV]	[FV]
answer	-9,502.83	-9,502.83	-9,502.83	-9,502.83

When using monthly compounding with the HP-12C, there is a short cut to enter the number of periods and the interest rate. In this example, 7 years can be entered as: 7 [g] [n], and 3.5% interest rate as: 3.5 [g] [i]. This short cut only works with monthly compounding. You must use the key strokes above with all other compounding periods.

❖ **Interpretation:** Because you do not earn interest until the money has been on deposit for the entire period, with a regular annuity you do not earn interest on the money deposited for the first period *or* the last period. This is another case where you must disregard the negative sign. Your answer of -9,502.83 means that you will have $9,502.83 in the account at the end of 7 years. If you get -9,530.54, you have your calculator set to the due or begin mode. Since you did not put an amount in present value, the answer shows up as a negative. Disregard the negative sign when reporting your answer. You will have $9,502.83 at the end of 7 years.

A stream of equal payments is called an **annuity** or an **annuity due**, and these are different from each other. The distinction is whether the payment is made at the beginning of the interest period or at the end. If the stream of equal payments is made at the beginning of the period, such as a deposit on the first day of every month to a savings account, this is referred to as an **annuity due**. This will require the use of the due or begin key of your calculator. When the stream of equal payments is made at the end of the period, as with a mortgage where you do not owe interest on the money until you have used it, this is referred to as an **annuity**. The default mode for your calculator is a regular annuity. You need to set the mode for annuity due. Be sure to set the mode back to the default before going to the next problem. For all calculators, except the BA-II Plus, the number of payments per year and the number of compounding periods per year must be the same. For example, if interest is compounded quarterly, then payments must be made quarterly.

B. Future Value of an Annuity Due

▼ **Example 1.2.2:** You deposit $50 into your savings account on the first day of every month for 5 years starting on January 1. Your account pays 3% interest compounded monthly. How much money will be in the account at the end of 5 years? Use the following key strokes.

Purpose	EL-733A	HP-10B	BA-II Plus	HP-12C
set to annuity due	[BGN]	□ [BEG/END]	[2nd] [BGN] [2nd] [SET] [2nd] [QUIT]	[g] [BEG]
setting compounding		12□ [P/Y]	[2nd] [P/Y] 12 [ENTER] [2nd][QUIT]	
starting amount	0 [PV]	0 [PV]	0 [PV]	0 [PV]
time period	5 [x]12[=] [n]	5 □[xP/Y]	5 [2nd] [xP/Y]	5[ENTER]12[X] [n]*
interest rate	3[÷]12[=] [i]	3 [I/YR]	3 [I/Y]	3[ENTER]12[÷][i]*
payments	50 [PMT]	50 [PMT]	50 [PMT]	50 [PMT]
future amount	[COMP][FV]	[FV]	[CPT][FV]	[FV]
answer	-3,240.42	-3,240.42	-3,240.42	-3,240.42

Caution: Reset your calculator to regular mode before you start a new problem.

❖ **Interpretation:** Every deposit earns at least one month's interest. This is another case when you disregard the negative sign in the answer. It appears there because you could not enter it in the present value register since that is zero. The answer is -3,240.42. This means you will have $3,240.42 in your account at the end of five years. If you get -3,232.34, you forgot to set your calculator to annuity due and therefore did not receive any interest on the first period or the last.

3. Present Value of a Single Sum[2]

A. Using Annual Interest

▼ **Example 1.3.1:** You have $3,000 today in a certificate of deposit (CD) that you purchased 6 years ago which earned 4% annual interest. How much did you deposit when you purchased the CD? Use the following key strokes.

Purpose	EL-733A	HP-10B	BA-II Plus	HP-12C
setting compounding		1 □ [P/Y]	[2nd] [P/Y] 1 [ENTER] [2nd][QUIT]	
starting amount	3000 [+/-][FV]	3000 [+/-][FV]	3000 [+/-][FV]	3000 [CHS][FV]
time period	6 [n]	6 [N]	6 [N]	6 [n]
interest rate	4 [i]	4 [I/YR]	4 [I/Y]	4 [i]
future amount	[COMP][PV]	[PV]	[CPT][PV]	[PV]
answer	2,370.94	2,370.94	2,370.94	2,370.94

Caution: If you forgot to clear your calculator, enter 0 in **[PMT]** *for all calculators before completing the last step.*

❖ **Interpretation:** You solve for present value whenever you are traveling to the left on the time line (e.g., you know the later value of a single sum or series of payments and you want to know how much they would be worth at an earlier date). It does not matter in what order you enter **[FV]**, **[n]**, **[i]**, and **[PMT]** as long as everything is entered before you complete the **[PV]** step. The answer means you deposited $2,370.94 six years ago.

B. Using Other Than Annual Interest

▼ **Example 1.3.2:** You received $3,000 today for a 6-year certificate of deposit (CD) that earned 4% interest compounded quarterly. How much did you deposit when you purchased the CD? Use the following key strokes.

Purpose	EL-733A	HP-10B	BA-II Plus	HP-12C
setting compounding		4 ☐ [P/Y]	[2nd] [P/Y] 4 [ENTER] [2nd][QUIT]	
starting amount	3000[+/-][FV]	3000[+/-] [FV]	3000[+/-] [FV]	3000 [CHS] [FV]
time period	6[x]4[=] [n]	6 ☐ [xP/Y]	6[2nd][xP/Y][N]	6[ENTER]4 [X] [n]
interest rate	4[÷]4[=] [i]	4 [I/YR]	4 [I/Y]	4[ENTER] 4[÷] [i]
future amount	[COMP][PV]	[PV]	[CPT][PV]	[PV]
answer	2,362.70	2,362.70	2,362.70	2,362.70

Caution: If you forgot to clear your calculator, enter 0 in **[PMT]** *for all calculators before completing the last step.*

❖ **Interpretation:** This means by having the interest on the CD compounded quarterly rather than annually you could deposit $2,362.70, instead of $2,370.94, and have the same amount when the CD matured.

4. Present Value of a Series of Equal Payments

A. Present Value of an Annuity

▼ **Example 1.4.1:** You take out a mortgage on June 1. Starting on July 1 you start making $600 a month payments. The mortgage has an interest rate of 8% compounded monthly for 30 years. How much is the mortgage? Use the following key strokes.

Purpose	EL-733A	HP-10B	BA-II Plus	HP-12C
setting compounding		12 □ [P/Y]	[2nd] [P/Y] 12 [ENTER] [2nd][QUIT]	
starting amount	0 [FV]	0 [FV]	0 [FV]	0 [FV]
time period	30 [x]12[=] [n]	30 □[xP/Y]	30[2nd][xP/Y][N]	30[ENTER]12[X] [n]
interest rate	8[÷]12[=] [i]	8 [I/YR]	8 [I/Y]	8[ENTER] 12[÷] [i]
payments	600 [PMT]	600 [PMT]	600 [PMT]	600 [PMT]
future amount	[COMP][PV]	[PV]	[CPT][PV]	[PV]
answer	-81,770.10	-81,770.10	-81,770.10	-81,770.10

❖ **Interpretation:** You borrowed $81,770.10. Remember that all loans are regular annuities because you do not make your first payment until you have used the money for a month. If you get -82,315.23, you have your calculator set to the due or begin mode. Since you did not put an amount in future value, the answer shows up as a negative. Disregard the negative sign when reporting your answer.

B. Present Value of an Annuity Due

▼ **Example 1.4.2:** You have just won the lottery. You will receive $150,000 on the first day of the year for 20 years. If you can earn 6% annual return on your money, how much of a lump sum payment today would be worth the same as the stream of payments? Use the following key strokes.

Purpose	EL-733A	HP-10B	BA-II Plus	HP-12C
set to annuity due	[BGN]	□ [BEG/END]	[2nd] [BGN] [2nd] [SET] [2nd] [QUIT]	[g] [BEG]
setting compounding		1 □ [P/Y]	[2nd] [P/Y] 1 [ENTER] [2nd][QUIT]	
starting amount	0 [FV]	0 [FV]	0 [FV]	0 [FV]
time period	20 [n]	20[N]	20 [N]	20 [n]
interest rate	6 [i]	6 [I/YR]	6 [I/Y]	6 [i]
payments	150000 [PMT]	150000 [PMT]	150000 [PMT]	150000 [PMT]
future amount	[COMP][PV]	[PV]	[CPT][PV]	[PV]
answer	-1,823,717.47	-1,823,717.47	-1,823,717.47	-1,823,717.47

Caution: Reset your calculator to regular mode when you have finished the problem.

❖ **Interpretation:** This is another case when you disregard the negative sign in the answer. It appears there because you could not enter it in the future value register since that is zero. If you get $1,720,488.18, you forgot to set your calculator to annuity due and therefore did not receive any interest on the first period. Thus, receiving $1,823,717.47 today and investing it for an annual return of 6% for 20 years is equivalent to receiving $150,000 per year and investing it at 6% for 20 years.

C. Present Value of a Series of Equal Payments When Future Value is Known

▼ **Example 1.4.3:** You would like to purchase a corporate bond with a $20 semi-annual interest payment and a maturity value of $1,000. If the current rate of interest on these bonds is 8% compounded semi-annually and years to maturity are 10, how much should you pay for the bond? Use the following key strokes.

Purpose	EL-733A	HP-10B	BA-II Plus	HP-12C
setting compounding		2 ☐ [P/Y]	[2nd] [P/Y] 2 [ENTER] [2nd][QUIT]	
starting amount	1000 [FV]	1000 [FV]	1000 [FV]	1000 [FV]
time period	10 [x] 2[=] [n]	10 ☐ [xP/Y]	10[2nd][xP/Y][N]	10[ENTER]2[X] [n]
interest rate	8[÷]2[=] [i]	8 [I/YR]	8 [I/Y]	8[ENTER] 2[÷] [i]
payments	20 [PMT]	20 [PMT]	20 [PMT]	20 [PMT]
future amount	[COMP][PV]	[PV]	[CPT][PV]	[PV]
answer	-728.19	-728.19	-728.19	-728.19

❖ **Interpretation:** The answer means that if you pay $728.19 for the bond you will earn a yield equivalent to the rate of current bonds (8% in this case). If your answer was 728.19 instead of -728.19, then you changed the sign when entering the payment which will not affect your answer. When you enter a future value **[FV]** and payments **[PMT]** and solve for the present value **[PV]**, do not change the sign of the future value, but just disregard the negative sign in the answer. If your answer is 184.58, you changed the sign of the future value.

5. Solving for the Number of Periods

A. Knowing Present and Future Value and Using Annual Interest

▼ **Example 1.5.1:** If you buy a certificate of deposit (CD) now with $3,000 at 4% annual interest, in how many years will the CD be worth $6,000? Use the following key strokes.

Purpose	EL-733A	HP-10B	BA-II Plus	HP-12C
setting compounding		1 □ [P/Y]	[2nd] [P/Y] 1 [ENTER] [2nd][QUIT]	
starting amount	3000[+/-][PV]	3000[+/-][PV]	3000[+/-][PV]	3000[CHS][PV]
interest rate	4 [i]	4 [I/YR]	4 [I/Y]	4 [i]
future amount	6000[FV]	6000[FV]	6000 [FV]	6000 [FV]
time period	[COMP] [n]	[N]	[CPT] [N]	[n]
answer	17.67	17.67	17.67	18

Caution: If you get the message "error 5" on the HP-12C or BA-II Plus, "no solution" on the HP-10B, or "E" on the EL-733A, you forgot to enter either the present value or the future value as a negative number. It does not matter which one you enter as a negative number. To clear the message use [Clx] *on the HP-12C,* [CE/C] *on the BA-II Plus,* [C] *on the HP-10B, and* [CE-C] *on the EL-733A.*

❖ **Interpretation:** The answer is about 18 years. When you know the interest rate and both the present and future value, or the interest rate and either the present or the future value and an equal stream of payments, you can solve for the number of periods. When solving for the number of periods, always round to the next full period since you do not make a part of a payment. The HP-12C will do it for you.

B. Knowing Present and Future Value and Using Other Than Annual Interest

▼ **Example 2.5.2:** If you buy a certificate of deposit (CD) now with $3,000 at 4% annual interest compounded quarterly, in how many years will the CD be worth $6,000? Use the following key strokes.

Purpose	EL-733A	HP-10B	BA-II Plus	HP-12C
setting compounding		4 □ [P/Y]	[2nd] [P/Y] 4 [ENTER] [2nd][QUIT]	
starting amount	3000 [+/-][PV]	3000 [+/-][PV]	3000 [+/-][PV]	3000 [CHS][PV]
interest rate	4[÷]4[=] [i]	4 [I/YR]	4 [I/Y]	4[ENTER] 4[÷] [i]
future amount	6000[FV]	6000[FV]	6000[FV]	6000[FV]
time period	[COMP] [n]	[N]	[CPT] [N]	[n]
answer	69.66	69.66	69.66	70

❖ **Interpretation:** This does not mean that you have to deposit the money for about 70 years. Remember your answer is in quarters since your compounding period is in quarters. Therefore, you must divide the answer by 4 to get the number of years as requested in the problem: 70/4 = 17.5, or 17 years 6 months.

C. Knowing Future Value and a Stream of Equal Payments

▼ **Example 1.5.3:** You currently have $6,000 in your savings account. In the past, you regularly deposited $50 a month on the first day of the month at 3% annual interest compounded monthly. How many years have you had the account? Use the following key strokes.

Purpose	EL-733A	HP-10B	BA-II Plus	HP-12C
setting compounding		12 □ [P/Y]	[2nd] [P/Y] 12 [ENTER] [2nd][QUIT]	
starting amount	6000[+/-][FV]	6000[+/-][FV]	6000[+/-][FV]	6000 [CHS][FV]
interest rate	3[÷] 12[=] [i]	3 [I/YR]	3 [I/Y]	3[ENTER]12[÷] [i]
payment amount	50[PMT]	50[PMT]	50[PMT]	50[PMT]
time period	[COMP] [n]	[N]	[CPT] [N]	[n]
answer	104.85	104.85	104.85	104.85

❖ **Interpretation:** This means you started the account 106 months ago, or 8 years 10 months ($8 \times 12 = 96$; $106 - 96 = 10$) ago.

D. Knowing Present Value and an Equal Stream of Payments

▼ **Example 1.5.4:** You purchase a municipal bond for $5,000 that pays $381.89 every six months. If the annual rate of return of the bond is 3.5%, how many payments will be received? Use the following key strokes.

Purpose	EL-733A	HP-10B	BA-II Plus	HP-12C
setting compounding		2 □ [P/Y]	[2nd] [P/Y] 2 [ENTER] [2nd][QUIT]	
starting amount	5000[+/-][PV]	5000[+/-] [PV]	5000[+/-] [PV]	5000 [CHS] [PV]
interest rate	3.5[÷]2[=] [i]	3.5 [I/YR]	3.5 [I/Y]	3.5[ENTER]2[÷] [i]
payment amount	381.89[PMT]	381.89[PMT]	381.89[PMT]	381.89[PMT]
time period	[COMP] [n]	[N]	[CPT] [N]	[n]
answer	15	15	15	15

❖ **Interpretation:** This means that you will receive 15 more payments or that your bond matures in 7 years 6 months($15/2 = 7.5$).

6. Solving for Rate

A. Knowing Present and Future Value and Using Annual Interest

▼ **Example 1.6.1:** Today a home costs $106,000. If the same home cost $95,000 five years ago, what has been the average annual inflation rate for the home? Use the following key strokes.

Purpose	EL-733A	HP-10B	BA-II Plus	HP-12C
setting compounding		1 ☐ [P/Y]	[2nd] [P/Y] 1 [ENTER] [2nd][QUIT]	
starting amount	95000[+/-][PV]	95000[+/-] [PV]	95000[+/-][PV]	95000 [CHS][PV]
future amount	106000[FV]	106000[FV]	106000 [FV]	106000 [FV]
time period	5 [n]	5 [N]	5 [N]	5 [n]
interest rate	[COMP] [i]	[I/YR]	[CPT] [I/Y]	[i]
answer	2.22	2.22	2.22	2.22

❖ **Interpretation:** The answer means that the average inflation rate over the past five years was 2.22%. When you know the number of periods and both the present and future value or the number of periods, the present value and an equal stream of payments, you can solve for the interest, the inflation, or the discount rate. **Interest**, **inflation**, and **discount rate** are different terms used to refer to the [i]] key.

B. Knowing Present and Future Value Using Other Than Annual Interest

▼ **Example 1.6.2:** If you put $3,000 in an investment account and the account has a balance of $6,000 at the end of ten years, what was the interest rate if the rate compounded daily? Use the following key strokes.

Purpose	EL-733A	HP-10B	BA-II Plus	HP-12C
setting compounding		365 ☐ [P/Y]	[2nd] [P/Y] 365 [ENTER] [2nd][QUIT]	
starting amount	3000[+/-][PV]	3000[+/-] [PV]	3000[+/-] [PV]	3000 [CHS] [PV]
future amount	6000[FV]	6000[FV]	6000[FV]	6000[FV]
time period	10[x]365[=][n]	10 ☐ [xP/Y]]	10[2nd][xP/Y][N]	10[ENTER]365[x][n]
interest rate	[COMP] [i]	[I/YR]	[CPT] [I/Y]	[i]
answer	.0190	6.93	6.93	.0190

❖ **Interpretation:** The answers from the different brands of calculators seem different, but they are not. The HP-10B and the BA-II Plus automatically compute the annual rate. You have to do it manually with the El-733A and the HP-12C. This means you earned .019% interest per day or 6.935% annually (.0190 X 365 = 6.935).

C. Knowing Present and an Equal Stream of Payments

▼   **Example 1.6.3:** You purchase an existing loan for $5,000 that pays $100 per month for 12 years. What is the annual discount rate earned on the loan? Use the following key strokes.

Purpose	EL-733A	HP-10B	BA-II Plus	HP-12C
setting compounding		12 □ [P/Y]	[2nd] [P/Y]12 [ENTER] [2nd][QUIT]	
starting amount	5000[+/-][PV]	5000[+/-] [PV]	5000[+/-] [PV]	5000 [CHS] [PV]
payment amount	100[PMT]	100 [PMT]	100 [PMT]	100 [PMT]
time period	12 [x] 12[=][n]	12[ ] [xP/Y]	12 [2nd][xP/Y][N]	12[ENTER]12[x][n]
interest rate	[COMP][i]	[I/YR]	[CPT][I/Y]	[i]
answer	1.859	22.31	22.31	1.859

Caution: If you get the message "error 5" on the HP-12C or BA-II Plus, "no solution" on the HP-10B, or "E" on the EL-733A, you forgot to enter either the present value or the future value as a negative number. It does not matter which one you enter as a negative number. To clear the message use [Clx] on the HP-12C, [CE/C] on the BA-II Plus, [C] on the HP-10B, and [CE-C] on the EL-733A.

❖   **Interpretation:** The 1.859 and the 22.31 are not different answers. The HP-10B and the BA-II Plus automatically compute the annual rate. You have to do it manually with the El-733A and the HP-12C. This means you earned 1.859% interest per month or 22.31% annually (1.859 X 12 = 22.31).

7. Solving for an Equal Stream of Payment

A. Knowing Present Value

▼   **Example 1.7.1:** You borrow $3,000 at 16.9% interest compounded monthly. What is the monthly payment for the loan if you plan to pay it off in 5 years? Use the following key strokes.

Purpose	EL-733A	HP-10B	BA-II Plus	HP-12C
setting compounding		12 ☐ [P/Y]	[2nd] [P/Y] 12 [ENTER] [2nd][QUIT]	
starting amount	3000[+/-][PV]	3000[+/-] [PV]	3000[+/-][PV]	3000 [CHS][PV]
interest rate	16.9[÷]12[=] [i]	16.9 [I/YR]	16.9 [I/Y]	16.9[ENTER]12[÷][i]
time period	5 [x]12[=] [n]	5 ☐[xP/Y]	5[2nd][xP/Y][N]	5[enter]12[x][n]
payment	[COMP][PMT]	[PMT]	[CPT][PMT]	[PMT]
answer	74.40	74.40	74.40	74.40

Caution: If you forgot to clear your calculator, enter 0 in **[FV]** *for all calculators before completing the last step.*

❖ **Interpretation:** It does not matter in what order you enter **[FV]**, **[PV]**, **[I]**, and **[N]** as long as everything is entered before you complete the **[PMT]** step. If your answer is -74.40, you forgot to enter the present value as a negative. The answer means that your monthly payment would be $74.40.

B. Knowing Present and Future Value

▼ **Example 1.7.2:** You take out a $30,000 second mortgage on your home at 8% interest compounded monthly for 5 years. In order to lower the payment amount, you agree to make a $15,000 single payment (a balloon payment) with the last payment. How much are your monthly payments? Use the following key strokes.

Purpose	EL-733A	HP-10B	BA-II Plus	HP-12C
setting compounding		12 ☐ [P/Y]	[2nd] [P/Y] 12 [ENTER] [2nd][QUIT]	
starting amount	30000 [+/-][PV]	30000 [+/-][PV]	30000 [+/-][PV]	30000 [CHS][PV]
interest rate	8[÷]12[=] [i]	8 [I/YR]	8 [I/Y]	8[ENTER]12[÷] [i]
future amount	15000[FV]	15000[FV]	15000[FV]	15000[FV]
time period	5 [x] 12[=] [n]	5 ☐ [xP/Y]	5 [x] 12[=][N]	5[ENTER]12[x][n]
payment	[COMP][PMT]	[PMT]	[CPT][PMT]	[PMT]
answer	404.15	404.15	404.15	404.15

❖ **Interpretation:** Your monthly payment would be $404.15. If your answer is -812.44, you forgot to enter a negative sign when entering the present value.

EXERCISE PROBLEMS

Future Value of a Single Sum

1. You put $3,000 in a certificate of deposit (CD) that pays 3% interest compounded annually. How much will the CD be worth when it matures in 2 years?

2. You deposit $5,000 in a savings account which earns 5% annual interest. How much money will you have at the end of 5 years, if interest is compounded
   a. annually?
   b. semiannually?
   c. quarterly?
   d. monthly?
   e. daily?
   (Hint: when compounding methods differ, all you need to change are the number of periods and the interest rate, then recompute the future value.)

3. If you earn $20,000 today, how much will you need to earn in 10 years to keep up with inflation if the average annual inflation rate over the next 10 years is 5%?

Future Value of a Series of Each Payment

4. You deposit $50 in a savings account each month. The account earns 2.5% annual interest compounded monthly. How much will be in the account at the end of ten years, if you
   a. make the deposit at the beginning of the month?
   b. make the deposit at the end of the month?

5. You deposit $2000 annually at the beginning of each year in a individual retirement account (IRA) that earns a 10% annual rate of return. How much will be in the account at the end of the tenth year?

Present Value of a Single Sum

6. Your certificate of deposit (CD) matured today and is worth $7,299.92. It earned 4% annual interest. How much did you deposit 5 years ago?

7. How much do you need to save today to have $100,000 when you retire in 30 years if you can average a 7% annual rate of return?

8. How much is one million dollars at retirement worth in today's dollars if inflation averages 4.5% annually and you have
   a. 45 years until you retire?
   b. 35 years until you retire?
   c. 20 years until you retire?

9. You have $538.90 in your savings accounts which pays 2.5% annual interest compounded monthly. You have not added to the account since you opened the account 3 years ago. How much money did you deposit when you opened the account? *(Hint: periods = 12 X 3 = 36)*

Present Value of a Series of Payments

10. You owe 37 more payments on your car. The interest rate on the loan is 16% compounded monthly. Your payment is $239 per month. What is the current principal balance of the loan?

11. A corporate bond has a semi-annual interest payment of $40 and will pay $1,000 when it matures in 10 years. How much should you pay for the bond if current interest rate is 6.5% compounded semi-annually?

12. Today is November 1 and you just won a sweepstakes. They want to know if you would like a check today for $500,000 or 20 annual payments of $50,000 on the first of November each year starting today. You can earn 8% annual return on your investments. If taxes are ignored, which alternative should you take?

Solving for Number of Periods

13. You purchased a certificate of deposit (CD) for $5,000 at 4% annual interest. Today your received $5,849.29. How many years did you have the CD?

14. You deposited $10,000 in a savings account that pays 3% annual interest compounded quarterly? Today you received $10,938.07. How many years did you have the account?

15. How many semi-annual payments are left on a $1,000 corporate bond that has $60 coupon payments if the current price of the bond is $1399.79 and the interest rate is 8% compounded semi-annually?

Solving for Rate

16. An investment that was worth $6,000 three years ago is worth $6,439 today. What is the average annual rate of return on the investment?

17. If your new $80,000, 30-year fully amortized mortgage has monthly payment of $678 (principal and interest only), what is the annual interest rate?

18. What is the annual rate of inflation if the monthly rate is .5%? *(Hint: you may solve this problem with three steps.)*

Solving for Payment

19. How much money do you have to save at the end of each year to have $100,000 in 10 years if your investments have an average annual rate of return of 7%.

20. How much would your monthly car payment be if you borrowed $8,000 for 5 years at 16% annual interest compounded monthly?

21. How much do you have to deposit at the beginning of each month to have $10,000 in 8 years if your savings account pays 4.5% annual interest compounded monthly?

22. You just paid $1,081.11 for a corporate bond that matures in 5 years. Current annual interest rates are 8% compounded semiannually. If the bond pays $1,000 at maturity, what is the amount of the coupon payment?

23. How much do you have to save at the beginning of each month to have a million dollars if your investments earn an average of 9% and you retire in
    a. 45 years?
    b. 35 years?
    c. 20 years?

ENDNOTES

1. A **certificate of deposit (CD)** is an interest earning savings instrument offered by an institution that accepts deposits for a fix amount of time.

2. A function "**NPV**" in financial calculators is to calculate the present value of cash flows. The use of this function is demonstrated in the section "Cost-Benefit Analysis of Graduate Education" found in Chapter 6, Career Planning Math.

Chapter 2
Personal Finance and The Computer

▼ Using Typed-in Formulas to Calculate Time Value of Money
▼ Using Built-in Functions to Calculate Time Value of Money
▼ Using Logical Operators
▼ Using Backsolver to Solve an Iterative Problem
▼ Enhancing Presentation of Financial Information
▼ Search for Personal Finance Information on the Internet

Chapter 2
Personal Finance and The Computer

Regina Chang and Sandra J. Huston[1]

OVERVIEW

As computers become more prevalent in the home and workplace there is reason to ponder the question, "What role does the personal computer have in managing personal finances?" The specific role a personal computer can have for you is dependent upon your own circumstances. Provided below is a discussion of the issues regarding personal finance and the computer.

The computer offers many useful features for managing personal finances. The major advantages of using a computer include powerful computation, sophisticated memory capacity, complex functions, speed, accuracy, convenience, and the ability of merging various sources and types of information. For example, computers can perform repetitive tasks, such as monthly updates, with accuracy and ease. Computers are particularly useful for creating financial scenarios which can help you to compare between periods or alternatives. Also, reports can be generated which present financial information in various combinations of formats—tables, charts, graphics, and text. You can use a computer to create a high quality, detailed report of your own personal financial plan. Moreover, the use of a computer can greatly assist you solving problems which require repetitious computations and/or an iterative (trial and error) process.

While computers have many attractive features for managing personal finances, there are some caveats to bear in mind. First, there is the expense. You need access to the hardware (the computer itself and a printer) and software (computer applications). Fortunately, computers are widely available and affordable. Second, there is the skill. You need to know how to operate the equipment and the relevant

---

[1]Regina Chang, Ph.D., Assistant Professor, Consumer and Family Economics, University of Missouri, Columbia, MO 65211. cfechang@mizzou1.missouri.edu; and Sandra J. Huston, Ph.D. Candidate, Consumer and Family Economics, University of Missouri, Columbia, MO 65211. c641349@mizzou1.missouri.edu

applications. Not knowing how to use a computer properly can be very frustrating and time consuming. Third, there is the software itself. If the financial software available does not meet your particular needs, then some modifications may be required. This will require time and expertise. Remember, personal computers will execute programs whether they are useful or not! Finally, it is important to remember that a computer is only a tool not a magician! A computer can certainly provide excellent support, but it is the human who is responsible for developing a sound financial plan. This includes knowing which personal finance mathematical formulas are appropriate for which situations.

Major uses of the computer in personal financial planning include spreadsheet applications, on-line services, and personal financial software. There are several types of computer software which can assist in managing personal finances. The three broad categories of software are (1) money management, (2) taxes, and (3) investment. Examples of various software packages in these three areas are listed below in the section, "Information and Computing Resources."

Money management software typically assists in maintaining home financial records, creating budgets, tracking expenditures, writing checks, keeping tax records, selecting and monitoring investments, and projecting retirement needs. Tax software is available to prepare both federal and state-level income tax returns. Tax programs often include tax-planning tips, audit warnings, and the ability to file your tax returns electronically. Finally, investment software is designed for researching, trading, and monitoring one's investment portfolio. Many of these investment programs are connected to on-line services to obtain current stock quotes and allow a buy and sell format for trading investments.

In terms of computer applications, in contrast to a word processor which manipulates text, an electronic spreadsheet manipulates numerical data. Electronic spreadsheets have been around for about two decades. The particular spreadsheet application used in the examples provided in this chapter is Lotus 1-2-3; however, there are many spreadsheet programs available for use on IBM compatible and MacIntosh computers, such as Excel, QuattroPro, SuperCal.

The following five examples will illustrate the usefulness of a computer spreadsheet application in solving personal financial problems: (1) using typed-in financial functions, (2) using built-in functions, (3) using logical operators, (4) using an iterative solving feature (e.g., backsolver), and (5) enhancing presentation of financial information.

This chapter also gives an example how to search for personal financial information in the Internet. The **Internet** is a global network of computers linked by high-speed data lines and wireless systems that allows people to share information and resources. Several approaches can be used to navigate the Internet, such as E-mail, newsgroup reader, FTP, Telnet, Gopher, and World Wide Web (WWW) browser. Numerous government agencies, educational institutions, companies, and other non-profit organizations in the world distribute information and other services on the Internet, especially WWW sites. Through Internet, you can get access to personal financial information and some financial services, such as on-line investment trading, home banking, and purchasing. Some terms commonly used in the Internet are included in the "Information and Computing Resources" section of this chapter.

EXAMPLES OF USING ELECTRONIC SPREADSHEETS AND INTERNET

1. Using Typed-in Formulas to Calculate Time Value of Money

Electronic Spreadsheet Operation: If there are no built-in functions available on the available spreadsheet software program, the appropriate formula can be typed into the spreadsheet. Relative and absolute cell referencing (described below) can be used to type in formulas to calculate time value of money as well as perform various other calculations. To enter a numeric formula, the following arithmetic operators are used:

    +   for addition
    -   for subtraction
    *   for multiplication
    /   for division
    ^   for exponentiation

▼ **Example 2.1:** If Andrew Peng expects to receive $50,000 from a trust fund in three years, calculate the current value of this amount given an annual interest rate of 8.25%, 10%, and 12.5%, using the formula: $PV = FV/(1 + i)^n$, where, PV = present value, FV = future value, i = interest rate, and n = number of years.

Solution: The operation procedure is demonstrated in Spreadsheet 1.

SPREADSHEET 1

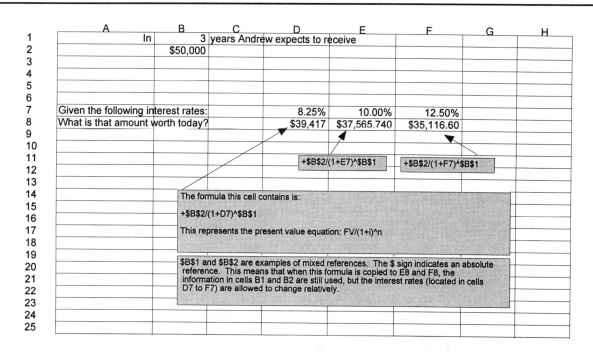

Step 1: type in the given information, such as number of years (Cell B1), future value (B2), interest rates (D7, E7, F7), and any narrative descriptions (optional).

Step 2: to calculate D8, type, +$B$2/(1+E7)^$B$1 and enter which reveals the answer, $39,417.25.

Step 3: copy D8 to E8 and F8, and two more answers will be shown.

❖ **Interpretation:** The answers are $39,417.25, $37,565.74, and $35,116.60, respectively. Because there are no built-in financial functions in Lotus 1-2-3 available for calculating the time value of a lump sum, the formula should be typed in the spreadsheet to perform the calculation. In this example, you may distinguish the difference between absolute and relative cell references. An **absolute cell reference** is indicated with "$" signs which does not change the value when it is copied. In this example, $B$1 is used in Cell D8, E8, and F8, and the value always is the same as B1, 3. For the same reason, $B$2 is also an absolute reference. However, a **relative cell reference** is one without a "$" sign and it will change the value when the cell changes. In this example, D7, E7, and F7 are relative cell references. Both types of references will have significance when the formula is copied from one cell to other cells. In this example, the mixed references (using both absolute and relative cell references) are used.

2. Using Built-in Functions to Calculate Time Value of Money

Electronic Spreadsheet Operation: There are many **built-in financial functions** in electronic spreadsheets that can be used to calculate time values of money. The following are three example of the functions available in Lotus 1-2-3:

@**PMT**   (principal, interest, term) that calculates the payment on a loan (principal) at a given interest rate for a specified number of payment periods (terms);

@**PV**   (payments, interest, term) that calculates present value given periodic payment, interest rate and term; and

@**FV**   (payments, interest, term) that calculates future value given periodic payment, interest rate and term.

For a complete listing of all the financial functions available to you, please consult your software documentation literature.

Note that Excel, another popular spreadsheet program, usually starts any calculations with "=" sign. For example, in Excel, to calculate "payment", type =pmt(...). Excel users may check the manual for detail.

▼ **Example 2.2:** Jim and Suzy Evans have decided to purchase a home which costs $125,000. They will be able to pay a 20% downpayment plus pay the closing costs from the proceeds of sale of their current residence. They want to have the new home paid in full in 15 years. Assuming the mortgage interest rate is 8.75% and there are no up front points, what is the monthly payment?

Solution: The operational procedure is demonstrated in Spreadsheet 2.

SPREADSHEET 2

	A	B	C	D	E	F
1	How much is Jim and	Suzy's monthly home payment?				
2						
3	Home price:	$125,000				
4	Down Payment	$25,000	20.00%	of home price		
5	Loan amount	$100,000				
6	Length	15	years	=	180	months
7	Annual Interest rate	0.0875		=	0.007292	monthly
8	Monthly Payment	$999.45				
9						
10						
11						
12		The function this cell contains is:				
13		@PMT(B5,E7,E6)				
14						
15		This represents the ordinary due payment function.				
16						
17						
18						
19						

Step 1: type in given information and descriptions (A1-8, B3, B6-7, C4, C6, D4, D6-7, F6-7);

Step 2: to calculate B4 (down payment), type +B3*C4, and press Enter, and then B4 will be shown as $25,000.00;

Step 3: to calculate B5 (loan amount), type +B3-B4, and press Enter, and then B5 will be shown as $100,000.00;

Step 4: to calculate E6 (number of months), type +B6*12, and press Enter, and then E6 will be shown as 180;

Step 5: to calculate E7 (monthly rate), type +B7/12, and press Enter, and then E7 will be shown as 0.73%; and

Step 6: to calculate B8 (monthly payment), type @PMT(B5, E7, E6), and press Enter, and then B8 will be shown as $999.45.

❖ **Interpretation:** The monthly payment will be $999.45. The built-in financial functions are very useful in solving quantitative financial problems. The example illustrated here used the @PMT (principal, interest, term) function that calculates the ordinary payment due (e.g., the payment made at the end of the period) on a loan of $100,000 (B5). *Caution: Note that before using the built-in function @PMT, two adjustments need to be made. The annual interest rate should be converted to a monthly rate (E7) and the number of years should be converted to the number of months (E6). Also note that in Steps 2 to 5, the typed-in formula approach is used.*

3. Using Logical Operators

The following case study provides an example of medical insurance payments to illustrate the use of logical operators in the @IF function

Electronic Spreadsheet Operation: The logical operators in the electronic spreadsheets can calculate two alternatives in personal financial decisions. The logical operator used in Lotus 1-2-3 is as follows:

@**IF**   (condition;x;y) that selects one of two values depending on the given condition. If condition is true, @IF returns x; if false, @IF returns y.

▼ **Example 2.3:** Jim Malcom has a medical insurance policy that pays 80% of medical bills in excess of the deductible with a cap of $1,000 as the maximum amount that will be paid. The deductible for this policy is $500 and the annual premium is $2000. Calculate the amount Jim has to pay if his accumulated medical expenses for the year are as follows:

Scenario 1: $489.28
Scenario 2: $574.76
Scenario 3: $9374.26

Solution: Spreadsheet 3 demonstrates the operation procedures (the formulas used are demonstrated in Column E).

Step 1: type in given information and descriptions (A1-22, B2-6, C2-6, D2-6, B20, C20, D20);

Step 2: to calculate B8 (deductible paid by Jim), type @IF(B6<B3, B6, B3), and press Enter and B8 will be shown as $489.28 since $489.28(B6)<$500.00(B3), and then $489.28 is selected;

Step 3: to calculate B10 (total bill submitted to insurance), type @IF(B6<B3, 0, (B6-B3)), and press Enter, and B10 will be shown as $0.00 since Jim's expense in this scenario is less than the deductible, and then he does not need to send the medical bill to the insurance company;

Step 4: to calculate B12 (copayment by Jim), type, @IF(0.2*B10>B4, B4, 0.2*B10), and press Enter, and B12 will be shown as $0.00 since Jim does not ask for the payment from the insurance company in this scenario, and then he does not need to make copayment;

SPREADSHEET 3

	A	B	C	D	E
1	Jim's Medical Insurance Plan				
2		Scenario 1	Scenario 2	Scenario 3	Lotus 1-2-3 Operations
3	Deductible ------>	$500	$500	$500	+B3 (value given)
4	Maximum Annual Copayment ------>	$1,000	$1,000	$1,000	+B4 (value given)
5					
6	Jim's medical bills	$489.28	$574.76	$9,374.26	value given
7					
8	Deductible paid by Jim	$489	$500	$500	@IF(E6<E3,E6,E3)
9					
10	TOTAL BILL SUBMITTED TO INSURANCE	$0	$75	$8,874	@IF(E6<E3,0,(E6-E3))
11					
12	COPAYMENT BY YOU (20% or cap)	$0	$15	$1,000	@IF((0.2*E10)>E4,E4,(0.2*E10))
13					
14	COPAYMENT by insurance company	$0	$60	$7,874	+E10-E12
15					
16	YOUR TOTAL ANNUAL COST				
17					
18	Deductibles	$489	$500	$500	+E8
19	Copayment	$0	$15	$1,000	+E12
20	Premium	$2,000	$2,000	$2,000	+B20 (value given)
21					
22	TOTAL ------>	$2,489.28	$2,514.95	$3,500.00	@SUM(E17..E20)
23					
24					

Callout (rows 3–8):
Medical expenses are less than the deductible amount. If this statement is true then the actual expenses (E6) is assigned to the cells in row 8, if not then the amount of the deductible ($500) is assigned to this cell instead.

To determine the bill submitted to the insurance company, the same argument applies, EXCEPT if the statement is false, then the value of bills-deductible is entered in the cells in row 10.

Callout (rows 17–20):
To determine Jim's share of copayment the condition is 20% of the bill submitted exceeds the maximum copayment ($1,000). If this statement is true then the cap amount is assigned to the cells in row 12. If the statement is false then 20% of the bill submitted to the insurance company is assigned to these cells.

Step 5: to calculate B14 (copayment by insurance company), type +B10-B12, and press Enter, and the B14 will be shown as $0.00;

Step 6: to calculate B22 (total insurance costs), type +B8+B12+B20, and press Enter, and B22 will be shown as $2,489.28; and

Step 7: to calculate all values between C8 to D22, copy B8-B22 to C8-D22.

❖ **Interpretation:** B22, C22, and D22 indicate the answers of this question. From this spreadsheet, we can determine that the maximum out-of-pocket expenses for Jim will not exceed $3,500. As the medical bills increase, the amount that Jim actually has to pay does not increase proportionally. As medical bills increase, Jim pays an increasing absolute amount at a decreasing rate.

This example demonstrates the use of the @IF function, a logical operator, to assign an appropriate value to a given cell depending on the given condition. For example, Step 2 is using @IF to assign a value of the deductible. If the medical expense is less than the value of the deductible, the value of the actual expense will be used, which is the case in B8. If the medical expense is greater than the deductible, the deductible value is used which is the case in C8 and D8. Step 3 is using @IF to decide if Jim needs to submit the medical bill to the insurance company. If the medical bill is less than the deductible, Jim does not need to send the bill which is the case in B10. But if the bill is greater than the deductible, Jim needs to send bill minus the deductible to the insurance company as indicated in C10 and D10. Step 4 is using @IF to decide the copayment amount by Jim. In B12, since Jim's expense is less than the deductible, he does not need to send the bill to the company; thus he does not need to make copayment. C12 demonstrates a case in which the copayment (20% of the medical expense submitted to the insurance company) is less than the maximum value of copayment, and D12 is a case in which Jim makes a maximum copayment.

4. Using Backsolver to Solve an Iterative Problem

Electronic Spreadsheet Operation: The **backsolver** refers to a trial-and-error approach to find a value for a cell that makes another cell with a formula using the value of the first cell to achieve a desirable value you specify.

▼ **Example 2.4:** Alonzo Binkly is 30, with an annual income of $35,000 and currently he has $4,000 in his investment account. Alonzo has decided to put aside 10% of his income every year for retirement. Assuming that Alonzo wants to retire at age 65 with $1,000,000, what is the rate of return Alonzo must have in his investment account for him to achieve the $1,000,000 goal?

Solution: Spreadsheet 4 demonstrates the operation procedures.

Step 1: type in given information and descriptions (A1 to D7, A45);

Step 2: type 5% in B45, in which 5% is an assumed initial value of interest rate;

Step 3: to calculate A8, type +A7+1, and press Enter, and A8 will be shown as 31;

SPREADSHEET 4

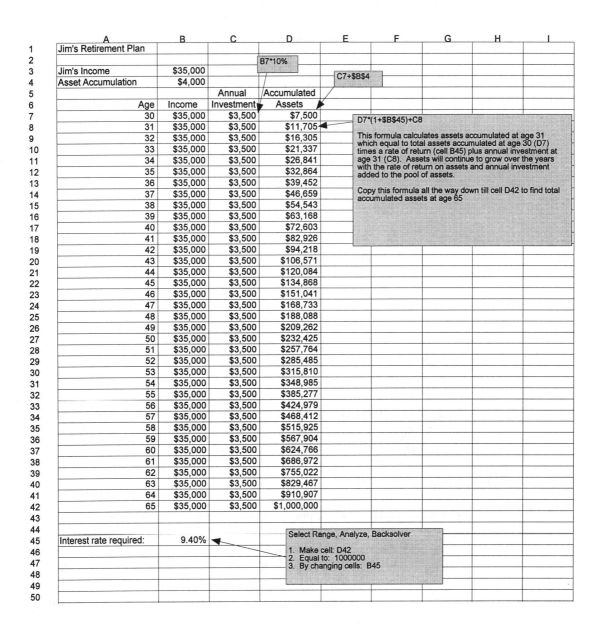

	A	B	C	D	E	F	G	H	I
1	Jim's Retirement Plan								
2				B7*10%					
3	Jim's Income	$35,000							
4	Asset Accumulation	$4,000			C7+$B$4				
5			Annual	Accumulated					
6	Age	Income	Investment	Assets					
7	30	$35,000	$3,500	$7,500					
8	31	$35,000	$3,500	$11,705	D7*(1+$B$45)+C8				
9	32	$35,000	$3,500	$16,305					
10	33	$35,000	$3,500	$21,337					
11	34	$35,000	$3,500	$26,841					
12	35	$35,000	$3,500	$32,864					
13	36	$35,000	$3,500	$39,452					
14	37	$35,000	$3,500	$46,659					
15	38	$35,000	$3,500	$54,543					
16	39	$35,000	$3,500	$63,168					
17	40	$35,000	$3,500	$72,603					
18	41	$35,000	$3,500	$82,926					
19	42	$35,000	$3,500	$94,218					
20	43	$35,000	$3,500	$106,571					
21	44	$35,000	$3,500	$120,084					
22	45	$35,000	$3,500	$134,868					
23	46	$35,000	$3,500	$151,041					
24	47	$35,000	$3,500	$168,733					
25	48	$35,000	$3,500	$188,088					
26	49	$35,000	$3,500	$209,262					
27	50	$35,000	$3,500	$232,425					
28	51	$35,000	$3,500	$257,764					
29	52	$35,000	$3,500	$285,485					
30	53	$35,000	$3,500	$315,810					
31	54	$35,000	$3,500	$348,985					
32	55	$35,000	$3,500	$385,277					
33	56	$35,000	$3,500	$424,979					
34	57	$35,000	$3,500	$468,412					
35	58	$35,000	$3,500	$515,925					
36	59	$35,000	$3,500	$567,904					
37	60	$35,000	$3,500	$624,766					
38	61	$35,000	$3,500	$686,972					
39	62	$35,000	$3,500	$755,022					
40	63	$35,000	$3,500	$829,467					
41	64	$35,000	$3,500	$910,907					
42	65	$35,000	$3,500	$1,000,000					
43									
44									
45	Interest rate required:	9.40%							
46									
47									
48									
49									
50									

Comment box (pointing to D8):

This formula calculates assets accumulated at age 31 which equal to total assets accumulated at age 30 (D7) times a rate of return (cell B45) plus annual investment at age 31 (C8). Assets will continue to grow over the years with the rate of return on assets and annual investment added to the pool of assets.

Copy this formula all the way down till cell D42 to find total accumulated assets at age 65

Comment box (pointing to B45):

Select Range, Analyze, Backsolver

1. Make cell: D42
2. Equal to: 1000000
3. By changing cells: B45

Step 4: to calculate B8, type +B7, and press Enter, and B8 will have the same value as B7;

Step 5: to calculate C8, type +C7, and press Enter, and C8 will have the same value as C7;

Step 6: to calculate D8, type +D7*(1+$B$45)+C8, and enter. The formula means 7500 X (1+0.05) + 3500 = 11375. If the interest rate is 5%, and Alonzo puts another $3,500 in his investment, he will have $11,375 at the end of the second year. Note that the value here is different from the one in D8 in Spreadsheet 4. Why? The reason is that now a 5% rate is used, instead of a 9.4% rate. Note that an absolute cell reference is used for B45 and relative cell references are used for other cells.

Step 7: copy A8-D8 to A9-D42. The values of A9 to C42 will be the same as ones in Spreadsheet 4, but the values of D9 to D42 are different.

Step 8: Lotus 1-2-3 has a feature available to help find the exact interest rate required. This feature is called "**Backsolver**." Choose Range, Analyze, Backsolver from the menu bar. In the "Make cell" text box, specify the cell containing the formula. In this example, it is the cell D42. In the "Equal to value" text box, enter the specific result you want for the formula. In this example, we want to make cell D42 equal to $1,000,000, so type 1000000 in the "Equal to value" text box. In the "By changing cell" text box, specify the cell containing the value you want to change. Here, it is the cell B45. Choose OK. Lotus 1-2-3 replaces the value in the cell B45 with the value that makes cell D42 equal the result specified, $1,000,000.

❖ **Interpretation:** If Alonzo plans to invest in the way he specifies, he needs an return rate of 9.4% to achieve his goal of having one million dollars in his investment account when he is 65 years old. When one has a specific financial goal to reach in a specified period of time, one needs to find an investment opportunity which may provide the necessary rate of return to reach the goal. You can use "Backsolver" to find the interest rate required.

5. Enhancing Presentation of Financial Information

Electronic Spreadsheet Operation: The format of a report can be created manually or by pre-selected templates (style gallery). A chart is an illustration of data in your worksheet. Charts are effective ways to present data. They can make relationships among numbers easy to comprehend because they turn numbers into shapes (lines, bars, slices of a pie), and the shapes can then be compared to one another. Using an electronic spreadsheet, you can set up a range so that it contains all the elements you need to create a basic chart.

▼ **Example 2.5:** Jim's personal monthly expenditures are displayed on the top portion of Spreadsheet 5. Create a report format and a pie chart using the data provided.

Solution:

(1) To create a **report format**, do the following:
   A. Highlight A10 to B16;
   B. Click on STYLE menu;
   C. Select GALLERY;

SPREADSHEET 5

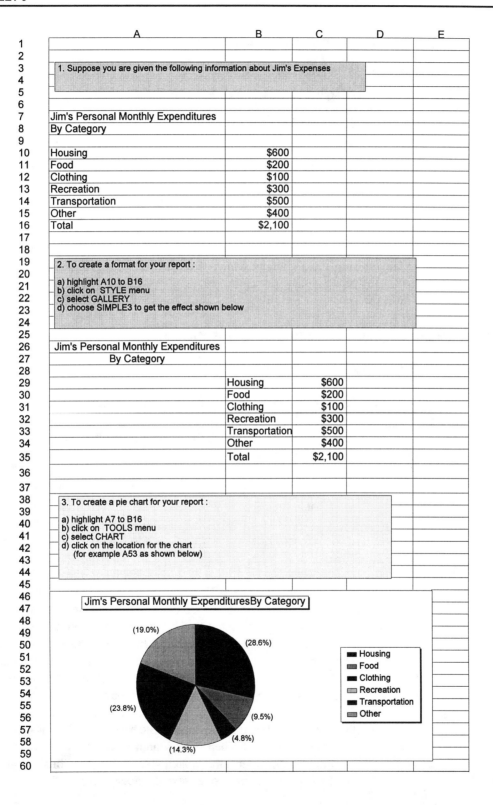

	A	B	C	D	E
1					
2					
3	1. Suppose you are given the following information about Jim's Expenses				
4					
5					
6					
7	Jim's Personal Monthly Expenditures				
8	By Category				
9					
10	Housing	$600			
11	Food	$200			
12	Clothing	$100			
13	Recreation	$300			
14	Transportation	$500			
15	Other	$400			
16	Total	$2,100			
17					
18					
19	2. To create a format for your report :				
20					
21	a) highlight A10 to B16				
22	b) click on STYLE menu				
	c) select GALLERY				
23	d) choose SIMPLE3 to get the effect shown below				
24					
25					
26	Jim's Personal Monthly Expenditures				
27	By Category				
28					
29		Housing	$600		
30		Food	$200		
31		Clothing	$100		
32		Recreation	$300		
33		Transportation	$500		
34		Other	$400		
35		Total	$2,100		
36					
37					
38	3. To create a pie chart for your report :				
39					
40	a) highlight A7 to B16				
41	b) click on TOOLS menu				
	c) select CHART				
42	d) click on the location for the chart				
43	(for example A53 as shown below)				
44					
45					
46					
47	Jim's Personal Monthly ExpendituresBy Category				
48					
49	(19.0%)				
50	(28.6%)				
51					Housing
52					Food
53					Clothing
54					Recreation
55	(23.8%)				Transportation
56	(9.5%)				Other
57					
58	(4.8%)				
59	(14.3%)				
60					

D. Choose SIMPLE3, and the effects are shown in the middle part of Spreadsheet 5.

(2) To create a **pie chart**, do the following:

A. Highlight A7 to B16;

B. Click on TOOLS menu;

C. Select CHART;

D. Click on the location for the chart, and the effects are shown in the bottom part of Spreadsheet 5.

❖ **Interpretation:** Given the data presented in the spreadsheet, a pie chart seems to be an effective way to illustrate budget allocation of monthly expenses. Depending upon the types of available data and the purposes required, you may choose different types of charts to enhance a presentation. You may further enhance a report with a Draw feature (Tools, Draw) which provides line, arrow drawing, text box, etc. Font & Attributes and Lines & Color (under STYLE) are also helpful tools that may be used to enhance a report.

6. Search for Personal Finance Information on the Internet

Search Steps:

1. Select Netscape on Windows by double clicking the icon.

2. Search for specific sites via the use of net search or enter a URL for a search engine home page.

3. If you know the URL of a specific site that may contain the information you need, enter the URL in the at the "Location" space on screen. It is important that you type in correct URL at the space provided to go to the desired site. If you do not know a site from which to obtain a stock quote, follow steps 4 and 5.

4. If you don't know the URL of a site and would like to conduct a search of a subject that you are interested in, click on "Net Search" box on the screen and you will be prompted to the Search Page. You may select any search engine, such as Alta Vista, Yahoo, Infoseek, and Lycos, to conduct the search by clicking on one particular search engine box. After selecting the engine box, type key words or concepts which describe what you are looking for in the text box on the Search page.

5. Once you have typed in the appropriate search words, click the "Search" or "Go get it" button. When your search is completed you will see a page showing the documents that match your search (the "hits"). Each document is a **link**. Click the link to retrieve the document.

▼ **Example 2.6:** Jerry Murphy currently holds 500 shares of Wal-mart stock. He would like to determine the value of his stock holding today. Use Internet to find the price quote for Wal-mart stock, and then use this information to calculate the total value of his stock. The web site that includes stock quotes for major companies is http://www.secapl.com/cgi-bin/qs.

Solution:

1. Select Netscape on Windows by double clicking the icon.
2. Type http://www.secapl.com/cgi-bin/qs at the "Location" space on screen and it will take you to a site where you can get a stock quote for the Wal-mart stock.
3. Take the per share value the stock at its last trade and multiply this figure by 500 shares to determine the current value of Jim's stock.

Useful Terminology: Following are explanations of common Internet terminology.

Internet is a global network of computers linked by high-speed data lines and wireless systems. Established in 1969 as a military communications system, it allows people of all ages, nationalities, and backgrounds to share information and resources.

WWW refers to World Wide Web that is a hypermedia information storage system linking resources around the world. Browsers allow highlighted words or icons, called hyperlinks, to display text, video, graphics, and sound on a local computer screen, no matter where the resource is actually located.

Hypermedia, also called **multimedia**, this describes the Web's integration of audio, video, graphics, and text.

Browser is a program that allows users to access the Web with the click of a mouse. Graphical browsers such as NCSA's Mosaic and Netscape's Navigator enable consumers to bypass plain text for slick sounds and graphics.

Hyperlinks are highlighted words or images on a Web page that, when clicked on by a mouse, can connect the user to a new location. For example, if the word Mars was a hyperlink, clicking on it would result in an image of Mars, an article about the planet or both to appear on screen.

URL means Universal Resource Locator.

HTML means HyperText Markup Language.

HTTP, for HyperText Transport Protocol, is the Internet standard that enables information to be distributed across the web. HTTP allows programmers to embed hyperlinks (using HTML) in documents.

INFORMATION AND COMPUTING RESOURCES

1. Following is a list of personal financial planning software (money management, taxes, and investment) as well as some computerized data bases for investors.

Money Management Software

Quicken Financial Planner
(800) 446-8848

Dollars and Sense
Monogram
8295 South La Cienega Blvd.
Inglewood, CA 90301
(213) 215-0355

Andrew Tobias Managing Your Money
MECA Software
285 Riverside Ave.
Westport CT 06880
800-962-5583
203-222-9087

Financial Independence
Charles Schwab & Co.
101 Montgomery St.
San Francisco CA 94104
800-334-4455
415-627-7197

Personal Financial Planner
Lumen Systems
P.O. Box 9893
Englewood NJ 07631
201-592-1121

Sylvia Porter's Your Personal
Financial Planner
Timeworks Inc.
444 Lake Cook Rd.
Deerfield IL 60015
800-323-9755
312-948-9200

J.K. Lasser's Your Money
    Manager
Simon & Schuster Electronic
Publishing
Gulf & Western Bldg.
One Gulf & Western Plaza
New York NY 10023
800-624-0023
212-333-3397

PC/PFP II
Best Programs
5134 Leesburg Pike
Alexandria VA 22302
800-368-2405
703-931-1300

The Home Accountant Plus
Continental Software
6711 Valjean Ave.
Van Nuys CA 91406
800-468-4222
818-989-5822

Financier II
Financial Software Inc.
P.O. Box 558
Hudson MA 01749

Investment Software

Value/Screen Plus
Value Line Inc.
711 Third Ave.
New York NY 10017

Stockpak II
Standard & Poor's Corp.
Micro Services Dept.
25 Broadway
New York NY 10004
800-852-5200
212-208-8581

Dow Jones Market Microscope
Dow Jones & Company
P.O. Box 300
Princeton NJ 08540
800-257-5114
609-452-2000

Computerized Data Bases for Investors

CompuServe
5000 Arlington Center Blvd.
P.O. Box 20212
Columbus OH 43220
800-848-8990
614-457-0802

Dow Jones News/Retrieval
    (DJN/R)
Dow Jones & Company
P.O. Box 300
Princeton NJ 08540
800-257-5114
609-452-1511

The Equalizer
Charles Schwab & Co.
101 Montgomery St.
San Francisco CA 94104
800-334-4455
415-627-7197

The Source
Source Telecomputing Corp.
1616 Anderson Rd.
McLean VA 22102
800-336-3366
703-734-7500

Tax Software

J.K. Lasser's Your Income Tax
Simon & Schuster Electronic
Publishing
Gulf & Western Building
One Gulf & Western Plaza
New York NY 10023
800-624-0023
212-333-3397

PC/TaxCut
Best Programs
5134 Leesburg Pike
Alexandria VA 22302
800-368-2405 (outside Virginia)
703-931-1300 (Virginia only)

The Tax Series
Financial Software Inc.
P.O. Box 558
Hudson MA 01749
617-568-0374

Forecast
Monogram
South La Cienega Blvd.
Inglewood CA 90301
213-215-0355

Swiftax
Timeworks Inc.
444 Lake Cook Rd.
Deerfield IL 60015
800-323-9755
312-948-9200

The Tax Advantage
Continental Software
6711 Valjean Ave.
Van Nuys CA 91406
800-468-4222
818-989-5822

Professional Tax Planner
Ardvark McGraw-Hill
1020 Broadway
Milwaukee WI 53202
414-225-7500

Turbo Tax
Chipsoft
5045 Shoreham Place
San Diego CA 92122-3954
800-782-1120
619-453-8722

Quick Tax
800-224-0991 ext. 500444

2. Popular personal financial web sites.

- *ACCI:* http://acci.ps.missouri.edu (information on membership, publications, and other services of the American Council on Consumer Interests).

- *AFCPE:* http://www.hec.ohio-state.edu/hanna/sh/index.htm (information of the journal and newsletter of Association of Financial Counseling and Planning Education)

- *Consumer Information Center:* http://www.pueblo.gsa.gov (the current issue of the Consumer Information Catalog and its publications).

- *Consumer Law:* http://consumerlawpage.com (extensive information related to many aspects of consumer law along with the National Consumer Complaint Center).

- *Federal Agencies:* http://www.law.vill.edu/Fed-Agency/fedwebloc.html (locate federal agencies).

- *GNN's Personal Finance:* http://gnn.com/gnn/wic/wics/persfin.new.html (a starting point for finding interesting web sites on financial planning).

- *Money Magazine:* http://moneymag.com (selected features and information from the latest issue of Money).

- *Personal Finance Employee Education:* http://www.chre.vt.edu/~/pfee/ (resources on personal finance employee education).

EXERCISE PROBLEMS

Using Typed-in Formulas to Calculate Time Value of Money

1. If you expect to receive $10,000 from a trust fund in five years, how much do you need to deposit into this fund today given an annual interest rate of 5.25%, 7.25%, and 9.5%?

2. John Smith purchased a plot of land for $25,000 four years ago. If the land has appreciated 12% each year, what is its value now? If the land has appreciated 15% each year, what is its value now?

Using Built-in Functions to Calculate Time Value of Money

3. Tom and Jane made a loan to their son, Matt. For the next 10 years, Matt is repaying his parents $2,000 every year. If the interest rate on the loan is 10%, what was the dollar amount of the original loan?

4. If Mary and Chris invest $2,000 at the end of each year in an investment providing an 11% annual return, what will be its value in 10 years?

Using Logical Operators

5. Jean has medical insurance where the insurance company pays 70% of medical bills in excess of the deductible with a cap of $1,500. The deductible for this policy is $750 and the annual premium is $1800. Calculate the amount Jean has to pay if her accumulated medical expenses for the year are as follows:

   Scenario 1: $1025.28
   Scenario 2: $ 669.76

6. Gilberto Gerruro has a taxable income $25,150, and as a single person he takes the standard deduction. If he was buying a home and could use the mortgage interest and property taxes as itemized deductions, his taxable income would be reduced to $20,930. What are his tax liabilities in both scenarios using the tax rate schedule below?

If Taxable Income is	Tax Rate
0 - $23,499	15%
$23,500 - $56,749	28%

7. The XYZ mail order company charges different shipping and handling fees according to amount of purchase as summarized below:

Purchase ($)	S & H charges ($)
$50 and below	$ 5
$51 - $100	$ 7
$101 - $150	$ 9
$151 - $200	$11
$201 and above	$15

   Use the @IF function to calculate total amount (purchase and S&H) a consumer needs to pay if he/she makes a purchase of $57. What will be the total charge if the purchases are $125 and $300?

Using Backsolver to Solve an Iterative Problem

8. Neil is 40 years old. He has an annual income of $45,000 and currently has $75,000 in his investment account. Neil has decided to put aside 12% of his income every year for retirement. Assuming that Neil wants to retire at age 55

with $1,000,000, what is the rate of return Neil must have in his investment account for him to achieve the goal?

9. Gene is 30 years old. He has an annual income of $35,000 and currently has $4,000 in his investment account. Gene decided to put his money in an investment which is expected to earn a rate of return of 12% rate annually. Gene would like to retire at age 65 with $1,000,000. What is the percentage of income Gene needs to put aside each year for him to achieve the retirement goal?

Enhancing Presentation of Financial Information

10. Use the data in Spreadsheet 5 to create a line chart and a bar chart. Print them out and compare them with the pie chart. Record any advantages and/or disadvantages of using different types of charts.

11. Use a report format and your own data to present a balance sheet (assets plus liabilities equals net worth).

12. Jim and Suzy have collected their monthly expenses information from June to November. They would like to see how their expenses changed month to month with help of some graphic illustration. Create a bar chart to show the monthly expenses from June to November.

June:	$1,355
July:	$1,567
August:	$1,665
September:	$2,205
October:	$1,458
November:	$1,675

13. Using the information provided above, create a line chart to show the monthly expenses from June to November.

Search for Personal Finance Information on the Internet

14. Use the "net search" function in Netscape with the key word "retirement planning" to find a formula to calculate your retirement needs.

15. John is thinking of investing $5,000 in a stock which will yield at least 15% annual return with moderate risk. He would like to review past performance of some stocks before making his decision. Use Internet to help John find the historical stock price information so he can decide which stock to invest.

16. Jeff expresses his interest of subscribing Kiplinger Personal Financial Magazine to his friend Jennifer. Jennifer tells Jeff "save your money, the magazine is on-line!"So the magazine is one-line! Use a browser and find the magazine's home page to prove it yourself.

SELECTED REFERENCES

Goldstein, D., & Flory, J. (1997). *The online guide to personal finance and investing*. Chicago: Irwin.

Fister, M. (1995). *A pocket tour of money on the Internet*. San Francisco: Sybex.

Kardas, E. P., & Milford, T. M. (1996). *Using the Internet for social science research and practice*. Belmont, CA: Wadsworth.

Massey, P. D., & Douglas, D. E. (1994). *Lotus 1-2-3 for windows: Acquiring functional skills*. Houston, TX: Dame Publications.

O'Leary, T. J., & O'Leary, L. I. (1994). *Lotus 1-2-3: Release 5 for windows*. Hightstown, NJ: McGraw-Hill.

Chapter 3
The Economic Environment of Personal Finance

▼ **Percentage Change in the Consumer Price Index**

▼ **Purchasing Power Based on Consumer Price Changes**

▼ **Inflation-Adjusted Income Change Rate**

▼ **Inflation- and Tax-Adjusted Investment Return Rate**

▼ **Using Inflation and Interest Rate Estimates to Plan for Future Goals**

Chapter 3
The Economic Environment of Personal Finance

Jean M. Lown[1]

OVERVIEW

Is now a good time to buy a home? Are mortgage rates heading up or down? Should I put off buying a vehicle until interest rates come down? Should I purchase a short term certificate of deposit or go for the longer term commitment? Will interest rates likely be higher or lower when my certificate of deposit (CD) comes up for renewal? An understanding of economic trends is essential to wise consumer decisions.

Fundamental to applying the concepts of personal finance mathematics is to understand the economic environment surrounding and affecting your decisions. Personal finance decisions are not made in a vacuum. Economic cycles and unanticipated national and world events will affect your finances. An **economic cycle** (or **business cycle**) is a wavelike pattern of economic activity that includes temporary phases that undulate from boom to bust: expansion, recession (or depression), and recovery. While no one has a crystal ball to forecast economic trends with certainty, understanding the phases of the economic cycle will enable you to improve the quality of your personal financial decisions.

Other components of the **economic environment** that will influence your financial life are interest rates and inflation. **Interest rates** are indicators of the cost of money, and the rates rise during times of high inflation. **Inflation** is a steady rise in the general level of prices. Inflation is measured in a number of ways but the most widely used measure for consumers is the **consumer price index (CPI)**. The CPI tracks prices of a market basket of goods and services for urban consumers. While not a direct reflection of an individual's costs, the CPI provides an estimate of the trends in consumer prices.

---

[1] Jean M. Lown, Ph.D., Professor, Department of Human Environments, Utah State University, Logan, UT 84321-2910. Lown@cc.usu.edu.

To economists, inflation is a steady rise in the general level of prices which affects purchasing power. Even at a moderate 5% annual rate, prices will double in only 14 years.

The best way to assess the current state of the economy and the phase of the business cycle is through regular attention to business and economic news. Personal finance magazines typically start each year with articles that forecast the economic future. Popular magazines include *Kiplinger's Personal Finance Magazine, Money, Smart Money,* and *Worth*. To become knowledgeable, you need to follow employment figures, interest rates, inflation reports, and general economic news. This will enable you to better time borrowing and saving decisions so that you might obtain the most advantageous rates. The actions of the Federal Reserve Board are widely reported amid speculation about anticipated changes in interest rates. Thus, it is not difficult for consumers to assess short-term interest rate trends.

Statistics that provide warnings of shifts in the economy are the consumer price index, gross domestic product, and the index of leading economic indicators. The **gross domestic product (GDP)** is the value of all goods and services produced by workers and capital located in the United States, regardless of ownership. Thus, it is a comprehensive measure of a country's economic activity. The **index of leading economic indicators (LEI)** is a composite index, reported monthly as a percentage by the federal government, that suggests the future direction of the U.S. economy. The LEI averages 11 components of growth from different segments of the economy, such as new orders for consumer goods and materials, new business formation, and new private housing starts.

While economists generally dislike inflation, borrowers actually benefit by being able to repay loans with cheaper dollars. Inflation often drives up wages as well as prices, making it easier for many people to repay existing fixed rate debts and mortgages, but, of course, inflation makes it more expensive to incur new debt. Inflation results in higher payments for variable rate mortgages, loans and credit cards. While inflation in the U.S. has held steady at about 3% in recent years, the annual rate has fluctuated considerably over time.

When planning your finances over the long term, it is reasonable to use 3% as a "real" interest rate, that is one that is adjusted for inflation. Being aware of inflation and interest rate trends can help consumers make better decisions about spending, saving, and investing. When prices and wages escalate, it is important to compare the relative rates of increase of both in order to determine whether one is getting ahead or falling behind.

While the CPI is the main measure of price levels for consumer goods and services, the other side of the coin is the cost of labor. Wages are another component of the cost of doing business. When wages increase without a concomitant increase in productivity, inflation results. Thus, a fundamental question for consumers is whether their wage increases are keeping pace with the rising costs of goods and services. When prices are rising faster than wages, workers suffer from a decline in purchasing power. Then consumers need to calculate their **real income** which is their income measured in constant prices relative to some base time period. **Nominal income** simply states income in dollars with no adjustment for purchasing power.

This chapter examines several mathematical examples related to the economics of personal finance, including changes in the consumer price index, inflation-adjusted income changes, and using inflation and interest rate estimates to plan for future goals.

EXAMPLES OF MATHEMATICAL CONCEPTS RELATED TO THE ECONOMICS OF PERSONAL FINANCE

1. Percentage Change in the Consumer Price Index

Formula 3.1:

$$r_{CPI} = \frac{CPI_2 - CPI_1}{CPI_1}$$

Where: r_{CPI} = percentage change of CPI; CPI_2 = CPI in the second period; and CPI_1 = CPI in the first period.

▼   **Example 3.1:** If the CPI increases from 122.9 to 128.4 in one year, what is the percentage change in prices?

Solution: r_{CPI} = (128.4 - 122.9)/122.9
$$= .045$$
$$= 4.5\%$$

❖   **Interpretation:** The consumer price index measures the increase in the prices of goods and services purchased by consumers. To find the percentage increase during a period of time, subtract the CPI for the first (beginning) time period from the CPI for the second time period and divide the result by the CPI for the beginning period. For this example, the annual inflation rate is 4.5%. In general, the CPI increases every year. Only during a severe economic recession or depression would the overall inflation figure be negative. Individual components of the CPI, however, show considerable variability over time.

2. Purchasing Power Change Based on Consumer Price Changes

Formula 3.2:

$$r_p = \frac{(CPI_2 - CPI_1)}{CPI_2}$$

Where: r_p = change rate of purchasing power; CPI_1 = CPI in the first period; and CPI_2 = CPI in the second period. Note that the positive r_p indicates the decreasing rate of purchasing power.

▼   **Example 3.2:** If consumer prices, as reflected in the CPI, increase 34% in a six-year period from 100 to 134, how much does purchasing power decline?

Solution: $r_p = \dfrac{(134 - 100)}{134}$

$= 0.254$

$= 25.4\%$

❖ **Interpretation:** The purchasing power will decrease at a rate of 25.4%. This means that the purchasing power decreased by $.254, or about ¼ of a dollar. When prices increase, purchasing power decreases, but not by the same percentage. If you compare Formulas 3.1 and 3.2, you will find that the only difference between the two is the denominator. Be aware of the differences that result in different interpretations.

3. Inflation-Adjusted Income Change Rate

Formula 3.3: $r_{adj} = r_n - r_i$

Where: r_{adj} = inflation-adjusted change rate; r_n = nominal change rate; and r_i = inflation rate.

▼ **Example 3.3.1:** If James receives a raise of 4.1% and inflation for the year (as measured by the CPI) was 4.9%, what is James' real raise after subtracting the effects of inflation?

Solution: $r_{adj} = 4.1\% - 4.9\%$

$= -.8\%$

❖ **Interpretation:** Since inflation exceeded the wage increase, James actually lost purchasing power despite a nominal wage increase. While the CPI accurately measures price increases, it may not accurately reflect the prices of the goods and services that consumers actually purchase. Thus such comparisons should be made with caution. For persons who have owned a home for a long time and are not purchasing a new vehicle, the CPI may overstate the increase in their cost of living. Since college costs have increased faster than the overall CPI in recent years, persons paying college tuition and expenses may be worse off than the general CPI calculations indicate. Similarly, renters in markets with low vacancy rates may be far worse off than what the CPI indicates when they compare their wage increases to rent prices. The federal government is considering reducing **cost of living adjustments (COLA)** (annual adjustments, typically increases, to reflect inflation) to reduce the deficit.

▼ **Example 3.3.2:** Manuel earned $30,000 last year and he was given a $1,000 raise this year. If inflation, as measured by the CPI, increased 3% during the same time period did Manuel's raise keep up with inflation?

Solution:
$$r_n = \frac{31,000 - 30,000}{30,000}$$
$$= .0333$$
$$= 3.33\%$$
Then, r_{adj} = 3.33% − 3% = .33%

❖ **Interpretation:** The $1,000 raise (3.33%) increased Manuel's salary by more than the increase in the cost of living which was 3%. While Manuel may feel better off as a result of the $1,000 raise, he should be cautious about incurring additional financial obligations since the amount of the raise was barely ahead of inflation. Most of the raise will be "eaten up" by increases in the prices of goods and services that Manuel normally buys.

4. Inflation- and Tax-Adjusted Investment Return Rate

Formula 3.4: $r_{adj} = r_n (1 - MTR) - r_i$

Where: r_{adj} = adjusted return rate; r_n = nominal return rate; MTR = marginal tax rate; and r_i = inflation rate. Note that $r_n (1 - MTR)$ is **tax-adjusted return rate**.

▼ **Example 3.4:** Margaret's money market mutual fund currently pays 6%, her marginal tax rate is 28%, and inflation is 4%. What is the increase in purchasing power over the year from Margaret's fund?

Solution: r_{adj} = .06 (1 − .28) − .04
$$= .043 - .04$$
$$= .003$$
$$= .3\%$$

❖ **Interpretation:** First calculate Margaret's rate of return after paying taxes at the marginal tax rate of 28%. Since interest on money market mutual funds is fully taxable, 28% of the interest earned must be paid in federal income taxes. Thus, the 6% return is reduced to 4.3% after taxes (6.0 × .72). Then subtract the 4% inflation rate which results in a net gain of .3%. This example demonstrates that taxes and inflation can greatly discount the nominal return rate. Consider the consequences of a savings account earning 3% under these conditions: .03 (1 − .28) − .03 = −.008 = −.8%, which means after considering the efforts of both federal income taxes and inflation, the saving account earning 3% interest actually is losing 8/10th of one percent annually. State and local income taxes will further erode the return rate.

5. Using Inflation and Interest Rate Estimates to Plan for Future Goals

Formula 3.5: $p_f = p_c (1 + r_i)$

Where: p_f = future price; p_c = current price; and r_i = inflation rate.

▼ **Example 3.5:** Assume that a new vehicle currently costs $14,000, a restaurant dinner costs $25, and a VCR costs $300, and that prices are expected to increase in the coming year as follows, vehicle 4%, dinner 6%, and VCR 3%, what will these items cost in one year?

Solutions: Vehicle: $14,000 × (1 + .04) = $14,560
                      Dinner: $25 × (1 + .06) = $26.50
                        VCR: $300 × (1.03) = $309

❖ **Interpretation:** The prices for vehicle, dinner, and VCR will be $14,560, $26.50, and $309, respectively, next year. Note that not all prices increase at the same rate, and price trends for various categories can vary widely. Sometimes prices decrease due to improved technology. For example, compact disc players cost about $1000 when first introduced and they have steadily fallen in price since then.

INFORMATION AND COMPUTING RESOURCES

1. For information on general economic conditions, business cycles, current interest rates, inflation rate, projections for economic conditions over the coming 12 to 18 months: *Kiplinger's Personal Finance Magazine* (especially the sections titled "The Months Ahead" and "Market Markers"), *Money* (see "Your Money Monitor," "Money Newsline," and the annual forecast issue), *The Wall Street Journal, Barron's, Fortune, Business Week,* and *U.S. News and World Report.*

2. A useful personal finance radio program is Sound Money, where economics analyst Chris Farrell provides a weekly commentary on the economic news.

3. Related WWW sites:

   ■ *Dr. Ed Yardeni's Economic Network*:
     http://www.yardeni.com

   ■ *Fed Economic Forecasts:* http://www.libertynet.org/fedresrv/fedpage.html

   ■ *Federal Reserve System:* http://www.bog.frb.fed.us

   ■ *FinanCenter:* http://www.financenter.com/resources

   ■ *Highest Bank rates:* http://gnn.com/gnn/meta/finance/res/mri.html

   ■ *Kiplinger's Personal Finance Magazine:*
     http://www.dc.enews.com/magazines/kiplinger

   ■ *Money:* http://pathfinder.com.money

   ■ *Sound Money Web site:*

http://www.mnonline.org/mpr/programs/smhome.htm

■ *U.S. News and World Report*: http://www.usnews.com

■ *USA Today:* http://www.usatoday.com

■ *Wall Street Journal Money and Investing Update:* http://update.wsj.com

EXERCISE PROBLEMS

Percentage change in the Consumer Price Index

1. The base for the CPI is 100 in 1982-84. The CPI was 156.6 in May 1996 and 152.2 in May 1995. What was the percentage change in prices from May 1995 to May 1996?

2. If the CPI increases from 152 to 155 what is the percentage increase in prices?

3. If the CPI increases from 134 to 140 what is the percentage increase in prices?

4. If tuition at a private college cost $5075 twenty years ago ($11,824 adjusted for inflation) and $23,880 today, how much did the price increase?

5. If a hand held calculator cost $150 twenty years ago ($349 adjusted for inflation), and $7 today, what is the inflation adjusted price change?

6. If a Toyota costs $2,180 ($5,079 adjusted for inflation) twenty years ago and $10,000 today, what is the inflation adjusted price change?

7. If a cross country plane ticket cost $488 twenty years ago (adjusted for inflation the cost was $760 in today's dollars) and $326 today, how much did the real cost of the ticket decline?

8. Anita is considering asking for a raise since she senses that her salary has not kept pace with inflation. She has decided to do some calculations to determine her purchasing power. Over the past five years, the CPI increased from 115 to 135 while her salary increased from $20,000 to $24,000. Can you do the calculation for Anita?

Purchasing Power Based on Consumer Price Changes

9. The base for the CPI is 100 in 1984. The CPI was 156.6 in May 1996. How much did it cost in 1984 dollars to buy in May 1996 what it cost $100 to buy in 1984?

10. The CPI was 156.6 in May 1996 and 152.2 in May 1995. How much did the purchasing power of the dollar decline from May 1995 to May 1996?

11. How much did the purchasing power of the dollar decline from 1984 (CPI = 100) to May 1996 (CPI = 156.6)?

12. If prices rose 34% over 6 years how much did purchasing power decline, assuming the CPI is 100 six years ago?

13. If gas costs $1.50/gallon, your vehicle gets 20 miles per gallon, you typically drive 10,000 miles/year, and if gas prices increase to $1.75/ gallon due to political turmoil in the Middle East in the coming year and you maintain the same number of miles of driving, what is your percentage increase in transportation costs resulting from the increased cost of gasoline?

14. (a) If you typically drive 12,000 miles/year and pay $1.35/gallon, what is your current cost for gas, assuming the car gets 25 miles per gallon? (b) Due to increased world-wide demand, gas prices are expected to increase to $1.48/gallon in the coming year. If you maintain the same level of driving (12,000 miles/year), how much should you budget for gasoline in the coming year? (c) What is the change rate of the purchasing power in terms of driving costs?

Inflation-Adjusted Income Change Rate

15. If you receive a raise of 3.2% and inflation for the year (as measured by the CPI) was 2.9%, what is your real raise?

16. Audrey started working for a computer company on September 1 four years ago at a salary of $25,600. She received a raise on September 1 of each of the next three years. The chart illustrates her raise and salary for each year, and the inflation rate. It is now the beginning of the fifth year.

Year	Date	Raise	Salary	Inflation Rate
1	9-1-92	—	$25,600	5%
2	9-1-93	$1200	$26,800	3%
3	9-1-94	$1400	$28,200	3%
4	9-1-95	$1650	$29,850	3%
5	9-1-96	?	?	3%

a. What would Audrey's salary have to have been at the beginning of the second, third, and fourth years to keep up with inflation each year?

b. What would her raise and salary need to be for the fifth year for her salary to simply keep up with inflation?

c. If Audrey receives a $1,000 raise at the beginning of the fifth year, would she be ahead or behind after inflation and by how much?

Inflation- and Tax-Adjusted Investment Return Rate

17. Assume you have $5,000 in a money market mutual fund earning 6% allocated for next year's tuition. If your marginal tax rate is 31% and inflation rate is 3%, how much will the $5,000 be worth in a year?

18. If your savings account pays 5% interest, your marginal tax rate is 31%, and inflation is 3%, what is your effective rate of return?

19. Juan earned 8% on his taxable savings and investments last year and he is in a 28% marginal tax bracket. (a) How much did he earn after taxes? (b) If inflation was 3%, what is Juan's return after taxes and inflation?

Using Inflation and Interest Rate Estimates to Plan for Future Goals

20. If the first year at State University costs $10,000, how much will years two to four cost if The College Board recommends adding 7% for the second year, 15% for the third year and 23% for year four? What is the total cost of the four years of college? *(Hint: always use the first year as base year.)*

21. (a) If the cost of housing is increasing at the rate of 3% annually and homes similar to what you would like to buy cost $100,000, how much will the home cost in 4 years? (b) If you need 20% of the cost for a down payment and closing costs, how much will that be in 3 years?

22. If during your first year at college, rent is $450/month for a two-bedroom apartment, how much will rent cost in years two, three, and four if rents are increasing at 6% annually?

23. After college graduation, you plan to buy a basic used vehicle which would cost $8,000 today. How much will a similar vehicle cost in 3 years at 4% annual inflation?

24. Vehicles generally depreciate very rapidly in the first year and then the depreciation rate gradually tapers off. If your $13,000 vehicle is depreciating at 6% annually, how much will it be worth in 3 years when you plan to sell it?

25. Your child just started college at an annual cost in tuition of $5,000 which is expected to increase at 5% per year. What is the expected cost of four years of tuition? *(Hint: calculate the cost for each year, using the previous year as base year. Then sum up the total cost.)*

SELECTED REFERENCES

Bodnar, J., & Wilcox, M. (1992, April). Cheer up, America. *Kiplinger's Personal Finance Magazine*, 71, 72, 74.

Garman, E. T. & Forgue, R. E. (1997). Understanding the economic environment of personal finance. In *Personal Finance*, (5th ed.). (pp 5-11) Boston: Houghton Mifflin.

Morgan, J. N., & G. J. Duncan (1982). *Making your choices count: Economic principles for everyday decisions.* Ann Arbor: The University of Michigan Press.

Shim, J. K., & J. G. Siegel (1991). *Theory and problems of personal finance*, New York: McGraw-Hill, Schaum's outline series.

Sivy, M. (1996, Forecast). Where to make money in the year ahead. *Money*, 32-38.

Tainer, E. M. (1993). *Using economic indicators to improve investment analysis.* New York: John Wiley & Sons.

Wilcox, M. (1995, May). Cola nuts. *Kiplinger's Personal Finance Magazine*, 53-55.

Wilcox, M. (1996, January). Still strong economy. *Kiplinger's Personal Finance Magazine*, 38-42.

Will you come out ahead if you relocate? *Money*, July 1996, p. 81(v. 25 # 7). Correction: *Money*, September 1996, p. 16.

Chapter 4
Time Value of Money

▼ Simple Interest
▼ Bank Discount Rate
▼ Compound Interest
▼ Effective Interest Rate
▼ Continuous Compounding
▼ Future Value of Annuity
▼ Future Value of Annuity Due
▼ Present Value of Annuity
▼ Present Value of Annuity Due

Chapter 4
Time Value of Money

M. J. Alhabeeb[1]

OVERVIEW

Would you be excited if you were announced as the winner of a $100,000 in cash? And, you probably would be disappointed if the announcer went on to say, "The prize will be paid 10 years from now." Your disappointment might even multiply if the announcer continued to say, "The $100,000 will be paid in ten annual payments of $10,000 each." What might your thought be if the announcer finally said that, "Any unpaid amount will earn interest throughout all the years from today"? This scenario illustrates the notion that money obtained later is universally considered less valuable than money obtained sooner. The phrase "A dollar today is worth more than a dollar tomorrow" signifies what we call the time value of money.

The **time value of money** is a key theoretical concept in personal finance. The central concept of the time value of money is that money value tends to decline over time primarily because of inflation. **Inflation** is a steady rise in the general level of the prices of goods and services. When the prices of goods and services increase, the purchasing power of money decreases because more money would be needed in the future to make the same purchases as were before the inflation.

However, even if inflation is zero, certain non-inflationary factors such as consumer impatience and life uncertainty would still contribute to make money of a lesser value in the future compared to the present. **Consumer impatience** refers to people's preference for today's satisfaction over tomorrow's satisfaction. The higher value of current money is attributed to the instant utility derived from the goods and services purchased immediately as opposed to the delayed utility that may be derived from the goods and services purchased in the future. **Life uncertainty** poses a great risk to the extension of time to utilize money. When the delivery of the prize in our scenario was postponed to ten years later, the disappointment of the winner can be

[1] M.J. Alhabeeb, Ph.D., Assistant Professor, Department of Consumer Studies, University of Massachusetts, Amherst, MA 01003. mja@constudy.umass.edu

appreciated when uncertainty is considered. One might think that he or she may die during the ten years before he or she can collect any part of the prize. Further, the rules and regulations governing the prize might change unfavorably during those years. The obligations and liabilities may become greater and taxes and fees may go higher. Many things might occur which jeopardize the utilization of the prize.

For all of these reasons—inflation, impatience, and uncertainty—people would be better off to utilize the money as soon as possible. If one has to wait and forgo the immediate satisfaction of current consumption, it is plausible to figure that a reward to compensate for the sacrifice should be due. This reward is what we call interest which is the focal point of the time value of money. **Interest** is defined as the price of money services. The **rate of interest** is the reward that would have to be paid by the borrower to the lender for the use of money borrowed. This rate is expressed as a percentage of the original amount of money borrowed, which is called the **principal**. Since money is generally characterized by being a store of value or worth, the rate of interest may reflect the opportunity cost of holding that value or wealth that could be earned on other financial alternatives.

The interest rate is one of the vital indicators of economic performance of a country. The rate of interest is often characterized as the most important regulator of the pace of business and the prosperity of nations. Interest rates are crucial to consumers whether they are borrowing to purchase a home or investing in the stock market to build funds for retirement.

In the calculation of time value of money, five key terms are involved: (1) present value, (2) future value, (3) period, (4) interest rate, and (5) payment. **Present value** refers to the worth of money today.[1] **Future value** measures the worth of money in a certain future date. **Period** refers to the time periods between the beginning and end of a calculation. **Interest rate** is the price of using the money for a certain period of time. **Payment** is a sum that is paid periodically to repay the money borrowed. All calculations of time value of money have one thing in common—to solve for one factor when other factors are given.

The time value of money can be calculated using any of four methods. In this chapter, you will learn the **formula method**. You learned how to use **financial calculator method** and the **computer method** to calculate time value of money in Chapter 1 and 2, respectively. Another type of calculation is the **table method**, which is shown in Appendix B.

Compared to the other methods, the formula method has several advantages. The formula method is straightforward and it indicates the process of how the focused value is solved. For any of these formulas, you can easily derive different forms of equations to solve for one value when other values are given. The formula method also can solve some problems for which there are no built-in functions in computers and financial calculators. Using the formula method, you may evaluate values with ordinary scientific calculators instead of more expensive financial calculators. However, disadvantages of the formula method include that some formulas are complicated and need lots of energy to remember. Using formula calculations is slower than using financial calculators and computers. Because of the disadvantages of formulas, most people use financial calculators, tables and computers instead. They do so primarily because calculations become easier for them. However, those who understand the formulas will better comprehend the results obtained from calculators, tables and computer spreadsheets. In life people use what is convenient.

This chapter will introduce several types of calculations of time value of money. The first is the **simple interest** method in which interest is assessed only on the principal. The second concept, **bank discount**, is when interest is deducted from the principal in advance. The third type of calculation examines the **compound interest** method in which interest is assessed not only on the principal but also on the interest earned in previous periods. **Effective interest rate** and **continuous compounding**, two concepts related to the compound interest method, are discussed in the following two sections. The last sections examine annuity and annuity due, respectively. **Annuity** means a future value when a series of equal payments are made at the end of each period. **Annuity due** is the same as annuity except that each payment is made at the beginning of each period.

EXAMPLES OF CALCULATING TIME VALUE OF MONEY

1. Simple Interest

Formula 4.1.1: $FV_s = PV(1 + r \cdot n)$

Where: FV_s = future value of money using simple interest method; PV = present value of money or the principal; r = interest rate; and n = number of periods.

▼   **Example 4.1.1**: Dave deposited $1,000 in his saving account which pays an annual interest of 10%. How much money will Dave have in his account three years later?

Solution: Since PV = $1,000, r = 0.10, n = 3,
Then, FV_s = $1,000 (1 + 0.10 × 3) = $1,300

❖   **Interpretation**: The money will be worth $1,300 in three years. Simple interest is the interest earned only on the principal sum of money. When earning interest, the initial amount of money (principal) will grow to a larger future value during a given term.

▼   **Example 4.1.2:** How many months would it take to raise $1,118 to $1,285 at 18% interest?

Solution: Since FV_s = $1,285, PV = $1,118, and r = 0.18, then

$1,285 = $1,118 (1 + 0.18 n) = $1,118 + $201.24 n
$1,285 - $1,118 = $167 = $201.24 n
n = $167/$201.24 = 0.83

❖   **Interpretation:** Since the annual interest rate is used in the calculation, the result of 0.83 years would approximately be equal to: 12 × .83 = 10 months. This example indicates that you can solve for any one of the factors with the formula, given the other three factors.

Note that Formula 4.1.1 can also be written as: $FV_s = PV + PV \cdot r \cdot n$, in which, $PV \cdot r \cdot n$ is the interest component. Then, we have the following formula:

Formula 4.1.2: $I_s = PV \cdot r \cdot n$

Where: I_s = interest component of a future value; PV = present value of money; r = interest rate; and n = number of periods.

▼ **Example 4.1.3**: Jill made a deposit of $3,250 in a money market account. If this account earns an annual interest of 5%, how much the total interest that she could collect in 10 months?

Solution 1: Since PV = $3,250, r = 0.05, n = 10/12 = 0.833,
          Then, I_s = $3,250 × 0.05 × 0.833 = $135.36

Solution 2: Since PV = $3,250, r = 0.05/12 = 0.00417, n = 10,
          Then, I_s = $3,250 × 0.00417 × 10 = $135.53

❖ **Interpretation**: The total interest will be about $135 in 10 months. The results from the two solutions are slightly different since we used different converting approaches. In solution 1, we converted the monthly term to an annual term (n = 10/12 = 0.833). In solution 2, we converted the annual interest to monthly interest (r = .05/12 = .00417). Remember that the period and interest rate should be consistent in the calculation. In this case, you may use both annual periods and interest rate, or both monthly periods and interest rate. Otherwise, you may get an incorrect result.

▼ **Example 4.1.4**: What is the interest earned on 60,000 for 90 days at 10% rate of interest, assuming that a year has 360 days? If a year is assumed to have 365 days, what is the interest?

Solutions: If a year has 360, and since PV = $60,000, r = 0.1, n = 90/360 = 0.25, then,
          I_s = $60,000 × 0.10 × .25 = $1,500

If a year has 365 days, and since PV = $60,000, r = 0.1, n = 90/365 = .2466, then,
          I_s = $60,000 × 0.10 × .2466 = $1,480

❖ **Interpretation:** Depending on whether a year has 360 or 365 days, the interest will be $1,500 or $1480. Interest can be calculated based on a time period (n) expressed in days. To convert the daily term into annual, the number of days is divided by either 360 as an approximate number of days in a year or by the exact number of days in a specific year which is either 365 or 366. If a denominator of 360 is used, the interest obtained is called **ordinary interest**. If a denominator of 365 or

366 is used, the obtained interest is called the **exact interest**. Due to using a smaller denominator, ordinary interest is slightly larger than the exact interest.

▼   **Example 4.1.5:** Megan has been told that at the end of nine months, she would have to pay an interest payment of $151.48 for her loan of $1,346.52. What must have been the interest rate?

Solution: Since I = $151.48, PV = $1,346.52, n = 9/12 = .75, then
$151.48 = $1,346.52 × .75 r = 1009.89 r
r = $151.48/1009.89 = 0.15

❖   **Interpretation:** The interest rate is 15%. This example demonstrates that if you know any three of the four factors in this formula, you can solve for the last one. In the same fashion, if I, PV, and r are given, you may solve for n with the formula.

2. Bank Discount Rate

Formula 4.2.1: P = M - M·d·n = M (1 - d·n)

Where: P = proceeds which refers to the amount received by a borrower when the interest (bank discount) is deducted out of the principal in advance; M = maturity value; d = bank discount rate; and n = number of period. Note that M·d·n is the total **bank discount**, P is the difference between the maturity value and total bank discount.

▼   **Example 4.2.1**: Paul wants to borrow $12,000 from his bank for one year. His loan officer informed him that bank would offer a discount rate of 12%. How much money will be discounted? And, how much money will Paul receive?

Solution: Since M = $12,000, n = 1, d = 0.12, then
M·d·n = $12,000 × 0.12 × 1 = $1,440
P = $12,000 - $1,440 = $10,560

❖   **Interpretation**: The total bank discount will be $1,440, and Paul will receive only $10,560. If the interest is deducted out of the principal in advance, the interest is called a **bank discount**. The amount received by the borrower is called the **proceeds** which is less than the principal by the amount of discount. The amount which the borrower will pay off is called the **maturity value**. In this example, the bank deducts its charges (the discount) of $1440 leaving Paul with only $10,560. But recall that Paul needed $12,000! What must he do to get the full amount that he needs? The answer is he has to apply for a larger amount that results in proceeds of $12,000 after discounting.

▼   **Example 4.2.2**: Find the right amount which Paul should apply for to get a net of $12,000.

Solution: Since P = $12,000, d = 0.12, n = 1, then
$12,000 = M (1 - 0.12 × 1) = M 0.88

$$M = \$12,000/0.88 = \$13,636$$

❖ **Interpretation:** If Paul needs a net of $12,000 from the bank, he needs to borrow $13,636.

▼ **Example 4.2.3**: Jack has been offered a rate of 15% to be either an interest or discount rate for a one year loan of $10,000. Would there be any difference in what he pays to the bank?

Solution: If Jack chooses the interest rate, the total interest he would pay at the end of one year is:

$$I_s = \$10,000 \times 0.15 \times 1 = \$1,500$$

If he chooses the discount rate, the total discount that he would pay now is:

$$M \cdot d \cdot n = \$10,000 \times 0.15 \times 1 = \$1,500$$

❖ **Interpretation**: Both methods result in $1,500. However, a $1,500 paid today may very well be worth more for Jack than a $1,500 paid a year from now. This is the reason why the amount discounted at the time of the loan should be less than the interest paid later. Therefore, from a borrower's standpoint, the interest rate method is more advantageous than the discount rate method if the two rates are the same. In other words, if a consumer would like to borrow the same amount of money from a bank when using either of the methods, the discount rate should be less than the interest rate. Formulas to calculate an interest rate equivalent to a bank discount rate, or vise versa, are given in Formula 4.2.2 and 4.2.3, respectively.

Formula 4.2.2: $$r = \frac{d}{1 - d \times n}$$

Where: r = interest rate; d = bank discount rate; and n = number of periods.

▼ **Example 4.2.4**: When Tom applied for a loan that he could pay back in 8 months, he was offered a discount rate of 9%. Since he preferred to go with an interest rate, how much would that rate be?

Solution: Since r = 9%, n = 8/12 = .667, then

$$r = \frac{0.09}{1 - 0.09 \times 0.667} = 0.096 = 9.6\%$$

❖ **Interpretation:** The equivalent interest rate will be 9.6%. Tom will borrow the same amount of loan with an 9.6% interest rate as he does with a discount rate of 9%.

Formula 4.2.3: $$d = \frac{r}{1 + r \times n}$$

Where: d = bank discount rate; r = interest rate; and n = number of periods.

▼ **Example 4.2.5**: If Jack chooses the discount method, what would be the discount rate that is equivalent to an interest rate of 15%? Assume that the period is one year.

Solution: Since r = 0.15, n = 1, then

$$d = \frac{0.15}{1 + 0.15 \times 1} = 0.13$$

❖ **Interpretation:** The equivalent discount rate should be 13%. With a discount rate of 13%, Jack will borrow the same amount of loan as he does so at an interest rate of 15% using the interest rate method.

▼ **Example 4.2.6**: Martha renovated her kitchen on July 20 at a cost of $5,000 which was financed by a home improvement contractor at 18% interest for 5 months. Because of an urgent need for cash, the contractor sold the loan instrument to a local bank on August 1st at a discount rate of 21%. What is the future value of the loan to Martha? How much proceeds did he receive from the bank? What is the contractor's financial loss in this case?

Solutions:

(1) FV from the loan.

> Since PV = $5,000, r = .18, n = 5/12 = .417, then using Formula 4.1.1
> FV = $5,000 (1 + 0.18 × 0.417) = $5,375
> Thus, the future value of the loan is $5,375, in which, $5,375 - $5,000 = $375 is the interest that is supposed to be earned.

(2) Proceeds received from the bank.

> Since August 1 is day 213 in the year and December 20 is day 354, then between the two dates there are (354 – 213) = 141 days, and M = $5,375, n = 141/360 = .392, d = 0.21, then using Formula 4.2.1
> P = $5,375 (1 – 0.21 × 0.392) = $4,933
> Thus, the contractor received proceeds of $4,933 from the bank.

(3) Financial loss.

> Since the interest loss is $375, and the principal loss is: $5,000 - $4,933 = $67, then, the total loss is: $375 + $67 = $442.

❖ **Interpretation**: In this example, the bank would give $4,933 in cash to the contractor which means that instead of earning $375 above his principal, the contractor lost $67 of his principal by accepting $4,933 for the work worth $5,000.

His total loss of $442 ($67 + $375) was the price paid for utilizing the cash he needed immediately as opposed to waiting for five months. The bank, however, will earn that $442 ($5,375 – $4,933) for the services rendered. This example demonstrates the application of the interrelationships between the interest and discount rates. The example also describes the situation of the **promissory note**, which is a negotiable financial instrument that can be sold to a third party without changing the original obligations. Promissory notes are often used in consumer credit and retail installment contracts.

3. Compound Interest[2,3]

Formula 4.3: $FV = PV (1 + r)^n$

Where: FV = future value using the compound interest method; PV = present value; r = interest rate; and n = number of periods.

▼   **Example 4.3.1**: Heather invested $8,000 at 9% interest. How much would her investment be worth in five years?

Solution: Since PV = $8,000, r = .09, n = 5, then
$FV = \$8,000 (1 + 0.09)^5 = \$12,308.99$

❖   **Interpretation:** She will have $12,308.99 in her investment account of which $4,308.99 is interest. Unlike simple interest, compound interest is accrued on both the principal and on the interest earned. It is often defined as "interest on interest".

The compound interest formula displays a positive relationship between the future value of an amount and each of the three other variables while holding the other two variables constant. This is to say that the higher the present value (PV) or the higher the interest rate (r) or the longer the term (n), the higher the growth in the future value (FV). The following table illustrates this point.

		r = 5%	r = 10%	r = 15%
100	n = 10	162.89	259.37	404.56
200		325.78	518.75	809.11
100	n = 20	265.33	672.75	1636.65
200		530.66	1345.50	3273.30
100	n = 30	432.19	1744.94	6621.17
200		864.38	3489.88	13242.35
100	n = 40	703.99	4525.92	26786.35
200		1407.99	9051.85	53572.70

▼   **Example 4.3.2**: If Dave's annual interest in Example 4.1.1 was calculated with a compound instead of simple interest method, would there be any difference in his future value?

Solution: $FV = \$1,000 (1 + 0.10)^3 = \$1,331$

❖ **Interpretation**: Dave will have $1,331 if the interest is compounded over three years. The difference between the simple and compound interest can be illustrated by looking at the two different ways in which interest accumulates. Under simple interest, Dave accumulated $300 in interest in the following way:

> In the first year, he earned 10% of $1,000 which is $100.
> In the second year, he earned 10% of $1,000 which is $100.
> In the third year, he earned 10% of $1,000 which is $100.
> Thus, the total interest earned in three years is $300.

With compounded interest, Dave would collect more than $331 for the same three years because each amount of earned interest also would earn interest.

> In the first year: 10% of $1,000 is $100, his balance would be $1,100.
> In the second year: 10% of $1,100 is $110, his balance would be $1,210.
> In the third year: 10% of $1,210 is $121, his balance would be $1331.

Thus, the difference between the simple and compound interest here would be $31.

▼ **Example 4.3.3**: $1,500 is deposited for 2 years in an account earning 19% interest. Find the future value of this investment by compounding the interest (1) annually, (2) semi-annually, (3) quarterly, (4) monthly, (5) weekly, and (6) daily.

Solution: In this question, PV = $1,500, and r and n will vary depending on the compounding frequencies.

(1) If compounded annually, n = 1, r = .19, then

$$FV = \$1,500 \ (1 + 0.19)^2 = \$2,124.15$$

(2) If compounded semi-annually, n = 2 × 2 = 4, r = 0.19/2 = 0.095, then

$$FV = \$1,500 \ (1 + 0.095)^4 = \$2,156.49$$

(3) If compounded quarterly, n = 2 × 4 = 8, r = 0.19/4 = 0.0475, then

$$FV = \$1,500 \ (1 + 0.0475)^8 = \$2,174.32$$

(4) If compounded monthly, n = 2 × 12 = 24, r = 0.19/12 = 0.01583

$$FV = \$1,500 \ (1 + 0.01583)^{24} = \$2,186.74$$

(5) If compounded weekly, n = 2 × 52 = 104, r = 0.19/52 = 0.00365

$$FV = \$1,500 \ (1 + 0.00365)^{104} = \$2,191.04$$

(6) If compounded daily, n = 2 × 365 = 730, r = 0.19/365 = 0.00052

$$FV = \$1,500 \ (1 + 0.00052)^{730} = \$2,192.33$$

❖ **Interpretation:** This example illustrates how the future value of a sum differs based upon changing the frequency of compounding while keeping the maturity term constant. Actually, with the same present value, length of term, and annual interest rate, the more frequently compounded, the more interest is earned. In this example, the future value using an annual compounding is only $2,124.15 with interest of $624.15 ($2,124.15 - $1,500). The future value using a daily compounding is the highest, $2,193.20, as it includes interest $693.20 ($2,193.20 - $1,500) given other factors. Since the annual interest rate and number of years are usually given in the personal finance questions, you must remember to check that the interest rate and number of periods are consistent in terms of compounding frequencies, otherwise you must make any necessary conversions. In this example, the interest rate and number of periods are converted to appropriate ones when different compounding frequencies are used. The only exception is for annual compounding, since the interest rate and number of periods are the same as given by the example.

▼ **Example 4.3.4**: In 6 years Bill will be able to receive $14,513 as his share of the family inheritance which is deposited in an account bearing 7.25% interest. What is the value of Bill's share now?

Solution: Since $n = 6$, FV = $14,513, $r = 0.0725$, then
$14,513 = PV (1 + 0.0725)^6 = PV\ 1.522$
$PV = \$14,513/1.522 = \$9,535.48$

❖ **Interpretation**: In the example, if Bill decides to receive his share now, it would be only $9,535.48. However, leaving this amount in the account for six more years allows it to grow to $14,513 due to compounding. Obtaining the present value out of the future value given a certain term and interest rate is called **discounting**. It is the reverse operation of compounding where money value is transferred back in time, from the future to the present. Discounting is a very powerful tool in financial and economic analysis. It allows the comparison of sums of different maturity or projects of different lives by finding out the worth of future money in terms of its value at the present time.

Derived from Formula 4.3, the present value can be expressed as: $PV = FV/(1+r)^n$, in which the term $1/(1+r)^n$ or $(1+r)^{-n}$ is called the **discount factor (DF)** which reflects the current worth of 1. In the example, the discount factor was $1/(1+0.0725)^6 = 0.657$. This means that withdrawing the share in the current time would result in discounting it by 65.7%. Using the same logic, it can be said that Bill would lose 34.3 cents of each dollar of his future share if he rushes to receive it now. The economic utility of money received now may seem higher than its economic utility received six years from now because people tend to prefer the utility derived from the immediate consumption over the utility derived from the postponed consumption. Economic utility or disutility should always be assessed in comparison to the financial gain or loss.

What if Bill had to wait longer, say 10 years instead of 6 years to get his share? The discount factor would be $1/(1+0.0725)^{10} = 0.497$. This means that his share would be discounted by 49.7% and Bill would lose even more than before (50.3%) if he takes the money now. Logically, we can infer that waiting for a shorter time, say for 4 years, would result in discounting the share by 75.6% and reducing the loss to 24.4%. What if the inheritance was left in an account bearing a higher interest rate, say 9% instead of 7.25%? The discount factor would be $1/(1+0.09)^6 = 0.596$, which means Bill would also lose more (40.4%) than he would with a lower interest rate.

Based on these different scenarios, we can generalize that the discount factor (DF) has a negative relationship with the interest rate (r) holding the term (n) constant and a negative relationship with the term(n) holding the interest rate (r) constant. This is to say the higher the r or the longer the n, the smaller the DF.

▼ **Example 4.3.5**: How long will it take Brian to collect $13,000 if he invests his $6,777 at 9.75%?

Solution: Since FV = $13,000, PV = $6,777, r = 0.0975, then
$13,000 = $6,777 $(1 + 0.0975)^n$
$13,000/$6,777 = $(1 + 0.0975)^n$, take logarithms for both sides, we have
ln ($13,000/$6,777) = n ln (1 + 0.0975)
ln 1.918 = n ln 1.0975
n = ln 1.918 / ln 1.0975 = 0.6513/0.093 = 7

❖ **Interpretation:** It will take seven years for Brian's investment to grow from $6,777 to $13,000. This example demonstrates how to solve for n with Formula 4.3 when FV, PV, and r are given. Note that the **natural logarithms (ln)** are used in this example. You may use the base-10 logarithms to calculate n following the same approach.

▼ **Example 4.3.6**: Lisa's goal is to have $15,485 in five years. If she invests what she has now, $7,700, what must be the interest rate to help her achieve her goal?

Solution: Since, FV = $15,485, PV = $7,700, n = 5, then
$15,485 = $7,700 $(1 + r)^5$
$15,485/$7,700 = $(1 + r)^5$, take logarithms for both sides, we have
ln ($15,485/$7,700) = 5 × ln (1 + r)
0.699 = 5 × ln (1+r)
0.699/5 = 0.1398 = ln (1+ r), which means: $e^{0.1398} = 1 + r$
1.15 = 1+ r
r = 1.15 - 1 = 0.15

❖ **Interpretation:** The interest rate should be at least 15%. This example displays how to calculate r with Formula 4.3 when FV, PV, and n are given.

▼ **Example 4.3.7**: Sam suggests that Melanie lends him $750. He offers to pay her back a total of $800 using the 3-year payment plan noted below. Is Sam's offer worthwhile if the interest rate is assumed to be 8.5% compounded annually?

Sam's payment plan:

First year:	$250
Second year:	$375
Third year:	$175
Total:	$800

Solution: Since there will be three returns in three different time periods, a sound decision can only be made if Melanie discounts these future values into their current values and sums the present value of the loan.

(1) First year, since FV = $250, n = 1, r = 0.085, then
$250 = PV (1 + 0.085) = PV 1.085
PV = $250/1.085 = $230.42

(2) Second year, since FV = $375, n = 2, r = 0.085, then
$375 = PV (1 + 0.085)^2 = PV 1.177
PV = $375/1.177 = $318.61

(3) Third year, since FV = $175, n = 3, r = 0.085, then
$175 = PV (1 + 0.085)^3 = PV 1.277
PV = $175/1.277 = $137.04

(4) Sum of present values
PV$_{sum}$ = $230.42 + $318.61 + $137.04 = $686.07

❖ **Interpretation**: Since the present value of the three payments is $685.96, it is not worthwhile for Melanie to accept Sam's plan. The $800 to be collected over the next three years would worth only $686.07 today.

4. Effective Interest Rates

Formula 4.4: $R = (1 + r/n)^n - 1$

Where: R = effective interest rate; r = nominal annual interest rate; and n = number of periods.

▼ **Example 4.4.1**: Find the effective rate for 8% interest compounded monthly.

Solution: Since r = 0.08, n = 12, then
$R = (1 + 0.08/12)^{12} - 1 = 0.083 = 8.3\%$

❖ **Interpretation**: If the nominal annual rate is 8%, then the effective interest rate compounded monthly will be 8.3%. The rate of interest usually quoted in financial transactions is a rate in name only and is often called the **nominal interest rate** or **stated rate**. The actual interest rate is called the **effective interest rate**, which is equal to the nominal rate only when the interest is compounded annually. The effective rate, therefore, depends on how many times in a given term the nominal rate is compounded. As shown on the table below, the effective rate increases positively with the number of conversion periods per year. The **interest conversion period (n)** is a basic time unit between successive interest calculations. Commonly n takes the values of 1, 2, 4, 12, 52, or 365 representing the frequency of compounding as annually, semiannually, quarterly, monthly, weekly, and daily, respectively. The following table shows how the effective interest rate varies according to different conversion periods.

Nominal Rate of 6% Compounded	Number of Conversion Periods	Effective Rate
Annually	1	6.0%
Semi-annually	2	6.09%
Quarterly	4	6.13636%
Monthly	12	6.16778%
Weekly	52	6.17782%
Daily	365	6.18383%

5. Continuous Compounding

Formula 4.5: $FV = PV \cdot e^{r \cdot n}$

Where: FV = future value of continuous compounding; PV = present value; e = 2.71828, the base of natural logarithms; r = interest rate; and n = number of periods.

▼   **Example 4.5.1**: If we continuously compound the 19% interest on the $1500 for 2 years, what is the future value?

Solution: Since r = 0.19, PV = $1,500, n = 2, then
$FV = \$1,500 \times 2.71828^{0.19 \times 2} = \$2,193.43$

❖   **Interpretation**: The future value will be $2,193.43 when continuous compounding is used. Recall that in Example 4.3.3, we calculated the future value when number of compounding frequencies increased from annually, semi-annually, quarterly, monthly, weekly, to daily. We noticed that the future value increases when the frequencies of compounding goes up, given other factors. The situation in which the number of compounding frequencies is infinite is called **continuous compounding**. We can prove that in the case of continuous compounding the future value can be calculated with Formula 4.5. Compared to the results with the ones in Example 4.3.3, the future value obtained by continuous compounding is about $70 larger than that obtained by the annual compounding ($2,124.15) and larger by only a few cents than that obtained by the daily compounding ($2,193.20). Example 4.3.3 and 4.5 together indicate that given other factors, the higher the compounding frequencies, the more interest is earned, but the increase rates are decreasing in the process, and the interest increase rate will become a constant, e, in the case of continuous compounding.

▼ **Example 4.5.2**: Richard noticed that a share of his mutual fund was valued at $10 on January 1, 1995 and at $12.50 on December 31, 1996. Given that interest is compounded continuously, what must be the interest rate?

Solution: Since FV = $12.50, PV = $10, n = 2, then
$12.50 = $10 \times e^{2r}$
$12.5/$10 = 1.25 = e^{2r}$, take logarithms for both sides
$\ln 1.25 = \ln (e^{2r}) = 2r$
$0.223 = 2r$
$r = 0.223/2 = 0.1115 = 11.15\%$

❖ **Interpretation:** The interest rate was 11.15%. This example demonstrates how to solve for r with Formula 4.5 when FV, PV, and n are given.

▼ **Example 4.5.3**: How long will it take Richard to see the value of his share growing from $10 to $14 if the interest rate drops to 10.75% compounded continuously.

Solution: Since PV = $10, FV = $14, r = .1075, then
$14 = $10 e^{0.1075n}$
$14/$10 = 1.4 = e^{0.1075n}$, take logarithms for both sides, then
$\ln 1.4 = 0.1075n$
$0.3365 = 0.1075n$
$n = 0.3365/0.1075 = 3.13$

❖ **Interpretation:** It will take 3.13 years, or about three years and two months ($0.13 \times 12 = 1.56$ months) to grow to $14. This example demonstrates how to solve n with Formula 4.5 when other factors are given. Example 4.5.2 and 4.5.3 are similar as natural logarithms have to be used to calculate the result.

▼ **Example 4.5.4**: Kim expects her investment to grow to $2,000 in 2 years. Given that she earns an 8% interest compounded continuously, what is her initial investment?

Solution: Since FV = $2,000, r = 0.08, n = 2, then
$2,000 = PV e^{0.08 \times 2} = PV\ 1.1735$
$PV = $2,000/1.1735 = $1,704.30$

❖ **Interpretation:** The initial investment must have been $1,704.30. This example illustrates how to calculate PV with the Formula 4.5, given other factors.

6. Future Value of Annuity

Formula 4.6:
$$FVA = \frac{A[(1 + r)^n - 1]}{r}$$

Where: FVA = future value of an annuity; A = annuity payment; r = interest rate; and n = number of periods.

▼ **Example 4.6.1**: Emily deposits $100 each month in her saving account which pays 6.5% interest compounded annually. How much will her balance be after three years?

Solution: Since A = $100 x 12 = $1,200, r = 0.065, n = 3, then

$$FVA = \frac{\$1,200[(1 + 0.065)^3 - 1]}{0.065} = \$3,839$$

❖ **Interpretation:** Emily's balance will be $3,839. This example exhibits the calculation of an annuity. An **annuity (A)** is defined as a stream of equal cash flows paid or received at regular time intervals. Although the name implies annual intervals, annuity in financial applications includes all regular time intervals. Mortgages and auto loan payments, premiums on insurance, interests payments on bonds, payments on installment purchases, and pension fund checks are all familiar examples of annuities. Annuities generally fall into three types (1) contingent annuity, (2) annuity certain, and (3) perpetuities. A **contingent annuity** is one for which the start or end of the payments or both are contingent upon a certain condition that cannot be predicted, such as the payments made to the beneficiary of a life insurance policy which would start upon the death of the insured. An **annuity certain** is one which has a definite term specified by a beginning and an end, such as the payment on a mortgage. A **perpetuity** is an annuity where the payments continue indefinitely, such as the interest payments on perpetual bonds. We will focus on the most common types of annuities certain which are the ordinary annuity and the annuity due. If the periodic payment of an annuity is made at the end of each period, the annuity is called **ordinary annuity**, **annuity-immediate**, or simply **annuity**.

▼ **Example 4.6.2**: Patrick needs $20,000 six years from now. How much a year should he save if his account pays 10% assuming the interest compounds annually? How much does he have to save every month if the interest is compounded monthly?

Solution:

(1) If the interest compounds annually, and since FVA = $20,000, r = 0.10, n = 6, then

$$\$20,000 = \frac{A[(1 + 0.1)^6 - 1]}{0.1}$$

$$\$20,000 \times 0.1 = \$2,000 = A\,0.7716$$

$$A = \frac{\$2,000}{0.7716} = \$2,592.02$$

(2) If the interest compounds monthly, and since FV = $20,000, r = 0.1/12 = 0.0083, n = 12 × 6 = 72, then

$$\$20,000 = \frac{A[(1 + 0.0083)^{72} - 1]}{0.0083}$$

$$\$20,000 \times 0.0083 = \$166 = A\,0.8133$$

$$A = \frac{\$166}{0.8133} = \$204.11$$

❖ **Interpretation**: To achieve his goal, Patrick should save $2,592.02 annually, or $204.11 monthly, depending on what compounding method is used. Obviously, he would benefit more with monthly payment and monthly compounding. This is because twelve deposits of $204.11 amounts to $2,449.32 which is less than the annual deposit of $2,590.02 due to the extra interest earned by monthly compounding compared to annual compounding. This example illustrates how to calculate annuity payment (a) with Formula 4.6 when other factors are given.

▼ **Example 4.6.3**: Vicki wants to accumulate $50,000 for her daughter's education. She is planning to deposit $4,000 a year in an annuity that pays 9.25% interest compounded annually. How long will it take Vicki to achieve her goal?

Solution: Since FVA = $50,000, A = $4,000, r = 0.0925, then

$$\$50,000 = \frac{\$4,000[(1 + 0.0925)^n - 1]}{0.0925}$$

($50,000 × 0.0925)/$4,000 = $(1 + 0.0925)^n - 1$
$1.15625 = 1.0925^n - 1$
$1.15625 + 1 = 2.15625 = 1.0925^n$, take logarithms for both side
$\ln 2.15625 = n \ln 1.0925$
$0.7684 = n\,0.008847$
$n = 0.7684/0.08847 = 8.685$

❖ **Interpretation:** It will take Vicki 8.685 years, or approximately eight years and nine months (.685 × 12 = 8.22 months), to achieve her goal. This example demonstrates how to use Formula 4.6 to solve for n, given other factors. In this example, natural logarithms are used. Actually, the base-10 logarithms can also be used in the similar fashion to calculate n.

▼ **Example 4.6.4**: Dan knows that he can afford to save $1,440 a year toward his goal of accumulating $10,000 in 5 years. If he invests his savings in an annuity that compound annually, what must be the interest rate that he should look for?

Solution:

We have to use the future value of annuity table (See Table A.3 in the Appendix) to solve the problem. Since FVA = $10,000, A = $1,440, n = 5, then

$$\$10,000 = \frac{\$1,440[(1 + r)^5 - 1]}{r}$$

Since the table is arranged based on the "amount of $1 per period," we have to divide both sides by 1440, then get:

$$6.9444 = \frac{[(1 + r)^5 - 1]}{r}$$

Now we refer to the Table A.3: Across the number of periods 5 (column 1, line 5) we can find two numbers with the closest values to our reduced future value of annuity (6.9444 in this case), which are 6.8771 with a corresponding interest rate of 16% and 7.0144 with a corresponding interest rate of 17%. We can conclude that our rate is somewhere in between 16 and 17%. For a closer estimate, we set up a **difference proportion equation** and solve for r:

$$\frac{r - 0.16}{0.17 - 0.16} = \frac{6.9444 - 6.8771}{7.0144 - 6.8771}$$

$$\frac{r - 0.16}{0.01} = \frac{0.0673}{0.1373} = 0.4902$$

$$(r - 0.16) = 0.4902 \times 0.01 = 0.004902$$

$$r = 0.004902 + 0.16 = 0.165 = 16.5\%$$

❖ **Interpretation:** The interest rate will be 16.5%. This example illustrates a **linear interpolation method** to estimate r using Formula 4.6 and the future value of annuity table, when other factors are given.

7. Future Value of Annuity Due

Formula 4.7:

$$FVAD = A(1 + r)\frac{(1 + r)^n - 1}{r}$$

Where: FVAD = future value of annuity-due; A = annuity payment; r = interest rate; and n = number of periods.

▼ **Example 4.7.1**: Cathy's $1,000 retirement contribution is made to her fund at the beginning of the year for 19 years. How much would the future value of these contributions be if the account bears a 10% interest?

Solution: Since A = $1,000, n = 19, r = 0.10, then

$$FVAD = \$1,000(1 + 0.1)\frac{(1 + 0.1)^{19} - 1}{0.1} = \$1,000 \times 1.1 \times 51.159 = \$56,275$$

❖ **Interpretation**: The future value of these contributions will be $56,275. When the periodic payment is made at the beginning of the term, this kind of annuity is called **annuity due**. Using Formula 4.7, we can also easily calculate the annuity payment (A) and number of payments (n) when other factors are given. These calculations are demonstrated in the following examples.

▼ **Example 4.7.2**: Dean wants to have $20,000 at his graduation. How much money must he deposit at the start of each of the next four years if the interest rate is 7%?

Solution: Since FVAD = $20,000, n = 4, r = .07, then

$$\$20,000 = A(1 + 0.07)\frac{(1 + 0.07)^4 - 1}{0.07} = A\,4.751$$

$$A = \frac{\$20,000}{4.751} = \$4,210$$

❖ **Interpretation:** Dean needs to put $4,210 every year to achieve his financial goal.

▼ **Example 4.7.3**: Omar is planning to accumulate $16,627. He plans to deposit $3,500 at the beginning of each year in an annuity that pays 7% interest compounded annually. How long will it take him to get what he wants?

Solution: Since FVAD = \$16,627, A = \$3,500, r = 0.07, then

$$\$16,627 = \$3,500 \ (1 + 0.07) \ \frac{(1 + 0.07)^n - 1}{0.07}$$

$\$16,627 = \$53,500 \ [(1 + 0.07)^n - 1 \ ]$
$\$16,627/\$53,500 = 0.3108 = 1.07^n - 1$
$0.3108 + 1 = 1.3108 = 1.07^n$, take logarithms for both sides, then
$\ln 1.3108 = n \ln 1.07$
$0.2706 = n \ 0.06766$
$n = 0.2706/0.06766 = 4$

❖   **Interpretation:** It will take 4 years for Omar to achieve his saving goal. The above examples demonstrate that by only remembering Formula 4.7, you can calculate the future value of annuity due, the annuity payment, or number of payments, given other factors. (Using Formula 4.7 to calculate interest rate is difficult, but not impossible, although it is not discussed in this book.)

8. Present Value of Annuity

Formula 4.8:

$$PVA = A \ \frac{1 - 1/(1 + r)^n}{r}$$

Where: PVA = present value of annuity; A = annuity payment; r = interest rate; and n = number of periods.

▼   **Example 4.8.1**: What is the present value of an annuity which pays \$200 at the end of each quarter of a 10-year term if the interest rate is 5%?

Solution: Since A = \$200, n = 10 × 4 = 40, r = .05/4 = .0125, then

$$PVA = \$200 \ \frac{1 - 1/(1 + .0125)^{40}}{.0125} = \$200 \times 31.3269 = \$6,265.38$$

❖   **Interpretation:** The present value of the annuity is \$6,265.38. The **present value of an annuity** is the sum of the current values of all the payments of the annuity. It is also referred to as the **cash equivalent of the annuity**. Since each payment is discounted to the present time, the **present value of an ordinary annuity** is obtained at one period before the first payment. The **present value of an annuity due** is obtained at the time of the first payment. The formula for calculating the present value for an annuity due will be introduced in the next section. The following examples illustrate how to use Formula 4.8 to calculate annuity payment and number of payments, when other factors are given.

▼ **Example 4.8.2**: To help her son Jason in his college expenses, Barbara deposits $20,000 in an account that is designed to send him a check at the end of each month for the next five years. If this account pays an 8% interest compounded monthly, how much would be the amount on Jason's check?

Solution: Since PVA = $20,000, n = 5 × 12 = 60, r = .08/12 = .0067, then

$$\$20{,}000 = A\,\frac{1 - 1/(1 + .0067)^{60}}{.0067} = A\,49.2719$$

$$A = \frac{\$20{,}000}{49.2719} = \$405.91$$

❖ **Interpretation:** Jason's monthly check will be $405.91.

▼ **Example 4.8.3**: Robert wishes to invest his $16,560 in a fund that would pay his granddaughter Rachel $5,000 at the end of each year. How long would it take Rachel to exhaust the fund given an interest rate of 8%?

Solution: Since PVA = $16,500, A = $5,000, r = .08, then

$$\$16{,}560 = \$5{,}000\,\frac{1 - 1/(1 + .08)^{n}}{.08}$$

$16,560 × .08/$5,000 = .26496 = $1 - 1/(1 + .08)^{n}$

$1 - .26496 = 1/(1 + .08)^{n}$
$.73504 = 1/1.08^{n}$
$1/.73504 = 1.3605 = 1.08^{n}$, take logarithms for both sides, then
$\ln 1.3605 = n \ln 1.08$
$.3079 = n\ .07696$
$n = .3079/.07696 = 4$

❖ **Interpretation:** It will take 4 years for Rachel to exhaust the fund.

9. Present Value of Annuity Due

Formula 4.9:

$$PVAD = A\left[\frac{1 - 1/(1 + r)^{n-1}}{r} + 1\right]$$

Where: PVAD = present value of annuity due; A = annuity payment; r = interest rate; and n = number of periods.

▼ **Example 4.9.1**: Upon his retirement, Professor Smith wants to see a $1,000 scholarship awarded at the beginning of each year and for the next 20 years to an outstanding student majoring in Personal Finance. If the department invest Smith's funds at 7.5%, how much should the Professor's deposit be?

Solution: Since A = $1,000, r = .075, n = 20, then

$$PVAD = \$1,000[\frac{1 - 1/(1 + 0.75)^{20-1}}{.075} +1] = \$1,000 \times 10.959 = \$10,959$$

❖ **Interpretation:** Professor Smith needs to deposit $10,959.

▼ **Example 4.9.2**: Susan invested $18,700 in a money market account providing a 6% return. She is planning to make a withdraw at the beginning of each month for the next 10 years? How much would that withdrawal be?

Solution: Since PVAD = $18,700, n = 10 × 12 = 120, r = .06/12 = .005, then

$$\$18,700 = A[\frac{1 - 1/(1 + .005)^{120-1}}{.005} +1] = A\,90.5238$$

$$A = \frac{\$18,700}{90.5238} = \$206.58$$

❖ **Interpretation:** Susan should withdraw $206.58 per month.

▼ **Example 4.9.3**: How many semi-annual checks of $2,520 can be received from an annuity presently valued at $60,000 if it earns 6% interest?

Solution: Since PVAD = $60,000, A = $2,520, r = .06/2 = .03, then

$$\$60,000 = \$2,520[\frac{1 - 1/(1 + .03)^{n-1}}{.03} +1]$$

$$\frac{\$60,000}{\$2,520} = 23.81 = \frac{1 - 1/(1 + .03)^{n-1}}{.03} +1$$

$$23.81 - 1 = 22.82 = \frac{1 - 1/1.03^{n-1}}{.03}$$

$22.81 \times .03 = .6843 = 1 - 1/1.03^{n-1}$
$1 - .6843 = .3157 = 1/1.03^{n-1}$
$1/.3157 = 3.1676 = 1.03^{n-1}$, take logarithms for both sides, then
$\ln 3.1676 = (n-1) \ln 1.03$
$1.153 = (n-1) .02956$
$n-1 = 1.153/.02956 = 39$
$n = 39 + 1 = 40$

❖ **Interpretation:** There will be 40 semi-annual checks.

INFORMATION AND COMPUTING RESOURCES

1. In *Mathematics of Finance* (Cissell, Cissell, & Flaspohler, 1990), many concepts of time values of money are discussed in detail.

2. Some functions, such as future value or present value of annuities, are available from many popular electronic spreadsheet programs and financial calculators. However, there are not built-in functions, such as simple interest rate, bank discount rate, effective interest rate, and continuous compounding in computers or calculators; thus the reader should use the formulas presented in this chapter to calculate the results.

EXERCISE PROBLEMS

Simple Interest

1. What is the simple interest on a 3-year loan of $2500 borrowed at 13%?

2. Calculate how much Jane will have in her saving account 5 years from now if she deposits $3250. The simple interest rate is 4.75%.

3. If the total interest cost for a $2110 loan is $759.60, and the rate is 6% simple,. what is the maturity of this loan?

4. Christie wants to have 6500 in 5 years but she only have $3688 to invest. What must the interest rate be to help achieve her goal?

5. Find the amounts of ordinary interest and exact interest that would be paid on $40,000 invested at 7.5% from May 21 to October 1.

Bank Discount Rate

6. Ben has a loan of $6800 , discounted at 10%, for 24 months. How much does he receive from the loan?

7. Cheryl has two offers for a 2-year loan, one from the town bank which discounts 7%, and the other from the city bank which charges 7.75% interest. What is the better offer for her?

8. Find the annual discount rate that is equivalent to an annual interest rate of 11%.

9. Find the annual interest rate that is equivalent to an annual discount rate of 9%.

10. Gretchen needed $9500 to finalize the deal on a new living room set. Her local bank agreed to offer this amount on a discounted note at 10.5% for 3 years. What is the maturity value of her loan?

11. Jeff applied for a 5-year $5600 loan. How much would his proceeds be if the bank discount the loan at 12%?

Compound Interest

12. If you invest $5150 at 7.75% compounded annually, how much will the investment worth 8 years later?

13. Compound semiannually to find the future value of $15,000 invested for 5 years at 11.50%. What is the future value if compounded quarterly, monthly, weekly, or daily (using 365 days as a year)?

14. In 5 years, Sharon will receive $13000 as returns to her investment. What is the present value of this return when the interest rate is 6.9%?

15. If $10,000 this year is doubled by investment 5 years later. Using monthly compounding, what rate of return is this investment yielding?

16. How many years will it take for Kelly's investment to grow from $2540 to $3512 when it is compounded monthly at 6.5%.

17. Find the present value of John's total return to his three investments: $618 and $1245 which are due two years from now, and $2370 which is due in four years, given that the interest rate is 6.25%.

18. Lisa and David have been married for two years. They have just decided the summer of 1999 should be spent in Switzerland. They figured out that to meet the cost of the entire vacation they would only have to dedicate what they already have in their saving account ($ 5,859.37) for that vacation, keeping their regular saving during the next three years for different purposes. Given that the interest rate would be 8.5%, find the following: (1) How much would they be able to spend for their vacation? (2) If the cost of vacation is $9,384.44, What would be the interest rate that would let their saving account accumulate to meet their vacation costs? (3) How many years would they have to wait if the interest rate is 10%, the cost of vacation is $12,000, and their saving account now has only $7451.05 ?

19. Calculate the present value of a couple's stream of returns to their five assets using an interest rate of 9.5%, assuming the current year is 1996.

Asset #	Return	Year
1	$ 1,530	1998
2	$ 2,320	1999
3	$ 900	1999
4	$ 3,456	2000
5	$ 2,113	2001

Effective Interest Rate

20. What is the effective rate of 12% interest compounded weekly?

21. If the annual rate is 10%, what is the effective rate if compounded quarterly?

Continuous Compounding

22. Compound continuously to find the future value of $15,000 invested for 5 years at 11.50%.

23. What is the future value of $2,000 if compounded continuously for six months with an interest rate of 5%?

24. If compounded continuously for three years with an interest of 9% to reach an amount of $4,000, what is the present value of the amount?

Future Value of Annuity

25. Joanne deposits $4500 at the end of each quarter for 5 years. How much will her balance be if the interest rate is 6% compounded quarterly?

26. How much should Liz have deducted from her monthly paycheck and deposited into an annuity paying 6% interest compounded monthly in order to secure an amount of $10,000 for her son's trip to Europe 5 years from now.

27. How many years will it take to have $10,000 in an annuity when a $269.89 deposit is made at the end of each quarter, and the interest is 8% compounded quarterly?

28. If a couple draws a new plan of saving for that vacation by putting aside $200 a month for the next three years, and if the cost of vacation will be $9,384.44, and the interest rate is 11%, (1) would the couple be able to take that vacation, (2) what must the interest rate be in order to make their saving plan, (3) what must their monthly saving payments be in order to make it to their vacation if the interest rate drops 5% below the rate you found in step (2)?

Future Value of Annuity Due

29. In an annuity paying 9% compounded semiannually, Kirk deposits $600 twice a year, the first is made at the beginning of the year while the second is made on July 1st. How much will he be able to collect when he retires 25 years from now?

30. In her daughter's wedding 3 years from now, Sue wants to give a $10,000 gift. If she saves in an annuity account that pays 8.5% and compound monthly, how much should she deposit at the beginning of each of the next 36 months?

31. Peter promised himself to save $100 at the beginning of each month from his current income as a customer service representative. His goal is to save of $5,000 to pay for a down payment of a new car. If the interest rate is 6%, how long can he reach his goal?

Present Value of Annuity

32. Dawn borrows $3,553 to be paid off in installments of $122 at the end of each quarter. (1) How many payments should she make to repay all the loan, given that the annual interest is 7%, (2) if the bank asks him to pay off the loan in 10 years, what is the quarterly payment, (3) if the bank reduces the interest rate by 1% and asks him to pay off the loan in 10 years with a quarterly payment of $120.34, how much he can borrow now?

Present Value of Annuity Due

33. Kevin makes his annuity payments of $400 at the beginning of each quarter for 10 years. If the interest is 8% compounded quarterly, what is the present value of his annuity?

34. The present value of Kristen's pension is $70,669. She receives two checks of $5,000 a year, one on Jan 1 and the other on July 1. (1) If the interest is 8%, how many years will she be able to receive those checks, and (2) if she hopes she should receive the checks for 12 years, how much is a check worth?

SELECTED REFERENCES

Bertisch, A.M. (1994). *Personal finance*. Orlando, FL: The Dryden Press.

Bliss, E. (1989). *College mathematics for business*. Englewood Cliffs, NJ: Prentice Hall.

Chottiner, S. (1978). *Mathematics for modern management*. New York, NY: Harper & Row Publishers.

Cissell, R., Cissell, H. & Flaspohler, D.(1990). *Mathematics of finance*. Boston, MA: Houghton Mifflin.

Copland,T.E. and Weston, J.F. (1979). *Financial theory and corporate policy.* Reading, MA: Addison-Wesley Publishing Co.

Dean, B.V., Sasieni, M.W, & Gupta S.K. (1979). *Mathematics for modern management.* Huntington, NY: Robert E. Krieger Publishing Co.

Garman, E. T., & Forgue, R. (1997). *Personal finance.* (5th ed.). Boston: Houghton Mifflin.

Gitman, L.J. (1989). *Basic managerial finance.* New York, NY: Harper and Row Publishers.

Gitman, L. J., & Joehnk, M. D. (1993). *Personal financial planning.* (6th ed.). Fort Worth: Dryden.

Greynolds, E.B., Aronofsky, J.S. & Frame, R.J.(1980). *Financial analysis using calculators: Time value of money.* New York, NY: McGraw Hill, Inc.

Howard, A., & Kolman, B. (1980). *Applied finite mathematics.* New York, NY: Academic Press.

Israelsen, C.L., & Weagley, R.O. (1992). *Personal and family finance workbook.* Dubuque, Iowa: Kendall/Hunt Publishing Co.

Kaczmarski, R.M. (1986). *Financial cookbook: A consumer's guide.* Cincinnati, OH: South-Western Publishing Co.

Kapoor, J.R., Dlabay, L.R., & Hughes, R.J. (1996). *Personal finance.* Chicago, IL: Irwin.

Khoury, S.J., & Parsons, T.D. (1981). *Mathematical methods in finance and economics.* New York, NY: North Holland.

Lang, L.R. (1993). *Strategy for personal finance.* New York, NY: McGraw Hill, Inc.

Langhout, J., & Der Meyden, F.V. (1986). *Introduction to the mathematics of finance.* Amsterdam: A.A. Balkema.

Mayo, H.B. (1983). *Investments.* Chicago, IL: The Dryden Press.

Sharpe, W., Alexander, G. J., & Bailey, J. V. (1995). *Investments* (5th ed.). Englewood Cliffs, NJ: Prentice Hall.

Shim, J.K., & Siegel, J.G. (1994). *569 Solutions to your personal finance problems.* New York, NY: McGraw Hill, Inc.

Shim, J.K., & Siegel, J.G. (1991). *Theory and problems of personal finance .* New York, NY: McGraw Hill, Inc.

Siegel, J.G., & Shim, J.K. (1989). *Personal financial planning and investment pocket guide.* New York, NY: McGraw Hill, Inc.

Simpson, T.M., Pirenian, Z.M., Crenshaw, B.H., & Riner, J. (1969). *Mathematics of finance.* Englewood Cliffs, NJ: Prentice Hall.

Thomsett, M.C. (1989). *A little black book of business mathematics.* New York, NY: American Management Association.

END NOTES

1.   Some books distinguish between current value and present value, but many others, such as Cissell, Cissell, and Flaspohler (1990), Garman and Forgue (1997), Gitman and Joehnk (1993), and Sharpe, Alexander, and Bailey (1995), treat the two terms as the same. This book follows the second approach, and the term "present value" is used as it refers to current value.

2.   Formulas in this chapter can be easily transformed to solve for a different factor given other factors. For example, Formula 4.3 can be transformed to Formula 4.3b (see below) to solve for present value of a single amount, given future value, interest rate and number of periods. It can also be transformed to solve for number of periods (Formula 4.3c) or interest rate (Formula 4.3d). For practice, you may use the Formulas 4.3b, 4.3c, and 4.3d to redo Examples 4.3.4, 4.3.5, and 4.3.6. In the following, we list transformations of several formulas that are used often.

(1) Future value of a single amount

Formula 4.3: $FV = PV(1+r)^n$

Formula 4.3b: $PV = FV(1+r)^{-n}$

Formula 4.3c: $n = \dfrac{\ln(FV/PV)}{\ln(1+r)}$

Formula 4.3d: $r = (FV/PV)^{1/n} - 1$

Where: FV = future value; PV = present value; r = interest rate; n = number of periods; and ln = logarithm

(2) Future value of annuity

Formula 4.6: $FVA = \dfrac{A[(1+r)^n - 1]}{r}$

Formula 4.6b: $A = \dfrac{FVA \cdot r}{(1+r)^n - 1}$

Formula 4.6c: $n = \dfrac{\ln[(FVA \cdot r)/A + 1]}{\ln(1+r)}$

Where: FVA = future value of annuity; A = annuity; r = interest rate; n = number of periods; and ln = logarithm. Note that there is not a simple transformation for solving for interest rate (r). You may use a linear interpolation method to solve for *r*, given other factors (see Example 4.6.4).

(3) Future value of annuity due

Formula 4.7: $FVAD = A(1+r)\dfrac{(1+r)^n - 1}{r}$

Formula 4.7b: $A = \dfrac{FVAD \cdot r}{(1+r)[(1+r)^n - 1]}$

Formula 4.7c:

$$n = \frac{\ln\{(FVAD \cdot r)/[A(1+r)]+1\}}{\ln(1+r)}$$

Where: FVAD = future value of annuity due; A = annuity; r = interest rate; n = number of periods; and ln = logarithm. Note that there is not a simple transformation for solving for interest rate (r). You may use a linear interpolation method to solve for *r*, given other factors.

(4) Present value of annuity

Formula 4.8:

$$PVA = A\frac{1-1/(1+r)^n}{r}$$

Formula 4.8b:

$$A = \frac{PVA \cdot r}{1-1(1+r)^n}$$

Formula 4.8c:

$$n = \frac{\ln(1-PVA \cdot r/A)}{-\ln(1+r)}$$

Where: PVA = present value of annuity due; A = annuity; r = interest rate; n = number of periods; and ln = logarithm. Note that there is not a simple transformation for solving for interest rate (r). You may use a linear interpolation method to solve for *r*, given other factors.

(5) Present value of annuity due

Formula 4.9:

$$PVAD = A[\frac{1-1/(1+r)^{n-1}}{r}+1]$$

Formula 4.9b:

$$A = \frac{PVAD}{[1-1/(1+r)^{n-1}]/r+1}$$

Formula 4.9c:

$$n = 1 - \frac{\ln[1-(PVAD/A - 1)r]}{\ln(1+r)}$$

Where: PVAD = present value of annuity due; A = annuity; r = interest rate; n = number of periods; and ln = logarithm. Note that there is not a simple transformation for solving for interest rate (r). You may use a linear interpolation method to solve for *r*, given other factors.

3.   The formula for compounding interest is the most critical formula in finance. The impressive mathematical multiplication of this formula is behind what is called, "The wonder of compounding." The British economist John Maynard Keynes called

the compound interest "magic," and Baron Rothschild, a banker with international stature, called compounding, "The eighth wonder of the world." Mathematicians and economists have been circulating several interesting historical scenarios to illustrate the wonder of compounding. For instance, what has become the heart of New York City now, Manhattan, was bought in 1624 from the native Indians for the sum of $24. If this amount was invested at, say 5% interest, it would have grown today to $1,922,293,931. When Benjamin Franklin died in 1790, he left to the city of Boston a bequest that was equivalent to $4,570. In his will, he wanted the money to earn interest for a century. He stipulated that part of the fund was to be spent on public projects and the remaining part was to be invested for another century. By 1890 the bequest had grown to $332,000. About $438,742 was spent in 1907 on the Franklin Institute while the rest of the fund was left to accumulate to $3,458,797 by 1980. In 1810, Francis Bailey, an English mathematician and astronomer, calculated that if a British penny was invested on the birth of Christ at 5% interest compounded annually, it would have grown to what could buy an amount of gold enough to fill 357,000,000 earths.

Chapter 5
College Financial Planning Math

▼ Future Value of Annual Cost of Attendance
▼ Future Value of Total Cost of Attendance for Number of Years
▼ Monthly Contributions to an Investment at the End of the Month
▼ Monthly Contributions to an Investment at the Beginning of the Month
▼ Contributions to Series EE Savings Bonds
▼ Educational Loan Repayments
▼ Parent's Ability to Borrow

Chapter 5
College Financial Planning Math

Abraham Mulugetta and Yuko Mulugetta[1]

OVERVIEW

The first step of college financial planning is to estimate the **future cost of attendance**. This is an approximation of how much will it cost to provide a child with the opportunity to attend college in the future. Costs that should be estimated include tuition, fees, room, board, books, supplies, transportation, and personal expenses.[1]

With the future cost of attendance estimated, the next steps are to choose appropriate investment vehicles to cover the cost of attendance, to determine the amount of regular contributions toward these investments, and, finally, to decide whether the child or the parent should maintain ownership of the investment portfolio. These decisions must be based upon careful consideration of several factors including the number of years available to invest; the estimated rate of return; local, state and federal tax consequences; and the family's financial ability and willingness to take calculated risk.

Many parents attempt to save utilizing investments that offer a relatively conservative return, perhaps 4 to 5 percent, typically in the effort to avoid placing funds earmarked for future college expenses at risk. They often choose low-return investment alternatives such as certificates of deposit, Series EE savings bonds, and state sponsored college tuition prepayment plans.

A **certificate of deposit** is an interest-earning savings instrument offered by a bank-like institution that accepts deposits for a fixed amount of time, commonly ranging from seven days to eight years, with no fees charged. Certificates of deposit

---

[1]Abraham Mulugetta, Ph.D., Associate Professor in the Department of Finance and International Business, Director of the Center for Trading and Analysis of Financial Instruments, Ithaca College, Ithaca, NY, 14850, Mulugett@Ithaca.edu and Yuko Mulugetta, Ph.D.,Director of Research and Planning Analysis for Admissions and Financial Aid, Cornell University, Ithaca, NY, 14853. ymm1@cornell.edu

are federally insured. Saving for college by investing in certificates of deposit, or specialized programs (such as the *CollegeSure CD* sold by the College Savings Bank in Princeton, NJ)[2]requires careful consideration of what features of these vehicles work best for each individual investors.

Investing in U.S. Treasury Series EE savings bonds is particularly convenient for most families, although they too provide only a conservative return. **Series EE savings bonds** are discount bonds of the U.S. government that are purchased for 50 percent of their face value. A **discount bond** is one sold at less than face value and the difference between its purchase price and its value at maturity represents the interest earned. The bonds offer a minimum interest rate of 4 percent after five years of investment, compounded semiannually.[3] Perhaps the most beneficial aspects of investing in Series EE savings bonds are that (1) the interest earned is free from local and state income taxes, and (2) federal taxes on the interest income are deferred until the bonds are redeemed.

The interest accrued on the Series EE savings bonds can be totally free of federal tax if three criteria are met: (1) the bonds are cashed in to pay for college tuition and fees of a dependent, or in the case of adult education, the bond purchaser or spouse;[4] (2) the bonds purchased after 1989 are registered in the name of a person who is 24 years of age or older; and (3) the adjusted gross income of bond purchaser does not exceed a federally determined threshold.[5]

Oftentimes, however, the 10- or 15-year return on conservative investments, like certificates of deposit and government savings bonds, do not sufficiently offset the inflationary increases in the costs of college. Several states have responded to rising college costs by offering **state sponsored college tuition prepayment plans** that provide parents a hedge against future cost increases.[6] A typical plan permits a parent (or grandparent) to prepay tuition costs, even though the child will not attend college for 10 or more years. Prepayments are made to a state trust fund that holds and invests the amounts until the child reaches college age. At that time, the parent's prepayment fully covers the tuition, regardless of how high it is. A refund is available is the child is not admitted, decides not to attend college, or dies. A few plans permit the prepayment to be used for out-of-state colleges. A 1996 law provides that the earnings on money in these plans is exempt from income taxes until the funds are withdrawn, and then the income will be taxed at the student's rate, provided it is used for college expenses.[7]

Being concerned about the potentially low returns of certificates of deposit and Series EE savings bonds, many parents instead invest in common stocks and mutual funds that invest in common stocks. **Common stock** is the most basic form of ownership in a corporation whereby each shareholder has a proportionate interest in the ownership and, therefore, in the assets and income of the corporation. Stocks have generated over time the highest potential rate of return in exchange for the highest level of exposure to financial risks. Historically, the average real rate of return on common stocks (adjusted for inflation) has hovered around 8 percent during the past 200 years of market activity;[8] it has been about 13 percent, including dividends, over the past 20 years. This return is more than double the annual rate of return from more conservative bond investments.

Mutual funds are investment companies that combine the funds of investors who have purchased shares of ownership in the investment company and then invests that money using a strategic management philosophy in a diversified portfolio of securities issued by other corporations or governments. **Stock mutual funds** include only common stock in their portfolios as the investment objective is to increase in value over the long term through price appreciation of the securities in its portfolio.

If a child is relatively young (e.g. more than 10 years away from entering college), investing in stock mutual funds may be an appropriate strategy. These funds emphasize capital appreciation over income and, as a result, are less susceptible to the high taxes found in income generated from most other investments. When the child is only a few years away from attending college, funds in the investments should be shifted to more conservative, fixed-income mutual funds, or similar safe investments, in an effort to reduce any financial risk to the principal.

Taking advantage of **financial aid programs** is also an important part of college financial planning. These are private and government programs designed to provide financial assistance to college students. There are two kinds of financial aid programs: (1) need based, and (2) non-need based.

Need based aid programs provide students with financial aid according to their demonstrated financial needs. Each family's financial need is determined by subtracting the **expected family contribution (EFC)** from the projected total cost of attending a particular college or university. The determination of EFC is a complex process largely driven by the Congressionally approved **need analysis methodology**, although it often is adjusted by individual institutions. The calculation of EFC involves: (1) a contribution from the parents' available income; (2) a contribution from the parents' discretionary assets;[9] (3) a contribution from the students' assets; and (4) the number of dependent children the family already has in college.

Non-need based aid programs offer students financial assistance based specifically upon the students' merits such as athletic prowess, academic abilities, extracurricular, and/or academic interests. It is in the best interests of families to seek sources of non-need based financial aid by taking full advantage of computerized information resources now available to the public. (See the end of this chapter for a list.)

A transfer of investment ownership to a child is often recommended by financial experts because of likelihood of saving on income taxes. If a child is under 14 years old, the first $650 of interest income each year is tax-exempt due to the standard deduction and the next $650 is taxed at the child's rate, which is 15 percent in most cases. All interest income over $1,300 ($650 + $650) is taxable at the parents' top tax rate. The IRS's **kiddie tax regulation** requires that investment income of a dependent child under age 14 in excess of $1,300 be taxed at the parent's marginal tax rate, typically 28, 31, 36, or 39.6 percent. For the child who is older than 14, all such income is taxed at the child's tax rate, which is 15 percent in most cases.

The **financial aid package** is the total amount of financial aid each student receives from various financial sources (federal, state, institutional and private) in various aid forms (grants, loans and employment) in order to meet a requirement for some degree of demonstrated financial need. To choose an appropriate loan program and repayment option, and to determine an adequate loan amount, families need to consider several factors: future earning capability of the student, future earning capability of the family, length of the loan repayment, and interest.

This chapter details calculations and interpretations associated with college financial planning math. Topics include future value (price) of the annual cost of attendance, future value of total cost of attendance for number of years, monthly contributions to an investment at the end of the month, monthly contributions to an investment at the beginning of the month, contributions to Series EE savings bonds, education loan repayments, and parent's ability to borrow.

EXAMPLES OF MATHEMATICAL CONCEPTS RELATED TO COLLEGE FINANCIAL PLANNING

1. Future Value of Annual Cost of Attendance

Formula 5.1 (same as **Formula 4.3**): $FV = PV (1 + r)^n$

Where: FV = the future value of annual cost of attendance of your child's college; r = annual growth rate; n = pre-college years; and PV = the present value of cost of attendance.

▼   **Example 5.1**: Mr. and Mrs. Jenkins would like to send their son Kevin, now 8 years old, to IVY University in the future. IVY University currently charges $20,000 for tuition and fees combined on a yearly basis. Assume that the average cost of tuition at four-year private institutions has increased at a rate of 5% annually in recent years. If this price trend continues, how much would Kevin's first year of education cost be ten years from now?

Solution:

Since, PV = $20,000, r = .05, n = 10, then
$FV = \$20,000 \times (1 + .05)^{10}$
= $32,577.89

❖   **Interpretation:** Kevin's first year of education cost can be estimated to cost $32,577.89 ten years from now. This formula enables one to estimate the future price of annual cost of attendance. That is, how much you would need to pay for the child's future education at the beginning of the first year of college. In this example, cost of attendance is simply future tuition and fees. If desired, one may include room and board as well as allowances for books, supplies, travel between home and college, and personal expenses in the calculation. According to the College Board, the 1995-96 average costs were $9,285 for public colleges and universities, and $19,762 for private colleges and universities.

2. Future Value of Total Cost of Attendance for Number of Years

Formula 5.2 (same as **Formula 4.6**): $FVA = A [(1 + r)^n - 1]/r$

Where: FVA = the future value of the cost of a child attending college; r = annual growth rate; n = number of periods; and A = the annual cost of attendance.

▼ **Example 5.2:** From the calculation above, Mr. and Mrs. Jenkins have estimated that they would need approximately $32,600 for Kevin's first-year of tuition and fees at IVY University. If the tuition and fees continue to increase at 5 percent per year, how much would Kevin's four-year tuition cost in total assuming that the payment occurs at the beginning of the year.

Solution:

Since, A = $32,600, r = .05, n = 4, then
FVA = $32,600 × [(1 + .05)^4 - 1]/.05
= $32,600 × 4.310115
= $140,510.08
The result may be verified by the following step-by-step calculation;

1st Year	$ 32,600.00
2nd Year	$ 34,230.00 = ($32,600.00) (1 + .05)
3rd Year	$ 35,941.50 = ($34,230.00) (1 + .05)
4th Year	$ 37,738.58 = ($35,941.50) (1 + .05)
Total	$140,510.08

❖ **Interpretation:** Once you calculate the cost of a child's yearly education, you will be able to calculate the future price of total cost of attendance for N number of years based on this formula. The total cost for four years of college attendance is estimated to be $140,510.08. In this example, the Jenkins will need $140,510.08 for Kevin's four-year education at IVY University, assuming that the tuition payment will occur at the beginning of each college year. This is equivalent to having $130,400 ($32,600 x 4) in saving at the beginning of Kevin's freshman year, so that Mr. and Mrs. Jenkins can pay $32,600 for Kevin's four-year education and invest the rest ($97,800) into a conservative fixed-income investment earning a five-percent annual rate of return.

3. Monthly Contributions to an Investment at the End of the Month

Formula 5.3: FVA = A [(1 + r)^n - 1]/r

Where: FVA = the future value of total college cost estimated; A = the periodic payments at the end of each months; r = interest rate; and n = number of periods. Note that Formula 5.3 is the same as Formula 5.2.

▼ **Example 5.3**: According to the calculations above, Kevin's first year education at IVY University is estimated to be $32,600. Mr. and Mrs. Jenkins need to save $130,400 for Kevin's four-year education by the time when Kevin enters into IVY University as a freshman. Assuming that the stock market has a 12% annual rates of return and Kevin's college entrance is 10 years away, how much money do Mr. and Mrs. Jenkins need to invest monthly in order to cover Kevin's first-year college cost? For simplicity, ignore the income tax consequences. Compute the answer under the assumption that the investment payment occurs at the end of each month.

Solution:

Note that in this example the factor to be solved is A instead of FVA. The following steps show how to solve A when other factors are given. This approach will be used very often in this book, such as Examples 5.4 and 5.6 in the following sections.

Since, FVA = \$130,400, i = .12/12 = .01, n = 10 × 12 = 120, then
$$\$130,400 = A\,[(1 + .01)^{120} - 1]/.01$$
$$= A * 230.0387$$
$$A = \$130,400/230.0387 = \$566.86$$

❖ **Interpretation:** The monthly payment needs to be \$566.86. An annuity whose payments occur at the end of each period is called an **annuity.** Example 5.3 is an application of an ordinary annuity. Payments made at the beginning or end of a period will results in different answers. The example in the next section will demonstrate a situation in which payment is made at the beginning of a period. Once one has figured out the cost of sending a child to college, the next step is to calculate how much monthly investment contribution is needed to make to reach that goal. As indicated by the example above, this method requires a calculation of future value interest factor that is going to be applied to each monthly contribution. If you choose bi-weekly or weekly contribution method, then the number of periods and interest rate must be adjusted accordingly before the calculation.

4. Monthly Contributions to an Investment at the Beginning of the Month

Formula 5.4 (same as **Formula 4.7**): $FVAD = A\,(1 + r)\,[(1 + r)^n - 1]/r$

Where: FVAD = the future value of total college cost estimated; A = the periodic payments at the beginning of each month; r = interest rate; and n = number of periods.

▼ **Example 5.4:** Under the same assumptions described above in Example 5.3, how much money would Mr. and Mrs. Jenkins need to invest on a monthly basis to cover Kevin's four-year college cost if the investment payment occurs at the beginning of each month instead of at the end of the month? Compare the two results.

Solution:

Since FVAD = \$130,400, r = .12/12 = .01, n = 10 × 12 = 120, then
$$\$130,400 = A\,(1 + .01) \times [(1+.01)^{120} - 1]\,/.01 = 232.3391$$
$$A = \$130400/232.3391 = \$561.25$$

❖ **Interpretation:** In Example 5.4, Mr. and Mrs. Jenkins need \$561.25 if their monthly investment occurs at the beginning of the month, whereas they need to invest \$566.86 if their investment is made at the end of the month as shown in Example 5.3. An annuity whose payments are due at the beginning of each period is called an **annuity due**. Example 5.4 demonstrates an application of an annuity due. The basic difference of the two annuity formulas is that in the case of an annuity due, each payment would be compounded for one extra period. Therefore, a payment under the annuity due method would be smaller than a payment calculated under the ordinary annuity method as demonstrated above.

5. Contributions to Series EE Savings Bonds

Formula 5.5: $FV = PV (1 + r)^n$

Where: FV = the future value of bond investment for your child's college; r = annual interest rate; n = number of periods; and PV = the present value of investment. Note that Formula 5.5 is the same as Formula 5.1.

▼ **Example 5.5:** Mr. and Mrs. Jenkins have estimated that they need approximately $130,400 for Kevin's four-year education by the time Kevin enters into IVY University. They have formed a strategy, first to invest in the stock market for seven years. And then they plan to transfer the investment to EE savings bonds in order to protect the accumulated capital against shifts in market prices. If Mr. and Mrs. Jenkins let the stock investments grow to the end of year 7, and then shift their investment to Series EE savings bonds, will it be sufficient enough to cover Kevin's four-year education? Assume that bond interest is compounded semiannually, that the bond yields 6% per year, and that monthly contributions after year 7 will be invested in an investment earning 6% annual interest. The solution requires three steps.

Solution:

(1) Use Formula 5.4 to calculate the value of the investment in 7 years.
Since, A = $561.25, r = .12/12 = .01, n = 7 × 12 = 84, then
$FVA = \$561.05 \times (1 + .01) [(1 + .01)^{84} - 1]/.01$
$= \$561.05 \times 131.979$
$= \$74,073$
Thus, by the end of year 7, the Jenkins will have $74,073 in investments.

(2) Use Formula 5.5 to calculate the value of Series EE savings bond transferred from the stock market in three years.
Since, PV = $74,073, r = .06/2 = .03, n = 3 × 2, then
$FV = \$74,073 \times (1 + .03)^6$
$= \$74,073 \times 1.19405$
$= \$88,447.036$

(3) Use Formula 5.4 to calculate the value of Series EE savings bond contributed monthly in the three years of college education.
Since, A = $561.25, r = .06/12 = .005, n = 3 × 12 = 36, then
$FVA = \$561.25 \times (1 + .005) \times [(1 + .005)^{36} - 1]/.005$
$= \$561.25 \times 39.53279$
$= \$22,187.78$

Thus, the total investment is expected to be worth $110,634.8 ($88,447,036 + $22,187.78).

❖ **Interpretation:** The result indicates that this strategy will not be able to yield sufficient funds to cover Kevin's education at IVY University. Mr. and Mrs. Jenkins will fall short by about $20,000 ($130,400 - $110,635 = $19,765). If Series EE savings bonds are used as an investment vehicle, this formula helps one estimate the amount of needed bond investment.

6. Educational Loan Repayments

Formula 5.6 (same as **Formula 4.8**): $PVA = A [1 - (1 + r)^{-n}]/r$

Where: PVA = the present value of loan principal; A = the amount of periodic payment; r = interest rate; and n = number of periods.

▼ **Example 5.6**: Assume that Mr. and Mrs. Jenkins' college investment falls short by $20,000 to pay the four years of college tuition for Kevin. Therefore, they would like to borrow $20,000 for their son's college education through the Federal PLUS Loan program. Assuming a 9 percent interest rate on the $20,000 loan and a 10-year repayment period, how much would the Jenkins have to repay on a monthly basis?

Solution:

Since PVA = $20,000, r = .09/12 = .0075, n = 10 × 12 = 120, then
$20,000 = A [1 - (1 + .0075)^{-120}]/.0075 = A\ 78.942$
A = $20,000/78.942
= $253.35

❖ **Interpretation:** The monthly payment should be $253.3. If you are considering borrowing for education, this formula will help you calculate your monthly repayments based on the repayment period, annual interest rate, and loan principal amounts. If you choose a bi-weekly or weekly repayment method, the interest rates and number of periods need to be adjusted accordingly.

7. Parent's Ability to Borrow

Conceptual Idea 5.7: Experts recommend that families maintain a **debt-to-income ratio (D/I)** equal to or less than 37% to have any capacity to repay amounts borrowed, in which D refers to total monthly household debt payments and I is total monthly household gross income. This percentage is often used by authorities in financial aid offices. (Note that different percentage limits [often lower] are used by other lenders, such as home mortgage lenders; see Chapter 8, Using Financial Ratios.)

▼ **Example 5.7:** From the previous problem, Mr. and Mrs. Jenkins know that their monthly repayment would be $253.35 if they borrow $20,000 for their son's education. The question is whether the Jenkins have the financial capability to manage this new debt. Assume that their annual gross income is $80,000 and that they have the following monthly payments: home mortgage $1,500, $350 for automobile loan, minimum of $180 for all credit cards, and $260 for an installment loan at a bank. Do you recommend Mr. and Mrs. Jenkins take a $20,000 loan? If you do not, how much would be appropriate for the Jenkins?

Solution:

(1) To determine if Jenkins can borrow using gross annual income.

Since D = $1,500 + 350 + $180 + $260 = $2,290, I = $80,000/12 = $6,666.67
Then, D/I = $2,290/$6,666.67 = 34.35% < 37%
Since the D/I ratio is below 37%, the Jenkins still could borrow in addition to their current debts.

(2) To determine how much additional monthly debt payment they can make.

($80,000/12) × .37 - ($1,500 + $350 + $180 + $260) = $176.67

(3) To determine how much they can borrow.

Using previous Formula 5.6, since,

A = $176.67, r = .09/12 = .0075, n = 10 × 12 = 120, then
$$PVA = \$176.67 \times [1 - (1+.0075)^{-120}]/.0075$$
$$= \$176.67 \times 78.942 = \$13,946.68$$

❖ **Interpretation:** Thus, the Jenkins still can take a new loan since D/I ratio is less than 37%. They would be able to manage a $176.67 new loan instead of $253.35 monthly. The recommended maximum amount that they should borrow is approximately $14,000 in total which is $6,000 less than the amount the Jenkins originally wanted to borrow. To determine if you can borrow more, use the three steps demonstrated in this example, (1) to determine if your D/I ratio is less than the benchmark 37%; (2) if the D/I ratio is less than 37%, to determine how much additional monthly debt payment allowed using the same 37% standard; and (3) to determine how much extra debts in total you can borrow. If you are considering borrowing for education, this example will help you evaluate whether a repayment plan associated with an educational loan would be feasible or not based on your current total income and existing debt payments. Most lenders will refuse to issue a loan if the total of one's monthly debt payments exceed 37% of gross income.

INFORMATION AND COMPUTING RESOURCES

1. Popular magazines such as *Money, U.S. News & World Report, Newsweek,* and *Business Week* publish useful information on the cost and quality of education at various universities and colleges.

2. Detailed financial aid information, such as application deadlines and academic requirements, can be obtained from the financial aid office and/or the admissions office of collegiate institutions. Most universities and colleges have WWW homepages where one can find detailed. Fort instance, you can find Cornell University's WWW homepage at http://www.cornell.edu and Ithaca College's at http:www.ithaca.edu.

3. You can also find lots of information regarding college costs, financial aid, and financial planning for college expenses at the following WWW sites:

   ■ *NASFAA (National Association of Student Financial Aid Administrators):* http://www.finaid.org/

   ■ *U.S. Department of Education:* http://www.ed.gov/prog_info/SFA/StudentGuide/

   ■ *The College Board:* http://www.collegeboard.org/

   ■ *The Peterson's Guide:* http://www.petersons.com/resources/tools.html

4. Numerous private sponsored scholarships, fellowships, grants, and loans can be searched at following WWW sites:

   ■ *fastWEB:* http://www.fastweb.com/

   ■ *fastWEB Canada:* http://www.fastweb.com/canada/

   ■ *SRN Express:* http://www.rams.com/srn/search.htm

   ■ *Yahoo Educational Grants:* http://www.yahoo.com/Education/Grants/

   ■ *Financial aid information:* http://www.cs.cmu.edu/afs/cs/user/mkant/Public/FinAid/finaid.html

   ■ *Signet Bank:* http://www.infi.net:80/collegemoney

   ■ *U.S. Bank:* http://www.usbanksl.com/

5. Check out the following useful sources of information:

   ■ The College Board publishes *College Costs and Financial Aid Handbook, Paying for College*, and *The College Guide for Parents*. The College Board also sells the video, *Financing a Future*.

   ■ Gale Research publishes the annual *Scholarships, Fellowships and Loans* as well as *Fund Your Way through College: Uncovering 1,700 Great Opportunities in Undergraduate Financial Aid.*

   ■ Peterson's Guides publishes a number of financial aid related books, including *USA Today Financial Aid for College, Paying Less for College 1996; Winning Money for College: A High School Student's Guide to*

Scholarship Contests, Financing Graduate School, and Sports Scholarships and College Athletic Programs.

■ Prentice Hall publishes *The Prentice Hall Guide to Scholarships and Fellowships for Math and Science Students.*

EXERCISE PROBLEMS

Future Value of Annual Cost of Attendance

1. Mr. and Mrs. Tanaka would like to send their daughter, Yoko, 10 years old, to Big-Ten State University, which currently charges $9,500 for annual tuition and fees. Assume that the increase in public university tuition is relatively stable, on average about five percent. How much would Yoko's first year of education cost eight years from now?

2. Cost of attendance usually includes tuition and fees, room and board, as well as books, supplies, and personal expenses. This year's IVY University charges are:

Tuition and fees	$20,000
Room and Board	$ 7,000
Books and Supplies	$ 1,000
Personal Expenses	$ 1,500

   Assume that tuition and fees grow at a rate of 6% annual rate and other items increase at a rate of 5.5%. How much will the cost of attendance of IVY University will be ten years from now?

3. *Money* magazine has predicted that tuition charge of four-year private universities will grow at a rate of 6% in the next two years, but the growth rate will slow down to 5% after that. If a child's enrollment is five years away from now, how much annual tuition charge will be, given the current tuition is $19,500?

4. *Out-of-Class Exercise* Find your college's current charge of tuition and fees, and its average growth rate of the last five years. If this trend continues, how much would you have to pay for your tuition and fees four years from now?

Future Value of Total Cost of Attendance for Numbers of Years

5. Mr. and Mrs. Mitchner have estimated that their son, Retta's first-year tuition would be approximately $14,000 at Big-Ten State University. How much would Retta's four-year tuition cost in total, assuming that the tuition payment occurs at the beginning of the year and its growth rate is 5%

6. *Out-of-Class Exercise* Daniel is thirteen years old, five years away from college entrance. How much will his parents need to save in order to enroll him to your

college/university for four years? Find your college's tuition charge of the current year as well as the last two years, and compute its average growth rate. Assume that tuition steadily increases at the growth rate you have just computed.

Monthly Contributions to an Investment at the End of the Month

7. Mr. and Mrs. Ursilo have estimated that they need approximately $14,000 for their son, Ryan's first year education at Big-Ten University. Assuming that the stock market has a 10% annual rates of return and Ryan's college entrance is 8 years way, how much money do Mr. and Mrs. Ursilo need to invest on a monthly basis in order to cover Ryan's first-year college cost? Monthly payments are due at the end of the month.

Monthly Contributions to an Investment at the Beginning of the Month

8. Under the same assumption described above, how much money would Mr. and Mrs. Ursilo need to invest on a monthly basis to cover Ryan's first-year college cost if the investment payment occurs at the beginning of each year?

9. Many colleges and universities offer families a multiple-year tuition payment option. Under this plan, families can lock in four-year tuition at the first-year tuition rate and pay that total amount at once at the beginning of a child's first-college year. Mr. and Mrs. Miller would like to utilize this plan for their daughter, Menna. Menna's first year education at IVY University is estimated to be $20,000. Assuming that the stock market has a 9.5% annual rates of return and Menna's college entrance is 7 years away, how much money do Mr. and Mrs. Miller need to invest on a monthly basis in order to cover Menna's four-year tuition? Monthly payments are due at the beginning of the month.

Contributions to Series EE Savings Bonds

10. If a child is 13 years old, 5 years away from college entrance. If his/her parents invest $80,000 to Series EE savings bonds, how much will they receive when the bonds are redeemed? Bonds are assumed to yield 5% annually and are compounded semiannually. Which will give more tax advantage, investing under the child's name or under the parent's name? Assume that the parents' AGI (adjusted gross income) is $95,000.

11. Big Red University' tuition charge is $19,000 this year and it will grow at a rate of 6% on a yearly basis. If Mr. and Mrs. Cheng would like to invest their money in Series EE savings bonds, how much will be sufficient to cover their son, Lin's first-year tuition at Big-Red University? Assume that bond interests are compounded semiannually and the bond yields 5.5%. Lin is now 8 years old, 10 years away from college entrance. (*Hint: You need to estimate Lin's first-year tuition at Big Red University.*)

12. *Out-of-Class Exercise* Assume that you have a younger brother who is 15 years old. If he would like to enroll in your college three years from now and your parent(s) would like to use Series EE savings bonds as an investment vehicle to pay a half of his first-year tuition, how would you advise your parent(s) in terms of: (1) the amount that should be invested; (2) under whose ownership it should be registered, if your family would like to take a tax advantage; and (3) a possible impact on the application for need-based financial aid.

13. *Out-of-Class Exercise* Investigate whether your state has a state pre-paid tuition program or not. If your state operates a program, obtain a brochure of the program and describe what would be advantages and disadvantages in comparison to other investment options.

Educational Loan Repayments

14. Mr. and Mrs. Thorpe would like to take a $20,000 parental loan from ABC Bank for their daughter, Yoko's college education. Assuming a 10 percent interest rate on the $20,000 loan and a 15-year repayment period, how much would the Thorpe have to repay on a monthly basis? What is the total interest to be paid?

15. Mary Smith has taken $18,000 Subsidized Stafford Loan in total while studying at IVY University as an undergraduate student. The interest on the subsidized Stafford Loan is paid by the federal government while the student is in school and during the 6 month grace period. The annual interest rate of the loan is currently 8.25% and Mary would like to repay this loan in ten years. How much does she need to make a monthly repayment?

Parent's Ability to Borrow

16. Assume that Mr. and Mrs. Thorpe's annual gross income is $82,000 while they pay monthly $1,400 for mortgage, $320 for automobile loan, minimum of $120 for all credit cards they owe, and $250 for an installment loan at a local bank. Do you recommend that Mr. and Mrs. Thorpe take a $20,000 PLUS loan? If you do not, how much would be appropriate for the Thorpes? [Hint: Use the result from Question 14].

SELECTED REFERENCES

Baum, S. (1994). Access, choice and the middle class, *The Journal of Student Financial Aid.* (No. 2), 17-25.

College Savings Bank (1995). *CollegeSure certificate of deposit: The guaranteed way to save for college.*

Hoffman, W.H., J. E. Smith, & Willis, E. (1995). *West's Federal taxation: Individual income taxes, 1996 annual edition.* New York: West Publishing Company.

Luciano, L. (1997, March). Worried about saving for college? Consider a prepaid-tuition plan. *Money*, 37.

Massachusetts Educational Financing Authority (1995, February). *The U. plan: The Massachusetts college saving program, program description and offering statement.*

Morris, K. M. & Siegel, A. M. (1992). *Guide to understanding personal finance.* Lightbulb Press.

Siegel, J.J. (1992), The equity premium: Stock and bond returns since 1802, *Financial Analysis Journal, 48,* 28-38.

U. S. Department of the Treasury (1994, October). *The Savings bonds question and answer book.*

_____ (1995, May). *U.S. savings bonds: Investor information.*

_____ (1995, March). *Some questions and answers about education savings bonds.*

ENDNOTES

1.   The cost of attendance, if applicable, may also include federal loan origination fees, dependent care, child care, and expenditures related to a disability.

2.   The *CollegeSure CD* is a federally insured certificate of deposit designed to meet the future cost of higher education by pegging its annual percentage yield rate tied to a college inflation index (the Independent College 500 Index published by the College Board in this instance) less 1.5 percent; a minimum 4% annual interest rate is guaranteed.

3.   Series EE savings bonds purchased on or after March 1, 1993 offer a guaranteed minimum rate of 4 percent interest, compounded semiannually. For the first five years, interest accrues through monthly increases in redemption value. After five years, while the minimum rate is guaranteed, Series EE savings bonds earn interest on a **market-based variable rate basis**. This is set at 85 percent of the average yield of five-year marketable U.S. Treasury securities, and the rate is announced each May 1 and November 1. Bonds held more than five years accrue interest semiannually.

4.   Interest earned on Series EE savings bonds purchased after 1989 can be partially or entirely free of federal income taxes if the bonds are cashed in during the same calendar year when tuition and fees for a qualified post-secondary educational institution are paid on behalf of the bond owner, the owner's spouse, or a dependent. Expenses for proprietary institutions, such as beautician or secretarial schools, sometimes do not qualify. Series EE savings bonds are zero coupon bonds and, therefore, there are no interest payments. Bond interest is exempt from local and state taxes and can be free of federal income taxes if the bonds are cashed in to pay college tuition and fees. Bonds issued in the name of a child as owner or co-owner, not as the beneficiary, are ineligible for the education tax exemption. Buying bonds in the child's name can, however, be a clever tax strategy when the parents' AGI exceeds the limit of the interest exclusion program because if bonds are redeemed after a child reaches 14 years of age, all deferred interest income will be taxable at the child's rate (15% in most cases) which is likely to be less than the parents' tax rate.

5.   Taxpayers are eligible for this education bond program unless their adjusted gross income exceeds certain threshold limits. The tax break goes into effect the year the bond is cashed. Married couples earning about $74,000 can take the full tax break; single people earning about $50,000 are also eligible for the full tax break. Married taxpayers with AGI between a threshold income of $74,000 and about $104,000 are eligible for a partial exemption with a decreasing percentage above the threshold income; this is true for singles earning about $50,000 to $64,000.
To qualify, the taxpayer's AGI must include the accumulated bond interest redeemed during that year. These threshold amounts are indexed for inflation annually.

6.   The *Massachusetts U Plan* is designed to make it possible for families to lock in tomorrow's college tuition at today's rates by permitting participants to invest in Massachusetts general obligation bonds. Specifically, parents may invest in Massachusetts bonds and redeem them at their maturity for a guaranteed percentage of tuition at any participating institution. The guaranteed percentage depends on each institution's tuition in the year the bond is purchased. For example, one may invest $1,000 in the bonds when a child is eight years old and obtain a Tuition Certificate. At the time of purchase, $1,000 may represent 10% of a year's tuition at College A, 15% at College B, and 25% at College C. Ten years later when the child is 18 years old and ready for college, the Tuition Certificate will still cover 10% of a tuition at College A, 15% at College B, and 25% at College C, regardless of the tuition increments actually implemented during the ten-year period.

7.   Another 1996 law provides that contributions to a state sponsored college tuition prepayment plan are exempt from the federal gift and estate tax.

8.   Refer to Siegel, J.J. (1992), The Equity Premium: Stock and Bond Returns Since 1802, *Financial Analysis Journal, 48:* 28-38.

9.   Transferring investment ownership to the child may not be the most appropriate strategy to optimize potential eligibility for need based financial aid because of higher assessments that may be applied to parental assets than to the child's assets.

Chapter 6
Career Planning Math

Chapter 6
Career Planning Math

Jill Lynn Vihtelic[1]

OVERVIEW

Decisions, decisions, decisions. What should I be? Should I further my education? Which job offer is the best? Where should I live? Should I work for someone else or myself? Are there tax consequences to consider?

Career planning addresses these and other life-defining issues. It is a process involving self-evaluating aptitudes and interests, gathering information about various careers, setting career goals, and developing a plan to achieve those goals. Many non-financial factors such as work conditions, work purposes, and work relationships should be considered when choosing a career. In this chapter the personal financial math skills necessary to complete the career planning process will be covered.

For most individuals, how well they live depends on how much money they can earn from working. Determining **earnings potential** is an important consideration for individuals choosing a career. Starting **salary** and **salary growth rates** vary by professions. The *Occupational Outlook Handbook*, found in the reference department of most libraries, provides the starting salary and the salary for experienced individuals for various careers.

Government data reveal a strong positive correlation between education and many measures of economic well-being. The higher the educational level attained, the higher the average family income, the higher the average lifetime family income, and the higher the family net worth. Some careers require graduate education for entry, while for others it is merely an option. A **cost-benefit analysis of graduate education** determines the net value of the advanced degree over a specific time period.

Having multiple job offers is an enviable position, but choosing which to accept demands careful calculation as job offer packages encompass much more than starting salary. **Employee benefits**, also called **fringe benefits**, include all compensation other

---

[1] Jill Lynn Vihtelic, CFP, Associate Professor, Business Administration and Economics, Saint Mary's College, Notre Dame, IN 46556. vihtelic@saintmarys.edu

than cash payments from wages, salary, or commissions. These typically include compensation for time not worked, employee security and health benefits, employer provided services, and perquisites provided to selected employees.

Valuing employee benefits to determine **total compensation** requires an understanding of the different tax treatments of employee benefits. A **tax-exempt** employee benefit is one on which the recipient never pays income taxes. **Tax-sheltered** employee benefits offer the employee tax savings by reducing, postponing, or deferring until later the taxing of benefits. Finally, certain employee benefits are **taxable** and increase the worker's current tax liability.

Another factor to consider in weighing job offers is the **cost of living index**. In the American Chamber of Commerce Researchers Association's publication *ACCRA Cost of Living Index* (found in most large libraries), data is reported in index form, with the "average cost community" given a rating of 100. Since the cost of living has regional differences, **total real compensation** should be determined as a gauge for comparing job offers in different cities.

Whether changing jobs or looking for the first, deciding on various search methods requires knowing what options exist. Employment firms are generally retained by the hiring organization which pays the fee. **Private employment agencies** are firms specializing in locating employment positions for certain types of positions. **Executive search firms**, or **headhunters**, attempt to recruit personnel, especially executive personnel to vacant positions. The quality of these operations and the people in them varies widely. Job seekers should check references and carefully review any contract before signing. Some employment services are offered for a fee that is paid by the job seeker. **Employment data banks** (also called employment registers, job-clearing house operations, or job banks) list resume' information to facilitate employment. Note that other employment services are free, such as most college and university placement services and E-Span Interactive Employment Network available through CompuServe and American Online (see the "Information and Computing Resources" section for a list of web sites that provide employment information and services).

Finally, tax considerations also enter into career planning. For example, self employed individuals may **write off** expenses to reduce taxable income, which reduces the net cost of the expense to the employee. The advantages of such favorable tax treatments must be compared to the disadvantage of an extra tax typically levied, the **self employment tax**, to weigh whether self-employment is a viable option or not. Similarly, working parents must consider the available options to determine the best way to handle child-care costs. A **flexible spending account (FSA)** may be used if available from the employer to allow the payment of child-care expenses to be reimbursed with pre-tax dollars. Another option to consider is the **child care credit**, which directly offsets the working parents' tax liability. Yet another career consideration is that some employees may have job flexibility and find it advantageous to work at home. One must calculate the applicable personal financial math to discover mathematical information to bear upon the decision.

EXAMPLES OF MATHEMATICAL CONCEPTS RELATED TO CAREER PLANNING

1. Determining Earnings Potential

Formula 6.1: $FV = PV (1 + r)^n$

Where: FV = future value of annual salary; PV = present value of starting salary; r = annual growth rate; and n = number of years estimated.

▼ **Example 6.1.1:** The average starting salary for accountants and auditors is $28,000. Individuals with ten years of experience earn an average salary of $58,000. What annual salary growth rate is implied?

Solution 1: Using the time value table

To solve this problem, two steps are needed.

(1) Calculate the factor of future value.

The factor of future value can be calculated by substituting numbers into the formula, $28,000 \times (1 + r)^{10} = 58,000$. Then,

Factor of FV = $(1 + r)^{10} = 58,000/28,000 = 2.071$

(2) Estimate the change rate.

From Appendix A-1 (FV Sum Table), the closest values of FV factor for 10 year period are 1.967 and 2.159, implying the change rate of the salary is between 7 to 8 percent. To estimate the change rate, the approach of comparing two ratios is used.

Since, $(1 + 7\%)^{10} = 1.967$, and $(1 + r)^{10} = 2.071$

Then, $r / 7 = 2.071 / 1.967 = 1.0529$

And, $r = 1.0529 \times 7 = 7.37$

The change rate of the starting salary is approximately 7.37 percent.

Solution 2: Using the financial calculator

Identify that in this question the following factors are given: present value ($28,000), future value ($58,000), and time period (10 years). Solve for the annual rate of change (equivalent to interest rate) equal to 7.55 percent. The result from the financial calculator is more accurate than the result from using the time table.

❖ **Interpretation:** Salary growth rate as well as starting salary determine earnings potential. Most desirable is a career with a high starting salary and a high earnings growth rate.

▼ **Example 6.1.2:** Average starting salary for college professors is $37,000. The annual salary growth rate over ten years is estimated at 3.659 percent. How does the earnings potential of college professors compare to that of accountants and auditors?

Solution 1: Using the time value table

To solve this problem, two steps are needed.

(1) Calculating the factor of future value.

Since, $(1 + 3.659\%)^{10}$ = FV factor, and $(1 + 4\%)^{10}$ = 1.480

Then, $4/3.659 = 1.480/\text{FV factor} = 1.093$

And, FV factor = 1.480 / 1.093 = 1.354

The future value factor is approximately 1.354

(2) Calculating the earnings potential.

Use formula 6.1, $s_f = s_p(1 + i)^n$, to solve. The earnings potential (future salary) equals the starting salary 37,000 times the future value factor 1.354 equals $50,098.

Solution 2: Using the financial calculator

In this question, the following factors are given: present value ($37,000), rate of growth in salary (equivalent to interest) of 3.659%, and time period (10 years). Solve for the future value (earnings potential) equal to $53,000. The result from the financial calculator is more accurate than the result from using the time table.

❖ **Interpretation:** Even though the average starting salary for professors is higher, over a ten year period the earnings potential is greater for accountants and auditors. The higher salary growth rate for the accounting career yields a higher earnings potential despite the initial lower starting pay.

2. Cost-Benefit Analysis of Graduate Education

Formula 6.2:
$$NPV_g = \sum_{p=1}^{n} [(b_p - c_p)/(1 + i)^p]$$

Where: NPV_g = net present value of graduate education; b_p = benefits of the degree in period p; c_p = costs of the degree in period p; i = opportunity cost or discount rate or inflation; and n = number of years estimated.

▼ **Example 6.2.1:** Jamie Lee, age 33, is earning $35,000 a year as a middle-level manager in a bank. She figures a master's degree in business administration (MBA) would help her get on the fast track for a more senior position. She can attend night school at a local university for an estimated cost of $7,500 a year. It will take her three years to complete the degree program. After completing the degree, Jamie believes she will be promoted and receive raises in excess of those she would have received without the MBA in the amounts of $3,500, $4,500, and $5,500 in years 4, 5, and 6. If the opportunity cost or inflation rate is 3%, what is the net present value of the MBA degree to Jamie over the six year period?

Solution 1: Using the time value table

To solve this problem three steps are needed.

(1) Determining the benefits and costs for each period.

A time line provides a helpful display of the period cash flows. Place outflows (costs) beneath the line, and inflows (benefits) above.

```
                           +3,500  +4,500  +5,500
    0--------1--------2--------3--------4--------5--------6
      -7,500  -7,500  -7,500
```

(2) Determining the present value of these cash flows at 3%.

(3) Summing the discounted cash flows.
$$-7,281.55 - 7,069.47 - 6,863.56 + 3,109.70 + 3,881.74 + 4,606.16$$
$$= -9,616.98$$

Solution 2: Using the financial calculator

Identify that in this question i = 3%, and the cash flows are displayed in the time line. With a HP 10B calculator, the following key strokes are used.

Purpose	HP-10B Key Stroke
Clear all registers	☐[CLEAR ALL]
Store periods per year	1 ☐ [P/YR]
Enter initial cash flow	0 [CFj]
Enter next cash flow	7500[+/-] [CFj]
Enter next cash flow	7500[+/-] [CFj]
Enter next cash flow	7500[+/-] [CFj]
Enter next cash flow	3500 [CFj]
Enter next cash flow	4500 [CFj]
Enter last cash flow	5500 [CFj]
Enter inflation rate	3 [I/YR]
Calculate NPV	☐[NPV]

The answer -9616.98 will be displayed.

❖ **Interpretation:** For the short-run, the costs of the MBA degree for Jamie exceed the benefits, which is negative $9,117. If, however, the raises continue to exceed her non-MBA raises beyond the six-year time frame, the degree may still yield positive economic benefits. Consider also that some employers will help pay for the graduate education of their employees. In Jamie's case, if her employer would pay half of the costs of the MBA, her educational benefits will exceed the costs (calculator solution: NPV = $990). Note that the opportunity costs are ignored in the calculation. The opportunity costs refer to the foregone salary when she goes to graduate school. If the opportunity costs are considered, it will take Jamie a longer time to receive net economic benefits from graduate education.

There are many other factors besides the lure of promotions and higher incomes that sway people to attend graduate school. Personal satisfaction and enjoyment or interest in a particular subject are also good reasons to attend. Going back to school requires a big commitment in time and effort, as well as giving up the opportunity to do other activities.

3. Determining Total Compensation

Total compensation should include both cash earnings (wages, salary, commissions, and bonuses) and fringe benefits. Two types of fringe benefits are discussed as follows: tax-exempt employee benefits and tax-sheltered employee benefits.

For tax-exempt employee benefits

Formula 6.3.1: TC = E + VFB / (1 - MTR)

Where: TC = total compensation; E = cash earnings (wages, salary, commissions, and bonuses); VFB = value of fringe benefits; and MTR = employee's marginal tax rate. Note that VFB/(1-MTR) is the pre-tax value of fringe benefits.

▼ **Example 6.3.1:** Mary Freeport has two job offers to consider. Potential employer A offers a salary of $35,000 with no health insurance benefits, while potential employer B offers $33,000 and free health insurance. Comparable health coverage would cost Mary $200 per month. Mary has a 28 percent marginal tax rate. Calculate total compensation to advise Mary on which job to accept.

Solution:

(1) Determine the total compensation offered by potential employer A.

TC_A = $35,000 + $0 = $35,000

(2) Determine the pre-tax value of the health insurance offered by potential employer B.

$2,400 / (1 - .28) = $3,333

(3) Determine the total compensation offered by potential employer B.

TC_B = $33,000 + $3,333 = $36,333

❖ **Interpretation:** All other things equal, Mary should accept the job offer from potential employer B, even though B offers the lower starting salary. Since Mary has to have health insurance, she is better off receiving the insurance as a tax-exempt employee benefit.

For tax-sheltered employee benefits

Formula 6.3.2: TC = E + SR • TTR

Where: TC = total compensation; SR = the salary reduction or income sheltered; and TTR = total tax rate (marginal tax rate plus the employee's marginal rate including Social Security FICA] and Medicare taxes). Note that SR • TTR is tax savings because of qualified tax-sheltered income.

▼ **Example 6.3.2:** Juanita Romero is a single mother of 12 year old twins, earning $48,000 per year. Her employer provides family health care coverage, but orthodontia work is not included. Both of her children require braces. The doctor estimates annual cost to be $1,800 per year per child for three years. Help Juanita determine the annual benefit of participating in her employer's flexible spending account (FSA) program. Juanita's marginal tax rate and the employee portion of FICA combine to total 35 percent. If she considers the tax savings of participating in FSA, what is Juanita's total compensation?

Solution:

Tax savings: $3,600 × .35 = $1,260
Total compensation: $48,000 + $1,260 = $49,260

❖ **Interpretation:** Juanita can save $1,260 per year by using the flexible spending account (FSA) to pay the orthodontist with pre-tax dollars. During the time that she can take advantage of using the FSA, her total compensation goes up to $49,260!

4. Comparing Salary Offers in Different Cities

Formula 6.4: $S_2 = S_1 I_2/I_1$

Where: S_2 = the equivalent salary in city 2; S_1 = the salary in city 1; I_2 = the living index in city 2; and I_1 = the living index in city 1.

▼ **Example 6.4.1:** The American Chamber of Commerce Researchers Association (ACCRA) compiles a Cost of Living Index on a quarterly basis. With the U.S. average serving as the baseline of 100, ACCRA facilitates the comparison of living costs in different U.S. cities. A person considering relocating should compare the relative living costs to wages and salaries in the cities being considered. For example, in a recent year, the cost of living index for San Diego was 130.6 and 114.9 for Miami. Janeen Gore is considering jobs in both cities. The San Diego job offers $38,000. Based on salary alone, how much would the Miami offer have to be to keep Janeen interested?

Solution:

$38,000 × (114.9 / 130.6) = $33,432

❖ **Interpretation:** $33,432 in Miami buys the same goods and services as $38,000 does in San Diego. An offer above $33,432 in Miami beats the San Diego offer.

▼ **Continuing example 6.4.2:** Now consider that the San Diego job includes employer provided health care benefits valued at $200 per month. The Miami offer arrives for $37,000, no fringe benefits. Which is better? Assume Janeen has a 28 percent marginal tax bracket.

Solution: Convert the San Diego job offer to total compensation, then find the Miami equivalent.

$$TC_{SD} = \$38,000 + \$2,400 / (1 - .28) = \$41,333$$

$$\$41,333 \times (114.9 / 130.6) = \$36,364$$

❖ **Interpretation:** The $37,000 Miami offer beats the San Diego offer even though employer provided health care is not included.

▼ **Continuing example 6.4.3:** Suppose the San Diego firm asks Janeen what it would take to get her there. How should she respond?

Solution: Reverse the formula.

$$\$37,000 \times (130.6 / 114.9) = \$42,055$$

$$\$42,055 - \$3,333 = \$38,723$$

❖ **Interpretation:** An equivalent offer in San Diego is for total compensation of $42,055. Subtracting out the pre-tax value of the tax-exempt employee benefit gets Janeen to the equivalent job offer of $38,723 salary, with employer provided health care.

▼ **Continuing example 6.4.4:** Using the average cost community (living index = 100) as the base, compute the total real compensation for the San Diego offer.

Solution:
$$\$41,333 \times (100 / 130.6) = \$31,649$$

❖ **Interpretation:** San Diego is a relatively expensive place to live. If Janeen earns total compensation of $31,648 in an average cost city, she needs to earn nearly $10,000 more a year to buy the same goods and services in San Diego. Considering costs of living, the real compensation of the San Diego job totals $31,649.

5. Comparing Suburban Versus City Living Costs

Conceptual Idea 6.5: Develop an annual budget for each location to compare costs.

▼ **Example 6.5:** Marilyn Squires has accepted a job located in the downtown of a major city. She figures she can live in a nice area of the city for monthly rent of $1,200. Public transportation is available for the half hour transit to work at a cost of $50 per month. Due to limited parking and very high insurance rates, she would not want to own a car, but figures she would rent a car several times over the year for visits to her parents and friends. With weekend rate deals, Marilyn estimates the rental fees will be $1,200 per year.

Another option Marilyn is considering is living in the suburbs. Rent is much more reasonable, $800 per month, but she would have to have a car. She checked into leasing and could get the car she wants for a monthly lease fee of $250. Auto insurance and license fees would cost another $150 per month. Train commuter passes are available for $130 per month plus monthly parking passes are $25. Total commuting time from the suburbs door to door totals 1 hour 15 minutes. Financially, how do these options compare?

Solution:

Develop an annual budget for each of Marilyn's options:

	City	Suburbs
Housing	$14,400	$9,600
Commuting Costs	600	1,860
Auto Leasing, license, insurance	1,200	4,800
TOTAL COSTS	$16,200	$16,260

❖ **Interpretation:** All things equal, city living is generally more expensive than suburban living—but all things are not equal. For example, commuting costs and times differ greatly. When Marilyn considers transportation as well as housing, the costs are virtually the same. To make her choice Marilyn must consider other lifestyle factors such as personal space preferences, schooling opportunities, the appeal of nightlife, and safety.

6. Tax Savings from Working at Home

Formula 6.6: $TS = (BE_{ho}n_{ho}/n)MTR$

Where: TS = tax savings; BE_{ho} = business expenses of the home office (including mortgage interest, real estate taxes, utility expenses, and cleaning and repair expenses); n_{ho} = number of rooms used exclusively for business; n = total number of rooms in the house; and MTR = marginal tax rate. Note that $BE_{ho}n_{ho}/n$ is business portion of home expenses.

▼ **Example 6.6:** Lynn Thompson is a computer programmer for a large company. She recently had her first child and is considering taking advantage of her employer's work-at-home option. Lynn's house has eight rooms. She would devote use of one of the bedrooms exclusively to her office. Her employer will provide the necessary office furnishings and computer. Lynn's mortgage interest over the next year will be $3,000 and real estate taxes are $1,800 per year. Utilities total $125 per month, and cleaning and repair fees amount to $130 monthly. How much can Lynn deduct per year as a business expense? If Lynn's marginal tax rate is 28%, how much she will save through home office business expenses deductions.

Solution:

(1) Calculate business portion of home expenses

$$(\$3,000 + \$1,800 + \$1,500 + \$1,560) \times 1/8 = \$982.50$$

(2) Calculate the tax savings

$$\$982.50 \times .28 = \$275.10$$

❖ **Interpretation:** The percentage of business use of the home is determined by dividing the number of rooms used for business purposes by the total number of rooms in the home. Business expense is reported on Schedule C of Form 1040, and offsets business income. Lynn's home office expense amounts to $982.50. The value of this tax savings depends on her circumstances. If Lynn typically takes the standardized deduction, her savings will be approximately equal to the allowable business expenses, $982.50, times her marginal tax rate. At 28% Lynn saves $275.10 in taxes just from having her office at home. Other savings such as reduced child care costs, clothing expenses, and commuting expenses will add to the total savings to Lynn.

7. Comparison Between Employment and Self-Employment

Conceptual Idea 6.7: List benefits and costs of both employment and self-employment situations, compare them, and make decisions.

▼ **Example 6.7:** Liz Sprout has also been contemplating going out on her own. At her present job she earns $35,000 in salary and her employer pays $2,500 for family group health insurance. Additionally, her employer matches her 7.65% of salary contribution to FICA (social security tax). If self employed, Lynn estimates that her cash revenues would be $50,000. She anticipates $10,000 in related business expenses. Non-group family health insurance equivalent to her employer provided plan would cost Lynn $300 per month, and her Self Employed (SE) tax would be 15.3%. Which option offers Lynn the better financial reward?

Solution: Determine the net cash income of employment and compare it to the net cash income of self employment.

Salary	$35,000.00
Employee paid FICA	-2,677.50
Net Employment Income	**$32,322.50**
Revenues	$50,000.00
Related expenses	-10,000.00
Self employment tax	
([$50,000-$40,000] × .153)	-6,120.00
Health insurance premiums	-3,600.00
Net Self Employment Income	**$30,280.00**

❖ **Interpretation:** In this scenario Lynn would be better off remaining an employee. The drawbacks of self employment (paying the SE tax and higher health insurance premiums) make it uneconomical for Lynn to go out on her own unless she can increase revenues substantially.

8. Child Care Tax Credit Considerations

Tax savings based on child care expenses can be achieved by two approaches: (1) child care tax credit, and (2) flexible spending account (FSA).

Child Care Tax Credit

Formula 6.8.1: $TC = QE \cdot r$

Where: TC = tax credit; QE = qualified expenses; and r = percentage of expenses allowed.

When determining the child care tax credit, realize that the maximum qualified expenses for child care calculates to $2,400 for one child and $4,800 for two or more children, and the percentage of expenses allowed is ascertained by using Table 6.1:

Table 6.1 IRS Section 21	
Dependent Care Tax Credit (for a recent year)	
% of Qualifying Expenses Allowed	**Adjusted Gross Income**
30	$ 0-$10,000
29	10,001- 12,000
28	12,001- 14,000
27	14,001- 16,000
26	16,001- 18,000
25	18,001- 20,000
24	20,001- 22,000
23	22,001- 24,000
22	24,001- 26,000
21	26,001- 28,000
20	28,001 and over

▼ **Example 6.8.1:** Karen Speaker spent $3,600 last year on qualified child care expenses for her two pre-teen children. Her marginal tax rate is 28%, and her adjusted gross income is well over $28,000. Determine her tax credit and the maximum credit she could claim under **IRS Section 21**.

Solution: Child care tax credit = $3,600 × .20 = $720; also the maximum child care tax credit available in this circumstance is $960 ($4,800 × .20)

❖ **Interpretation:** The tax credit reduces Karen's tax liability by $720. Given her income, the maximum tax credit available for dependent care of her two children is $960.

Tax Savings from the Flexible Spending Account

Formula 6.8.2: TS = AE • MTR

Where: TS = tax savings; AE = allowed expenses; and MTR = marginal tax rate.

▼ **Continuing example 6.8.2:** Karen's employer has a flexible spending account (FSA) benefit plan which allows her to reduce her salary by a maximum of $5,000 per year to pay dependent care costs with pre-tax dollars. Considering only her federal income taxes, is this a better plan for Karen? What would Karen's maximum savings be under this option?

Solution:

Tax savings = $3,600 × .28 = $1,008
Maximum tax savings = $5,000 × .28 = $1,400

❖ **Interpretation:** Since it is available, Karen should participate in her employer's salary reduction FSA. This option saves her more money ($1,008 - 720 = $288) and has a higher maximum benefit ($1,400). Karen will gladly forgo the IRS Section 21 tax credit and pay her child care expenses with pre-tax dollars instead. Note that to choose which option is best, use the IRS Section 21 tax credit when the percentage of expenses allowed is greater than the taxpayer's marginal tax rate.

INFORMATION AND COMPUTING RESOURCES

1. There are many useful books available through the library, the career planning and placement center at you college, or in bookstores. Some examples of these are *What Color is Your Parachute? A Practical Manual for Job-Hunters and Career-Changers*, by R.N. Bolles (Berkeley, CA: Ten Speed Press, 1996); *Careers for the 1990s and Beyond*, by the Research and Education Association (1994); *How to Survive Without Your Parents' Money: Making It From College to the Real World*, Revised Edition, by Geoff Martz (Random House, 1996); *Your Career: Choices, Chances, Changes*, by D.C. Borchard, J.J. Kelly, and

N.P.K. Weaver (Dubuque, IA: Kendall/Hunt, 1990); *The Directory of Executive Recruiters*, (Fitzwilliam, New Hampshire: Kennedy Publications, 1996).

2. Examples of employment data banks include the National Resume' Bank [(813) 896-3694], Mainstream Job Bank [(800) 296-1872], SkillSearch [(800) 258-6641], HispanData [(805) 682-5843], University ProNet [(800) 726-0280], and Peterson's Connexion [(800) 338-3282].

3. Useful information is also available on the Internet. Check the following sites:

    ▪ *Business pages at:* http://www.yahoo.com
    ▪ *Online Career Center:* http://www.occ.com
    ▪ *Career Path:* http://www.careerpath.com
    ▪ *CareerMosaic:* http://www.careermosaic.com
    ▪ *Working at home:* http://www.att.com/telecommute_americak
    ▪ *The Monster Board:* http://www.monster.com

4. Many business or general magazines, such as *Business Week, Fortune, Kiplinger's Personal Finance Magazine, US News and World Report,* and *Money*, and daily newspapers, such as the *Wall Street Journal,* report on career and employment statistics, outlooks, and trends. Specific industries and companies may also be featured.

5. Specific Industry information is available in the library. See, for example, *Moody's, Standard and Poor's,* and *ValueLine* publications. These same references may be used to investigate particular companies. Company annual reports are often available at the library or may be obtained by calling the company.

EXERCISE PROBLEMS

Determining Earnings Potential

1. Average starting salary for metallurgical engineers is $38,000. Average salary of experienced individuals is $55,000. If ten years of work is required to become experienced, what is the average salary growth rate of this profession? How does your answer change if to become experienced only takes seven years?

2. Average starting salary for a veterinarian is $30,000. The annual salary growth rate is quite high at 8.8%. How much per year could a veterinarian expect to make in five years?

3. *Out-of-Class Exercise* Use the *Occupational Outlook Handbook* to determine the salary growth rates for three careers, assuming that all require eight years to become experienced.

Cost-Benefit Analysis of Graduate Education

4. Jenna David earns $30,000 as a department manager in a retail store. She figures a master's degree in business administration would help her to move beyond her present position. Since she can schedule her work hours on the weekends, she can attend the local university's daytime program and complete the degree in two years. Tuition and books would cost $10,000 each year. After completing the program, Jenna expects to receive raises in excess of those she would have received without the MBA in the amounts of $4,000, $5,000, and $6,000 in years 3, 4, 5. If the inflation rate is 2.5%, what is the net present value of the MBA degree to Jenna over the five year period?

5. Mitsy Wu's employer reimburses employees one half the cost of tuition and books for graduate education. Mitsy can attend the local university at a total cost of $8,000 per year, half of which she would have to pay. If it takes Mitsy three years to complete a MBA degree, what is the present value of her costs for the MBA? Give Mitsy an idea of the additional raises she would need to expect in years 4, 5, and 6 in order to break even over the six year period if the inflation rate is 3%. (*Hint: use an trial-and-error approach to achieve a positive less than $100 NPV.*)

Determining Total Compensation

6. Jean Stamp has two job offers to consider. Potential employer A offers a $37,000 salary and free health insurance worth $250/month to Jean. Potential employer B offers no fringe benefits, but the salary is $40,000 per year. Jean has a marginal tax rate of 28%. Determine which offers the higher financial reward.

7. Lorena Messenger received a job offer of $34,000 in salary, employer provided family health care coverage worth $400 per month, and the option to participate in a flexible spending account (FSA) to pay for non-covered wellness exams and dental expenses. These typically costs Lorena $1,500 per year for her family. Assuming her marginal tax rate is 28%, determine the total compensation value of the job offer.

8. *Out-of-Class Exercise* Obtain two quotes for individually purchased health care insurance through local insurance agents. Are you presently covered under a group plan? If yes, calculate the pre-tax value of your health insurance benefits.

Comparing Salary Offers in Different Cities

9. Consider two job offers, one in Boston and the other in Chicago. The Boston total compensation package amounts to $39,000, compared to $37,500 in Chicago. Calculate the relative values of the offers if the cost of living index is 128 for Boston versus 120 for Chicago. Which offer is better? Show the calculations from the perspective of both salary offers.

10. Sarah Bishop works in Chicago and earns $35,000 in salary with employer provided health care coverage valued at $250 per month. Her marginal tax rate is 28%. She is considering a lateral move to a similar position in San Diego. The cost of living index in Chicago is 120 while San Diego's is 130.6. How much will the San Diego offer have to be in order for Sarah to maintain her present standard of living?

11. *Out-of-Class Exercise* Choose two locations that appeal to you. Using the *AACRA Cost of Living Index*, determine the relative value of earning $32,000 at each location. Show the calculations from the perspective of each location.

Comparing Suburban Versus Urban Living Costs

12. Luella Fitzgerald lives in the Near North side of Chicago, and works in the Loop. Rent on her studio apartment is $1,300 per month. She takes public transportation or walks to work each day at an annual cost of $475. Last year she paid $825 in car rental fees for weekend trips and a summer vacation to Michigan. Luella is considering moving to a Western suburb where rents are much more reasonable. She figures she would have to have a car which she estimates will cost $4,620 per year. Rail commuter passes will cost Luella $140 per month. How much can Luella spend on rent in the suburbs in order to break-even with what she spends in the city?

13. *Out-of-Class Exercise* Develop a budget for housing and transportation expenses using actual quotes obtained from local newspapers, Realtors, transportation authorities, auto dealers, and car rental agencies.

Tax Savings from Working at Home

14. Pat Andrews has recently moved her office home. She has a nine room house and one room will be devoted exclusively to business use. Pat's mortgage interest over the next year will amount to $3,500, and real estate taxes will be $1,250. She spends $120 a month on utilities and cleaning and repair fees should total $1,200 for the year. Determine Pat's deductible home office business expense for the coming year. What other savings can Pat expect from working at home?

Comparison between Employment and Self-employment

15. Sue Hayden is a successful self employed Broker/Realtor. She has annual revenues of $65,000 with related business expenses of $12,500. Sue buys family health insurance coverage for $400 per month. What is her net self employment income if the self-employment tax rate is 15.3%?

16. Veronica Taylor earns $38,500 as a salaried computer consultant. Her employer provides health care coverage which would cost her $350 per month to buy on her own. Veronica is considering going out on her own. She figures her related business expenses would be $12,000 in her first year. How much in revenues

will Veronica need to produce in order for her net self employment income to be equal to her net employment income?

17. *Out-of-Class Exercise* Explore the Web sites given in the Information and Computing Resources section. Prepare a summary report of your discoveries to share with the class.

18. *Out-of-Class Exercise* Visit the career and placement center for your campus. Prepare a report on the services offered for free to students. Be sure to inquire about the availability of interest tests.

19. *Out-of-Class Exercise* Inquire as to the costs and requirements for listing your resume with a employment data bank. Share your findings with classmates to compare various options.

Child Care Tax Credit Considerations

20. Andrea Patrick has adjusted gross income of $22,000 for the year. She spent $2,050 for child care expenses for her baby daughter. Using Table 6.1, determine Andrea's Dependent Care Tax Credit. Since Andrea has a 15% marginal tax rate, should she be paying her child care expense with pre-tax dollars through her employer's FSA? Explain.

SELECTED REFERENCES

Consumer Information Center. (1996). *Is there another degree in your future?* (no. 142B). [Brochure]. Pueblo, CO: Author.

Garman, E. T., & Forgue, R. E. (1997). *Personal finance.* (5th ed.) Boston: Houghton Mifflin.

Kotlarsky, M. (1989). Dependent care assistance plans in 1989. *Taxes: The Tax Magazine, 67*, 5: 324-327.

Consumer Information Center. (1995). *The job outlook in brief: 1995-2005.* (no. 103B). [Brochure]. Pueblo, CO: Author.

Great for grads job mart. (1996, January). *Kiplinger's Personal Finance Magazine*, 51-53.

Good jobs for fresh grads. (1995, March). *Kiplinger's Personal Finance Magazine*, 110-118.

The fifty hottest jobs in America. (1995, March). *Money*, 114-117.

Shim, J. K., & Siegel, J. G. (1991). *Theory and problems of personal finance.* New York: Schaum's Outline Series, McGraw-Hill, Inc.

Great towns with great jobs. (1996, April). *Money*, 124-134.

Vihtelic, J. L. (1989). Allocating child care expenses between a salary reduction plan and the tax credit. *Taxes: The Tax Magazine, 76*(2), 83-87.

Vihtelic, J. L. (1989). In defense of a mixed allocation strategy. *Taxes: The Tax Magazine, 67*(5). 328-329.

Chapter 7
Financial Statements and Budgeting

Chapter 7
Financial Statements and Budgeting

Sherman Hanna[1]

OVERVIEW

Financial statements are tools that can help households evaluate their financial positions and plan to reach goals in the future. As with business financial statements, there are many possible purposes of household financial statements. In addition to using financial statements for personal financial planning, financial statements may be needed for income tax purposes, for calculation of estate taxes, for loan applications, for student financial aid applications, for property insurance, for analysis of life insurance needs, and other purposes. This chapter will focus on the use of financial statements in personal finance.

The most basic financial statement is the **net worth statement**, also known as the **balance sheet**. The net worth statement consists of a listing of all assets and the current values of each asset; a listing of all amounts owed to others (**liabilities**) and the balance due on each liability, and the total value of the assets minus the total value of the liabilities on a particular day, or the **net worth**. If a household sold everything it owned and paid off all its debts, the amount of money it had left would be its net worth. If it did not have enough money from selling its assets to pay off all debts, it would have negative net worth.

Normally, a household would have a goal of increasing its net worth each year, unless it needed to sell or withdraw from assets to finance an education or to maintain living standards during retirement. However, many U.S. households have very low levels of net worth. As a result, instead of increasing their net worth every year they rely on current income from salaries, or on pensions in retirement. In a recent year, the median net worth of U.S. households was $37,587—in other words, half of the households had a net worth lower than $37,587. Eleven percent of households that year had zero or negative net worth. For many U.S. households, the

[1] Sherman Hanna, Ph.D., Professor, Consumer and Textile Sciences Department, The Ohio State University, Columbus, OH 43210-1290. hanna.1@osu.edu.

home is the only major asset, and their net worth increases over time simply because the home mortgage is gradually paid off. The median net worth level increases with age, as shown below.

Age	1993 Median Net Worth	
	Including home	Excluding home
Under 35	$5,786	$3,297
35–44	29,202	8,219
45–54	57,755	14,499
55–64	91,481	25,108
65 and over	86,324	20,642

(Source: U.S. Census Bureau, "Asset Ownership of Households: 1993." Series P70-47, 1995.)

The amount of net worth needed by a household depends on its particular goals and needs. Someone who wanted to retire at age 55 would typically need to accumulate a very large amount of net worth, perhaps as much as one million dollars, if it did not have an income from a pension to rely on. At the other extreme, someone who rented a home, did not want to buy housing, had a steady salary, and expected a generous pension upon retirement, might have relatively little need to accumulate a large amount of net worth.

Budgeting is the process of projecting, organizing, monitoring, and controlling future income and expenditures (including cash and credit purchases as well as savings). And within the budgeting process is a certain amount of recordkeeping.

You should know that most people use **cash-basis** budgeting to record their expenses and income as this system recognizes earnings and expenditures when the money is actually received or paid out. A more accurate method of maintaining financial records and budgeting is the **accrual basis** as it recognizes earnings and expenditures when the money is earned and expenditures are incurred, regardless of when money is actually received or paid. Both methods will work as long as they are used consistently.

Of course, the preparation of financial statements, like the net worth statement, reflects the type of recordkeeping that a household follows. Another important financial statement is the **cash flow statement** (also called an **income and expense statement**). It is very different from a net worth statement. Whereas the net worth statement shows one's financial condition at a single point in time, the income and expense statement summarizes the total amounts that have been received and spent over a time period, such as the previous year. The net worth statement lists income and expense items and it also calculates any surplus or deficit. In sum, it provides a very simple method of keeping track of money received and money spent.[1]

Note that the method used in this chapter will be the **accrual based** system. With this method, expenses are counted when incurred, so that, for instance, if you use a credit card to buy groceries, you would count the expense on that day, but you would not count the payment the following month to the credit card company as an expense. Also, when using the accrual method all income received during a period of time is counted, except that some amounts of money received, such as proceeds from loans, are not counted. Loans are not really a form of income, and that is why they are excluded from the definition. Moreover, one should count something as

income only when it represents a potential increase in wealth. For example, if you received money and did not spend it, would your net worth be higher? If the answer is "no" then it cannot be income.

The advantage of the accrual approach over the cash flow approach is that we can define the difference between total income and total expenses during a period as the **surplus**. As we will see, the net worth values at the beginning and the end of a period are related by the surplus during the period. Many households have trouble keeping accurate track of all of their expenses, so that the amount by which the net worth changes during a period can give an estimate of the surplus. The accrual basis does this job well.

The projected surplus in the future can be used to plan a budget. Future goals can be reached by accumulating adequate surpluses. If a surplus is not sufficient to reach a goal, some combination of the following actions must be taken:

(1) Expenses must be reduced;

(2) income must be increased;

(3) assets must be reallocated to increase the earnings of assets;

(4) liabilities must be reallocated to reduce the interest owed on loans; and/or

(5) goals must be revised.

Some households find it difficult to keep track of all of their expenses. Many find that after some experience, they can monitor their financial progress by calculating their net worth once or twice a year. Consider the analogy to a person's weight control. The net worth statement is similar to weighing yourself. If you weigh 160 pounds today and weighed 150 pounds a month ago, your surplus of calories ingested over calories burned was equivalent to 10 pounds of weight. You did not need to record every item of food consumed and the time for every physical activity during the month. However, if you feel that the 10 pound weight gain is a problem, one possible method to improve the situation is to keep track of your calorie consumption and physical activities, to better help you identify ways to prevent future weight gains.

EXAMPLES OF MATHEMATICAL CONCEPTS RELATED TO FINANCIAL STATEMENTS AND BUDGETING

1. The Net Worth Statement

Conceptual Idea 7.1: Net worth is the difference between total assets and total liabilities of a household on a particular day. The typical net worth statement has following items of assets and liabilities:

Total Assets
    Monetary assets
        Cash on hand
        Savings Accounts
        Checking accounts
        Tax refund due
        Rent receivable
    Tangible Assets
        Home
        Personal Property
        Vehicle
    Investment Assets
        Mutual funds
        Stocks
        Bonds
        Life insurance cash value
        Retirement accounts such as IRAs, Keogh Plans, 401(k) plans
        Real estate investments

Total Liabilities
    Short-term liabilities
        Utilities (only if due but not yet paid)
        Credit cards (list payoff balance, not minimum payment)
    Long-term liabilities
        Auto loan (payoff balance)
        Home mortgage (payoff balance)

Net Worth (Total Assets − Total Liabilities)

▼ **Example 7.1:** John just graduated from medical school with $100,000 in student loans. He owns a car he bought 4 years ago for $12,000, but the wholesale value today is only $5,000. He bought a computer 4 years ago for $4,000, but now they are worth $2,000. He has no debts other than his student loans. He has $500 in his checking account on July 1, 1998. He has no other assets or loans. His income in July will be $5,000. His rent of $1,000 will come due on July 10. What is his net worth on July 1, 1998?

Solution: In this example, the current values of **durable goods** (those that are expected to last more than one year) should be used and both the values of car and computer should be put into the net worth statement, $5,000 and $2,000, respectively. John does not expect to receive his salary on July 1, 1998, thus the $5,000 income should not be put in the statement. For the same reason, his rent will be due on July 1 and should not be included in the statement. Thus, John's net worth statement on July 1, 1998 should be as follows.

John's Net Worth Statement
July 1, 1998

ASSETS:

Monetary assets:

Checking account	$ 500
Total monetary assets	$ 500

Tangible assets:

Automobile (current market value)	$5,000
Furniture and computer (current value)	2,000
Total tangible assets	$7,000
TOTAL ASSETS	$7,500

LIABILITIES:

Long-term liabilities:

Student loans	$ 100,000
TOTAL LIABILITIES	$ 100,000
NET WORTH	$ – 92,500

❖   **Interpretation:** John has a negative net worth of $92,500. Can net worth be negative? As this example shows, it is certainly possible. A low net worth, or a negative one, signals a need to build up some cash reserves for investing toward future goals.

Note that for the purpose of personal financial planning, it is appropriate to value the car and computer at what those items could be sold for, rather than the cost of replacing them or the original purchase price. For insurance purposes, a different approach might be appropriate (see Chapter 12). Generally, **tangible assets** (physical items that have fairly long lifespans and could be sold to raise cash but whose primary purpose is to provide maintenance of a lifestyle) should be valued at what they could be sold for on a particular day. The value of a home might go up or down, depending on the local real estate market and the condition of the structure. The value of personal property typically decreases as it wears out. The value of vehicles will decrease rapidly—perhaps as much as 20 percent per year.

This example also demonstrates that different dates may result in different values of a household's net worth. Note that John's income this month and the rent that will be due in 10 days are not listed anywhere in the net worth statement. If the rent were already due but not yet paid, it should be listed as a short-term liability. In general, be careful not to list expenses as liabilities, unless they are bills due but not yet paid. Income should never be listed as an asset, although it will show up indirectly in the form of assets. Observe, too, that the day of the month will make a difference. On the day a monthly paycheck is received, assets may be much higher than the day before. That is why it is important to use the same day of the month for each net worth statement calculated over a period of time.

2. Income and Expense Statement

Conceptual Idea 7.2: The income and expenses statement lists income and expense items and also calculates any surplus or deficit. The positive difference between expenses and income is surplus, and the negative one is deficit. A typical format of an income and expenses statement is as follows.

Income
> Salaries and wages
> Scholarships
> Capital gains of selling assets
> Other incomes

Expenses
> *Fixed Expenses*
> > Rent
> > Auto lease payment
> > Tuition
> > Other expenses
> *Variable Expenses*
> > Food
> > Clothing
> > Income taxes
> > Other expenses

Surplus/Deficit (total income – total expenses)

Note that if after-tax income is used in the income and expenses statement, the income and payroll taxes should not be included in the expenses. Also observe that since an accrual basis approach is used in this chapter, definitions of some income and expense items are different from ones in the cash basis approach.[2] With an accrual basis approach, the following are not considered as income: proceeds of a student loan, other personal loans, a cash advance from a credit card, federal income taxes, etc. Using the same thinking, loan repayments also are not considered, but finance charges on the loan are judged as expenses.

▼ **Example 7.2:** Jon Fox is a college student, with an income of $15,000 in 1997. On January 3, 1997 he received a scholarship for $5,000. He used the scholarship to help pay for his tuition of $6,000. On January 5, 1997, he received disbursement of a $8,000 student loan. During 1997 he paid $6,600 in rent, $3,200 in food, $2,000 in clothing, $3,600 in auto lease payments, $3,000 in income taxes, and $3,600 in other expenses. What was his surplus/deficit during 1997?

Solution: Since the $8,000 loan disbursement is not considered as income, and it is not included in the income and expense statement. Then, we have the statement as follows.

Income and Expense Statement
Jon Fox
January 1, 1997 - December 31, 1997

Income:

Scholarship	$ 5,000
Jon's salary	15,000
TOTAL INCOME	$ 20,000

Expenses:

Fixed Expenses:

Rent	$ 6,600
Auto lease payments	3,600
Tuition	6,000
Total Fixed Expenses	$ 16,200

Variable Expenses:

Food	$ 3,200
Clothing	2,000
Income Taxes	3,000
Other	3,600
Total Variable Expenses	$ 11,800
TOTAL EXPENSES	$ 28,000
Deficit	$- 8,000

❖ **Interpretation:** Jon has a deficit of $8,000, which happened to be matched by a student loan of $8,000. Having a deficit is not uncommon. Part of the reason is the timing of income and spending. If you measured your surplus on the basis of a particular week, and you did not get paid that week, you would have a deficit. Even on an annual basis, 40 percent of households in the United States seem to run deficits, although half of the households have a surplus that amounts to at least 11 percent of their after-tax income.[3] Most households need to run a surplus in order to pay off debts and reach savings goals, such as having a comfortable retirement. For a household which rents its home, leases its vehicles, and owns no assets that fluctuate in value, the concept is very simple. For them, if income is greater than expenses, the surplus is positive and the household's net worth will increase. If income is less than expenses, the household is running a deficit, and the household's net worth will decrease.

Do you need to record every dollar of expenses? Most people should do this for a few months whenever there is a substantive change in their situation, such as a marriage or a new child. The information will help the household plan their finances better in the future. While some people might need to record every expense forever, others could go through most of their lives just keeping track of major expenses and lumping together miscellaneous cash expenses.

3. Relating the Net Worth Statement and the Income and Expense Statement

Conceptual Idea 7.3: If a household owns no assets that fluctuate in value, and leases a home and vehicles, the surplus in the income and expenses statement equals the difference between the net worth at the end of a period and the initial net worth.[4]

Note that if a household possesses assets that fluctuate in value and/or owns a home and cars, the calculation will be more complicated (see Endnote 2 for details).

▼ **Example 7.3.1:** Mary and Bill had income of $38,000 in 1997. They lease their cars and rent a townhouse. They own no financial assets that fluctuate in value. On January 1, 1997, their net worth was $12,000. On January 1, 1998, their net worth was $14,200. What is the surplus/deficit?

Solution: Since Mary and Bill lease their cars and rent a house, the initial net worth equals $12,000, and the net worth at the end of the period equals $14,200. Then

Surplus = $14,200 – $12,000 = $2,200

❖ **Interpretation:** They have a surplus of $2,200. This example demonstrates that if a household has no assets, such as **investment assets** (also known as **capital assets**, investment assets are tangible and intangible items acquired for the monetary benefits they provide, such as generating additional income and increasing in value), home, or cars that will change values over the period, a much easier way to calculate surplus/deficit is to simply to compare the net worth values between the end and beginning of the period.

▼ **Example 7.3.2:** Mary and Bill tried to keep track of their income and expenses during 1997. According to their records, their total expenses amounted to $33,200. Their income and net worth have been reported in Example 7.3.1. Is the total expense reported by them accurate?

Solution: Since income during the period equals $38,000, the net worth change equals $14,200 – $12,000, or $2,200, and in this case, the surplus equals the net worth change because of the simple finance of this couple. Then,

Expenses = $38,000 – $2,200 = $35,800

The calculated expenses are greater than the sum they tracked down by $2,600 ($35,800 – $33,200). Apparently, they missed $2,600 in their record-keeping.

❖ **Interpretation:** Many households have trouble keeping accurate track of all of their expenses, although they usually know their incomes. As illustrated in this example, if you know your income and know your net worth on January 1 and on December 31, you probably can easily calculate the actual expenses. This is true if your personal finances are relatively simple, such as no investment assets that fluctuate in value and you do not own a home or vehicle. If you have more complicated personal finances, the method in this example is inappropriate, and you need a more complicated approach to calculate the actual expenses.

4. Calculating Needed Surplus

Conceptual Idea 7.4: Surplus in the income and expenses statement can be planned to meet short- and long-term financial goals.

▼ **Example 7.4:** Tom and Jere have $5,000 in credit card debt, which they would like to start paying off this year. They would like to begin contributing $4,000 per year to their retirement plans next year. They also would like to have $24,000 accumulated for a down payment for a home 4 years from now. How much of a surplus should they run this year and next year, if the interest rate is ignored?

Solution:

(1) The surplus needed for this year: Since, credit card payment equals $5,000, the down payment to be saved annually equals $24,000/4, or $6,000, then the surplus needed for this year equals $5,000 + $6,000, or $11,000.

(2) The surplus needed for next year: Since, retirement account payment equals $4,000, down payment to be saved annually equals $24,000/4, or $6,000, then the surplus needed for next year equals $10,000.

❖ **Interpretation:** To achieve their financial goals, such as paying off credit card debts, saving for down payment for a home, and saving for retirement, Tom and Jere have to manage to have surplus of $11,000 this year, plus $10,000 next year. This example indicates a simple case in which the interest rate is ignored. If the interest rate is included, the calculation will be little complicated, but the logic will remain the same. The sacrifice needed for the next two years would be less for Tom and Jere than it might appear because once the credit card debt is paid off, the expense item for finance charges would decrease substantially, and the down payment fund might earn some interest. The sacrifice needed for the contribution for the retirement fund will also be less than it appears, if the fund qualifies for a tax-deductible contribution (a **qualified plan**).

5. Budgeting for Financial Goals

Conceptual Idea 7.5: Based on this year's income and expenses statement to make next year's annual budget, use following steps to estimate your spending, estimate your income, and calculate your surplus. The steps are as follows.

1. Estimate your spending next year by starting with expenses this year, and making obvious adjustments (e.g., rent increase, paying off auto loan);

2. estimate your income next year;

3. calculate your surplus; and,

4. if a surplus (income greater than spending) is projected, calculate whether it is enough to reach your goals.

If the projected surplus is not satisfactory, or you have a deficit, what can you do? (A) increase your income, (B) cut back expenses, (C) do both, or (D) consider changing your goals. Note that one or two months' of expenses may not provide a good basis for projecting annual expenses, as some expenses, such as insurance premiums, may be due annually or quarterly.

▼ **Example 7.5.1:** On January 1, 1997, Joe and Jill have $2,000 in a checking account, $4,000 in a money market account, and own a Saturn automobile with a value of $9,000. The balance on the Saturn loan is $8,000. They rent a townhouse, and have furniture worth $4,000. They lease a BMW automobile for $500 per month. They own 100 shares of Networld stock, currently valued at $60 per share. Joe's retirement plan has a value of $4,000. They have a $1,000 balance on a Mastercard and owe Jill's mother $2,000.

Joe's salary in 1996 was $27,000, and Jill's was $27,000. The Networld stock was purchased on December 31, 1996, so they received no dividends during 1996. The checking account paid no interest. The money market account paid $160 in interest during 1996. Expenses in 1996 were rent and utilities, $11,000; life insurance, $600; income taxes, $4,000; Saturn loan payments, $250 per month; auto registration and taxes, $200 per year; BMW lease payments, $500 per month; groceries cost $4,000; eating out cost $4,000; telephone bills totaled $600; clothing and clothing care cost $3,000; vacations cost $3,000, and miscellaneous expenses totaled $12,000.

They would like to buy a home on January 1, 1998 for $100,000 by making a $20,000 down payment and taking out a home mortgage loan. They would like to start contributing $10,000 per year to retirement accounts in order to try to retire at age 55. Help the couple construct a net worth statement for January 1, 1997.

Solution:

Net Worth Statement
Joe and Jill
January 1, 1997

Assets:

Monetary assets:	
Checking account	$ 2,000
Money market account	4,000
Total monetary assets	$ 6,000
Tangible assets:	
Saturn automobile (current market value)	$ 9,000
Furniture (current value)	4,000
Total tangible assets	$13,000
Investment assets:	
Stock (100 shares of Networld, current value = $60/share)	$ 6,000
Retirement plan (diversified stock fund)	4,000
Total investment assets	$10,000
TOTAL ASSETS	$29,000

Liabilities:

Short-term liabilities:

MasterCard balance	$ 1,000
Loan from Jill's mother	2,000
Total short-term liabilities	$ 3,000

Long-term liabilities:

Balance on Saturn auto loan	$ 8,000
TOTAL LIABILITIES	$11,000
NET WORTH	$18,000

❖ **Interpretation:** Note that the BMW auto lease should not be entered on the net worth statement as an asset or as a liability. Because of the cancellation penalties with some long-term vehicle leases, consumers should probably consider them as being similar to installment loans. However, the most common practice for consumers is to ignore leases when constructing net worth statements.

Observe also that salaries and expenses do not appear on the net worth statement. If on January 1, 1997, the monthly rent of $900 was due but not yet paid, it would be appropriate to list it as a short-term liability.

The value placed on each tangible asset should be based on how much that asset could be sold for that day. Therefore, for instance, even if the furniture cost $10,000 to purchase, it would probably be worth much less than that after a year or more.

The value listed for each liability should be the **pay-off balance**, the total amount required to liquidate the loan by paying it in full. For instance, if 40 months remained on the Saturn loan payments, a total of $10,000 (40 × $250) more will be paid if the loan payments are completed as scheduled. However, if Joe and Jill wrote a check for $8,000, that would pay off the loan in full, saving them $2,000 in finance charges. Therefore, $8,000 is listed as the liability, rather than the $10,000 in remaining payments.

▼ **Example 7.5.2:** Use the information given in Example 7.6.1 to construct an income and expense statement for 1996. What was the surplus in 1996?

Solution:

**Income and Expense Statement
Joe and Jill
January 1, 1996 - December 31, 1996**

Income:

Joe's salary	$27,000
Jill's salary	27,000
Interest from money market account	160
TOTAL INCOME	$54,160

Expenses:

Fixed expenses:

Saturn loan payments	$ 3,000	
Rent and utilities	11,000	
BMW lease payments	6,000	
Life insurance premiums	600	
Auto registration and taxes	200	
Total fixed expenses		$20,800

Variable expenses:

Groceries	$ 4,000	
Restaurants and other eating out	4,000	
Telephone	600	
Clothing and clothing care	3,000	
Vacations	3,000	
Income taxes	4,000	
Miscellaneous	12,000	
Total variable expenses		30,600
TOTAL EXPENSES		$51,400
SURPLUS		$ 2,760

❖ **Interpretation:** Which expenses are variable and which are fixed? **Fixed expenses** are usually paid in the same amount during each time period; they are often contractual (e.g., rent, vehicle installment loan). **Variable expenses** are expenditures over which an individual has considerable control (e.g., food, entertainment, clothing). A very simple guideline for categorizing expenses as fixed or variable is whether there can be a substantial cut in expenses without a penalty. Therefore, for instance, an auto lease should be counted as fixed, as typically there would be a penalty for ending a lease before the term of the lease is completed. The category "Misc." is large in this example to save space. However, it is not a good idea for households to have a large category for miscellaneous expenses. Joe and Jill have a surplus of $2,760. However, as we shall see below, this may not be a large enough surplus, given their goals.

▼ **Example 7.5.3:** Construct a budget for Joe and Jill for 1997. Discuss how it is consistent with their situation and their goals.

Solution:

Budget
Joe and Jill
January 1, 1997 - December 31, 1997

Income:

Joe's after tax salary	$28,200
Jill's after tax salary	28,200
Interest from money market account	160
TOTAL INCOME	$56,560

Expenses:

Fixed expenses:

Saturn loan payments	$ 3,000	
Rent and utilities	11,000	
BMW lease payments	6,000	
Life insurance premiums	600	
Auto registration and taxes	200	
Total fixed expenses		$20,800

Variable expenses:

Groceries	$ 4,000	
Restaurants and other eating out	2,000	
Telephone	600	
Clothing and clothing care	3,000	
Vacations	1,000	
Income taxes	4,400	
Miscellaneous	5,000	
Total variable expenses		20,000
TOTAL EXPENSES		$40,800
PROJECTED SURPLUS		$15,760

❖ **Interpretation:** We are assuming that Joe and Jill cannot break the BMW lease. If they could, that might be a good choice for cutting expenses. They need to find sufficient dollars to cut from expenses to increase the projected surplus enough to meet the goal of having enough money for a down payment on a home by January 1, 1998. They have 100 shares of Networld stock, but for budget planning with a limited one- or two-year timeframe, they should not assume any increase in the value of the stock because it probably will not occur. They already have $4,000 in a money market account. If they achieved the projected surplus of $15,760 and took $240 out of their checking account, they would have enough for the down payment of $20,000 on January 1, 1998. During 1997, they should also pay off their Mastercard balance of $1,000. They might have to sell some of their stock to cover other costs of buying a home, such as furnishings and closing costs, or they could cut spending more during 1997, or try to increase their incomes. Once they bought their home, they might be able to start using part of their surplus each year for contributions to retirement accounts. We are also assuming that their salaries both increase by $1,200 per year, from $27,000 to $28,200 and income taxes will be $4,400. One should be very cautious about making projections for salary increases, as the consequences of being too optimistic are worse than the consequences of being too pessimistic.

6. Fitting the Cost of a Major Purchase into One's Budget[2]

Formula 7.6: $S = Y - E_1 - E_2$

Where: S = cash surplus; Y = income; E_1 = expenditures before potential purchase; and E_2 = expenditure for new purchase.

---

[2]This example was contributed by Vickie L. Hampton, Associate Professor, Human Ecology, The University of Texas, Austin, TX 78712. v.hampton@mail.utexas.edu

▼   **Example 7.6.1:** Jane is a college junior who has just moved from the dorm into a new apartment with two of her best friends. To help furnish the apartment, Jane would like to purchase a 25-inch television that she saw advertised for only $279.99. Including sales taxes, the television would cost approximately $300. Since Jane has just finished paying off her credit cards, she prefers to pay cash for the television. As a part-time worker, Jane's monthly take-home income includes $350 wages, $200 student loan proceeds, and $150 from her parents. Her monthly expenditures include $200 rent, $50 utilities, $150 food, $100 clothing, $50 entertainment, and $50 education expenses. Does the television purchase fit into Jane's budget?

Solution:

$$S = (\$350 + \$200 + \$150) - (\$200 + \$50 + \$150 + \$100 + \$50 + \$50) - \$300$$
$$S = (\$200)$$

The television does not fit into Jane's monthly budget since its purchase creates a $200 cash deficit. In order to purchase the television, Jane will need to increase her income and/or decrease her other expenditures. She might decide to work more hours or ask her parents for more money to help purchase the television. She could also consider cutting some of her variable expenses for a month. She might be able to cut her food budget by $50 and forgo any clothing or entertainment in the month she purchases the television. She might also consider saving for two or three months to purchase the television or perhaps select a less expensive television.

▼   **Example 7.6.2:** Anna, one of Jane's roommates, wants to purchase a car now that she is living off campus. Anna is looking at car which costs $10,000, and she has $3,000 in savings to make a down payment. She calculates that she could finance the $7,000 difference over three years at a 10 percent rate of interest. Her monthly payments would be $226. Anna's monthly take-home income is $400 wages, $300 allowance, and $150 investment income. Her monthly expenditures include $200 rent, $50 utilities, $100 long-distance telephone calls, $200 food, $150 clothes, and $50 entertainment. Does the automobile purchase fit into Anna's budget?

Solution:

$$S = (\$400 + \$300 + \$150) - (\$200 + \$50 + \$100 + \$200 + \$150 + \$50) - \$226$$
$$S = (\$126)$$

Anna will not be able to purchase this car without making some changes in her income and/or expenditures. However, if she really wants the car she can probably squeeze $126 from her other expenditures. This $126 might come from cutting long-distance calls ($50), reducing clothing purchases ($50), and cutting back on food and/or entertainment ($26). While these may not seem to be difficult reductions, Anna must consider that she is committing to these cutbacks for a 36-month period.

❖   **Interpretation:** Examining whether a purchase fits into one's budget is an important way to figure out whether you can afford to make a specific purchase. This is critical is managing expenditures and will help keep one from making impulse purchases and uninformed purchases which end up jeopardizing financial well being. If its a cash purchase, a questionable expenditure may cramp the budget for only a month or two. However, a long-term installment purchase that turns out to be unaffordable can make one feel "poor" for a long period of time and it could possibly lead to serious credit problems.

INFORMATION AND COMPUTING RESOURCES

1. A common problem in budgeting is how to cut back on spending, either to increase the surplus or to deal with an income drop. Some resources on the web include:

   ■ *Links to budgeting and credit web resources, including some of those listed below*: http://www.hec.ohio-state.edu/cts/osue/credit.htm

   ■ *Steps To Successful Money Management:* http://www.ces.msstate.edu/pubs/pub1738.htm

   ■ *When Your Income Drops:* http://www.ces.msstate.edu/pubs/pub1618.htm

   ■ *Money Management Home Study Course:* http://www.ag.ohio-state.edu/~ohioline/home/money/money1.html

   ■ *Families Taking Charge Series:* http://www.ext.vt.edu/mgt-house-cons/resource-mgmt/

   ■ *Budgeting advice:* http://www.financenter.com/budget.htm

   ■ *66 Ways to Save Money:* http://www.chineseonline.com/cs/life/save.htm

   ■ *Links to resources on frugal living:* http://www.best.com/~piner/frugal.html

   ■ *Household budget management:* http://www.netxpress.com/users/hadap/budget.html

2. A related issue is wise use of credit. There are a number of resources available on this topic, including:

   ■ *National Foundation for Consumer Credit:* http://www.nfcc.org/

3. There is much information on financial statements on the Web, although most is related to business accounting rather than household accounting.

   ■ American Express provides simple, clearly documented worksheets for net worth and cash flow: http://www.americanexpress.com/advisors/assess/

   ■ This is a simple worksheet for a cash flow statement—you can enter income and expenses as weekly, monthly, or annual amounts, and the net cash flow is calculated: http://www.fleet.com/calculators_temp/expense-planner.html

   ■ This is a simple budgeting calculator: http://www.smartcalc.com/cgi-bin/smartcalc/bud3.cgi

   ■ Merrill Lynch net worth calculator: http://www.merrill-lynch.ml.com/investor/worthform.html

- A good primer on income/expense statements, budget planning, and related topics: http://www.iftech.com/centers/finance/finance1.htm

- A hidden expense calculator, helps plan for irregular expenses, although it may not work on some older web browsers: http://www.iftech.com/centers/finance/HiddenCalc.htm

4. The U.S. Department of Labor publishes national representative statistics of consumer income and expenses based on the data from the Survey of Consumer Expenditures. The latest results and definitions of expenditure and income categories can be found in a site created by the Department of Labor: http://state.bls.gov:80/csxhom.htm

EXERCISE PROBLEMS

Net Worth Statement

1. Allen bought a home for $300,000 in Southern California on January 1, 1994, with a $270,000 loan. On January 1, 1997 the home was worth $230,000, and Allen still owed $260,000 on the loan. On both dates, Allen had $1,000 in a checking account, leased his car, and all of his personal possessions had little value. What was his net worth on January 1, 1994, and on January 1, 1997?

2. The Smith family had an income after income taxes and FICA withholdings of $60,000 in 1997 and expect to have the same income in 1998. Spending in 1997 was food $7,000, clothing $4,000, auto leases $6,000, other transportation $4,000, rent $9,000, entertainment $2,000, insurance $3,000, and other expenses (including finance charges) $14,000. On Jan 1, 1997, their checking account had a balance of $1,000. Their Visa card had a balance of $2,500. Their Mastercard had a balance of $3,500. They had no savings accounts or investments. What was the family's net worth on Jan. 1, 1997?

3. On June 30, 1997, Jerome had $300 in his checking account and owned a car worth $10,000. He owed his father $500. On July 1, he received his monthly paycheck of $2,000. During July, he spent $400 on food, $500 on rent and $500 on other items. He paid his father the $500 he owes him. What was Jerome's net worth on June 30, 1997?

4. The Schultz family had an income after income taxes and FICA withholdings of $80,000 in 1997. Spending in 1997 was: food $8,000, clothing $5,000, auto leases $7,000, other transportation $4,000, mortgage payments $12,000, entertainment $2,000, insurance $3,000, and other expenses $20,000. On Dec. 31, 1997, their checking account had a balance of $2,000. Their savings accounts had a balance of $24,000. Their home had a market value of $200,000. The balance on their home mortgage was $140,000. What was the family's net worth on Dec. 31, 1997?

Income and Expense Statement

5. Use the information of Exercise 2 to calculate the family's surplus during 1997?

6. What was the family's surplus during 1997 if the information of Exercise 4 is used?

Relating the Net Worth Statement and the Income and Expense Statement

7. Use the information of Exercise 2 to calculate Smith family's net worth be on Jan. 1, 1998?

8. The Schultz family's financial information is presented in Exercise 4. Assume the family will have the same spending and income in 1998 that it had in 1997. What will its net worth be on December 31, 1998, if we ignore the changes of both the market price of the home and the mortgage loan balance? Also discuss if we do not ignore the two changes, what is the net worth on December 31, 1998?

9. The following is Joe and Jill's net worth statement on December 26, 1997. Assume that on January 1, 1998, Joe and Jill buy a home for $100,000, making a $20,000 down payment. Closing costs amount to $2,000. Construct a net worth statement on January 1, 1998 for the couple and state your assumptions.

Net Worth Statement
Joe and Jill
January 1, 1998

Assets:

Monetary assets:

Checking account	$ 2,000
Money market account	18,760
Total monetary assets	$ 20,760

Tangible assets:

Saturn automobile (current market value)	$ 7,000
Furniture (current value)	3,000
Total tangible assets	$10,000

Investment assets:

Stock (100 shares of Networld, current value = $60/share)	$ 6,000
Retirement plan (diversified stock fund)	6,000
Total investment assets	$12,000
TOTAL ASSETS	$42,760

Liabilities:

Short-term liabilities:

MasterCard balance	$ 0
Loan from Jill's mother	2,000
Total short-term liabilities	$ 2,000

Long-term liabilities:

Balance on Saturn auto loan	$ 5,500
Total long-term liabilities	$ 5,500
TOTAL LIABILITIES	$ 7,500
NET WORTH	$ 35,260

10. Assume that the Gee family's income after taxes was $102,000 in 1996. Mr. Gee estimates that expenditures (measured in the way shown in this chapter) totaled $92,000 in 1996, so the surplus equaled $4,000. However, balance sheets on January 1, 1996 and January 1, 1997 showed the following:

> January 1, 1996 net worth = $100,000
> January 1, 1997 net worth = $101,000
> Increase in value of home = $2,000
> Decrease in home mortgage balance = $1,500
> Depreciation on vehicles = $1,300
> There were no vehicle loans.

Is the estimate of the surplus (based on the income and expense statement) accurate?

Calculating Needed Surplus

11. Mary and Steve have $50,000 in mutual funds, $50,000 of net equity in their home, and no debts other than their home mortgage. In 1997, they had a surplus of $10,000. They are expecting a baby on January 1, 1998, at which time Mary will stop working full-time, and they will have to rely on Steve's income of $40,000 (before taxes) and income from their mutual funds of $2,500. Mary had a gross income of $45,000 in 1997. Mary plans to return to half-time work in 1999 and full-time work in 2001. What should their surplus be in 1998?

12. Use the information in Exercise 4 and assume the Schultz family wants to save cnough to pay $99,000 cash for a vacation home on Dec. 31, 2000. Assume the family wants its monetary assets on Dec. 31, 2000 to be at the same level as on Dec. 31, 1997. During 1998, 1999, and 2000, by how much should the family should cut its annual spending?

Budgeting for Financial Goals

13. On January 1, 1999, Sam and Debby have $500 in a checking account and lease two cars for a total of $400 per month. They rent an apartment and have furniture worth $2,000. They have a $3,000 balance on a Mastercard and owe $15,000 in student loans. Sam's after-tax salary in 1998 was $20,000, and Debby's was $22,000. Other expenses in 1998 were tent and utilities, $600 per month; auto registration and taxes, $100 per year; groceries cost $60 per week; eating out, $100 per week; telephone bills, $90 per month; clothing and clothing care, $3,000 during 1998; vacations cost $3,000; and miscellaneous expenses cost $9,000. They would like to be out of debt by the end of the year 2000, and then start saving to buy a home. What cuts in spending should they make in 1999?

Fitting the Cost of a Major Purchase into One's Budget

14. Kim would like to purchase a black-and-white laser printer to accompany the computer her parents gave her for her birthday. The model she likes costs $540 including taxes and can be paid over six months with no interest charges. Kim's monthly income includes $230 wages and $150 allowance from her parents. Her typical monthly expenses include $55 food, $150 entertainment, and $100 clothing. Kim's parents pay for her other expenses. Will the printer fit into Kim's budget?

15. Russell would like to buy an electric shaver for his father, but the one he prefers costs $75. Since Russell is a full-time student on a limited budget, he needs to check his budget before making the purchase. Russell's monthly income includes $200 from his scholarship, $300 withdrawals from summer savings, and $150 from wages. His monthly expenditures include $200 rent, $50 utilities, $150 auto expenses, $200 food, and $50 school expenses. Will the shaver fit into Russell's budget?

SELECTED REFERENCES

Garman, E. T., & Forgue, R. E. (1997). *Personal finance* (5th ed.). Boston: Houghton Mifflin.

Jayathirtha, C., & Fox, J. J. (1996). Home ownership and the decision to overspend. *Financial Counseling and Planning, 7,* pp. 97-106.

ENDNOTES

1. See Garman and Forgue (1997, pp. 72–75) for a discussion of cash flow basis budgeting. The example of the "Income and Expense Statement for a College Student" (Table 3.4 on p. 75) has two features that are inconsistent with the accrual-basis accounting used in this chapter: the Government Loan and the Loan from Parents are counted as income. In accrual-basis household accounting, proceeds from loans should not be counted as income.

2. Unlike the cash basis approach to income and expense statements, not all money received is counted as income when the accrual basis is used. In most cases, the definition of **income** in accrual basis household accounting is similar to that used by the Internal Revenue Service for federal income taxes. For instance, a salary is income, but a student loan is not income. Some non-taxable money receipts should be counted as income in accrual basis household accounting. For instance, even if a scholarship is not taxable, it should be counted as income. The logic of the definition of income for accrual basis household accounting is quite simple: if you receive money or other items of value, with no future obligation for repayment, and not in repayment of a past loan you made, it should be counted as income. Thus, federal income tax refunds should not be counted as income, as they are simply repayment for your "loan" to the government. Note that a state income tax refund

might be counted as income for federal income tax purposes, if you had in the previous year deducted the full amount of the state income taxes withheld. The proceeds of a student loan, other personal loan, or a cash advance from a credit card, therefore, should not be counted as income. The proceeds from the sale of an asset you own should not be counted as income, if you sell it for the same price you paid for it; if you sell it for more than you paid for it, then the increase (the capital gain) should be counted as income.

With accrual basis household accounting, expenses should be counted when purchases are made. For instance, if you use a credit card to buy clothing this month, and pay your credit card bill in full next month, the expense should be counted this month, not next month. A loan repayment should not be counted as an expense. Finance charges on a credit card or other loan should be counted as expenses. If a balance of $145 is carried over on a credit card and if a payment of $50 is made, the finance charge listed on the statement, perhaps $15, should be counted as an expense. The $50 payment represents an expense already counted when the charges were incurred.

Loans on large durable items such as a vehicle or a home present a special challenge. The Bureau of Labor Statistics (BLS) of the U.S. Department of Labor counts the full value of a vehicle purchase in the year it is acquired, even if the consumer takes out a loan for the full value of the vehicle. After the year of purchase, only the finance charge portion of the installment payments is counted as a vehicle expenditures. In contrast, the purchase of a home does not show up at all in consumer expenditures as tabulated by BLS. Only the finance charge portion of home loan payments and related expenses, such as property taxes, are counted as expenses. The difference in BLS treatment comes from the typical durability of the items—a vehicle may have substantial value for less than 10 years, whereas a home may have value forever.

The ideal way from an economic viewpoint for recording expenses for durable goods is to count only finance charges and depreciation. Therefore, for instance, if you paid $20,000 in cash for a car, nothing would be counted on that day as an expense. A year later, the car might only be worth $16,000, so the cost of the car during the year would be the depreciation of $4,000. **Depreciation** represents the decline in value of an asset over time due to normal wear and tear and obsolescence. Because homes are more likely to maintain value than are vehicles, and the lots on which homes sit are even less likely to decrease in value over the long run, buying a home might seem to result in no expense. In reality, maintaining the value of a home usually requires much expense and/or labor in repairs and improvements. Ignoring this detail, however, it is exactly right from an economic viewpoint to record a home purchase for cash as involving no expense. Here you have exchanged one asset (e.g., a savings account) for another asset, the home.

However, this approach would be a rather radical departure from the usual way of viewing household expenses. Therefore, the approach we are suggesting requires the following:

A. Recording mortgage payments and vehicle loan payments as expenses. This may be a reasonable approximation to the economic approach in most cases. This is because the home mortgage payments on a loan with a 30-year term are made up of mostly financing costs during the first years of payments, plus the principal portion of vehicle loan payments may be roughly offset by the depreciation in the value of the vehicle.

B. Making an adjustment at the end of each year in the formula for ending net worth to reflect the change in value of the home and of the vehicle, and the decrease in the balance on the vehicle loan.

3.   Jayathirtha and Fox (1996) analyzed a nationally representative sample of households for the years 1990-1992. Some of the overspending was related to the way that the United States Bureau of Labor Statistics measured spending. For instance, if you purchased a vehicle this year, the entire price of the vehicle would be counted as current spending. Still, over a third of those who did not purchase a vehicle had a deficit.

4.   The net worth is a *stock*, similar to the level of water in a container. The *surplus* is a flow, similar to the flow of water into a container. If a container has a 10 liters of water, and I add 2 liters, it will then contain 12 liters. In a similar manner, I can predict future net worth based on initial net worth and the surplus during the period in between net worth statements.

The net worth statement and the income and expense statement can be tied together by the following equation:

Net worth at end of period = initial net worth + surplus during period + unrealized changes in asset values + changes in loan balances not accounted for in expenses.

An example of a change in an asset value is an increase in the value of a home. Many households own no assets that fluctuate in value, and lease a home and vehicles, so the equation becomes the simplified version below:

Net worth at end of period = initial net worth + surplus during period

This equation can be used to estimate the true surplus of a household, if it is rearranged:

Surplus = net worth at end of period - initial net worth

Chapter 8
Using Financial Ratios

▼ **Liquidity Ratio**

▼ **Assets-to-Debts Solvency Ratio**

▼ **Savings Ratio**

▼ **Debt-to-Income (or Debt-Safety) Ratio**

▼ **Debt-Service Ratio**

▼ **Front-End Housing Affordability Ratio**

▼ **Back-End Housing Affordability Ratio**

▼ **Capital Accumulation Ratio**

▼ **Assets-to-Income Ratio**

Chapter 8
Using Financial Ratios

Sharon A. DeVaney[1]

OVERVIEW

A **financial ratio** is an index which relates two items of financial data to each other. Financial ratios originated with the credit industry. Through most of the 1800s the amount of credit to be provided to a customer (mostly businesses) was based upon the three C's of credit: character, capacity, and capital. In the late 1800s the credit industry sought a more quantifiable approach to the granting of credit. The current assets of a business firm were compared to the current liabilities of a firm and the current ratio was developed. A benchmark for the current ratio of 2 to 1 became well established and appeared in early literature as "the two-for-one rule."

Although the use of ratios began with the credit industry, managers of business firms began to see the advantages of **financial ratio analysis**, techniques for measuring related financial data and reported in an index format. The ratios for gross profit, rate of return, and inventory turnover were suggested in the twentieth century. Soon credit agencies, such as Robert Morris Associates and Dun & Bradstreet, began to compile financial ratios for different companies as a service to their customers.

As proof of the growth in the acceptance of financial ratios, the first critics of financial ratio analysis appeared about this time. The critics questioned the use of financial ratio analysis for its lack of theory, the use of normative financial ratios, and the effects of firm size on the relationship between the numerator and denominator.

In the 1930s with the formation of the Security and Exchange Commission, the accuracy and consistency of financial statement information improved. Along with an increase in the number of financial statements publicly available, interest in ratio analysis grew since normative ratios could now be developed from a number of different companies in a particular industry. Authors identified their favorite ratios

---

[1] Sharon A. DeVaney, Ph.D., AFC, Assistant Professor, Consumer Sciences and Retailing, Purdue University, West Lafayette, IN 47907-1262. sdevaney@purdue.edu

based on their experience and expertise in financial analysis. During the 1930s and 1940s, several researchers sought to determine if financial ratios could be effective as predictors of business failure.

Since 1985, ratio analysis has been recommended to be applied to personal financial statements.[1] Up until then, financial planners and counselors typically advised clients to prepare an annual financial statement but seldom explained how to judge the implications of the information contained in the statements. Financial ratios were developed to represent four important concepts: (1) liquidity, (2) debt, (3) inflation protection, and (4) derivatives of net worth. Others have proposed financial ratios to determine financial strength in the areas of consumption, investment, and credit.[2]

Today, financial ratios are used to compare the debt and equity of firms and households. Besides being used as guidelines in personal financial planning, financial ratios are also used to predict **insolvency** (having more liabilities than assets). A study found that households were more likely to be insolvent if they met one or more of the following conditions: Liquid assets were less than one-fourth of their annual take-home income, annual payments for housing and consumer debt were larger than 35% of their annual take-home income, and total assets were less than total liabilities.[3] Though no ratio can be considered an absolute indicator of financial health, each remains a powerful tool for those interested in a quick, accurate, and objective tool.

Moreover, financial ratios are a "numerical objective yardstick" designed to help in evaluating current financial strength and changes over time. Because the items used as numerators and denominators in the ratios are obtained from financial statements, the importance of preparing even very simple financial statements is reinforced for clients. Although different terminology may be used in naming categories on the financial statements and the ratios themselves may be identified by slightly different names, the intent is the same. The overall purpose of using financial ratios is to evaluate **liquidity**, **solvency**, and **burden of debt**. Although guidelines or rules of thumb are suggested in the evaluation, each ratio should be considered with the household's particular needs and circumstances in mind considering such factors as financial goals, stage in the life cycle, marital status, health, number of earners, and income.

In using ratios, there is one mathematical convention that needs to be observed. It is impossible to divide by zero. For example: Clients may have indicated that they have no financial assets or that their net worth is equal to zero and this item is the denominator of a ratio. By changing the zero to one, it is possible to complete the division and obtain a ratio value. The rationale for using a one in place of a zero is that the numerical difference between one and zero is minimal. Occasionally, one of the values used in the numerator or denominator of the ratio is negative. While negative values are usually left unchanged, it is not intuitively easy to explain a negative ratio value.

This chapter examines a number of key mathematical concepts related to financial ratios. There are several classification terms used within the accompanying balance sheet and cash flow statement. **Monetary assets** (also known as **liquid assets**) include cash and near-cash items that can be readily converted to cash. Examples include cash on hand, checking and savings accounts, tax refunds due, and rents receivable. Monetary assets are primarily used for maintenance of living expenses, emergencies, savings, and payment of bills. **Tangible assets** are physical items that have fairly long lifespans and could be sold to raise cash but whose primary purpose is to provide maintenance of a lifestyle. Examples include a home, jewelry, furniture, and vehicles. Tangible assets generally depreciate over time. **Investment assets** (also known as **capital assets**) include items acquired for the monetary benefits they might provide, such as generating additional income and increasing in value. Examples include mutual funds, stocks, bonds, and retirement accounts.

    Total income is the total of all income received, usually on an annual basis; it is also known as **gross annual income**. **Fixed expenses** are usually paid in the same amount during each time period, and they are often unalterable in the short run or contractual. Examples include rent payments and vehicle installment loans. **Variable expenses** are expenditures over which an individual has considerable control. Examples include food, entertainment, and clothing.

EXAMPLES OF MATHEMATICAL CONCEPTS RELATED TO FINANCIAL RATIOS

1. Liquidity Ratio

    Formula 8.1: $LR = MA/ME$

    Where: LR = liquidity ratio; MA = monetary assets; and ME = monthly expenses.

    ▼ **Example 8.1:** Harry Chase, aged 44, is a news engineer for a local TV station. And his wife Donna, also 44, is a personnel operations supervisor for a large corporation. The following amounts are obtained from their financial statements which are shown in an abbreviated format. Based on the information from their financial statements, what is the liquidity ratio?

Balance Sheet
December 31, 19XX

ASSETS		LIABILITIES	
Monetary assets	$ 19,500	Short-term liabilities (Credit card balance, $5,500)	$ 5,500

Investment assets (Stocks and mutual funds, $18,335; pension plans, $21,826)	40,161	Long-term liabilities:
		   Home mortgage
		   Vehicle
			127,886
			12,983

Tangible assets	209,275	Total Liabilities	$146,369
		Net worth	122,567
Total Assets	$268,936	Total liabilities and net worth	$268,936

Cash Flow (Income and Expense) Statement
January 1, 19XX - December 31, 19XX

Inflows of Income		Outflows of Funds		
Salary income	$61,150	Annual Savings and Investments		
Interest Income	350	(Company savings plan, IRA, and mutual funds)		$ 6,576
		Fixed Expenses:		
		Income and social security taxes	$19,645	
		Mortgage	10,393	
		Real estate taxes	1,500	
		Homeowner's insurance	1,000	
		Vehicle repayments	4,548	37,086
		Variable expenses		17,838
Total income	$61,500	Total outflows		$61,500

Solution: Find monetary assets ($19,500) on the balance sheet as well as fixed ($37,693) and variable expenses ($17,838) on the cash flow statement. Calculate monthly expenses by adding fixed expenses and variable expenses and dividing by 12 (months). Then divide monetary assets by the amount of monthly expenses to obtain number of months that bills can be paid.

$$LR = \$19,500/([\$37,086 + \$17,838]/12)$$
$$= \$19,500/\$4,577$$
$$= 4.26$$

❖ **Interpretation:** The **liquidity ratio** is determined by dividing monetary assets by monthly expenses and this reveals the number of months that bills can be paid given today's current monetary assets. Harry and Donna have enough monetary assets to cover more than 4 months of fixed and variable expenses which is within the recommended range of 3 to 6 months. But, they should consider health and job stability before deciding whether or not monetary assets are sufficient. Since Harry is partially disabled, they may want to increase their monetary assets to equal 6 months of expenses. Other factors to consider are availability of unemployment benefits and having a ready source of credit. Note: if information on fixed and variable expenses is not available, take-home income could be used in place of expenses. **Take-home income** is determined by subtracting from one's **gross annual income** (income from all sources in a given year) all amounts typically withheld by employers for income and social security taxes. Depending upon the situation, one also might subtract amounts withheld for health insurance premiums and contributions to a retirement plan to obtain a figure for take-home income.

2. Assets-to-Debts Solvency Ratio

Formula 8.2: SR = TA/TL

Where: SR = solvency ratio; TA = total assets; and TL = total liabilities.

▼ **Example 8.2:** Based on the information from the financial statements, what is the assets-to-debts solvency ratio?

Solution: Find total assets ($268,936) and total liabilities ($146,369) on the balance sheet. Divide total assets by total liabilities to obtain the solvency ratio value.

$$SR = \$268,936/\$146,369$$
$$= 1.84$$

❖ **Interpretation:** A **solvency ratio** reveals the relationship between a household's assets and debts and it can be determined in two ways. The first way is the **assets-to-debts solvency ratio.** It can be determined by dividing total assets by total liabilities and this reveals whether a household would be able to pay all outstanding debts by liquidating all assets. If the ratio yields a number greater than one, the household is solvent; if otherwise, the household is technically insolvent. Harry and Donna are solvent because their solvency ratio value is 1.84. They own almost twice as much as they owe, $1.84 in total assets for every $1 in total liabilities. Although current income may be adequate to pay current bills, the solvency ratio reveals whether a household would be able to pay all debts by liquidating all assets. Note that the solvency ratio can be presented in its reverse form to obtain a debt-to-assets ratio value.

3. Savings Ratio

Formula 8.3: $SR = ASI/AI$

Where: SR = savings ratio; ASI = annual savings and investments; and AI = annual income. Note that annual income can be either gross or take home income.

▼ **Example 8.3:** Use the information from the same financial statements to calculate the savings ratio.

Solution: Find annual savings and investments as well as gross annual income on the cash flow statement.

$$SR = \$6,576/\$61,500$$
$$= .107$$
$$= 10.7\%$$

❖ **Interpretation:** A **savings ratio** is determined by dividing a household's annual savings and investments by the amount of its annual income and this reveals the relationship between a household's annual savings and investments and its income. Although 10 percent is widely regarded as an appropriate savings goal for most people (those nearing retirement should be saving even more), on average, American families save about 5 to 8 percent a year. Harry and Donna save more than the average family. Households should consider all possibilities available for tax advantaged forms of savings, such as 401(k) contributions, individual retirement accounts, and tax deferred annuities. To boost one's savings ratio, it initially may be wiser to reduce debt that requires high finance charges than to save at relatively low interest rates. Note that the savings ratio can be presented using **take-home income**, rather than gross annual income, and this is demonstrated in the next formula. Continuing the example, take-home income is obtained by subtracting federal and state taxes ($19,645) from gross annual income ($61,500) which is found on the cash flow statement.

$$
\begin{aligned}
SR &= \$6,576/(\$61,500 - \$19,645) \\
&= \$6,576/\$42,035 \\
&= .156 \\
&= 15.6\%
\end{aligned}
$$

Harry and Donna save and invest over 15 percent of their take-home income, which is well above average.

4. Debt-to-Income (or Debt-Safety) Ratio

Formula 8.4:   DIR = ADR/AI

Where: DIR = debt-to-income ratio; ADR = annual debt repayments; and AI = annual income. Note that annual income can be either gross or take home income.

▼ **Example 8.4:** Calculate the debt-to-income ratio for the Chases.

Solution: Find credit card balance ($5,500) within the short-term liabilities section of the balance sheet. Looking at the cash flow statement, find the amounts for annual vehicle repayments ($4,548) and income and social security taxes ($19,645). (If balances for loans were wrongly obtained from the balance sheet, they would likely represent debt repayment for several years; thus, obtaining balances for loans from the cash flow statement assures that only the annual repayment amount is used in making the comparison.)

Using gross income,

$$
\begin{aligned}
DIR &= (\$5,500 + \$4,548)/\$61,500 \\
&= \$10,048/\$61,500 \\
&= .16 \\
&= 16\%
\end{aligned}
$$

Using take-home income,

$$
\begin{aligned}
DIR &= (\$5,500 + \$4,548)/(\$61,500 - \$19,465) \\
&= \$10,048/\$42,035 \\
&= .24 \\
&= 24\%
\end{aligned}
$$

❖ **Interpretation:** A **debt-to-income ratio** (or **debt-safety ratio**) is used to compare income to a household's annual consumer debt repayments. This reveals the proportion of income used to repay consumer debt. **Consumer debt** excludes home mortgage debt. The debt-to-income ratio may be calculated using either gross income or take-home income. The reason to exclude mortgage debt from the numerator is that debt undertaken to finance a home, a mortgage, is widely considered as financing an investment which is in contrast to consumer debt which is used to finance a variety of goods and services. Further, homes have an expected life of 50 years or more in contrast to most consumer goods which may have a life ranging from a few minutes to perhaps five years. Also, government agencies and private lenders commonly distinguish between mortgage debt and consumer debt. Most experts regard 20 percent as the maximum amount of consumer debt that should be carried and strongly recommend **debt-to-income ratios** of only 10 to 15 percent. The calculations using both gross and take-home income show that Harry and Donna are carrying a burden of debt that is higher than recommended. These calculations assume that credit card balances will be repaid within one year; however, in actual practice, households may use even longer time periods for repayment of credit card balances.

5. Debt-Service Ratio

Formula 8.5:   DSR = GADR/AI

Where: GADR = gross annual debt repayments, including a home mortgage and various consumer loans; and AI = annual income. Note that annual income can be either gross or take home income.

▼ **Example 8.5:** Based on the information of Chase's financial statement, what is the debt-service ratio?

Solution: Find the credit card balance ($5,500) from the short-term liabilities section on the balance sheet. Also, find the annual mortgage repayments ($11,000) and annual vehicle repayments ($4,548) from fixed expenses section on the cash flow statement. (If the balances for the loans were wrongly obtained from the balance sheet, these would likely represent debt repayment for several years; obtaining amounts from the cash flow statement insures that only the annual repayment amounts are used in making a comparison.) Income, either gross ($61,500) or take-home ($41,855 [61,500 - $19,465]), is found on the cash flow statement.

Using gross income,

> DSR = ($5,500 + $4,548 + $10,393)/$61,500
>   = $20,441/$61,500
>   = .33
>   = 33%

Using take-home income,

$$DSR = (\$5,500 + \$4,548 + \$10,393)/(\$61,500 - \$19,465)$$
$$= \$20,441/\$41,855$$
$$= .488$$
$$= 49\%$$

❖ **Interpretation:** A **debt-service ratio** includes the household's annual home mortgage repayments as well as repayments amounts for consumer debt, such as for vehicles and credit cards. Note that there is reduced financial flexibility for households with substantial mortgage and vehicle repayments because they are required to make regular payments to avoid foreclosure or loss of property. Experts recommend maximum debt-service ratio values of less than .30 or .35 when using gross income and .40 or lower when using take-home income. The ratio value should decrease as people age for three reasons: (1) incomes should increase relative to debt, (2) households usually need fewer durable goods later in life, and (3) households should increase savings to use later in life. The debt-service ratio values for Harry and Donna are not good. They need to consider ways to improve the values. Reducing consumer debt is probably the most feasible solution.

6. Front-End Housing Affordability Ratio

Formula 8.6: FAR = HE/AI

Where: FAR = front-end affordability ratio; HE = housing expense repayments for mortgage, taxes and insurance associated with housing; and AI = annual gross income.

▼ **Example 8.6:** What is the front-end affordability ratio, according to the information from Chase's financial statements?

Solution: Find mortgage ($10,393), real estate taxes ($1,500), and homeowner's insurance ($1,000) under fixed expenses on the cash flow statement as well as gross income ($61,500).

$$FAR = \$12,893/\$61,500$$
$$= .21$$
$$= 21\%$$

❖ **Interpretation:** Lenders use two rules of thumb to evaluate a household's housing affordability, the front-end ratio and the back-end ratio. These are in essence **housing affordability ratios** because mortgage loan applicants are typically denied credit if their debt repayments exceed the established standards. The **front-end affordability ratio** compares a household's gross income to their housing related debt repayments. The **back-end affordability ratio** compares a household's gross income to the total of all housing related debt repayments and amounts for any consumer debt repayments (see the next example). Private lenders and government housing programs typically require that housing related expenses not exceed 25 to

28 percent of gross income. Harry and Donna have a ratio value of 22 percent, which is acceptable.

7. Back-End Housing Affordability Ratio

Formula 8.7:   BAR = (HE + DR)/AI

Where: BAR = back-end affordability ratio; HE = housing expense repayments for mortgage, taxes and insurance associated with housing; DR = annual debt repayments for vehicle loans and other consumer loans; and AI = annual gross income.

▼ **Example 8.7:** Using the information from the financial statements of the Chases, calculate the back-end affordability ratio.

Solution: Find mortgage ($10,393), real estate taxes ($1,500), and homeowner's insurance ($1,000), and vehicle repayment ($4,548) under fixed expenses on the cash flow statement as well as credit card balance ($5,500) on the balance sheet.

BAR = ($12,893 + $4,548 + $5,500)/$61,500
       = $22,941/$61,500
       = .37
       = 37%

❖ **Interpretation:** Both private lenders and government agencies generally require that the ratio of repayments for both housing related debt and consumer loan repayments to gross income should not exceed 30 to 36 percent. In order to qualify for a new mortgage loan in the future, Harry and Donna will need to reduce their credit card balances to meet this lending requirement.

8. Capital Accumulation Ratio

Formula 8.8:   CAR = IA/NW

Where: CAR = capital accumulation ratio; IA = investment assets; and NW = net worth.

▼ **Example 8.8:** What is the capital accumulation ratio of the Chases?

Solution: Find investment assets ($40,161) and net worth ($122,567) on the balance sheet.

CAR = $40,161/$122,567
       = .327, or 33%

❖ **Interpretation:** The **capital accumulation ratio** compares the value of investment assets to net worth. At least 25% of a household's assets should be held in investment assets, with an increase as families near retirement. Younger households often have less than 20% of their net worth in investment assets. Harry and Donna have an appropriate value for this ratio. However, at their age (both are 44), Harry and Donna should aim to increase this ratio annually by increasing their investment assets. The value should be calculated on an annual basis to show changes over time.

9. Assets-to-Income Ratio

Formula 8.9:   AIR = (MA + NPIA)/GAI

Where: AIR = assets-to-income ratio; MA = monetary assets; NPIA = non-pension investment assets; and GAI = gross annual income.

▼ **Example 8.9:** To calculate the assets-to-income ratio based on the information from Chase's financial statements.

Solution: Find monetary assets ($19,500) and non-pension investment assets on the balance sheet ($18,335). Find gross annual income on the cash flow statement ($61,500).

($19,500 + $18,335)/$61,500
= $37,835/$61,500
= .615, or 62%

❖ **Interpretation:** This **assets-to-income ratio** compares the amount held in monetary and non-pension investment assets to income to show what assets are available if income is interrupted for a relatively lengthy period of time. It is intended to measure what amount would be available in addition to monetary assets in case a crisis occurred. It assumes that the household would need to redeem investment assets such as mutual funds and stocks. A rule of thumb of 6 months of income or 50% of annual income is recommended for this ratio. The ratio value of 62 percent suggests that Harry and Donna could manage for more than half a year if a financial crisis occurred. Although Harry and Donna would probably prefer not to cash in their investment assets, these assets could be used to cover living expenses if needed. When all the ratios are considered, it is apparent that Harry and Donna need to improve their debt-to-income ratios and everything else looks alright.

INFORMATION AND COMPUTING RESOURCES

1.   Journals such as *Financial Counseling and Planning*, the *Journal of Consumer Affairs*, and *Financial Services Review* include current research on the use of financial ratios.

2.   Conference proceedings such as the *Proceedings of the Association of Financial Counseling and Planning Education* and *Consumer Interests Annual* from the

American Council on the Consumer Interest are additional sources of current research on financial ratios and household financial status.

3. Personal finance magazines such as *Money*, *Kiplinger's Personal Finance*, *Smart Money*, and *Worth* feature articles on evaluation of household finance. It is likely that debt-safety and housing cost ratios will be most frequently mentioned because households have carried increasingly larger amounts of consumer debt.

4. The *Wall Street Journal* includes numerous articles on personal finance. Debt-safety, debt-service, and liquidity are often referred to although having a previous understanding of financial ratios as presented in this chapter will help in understanding the significance of articles.

5. Accounting textbooks, such as *The Analysis and Use of Financial Statements* by White, Sondhi & Fried (1994), include financial ratio analysis, but they will use different terminology and will evaluate a business rather than a household. A book by Ketz, Doogar, & Jensen (1990) compare financial ratios across several industries in *A Cross-industry Analysis of Financial Ratios: Comparabilities and Corporate Performance*.

6. The World Wide Web may be a source of articles on financial ratios. Suggested topics for searching include financial ratios, personal finance, and financial statements.

EXERCISE PROBLEMS

Liquidity Ratio

1. Problems using financial ratios to analyze financial strength are presented for Susan Estill, aged 49, a consumer behavior analyst for a large drug manufacturer. She has a 15 year old daughter, Amy, who plans to attend college in 3 years. Susan is beginning to think seriously about her retirement at 62 or 65. Is Susan adequately prepared for emergencies? (How many months could Susan manage if she lost her job?) Her salary is $65,850. She has $15,000 in monetary assets. Her annual expenses are: fixed expenses, $31,639 and variable expenses, $27,233.

Assets-to-Debts Solvency Ratio

2. Susan has total assets of $230,500. Her only liabilities are those on her home ($29,211) and vehicle ($13,800). How would you describe her level of solvency? Given her situation and goals, is this an acceptable level?

Savings Ratio

3. What is Susan's annual rate of savings? Is it adequate considering her objectives? She deposits $3,951 into the company savings plan. Her salary is $65,850. Her taxes including social security, Medicare, federal, state, and county taxes equal $20,266.

Debt-to-Income (or Debt-Safety) Ratio

4. Susan's annual mortgage payments equal $6,606. Her annual repayments for her vehicle amount to $2,280. Susan uses two credit cards and pays the balance in full each month on both cards. What is her debt-safety ratio for (a) gross income and (b) take-home income? Use information on income and taxes given in previous questions to help solve the problem.

Debt-Service Ratio

5. Susan has a $29,211 balance remaining on her mortgage. Her annual mortgage payments equal $6,606. She has a $13,800 balance remaining on her vehicle, a 3-year old Toyota Camry. Her annual repayments for the vehicle amount to $2,280. Using information about income and taxes from previous questions, calculate and evaluate Susan's debt-service ratio for (a) gross income and (b) take-home income.

Front-End and Back-End Housing Affordability Ratios

6. Evaluate Susan's housing costs using (a) the front-end affordability ratio and (b) the back-end affordability ratio. Her homeowner's insurance costs $987 and her real estate taxes are $1,586.

7. Susan is considering some repairs and renovation for her house. Can she take on more consumer debt?

SELECTED REFERENCES

DeVaney, S. A. (1993). Change in household financial ratios between 1983 and 1986: Were American households improving their financial status? *Financial Counseling and Planning, 4*, 31-46.

DeVaney, S. A. (1994). The usefulness of financial ratios as predictors of insolvency: Two perspectives. *Financial Counseling and Planning, 5*, 5-24.

DeVaney, S. A., & Lytton, R. H. (1995). A review of household debt repayment, delinquency, and bankruptcy. *Financial Services Review, 4* (2), 137-156.

Griffith, R. (1985). Personal financial statement analysis: A modest beginning. In G. Langrehr (Ed.) *Proceedings, Third Annual Conference of the Association of Financial Counseling and Planning Education*, 123-131.

Lytton, R. H., Garman, E. T., & Porter, N. M. (1991). How to use financial ratios when advising clients. *Financial Counseling and Planning, 2,* 3-23.

Prather, C. G. (1990). The ratio analysis technique applied to personal financial statements: Development of household norms. *Financial Counseling and Planning, 1,* 53-69.

ENDNOTES

1. The use of financial ratios in family financial planning was first proposed in Griffith (1985).

2. Research on financial ratios in *Financial Counseling and Planning* include articles by Prather (1990), Lytton, Garman & Porter (1991), and DeVaney (1993, 1994). Prather (1990) presented the median values of all 16 ratios originally suggested by Griffith in 1985 using the 1983 Survey of Consumer Finances. Lytton, Garman and Porter (1991) presented a case study and interpreted nine financial ratios. DeVaney (1993) showed changes in the proportion of households meeting financial ratio guidelines between 1983 and 1986. DeVaney (1994) predicted household insolvency using financial ratios. Johnson and Widdows compared emergency fund levels of households in 1977 and 1983. They found that the majority of households in 1983 had insufficient funds to cover income during the average time that a household could be out of work (*Proceeding of the American Council on Consumer Interests*, 1985). Hanna, Chang, Fan and Bae used a similar measure of emergency funds and analyzed emergency preparation using the 1990 Consumer Expenditure Survey. They showed that only 19 percent of families had sufficient liquid assets to cover six months of pre-tax income (*Proceedings of the American Council on Consumer Interests*, 1993). A panel (*Consumer Interest Annual*, 1995) compared results from different years and national data sets and reached similar conclusions about adequacy of emergency funds. Members of the panel and data used include Chang (1983 and 1986 Survey of Consumer Finance), DeVaney (1977 and 1989 Survey of Consumer Finance), and Hanna and Wang (1990 Consumer Expenditure Survey).

3. See the study by DeVaney (1994).

Chapter 9
Consumer Credit Mathematics

▼ Simple Interest With a Single Payment Loan
▼ Annual Percentage Rate With a Single Payment Loan
▼ Annual Percentage Rate With a Single Payment Discounted Loan
▼ Annual Percentage Rate of an Installment Loan with an Add-on Method
▼ Determining the Monthly Installment Loan Repayment Amount with a Calculator
▼ Determining a Possible Loan Amount from an Available Monthly Sum with a Calculator
▼ Effects of Full Payments and Daily Balances on Credit Card Finance Charges
▼ Determining the Annual Cost of a Credit Card

Chapter 9
Consumer Credit Mathematics

Cathy Faulcon Bowen[1]

OVERVIEW

The word **credit** describes purchase agreements in which products, services, or money are exchanged for a promise to pay a definite amount of money at a later date. **Interest** is the money one pays for the privilege of using credit. In other words, interest is the price, or fee, one pays for using credit. There are two types of credit used by most consumers: **installment credit** (also called **closed-end credit**) and **noninstallment credit** (also called **open-end credit**).

Installment credit is a loan for a predetermined amount which requires repayment in a specific number of payments, usually monthly. Each payment typically is the same amount. For example, if a person borrowed $5,000 to buy a car, and agreed to pay the loan back in 3 years (36 months), the monthly payment would be $138.90 per month until the loan was repaid ($5,000/36). With installment credit contracts, one does not have the option of getting more money under the original loan agreement.

Noninstallment credit is a loan for amounts that do not require repayment spread over a specific number of payments. Noninstallment credit loans may be repaid with one payment; sometimes such loans give the borrower a choice of whether to repay in full at a certain point or to repay in one or more monthly payments. If repayment occurs over several months, the monthly payments can be the same amount or a different amount.

Noninstallment credit includes single payment loans and open-end credit. A **single-payment loan** requires repayment in full at some point in time. Examples include bills for utility service and physician services. With **open-end credit**, credit up to a preset limit is extended before any items or services are bought. The borrower

[1]Cathy Faulcon Bowen, Ph.D., CFCS, Consumer Issues Programming, Department of Agricultural and Extension Education, College of Agricultural Sciences, The Pennsylvania State University. cfb4@psu.edu

may make as many charges as he or she likes as long as the **credit limit** (the maximum pre-approved amount one may borrow) is not exceeded. Penalty fees may be assessed if the credit limit is exceeded. When there is an account balance remaining from one lending period to another, the borrower's monthly statement typically requests that a minimum amount is due. Open-end credit is also known as **revolving credit** or **charge account credit**.

Regardless of the type of credit being used, installment or open-end, the key to comparing the cost of credit charged by lenders is the annual percentage rate. The **annual percentage rate (APR)** is the relative cost of credit on a yearly basis expressed as a percentage rate. Generally, the lower the annual percentage rate, the less one pays to use credit.

Finance charge is a term credit users should understand. This is the total dollar amount one pays to use credit. It includes the loan interest, service charges, credit-related insurance premiums and other costs required by the lender. The greatest part of the finance charge is the cost of the interest. (Technically, the finance charge only includes costs that are required as a condition of lending, perhaps, for example, for some type of insurance.) In addition to the finance charge, credit card issuers have additional fees that can increase costs for consumers who use credit. These fees vary among issuers and may include items such as **late fees** (for not repaying a bill by the due date), **over-the-limit fees** (for exceeding pre-approved credit limits), **cash advance fees** (for the privilege of obtaining a cash advance using a credit card), and **annual membership fees** (for the privilege of using a card for one year).

This chapter examines several methods used to assess finance charges on credit transactions. These range from the relatively straightforward simple interest calculated on a single payment loan to the more confusing technique that averages daily balances but excludes new purchases.

EXAMPLES OF MATHEMATICAL CONCEPTS RELATED TO CONSUMER CREDIT

1. Simple Interest with a Single Payment Loan

Formula 9.1: $I = p \cdot r \cdot n$

Where: I = interest; p = principal (in dollars); r = interest rate for the time period; and n = number of time periods for the loan.

▼   **Example 9.1:** Julia needs a car to complete a summer internship during her junior year of college. Her parents loaned her $2000 to buy a reliable car that should be operable for 4 or 5 years after her scheduled graduation. They are charging her 5% interest. She plans to repay the entire amount in a single payment in three years, one year after graduating from college. How much will Julia pay her parents in interest?

Solution:

Since, p = $2000, r = .05, and n = 3, then
I = $2000 × .05 × 3 = $300

❖ **Interpretation:** The total interest Julia should pay is $300. **Simple interest** is the interest calculated on the **principal**, the amount borrowed, without any compounding. This method of determining interest is one of many ways that might be used by lenders. It is also the least costly method of calculating interest. Lenders sometimes quote a simple interest rate of interest as a **stated rate**, which is defined as any verbal interest rate quoted by a lender. Confusion about stated rates of interest gave rise to the annual percentage rate, which is discussed in the next section.

2. Annual Percentage Rate with a Single Payment Loan

Formula 9.2:   APR = AAI/L

Where: APR = annual percentage rate; AAI = average annual interests; and
                 L = the loan received.

▼ **Example 9.2:** Mike receives a loan of $10,000 to be repaid in a single lump sum two years later. The total amount of interest to be charge on the loan is to be $1,800. What is the annual percentage rate for the loan?

Solution:

Since, AAI = $1,800/2 = $900, L = $10,000, then
APR = $900/$10,000 = .09 = 9%

❖ **Interpretation:** The annual percentage rate will be 9%. The federal Truth in Lending Act requires lenders to disclose to credit applicants the interest rate expressed as an annual percentage rate (APR) as well as the finance charge in dollars. Borrowers can then compare for the best deal. This regulation attempts to avoid confusion caused by lenders who sometimes quote a stated rate of interest. The law requires that all advertising and contractual paperwork dealing with credit transactions report the APR.

Methods of determining the APR vary according to the type of loan being given. The method used above is appropriate for a single payment loan. When the simple interest method is used to determine the interest cost of a loan, the annual percentage rate and stated interest rate are the same. In other types of loans, financial calculators, annuity tables, or computer programs provide greater accuracy than APR formulas.

3. Annual Percentage Rate with a Single Payment Discounted Loan

Formula 9.3:   L = p - PI

Where: L = loan received by the borrower; p = principal of the loan; and PI = prepaid interest charges.

▼ **Example 9.3:** Jane's parents are unable to loan her $2000 to buy a car. They were willing though, to co-sign a loan for Jane at the local finance company. The finance company is trying to increase business and currently has a limited number of loans at 5% interest for qualified first-time borrowers. Joan could get a single payment loan, repayable in 3 years, one year after she graduates from college. The lender used the discount method to determine the finance charges. How much prepaid interest does Jane pay? How much cash does Jane get from the loan company? What is the APR for the loan?

Solution:

(1) Prepaid interest.

> Since, p = $2,000, r = .05, n = 3, using Formula 9.1, then
> I = $2,000 × .05 × 3 = $300

(2) Loan received.

> Since, p = $2,000, PI = $300, using Formula 9.3, then
> L = $2,000 - $300 = $1,700

(3) APR.

> Since, AAI = $100, L = $1,700, using Formula 9.2, then
> APR = $100/$1,700 = .058 = 5.8%

❖ **Interpretation:** After prepaying $300 in interest, Jane gets $1,700 from the finance company, and the APR is 5.8%. When the loan payment is due, Jane will repay the lender $2,000. When the discount method is used, the interest from the loan amount is deducted up front and Jane receives the loan proceeds. When this method is used, the consumer prepays the loan interest. The net result is that the consumer has less money to use and he or she pays a higher annual percentage rate than any stated interest rate.

4. Annual Percentage Rate of an Installment Loan with an Add-on Method

Formula 9.4:
$$APR = \frac{Y\ (95n + 9)\ I}{12n\ (n + 1)\ (4p + I)}$$

Where: APR = annual percentage rate; Y = number of payment periods in 1 year; n = number of scheduled payments; I = total interests; and p = principal of the loan.

▼ **Example 9.4:** Faulcon Alston borrowed $3,000 for 2 years at a 7% stated rate, actually an add-on interest rate, to get his lawn service established. Calculate the total interest for the loan and the annual percentage rate for the loan if the payments will be made monthly.

(1) Total interest to be paid.

Since, p = $3,000, r = .07, n = 2, using Formula 9.1, then
I = $3,000 × .07 × 2 = $420

(2) APR.

Since, Y = 12, n = 24, I = $420, p = $3,000, using Formula 9.4, then

$$\text{APR} = \frac{12\,[95(24) + 9)]420}{12(24)\,(24 + 1)\,[4(3,000) + 420]}$$

$$= \frac{[95(24) + 9)]420}{(24)\,(24 + 1)\,[4(3,000) + 420]}$$

$$= \frac{961,380}{7,452,000}$$

$$= .129$$

$$= 12.9\%$$

❖ **Interpretation:** The add-on method is a common technique for computing finance charges on installment loans. Note that the calculated estimate of the APR (12.9%) is nearly twice that of the add-on rate (7%). Whenever a borrower does not have complete use of the full amount borrowed for the entire length of the loan, the APR will be higher than an add-on interest rate. This also occurs in loans when the discount method is used in loan transactions.

5. Determining the Monthly Installment Loan Repayment Amount with a Calculator

Conceptual Idea 9.5: The monthly installment loan repayment amount can be calculated easily with the financial calculator. The total of the loan and interest is determined by multiplying the monthly payment times the number of payments. The total interest is the difference between the total amount to be paid and the loan amount.

▼ **Example 9.5:** What is the monthly payment amount for a 3, 4 or 5 year loan of $14,000 at an interest rate of 14%?

Solution:

(1) Monthly payment.

Using a Texas Instrument BAII PLUS Financial Calculator, perform the following steps:

Purpose	BA-II Plus Keystrokes
Clear TVM registers	**[2nd][QUIT]** **[2nd] [CLR TVM]**
Set compounding methods	**[2nd] [P/Y]** 12 **[ENTER]**
PV of loan amount	14000 **[PV]**
Time periods: month	3[x]12[=][N]
Interest rate	14 **[I/Y]**
Result: payment	**[CPT] [PMT]**

The screen will show: −478.49, which means the monthly payment is $478.49. To calculate the monthly payment for the 4 year loan, use the information stored in the calculator, and add a couple of steps.

Purpose	BA-II Plus Keystrokes
Time periods: month	4[x]12[=][N]
Result: payment	**[CPT] [PMT]**

The screen will show: −382.57, which means the monthly payment for the 4 year plan is $382.57. The monthly payment for the 5 year loan can be calculated by performing a few extra steps.

Purpose	BA-II Plus Keystrokes
Time periods: month	5[x]12[=][N]
Result: payment	**[CPT] [PMT]**

The screen will show: −325.76, which means the monthly payment for the 5 year loan is $325.76.

(2) Total amount of loan and interest and total interest.

Using the results from (1), which are presented in Row (d) in the following, the total amount of loan and interest in Row (e) and the total interest in Row (f) can be easily calculated as follows.

(a) Loan size	$14,000	$14,000	$14,000
(b) Number of Years	3	4	5
(c) Number of Payments: 12 × (b)	36	48	60
(d) Amount of Each Payment	$478.49	$382.57	$325.76
(e) Total Amount Repaid: (c) × (d)	$17,225.53	$18,363.39	$19,545.33
(f) Total Interest: (e) − (a)	$3,225.53	$4,363.39	$5,545.33

❖ **Interpretation:** The above example illustrates clearly that "more time is more money." The longer the term of a loan, the more the interest costs are. Consumers who are concerned only with the lowest payment amount, and contract for such terms, will spend considerably more money on interest than those who value more highly the time period and other costs of borrowing.

This example also demonstrates a tip when using a financial calculator. If you want to see the effects when one factor changes, you can change only that factor without changing the other factors in the calculator. In the example above, you need only to change the number of time periods by making a few extra key strokes.

6. Determining a Possible Loan Amount from an Available Monthly Sum with a Calculator

Conceptual Idea 9.6: Financial calculators can be easily used to decide the amount of loan requested when the amount of monthly payment available is known.

▼ **Example 9.6:** John would like to pay for the furnishings in his new apartment in 2 years. After meeting all financial obligations, including savings, he determined that he could spend $350 on furnishings. What is the maximum loan amount John can handle if the interest rate is 9%?

Solution: Using a Texas Instrument BAII PLUS Financial Calculator, perform the following steps:

Purpose	BA-II Plus Keystrokes
Clear TVM registers	[2nd][QUIT] [2nd] [CLR TVM]
Set compounding methods	[2nd] [P/Y] 12 [ENTER]
Monthly payment	350 [+/-] [PMT]
Time periods: month	2[x]12[=][N]
Interest rate	9 [I/Y]
Result: loan size	[CPT] [PV]

❖ **Interpretation:** The screen will show 7661.20, which means the affordable loan size will be $7661.20. Borrowers often know how much monthly income is free to spend on additional needs or wants. By using the above procedure, people can determine the maximum amount of money they can spend for a given loan period. This can be a useful tool when shopping and can help consumers stay within manageable budgets when they sit down with a salesperson who might try to persuade them to spend more than they want to.

7. Effects of Full Payments and Daily Balances on Credit Card Finance Charges

Conceptual Idea 9.7: One method of calculating credit card finance charges involves multiplying the average daily balances times the monthly interest rate(s). When using the average daily balances method, card issuers may include or exclude new purchases in the daily balances. Finance charges differ when new purchases are excluded or included. Finance charges can be avoided altogether when monthly bills are paid in full by the due dates.

▼ **Example 9.7.1:** Following is a monthly credit card bill. Since government regulations permit the average daily balance to be calculated in different ways, credit card companies use different ways to calculate **average daily balances.** If a company calculates the average daily balance including the previous balance and new purchases if you do not make full payment within the grace period, what is the finance charge?

Credit Card Monthly Bill		
Previous balance = $100, APR = 18%, and monthly interest rate = 1.5%		
April	April	April
1	11	21
2	12	22
3	13	23
4 — charged $200	14	24
5	15	25
6	16 — charged $200	26
7	17	27
8	18	28 — charged $50
9 — payment of $40	19	29
10	20	30

Solution:

The average daily balance is calculated as follows.

Date (a)	# of Days (b)	Current Balance (c)	Total Balance in Period (d) = (b) × (c)
April 1-3	3	$100	3 × $100 = $ 300
April 4-8	5	$100 + $200 = $300	5 × $300 = $ 1,500
April 9-15	7	$300 - $40 = $260	7 × $260 = $ 1,820
April 16-27	12	$260 + $200 = $460	12 × $460 = $ 5,520
April 28-30	3	$460 + $50 = $510	3 × $510 = $ 1,530
Total Balance			$10,670

Then, the average daily balance is $10,670/30 = $355.67

Thus, the finance charge is $355.67 × .015 = $5.34

❖ **Interpretation:** The finance charge is $5.34. The average daily balance method of calculating the finance charges on a credit card or other open end credit account is viewed as the most favorable for consumers because the interest charges are the lowest compared to other methods of assessing interest. If a consumer usually carries over a balance from month to month, a card that uses this method to calculate the finance charge will save money. The larger one's monthly payment, the less one pays in interest. Note that a card issuer may charge other fees that add to one's cost of using a credit card.[1]

▼ **Example 9.7.2:** What is the finance charge if the company calculates the average daily balance including previous balance but excluding new purchases and full payment is not made within the grace period?

Solution:

Date (a)	# of Days (b)	Current Balance (c)	Total Balance in Period (d) = (b) × (c)
April 1-8	8	$100	8 × $100 = $ 800
April 9-30	22	$100 - $40 = $60	22 × $60 = $1,320
Total Balance			$2,120

Average daily balance = $2,120/30 = $70.67

Finance charge = $70.67 × .015 = $1.06

❖ **Interpretation:** Excluding new purchases from the average daily balance results in the lowest finance charge for consumers, and a limited number of cards have this feature. When compared to the finance charge in Example 9.7.1, which has the same credit card charges and payments, there is a $4.28 difference in the monthly finance charge.

▼ **Example 9.7.3:** If you make full payment within the grace period, what is the finance charge?

Solution: Since you make full payment within the grace period, the average daily balance will be zero, therefore, the finance charge is $0 × 0.015 = $0.

❖ **Interpretation:** The cardholder incurs no finance charges because the previous balance was paid in full. Paying each monthly bill in full is the best way to reduce interest charges associated with credit cards. Consumers who routinely pay their monthly bills in full, **convenience users**, avoid finance charges but they may be assessed annual membership fees by the card issuer.

8. Determining the Annual Cost of a Credit Card

Formula 9.8: $ACC = f + APR \cdot b$

Where: ACC = annual cost of credit card, f = annual fee, and b = average daily balance.

▼ **Example 9.8:** Hope is setting up her apartment and adjusting to her first job since graduating from college. She has to rely on her credit card for about one year. Hope is evaluating four different credit cards. She estimates that her average daily balance will be about $400 per month. Which of the four cards is projected to cost Hope the least?

Solution:

$ACC^1 = \$15 + .16 \times \$400 = \$79$

$ACC^2 = \$15 + .18 \times \$400 = \$87$

$ACC^3 = \$15 + .20 \times \$400 = \$95$

$ACC^4 = \$15 + .22 \times \$400 = \$103$

Credit card number 1 will cost the least, $79.

Card No.	Annual Fee	APR	Average Daily Balance
1	$15	16%	$400
2	15	18	400
3	15	20	400
4	15	22	400

❖ **Interpretation:** If all other features of several credit cards are equal, a card with the lowest annual percentage rate (APR) will save the most money in finance charges. Many consumers correctly believe that paying credit card bills in full by the due date is the best way to reduce or eliminate most of the costs of having a credit card. Still, however, about one-third of users maintain outstanding balances. Making monthly payments in excess of the card issuer's "suggested minimum amount due" (sometimes as little as 2 percent of the balance) can help reduce the average daily balance in an account. To lower total costs over time, one should get a card with the lowest APR because it will save the most money.

INFORMATION AND COMPUTING RESOURCES

1. Bankcard Holders of America for $4 (540-389-5445) and CardTrak for $5 (800-344-7714) offer monthly updates listing the lowest-cost bank credit cards in the United States.

2. Equifax (800-685-1111), TransUnion (800-916-8800), and Experian (formerly TRW) (800-682-7654) provide consumers with copies of their credit report for a nominal fee.

3. Most basic textbooks on personal finance will have formulas for many of the calculations used in credit transactions. They will also contain details about using credit effectively.

4. Payment tables are often available in basic personal finance textbooks. The tables can be used to find the monthly payment on a mortgage or installment loan. One source for mortgages or installment loans (ranging from $100 – $250,000) is *Barron's Financial Tables for Better Money Management —Mortgage Payments*. Instructions are included for how to calculate payments for loan amounts not in the booklet.

5. On-line sources of information. Calculators on the World Wide Web can be used to help you determine the cost of credit and related details associated with using credit. Below are a few sites to get you started. Be aware that the web sites might change or relocate. Technology changes so fast that becoming outdated can happen in weeks or a few months. Conduct a general web search using the key words: debt calculator, debt consolidation calculator, or financial calculators, and it will generate a long list of sites with calculators. A few are listed below. More than one site may be listed for some types of calculations.

   - *Determine the Monthly Payment:*
     http://www.bankamerica.com/tools/auto_payment.html

   - *Monthly Mortgages (or other Installment Loans):*
     http://www.lifenet.com/home.html#mortg
     http://www.bankamerica.com/tools/improve_payment.html

   - *Credit Cost and Length of Repayment:*
     http://www.ml.com/personal/liabil/credcalc.html (Enter the balance on your credit card, the annual percentage rate, and the amount you plan to repay each month and you will get total amount of interest you will repay and the number of months it will take you to repay the loan.)

- *Multiple Calculators:*
  http://pawws.secapl.com/1stSrc_phtml/finance/loancalc.shtml
  The site leads to several calculators that can be used in personal financial planning. You can click on the desired calculator listed below. If you wish, you can go directly to each site.

  Loan Payment Calculator
  http://pawws.secapl.com/lstSrc_phtml/finance/loancalc.shtml
  (Find out what level of payments fits your budget and lifestyle.)

  Mortgage Payment Calculator
  http://pawws.secapl.com/lstSrc_phtml/finance/husecalc.shtml
  (Why wait to find out if you can afford that home you have fallen in love with?)

  Savings Planning Calculator
  http://pawws.secapl.com/lstSrc_phtml/finance/invcalc.shtml
  (Plan today for your future.)

  Debt Consolidation Calculator
  http://pawws.secapl.com/lstSrc_phtml/finance/debtcalc.shtml
  (Restructuring your debt will save money and also may be tax deductible!)

- *Multiple Calculators:*   http://alfredo.wustl.edu/mort_links.html
  http://www.usatodaycom/money/calculat/mcfront.htm (This site has calculators for the following consumer transactions: Consumer loans, tuition, new vehicles, mortgages, and retirement.)

- *Calculating by Hand:*   http://alfredo.wustl.edu/mort/formula.html   (For those who prefer to calculate by hand and don't have a textbook, this site contains the formula; and directions to calculate monthly payments and amortization tables by hand.)

- *BankCard Holders of America:* http://www.epn.com:80/bha/   (objective and practical credit card information for consumers)

- *Bankruptcy Creditors' Service:* http://bankrupt.com/ (news, information, and resources for financially troubled individuals and companies)

- *CardTrak:* http://www.ramresearch.com/ct_main.html (updated listing of the lowest-cost bank credit cards in the U.S.)

- *Credit Bureaus:*
  Equifax: http://www.equifax.com/
  Experian: http://www.experian-com/
  TransUnion: http://www.tuc.com/

- *Credit Card Network:*   http://www.creditnet.com (a collection of links to online applications for credit cards)

- *Credit Union National Association:* http://www.cuna.org (including a calculator to compare various financing alternatives when buying a motor vehicle)

- *Debt Counselors:* http://shops.net/shops/GET_OUT_OF_DEBT (information on consumer debt)

EXERCISE PROBLEMS

Simple Interest With a Single Payment Loan

1. Jackie received a $6,500 loan at 10% interest rate for one year. When the single repayment amount is due, how much will Jackie repay in (a) principal, (b) interest, and (c) total amount?

2. Bob borrowed $7,000 from a local bank at an interest rate of 7%. He will repay the loan with a single payment in 24 months when a certificate of deposit he has matures. How much will Bob repay in (a) principal, (b) interest, and (c) total amount?

3. Hope borrows $800 at a 6% interest rate to pay for her college textbooks. She plans to repay the loan in a single repayment after one year using money earned from next summer's employment. How much will Hope repay in interest?

Annual Percentage Rate With a Single Payment Loan

4. Bob saw only a portion of a television advertisement for a local finance company. The portion that Bob saw stressed, "a limited time single payment loan offer of $1500 for two years with yearly finance charges totaling $250." If he took that loan, at the end of the two years how much would Bob repay in (a) interest, and (b) what is the annual percentage rate for the loan?

5. Sally has a single payment loan with the following conditions: principal borrowed $7,000, loan period of 18 months, and yearly interest amount due $490. At the end of the loan period, how much will Sally repay in (a) interest, and (b) what is the annual percentage rate for the loan?

6. Mischelle received a loan of $8,500 to be repaid in a single lump sum one year later. The total amount of interest to be charged on the loan is to be $935.00. What is the annual percentage rate on this loan?

Annual Percentage Rate With a Single Payment Discounted Loan

7. Joyce took out a one year loan for $6,500 at a 13% discounted interest rate to buy furniture for her home. (a) What is the amount of interest for the loan? (b) How much money did Joyce receive from the lender? (c) How much money will Joyce repay the lender at the end of the loan period? (d) What is the annual percentage rate for the loan?

8. Bob saw only a portion of a television advertisement for a local finance company. The portion that Bob saw stressed, "a limited time single payment loan offer of $1,500 for two years with yearly finance charges totaling $250." (a) How much cash would Bob receive if the lender used the discount method for determining the interest charges?, and (b) what is the annual percentage rate?

9. Hope borrows $800 at a 6% interest rate to pay for her college textbooks. She plans to repay the loan in a single repayment after one year using money earned from next summer's employment. (a) How much cash would Hope receive if the lender used the discount method for determining the interest charges?, and (b) what is the annual percentage rate?

Annual Percentage Rate of an Installment Loan with an Add-on Method

10. Mary borrowed $4,000 for 3 years at a 9% add-on interest rate for a trip to England. What is (a) the total interest, or finance charge, for the loan, and (b) the annual percentage rate?

11. Cynthia bought a computer system to help manage her home-based business using $4,500 in borrowed funds at an add-on interest rate of 8% for 2 years. What is (a) the total interest, or finance charge, for the loan, and (b) the annual percentage rate?

Determining Monthly Payments of an Installment Loan with a Calculator

12. What would be the monthly payment amount for a $25,000 loan at 12% interest payable over a) three years, b) four years, and c) five years?

Loan size	$25,000	$25,000	$25,000
Number of Years	3	4	5
Number of Payments	36	48	60
Amount of Each Payment			
Total Amount Repaid			
Total Amount of Interest Paid			

Determining a Possible Loan Amount from an Available Monthly Sum with a Calculator

13. Jesse has $250 per month that he can spend on a car payment. How much can Jesse afford to borrow if he desires to repay the loan in 36 months (3 years) and the going interest rate at his credit union for new cars is 8%?

14. Lori has $50 a month that she can spend on a new washer for 12 months. What is the maximum amount she can borrow if the interest rate is 9% at her local appliance store?

Effects of Full Payments and Daily Balance on Credit Card Finance Charges

15. What would be the finance charge if (1) the average daily balance is calculated includes both previous balances and new purchases when a consumer does not make full payment within the grace period, (2) the average daily balance is calculated includes previous balances but excludes new purchases when a consumer does not make payment within the grace period, and (3) the consumer makes full payment within the grace period?

Previous balance = $200, APR = 18%, and monthly interest rate = 1.5%		
April	April	April
1	11	21
2	12	22
3	13	23
4 — charged $400	14	24
5	15	25
6	16 — charged $400	26
7	17	27
8	18	28 — charged $100
9 — payment of $80	19	29
10	20	30

170

The Mathematics of Personal Finance

Determining the Annual Cost of a Credit Card

16. If all other features of credit cards 1, 2, 3, and 4 are the same, which would cost the least to use if during the year if the average daily balance for each month is $670?

Card No.	Annual Fee	APR	Average Daily Balance	Yearly Cost
1	$25	16%	$670	
2	25	18	670	
3	25	20	670	
4	25	22	670	

17. Which credit card costs the least to use for one year if the average daily balance for each month is $700?

Card No.	Annual Fee	APR	Average Daily Balance	Yearly Cost
1	$25	16%	$700	
2	35	18	700	
3	20	20	700	
4	0	22	700	

SELECTED REFERENCES

Detweiler, G. (1993). *The ultimate credit handbook*. New York: Penguin Books.

Fitch, T. (1993). *Dictionary of banking terms*. Hauppague, NY: Barron's Educational Series.

Garman, E. T., & Forgue, R. E. (1997). *Personal finance*, (5th ed.). Boston: Houghton Mifflin.

Israelsen, C. L., & Weagley, R. O. (1992). *Personal and family finance workbook*. Dubuque, IA: Kendall/Hunt Publishing Co.

Morris, K. M., & Siegel, A. M. (1992). *The Wall Street Journal guide to understanding personal finance*. New York: Simon & Schuster.

Shim, J. K., & Siegel, J.G. (1991). *Theories and problems of personal finance*. New York: McGraw-Hill, Inc.

Solomon, S. S., Marshall, C. & Pepper, M. (1992). *Barron's financial tables for better money management—Mortgage payments*. Hauppague, NY: Barron's Educational Series.

Trainer, R. D. C. (1984). *The arithmetic of interest rates*. New York: Federal Reserve Bank of New York.

ENDNOTES

1.   Other methods of calculating credit card finance in descending order of fairness to consumers are two-cycle average daily balance excluding new purchases, average daily balance including new purchases, and the two-cycle average daily balance including new purchases, although they are not illustrated in this chapter.

Chapter 10
The Mathematics of Income and Estate Taxes

Chapter 10
The Mathematics of Income and Estate Taxes

Robert O. Weagley[1]

OVERVIEW

Most people pay taxes in one or more ways. These include sales taxes, excise taxes, income taxes, Social Security taxes, and property taxes. Following their demise, the assets of affluent Americans are subject to estate taxes. This chapter examines the mathematics of both income taxes and the estate taxes.

For consumers trying to maximize their well-being in today's economy, taxes provide the revenue for many of the public goods and services on which our level of living depends. Each day we consume the products of our taxes, including such things as interstate highways, national defense, federally subsidized student grants and loans, libraries, public schools, community colleges, universities, medicines developed from federally funded research, police and fire protection, and weather forecasts. Thousands of additional services would not be available if it were not for the governments of our country.

To ensure that we pay for these services, each level of government has a system of taxes which attempts to collect each person's fair share of the cost of these services. Our fair share is the amount that we are legally liable to pay—no more and no less. Taxpayers need to be alert to many of the details of the various tax systems in order to avoid taxes by reducing tax liability through legal techniques. This is known as **tax avoidance**. Deliberately and willfully hiding income, falsely claiming deductions, or otherwise cheating the government out of taxes owed is illegal **tax evasion**. Understanding the mathematics of taxes also increases the chance of paying proper payment. One's eventual **tax liability**, the amount actually owed the government for a particular year, is based upon a person or household's **taxable**

---

[1]Robert O. Weagley, Ph.D., CFP, Associate Professor, Department of Consumer and Family Economics, University of Missouri-Columbia, Columbia, MO 65211. Robert_O._Weagley@muccmail.missouri.edu

income, which is determined by subtracting allowable exclusions, adjustments, exemptions, and deductions from total income. The key idea in tax avoidance is to reduce one's taxable income as much as possible, and this in turn reduces final tax liability.

While there are frequent changes in the legislation that affect federal income taxes, the basic process for the calculation has not changed through the years. The taxpayer begins by summing all the items that are included as a part of his/her **gross income**. This consists of all income received in the form of money, goods, services, and property that are reportable, less certain income that is excluded. **Exclusions** are not legally considered as income for federal income tax purposes, and they are in effect income that is **tax-exempt** or free from taxation. Once the taxpayer has completed the summation of the income items that are included in gross income, he or she may be able to further reduce taxable income from taxation by subtracting any **adjustments to income**. These particular reductions (such as some contributions to individual retirement accounts, contributions to flexible benefit programs, and certain moving expenses) are available to the taxpayer regardless of whether they itemize their deductions to income (described below). Once these adjustments to income have been subtracted from gross income, the remainder is known as **adjusted gross income (AGI)**, and this amount is used to determine eligibility for many further items of the tax code. The taxpayer must next determine his/her **itemized deductions** and compare that sum with the standard deduction. **Standard deduction** is the amount that all taxpayers (except some dependents) who do not itemize deductions may subtract from their AGI whenever they file an income tax return.

To reduce one's eventual income tax liability, the taxpayer should choose to itemize only when the sum of the itemized deductions exceeds the available standard deduction. For returns filed in 1997, the standard deduction amounts are $4,000 for single individuals and $6,700 for married people filing jointly. Itemized deductions are separated into six classifications for reporting on the household's 1040 form: (1) medical, dental, and hospital expenses (not paid by insurance) in excess of 7.5 percent of adjusted gross income, (2) taxes (but not sales taxes), (3) interest expenses, (4) charitable contributions, (5) casualty or theft losses (not paid by insurance) in excess of 10 percent of adjusted gross income, and (6) miscellaneous expenses in excess of 2 percent of adjusted gross income (although there are some miscellaneous expenses allowed as 100 percent deductions).[1] (See Garman & Forgue, Chapter 4, "Managing Taxes," for a rather detailed discussion of what items may be legally deducted.)

Personal exemptions further reduce the taxable income of the taxpayer. For returns filed in 1997, taxable income is reduced by $2,550 for each person whose livelihood depends on that income.[2]

At this stage, taxable income is actually known and the determination of the amount of the tax liability may be calculated. The taxpayer can use either the **tax table** or the **tax-rate schedule** (legal tables used to calculate income tax liability) for the appropriate filing status, and for all practical purposes the resulting calculations are the same. The 1997 tax-rate schedule for taxpayers who are single or who are married filing jointly is shown in Table 10-1.

Table 10-1
1997 Tax-Rate Schedule[3]

If 1996 Taxable Income is

Over	But not Over	The Tax is	Plus the Following Percent	Of Amount Over
Single Return				
$ 0	$ 24,000	$ 0	15	$ 0
24,000	58,150	3,600.00+	28	24,000
58,150	121,300	13,162.00+	31	58,150
121,300	263,750	32,738.50+	36	121,300
263,750		84,020.50+	39.6	263,750
Married Filing Jointly				
$ 0	$ 40,100	$ 0	15	$ 0
40,100	96,900	6,015.00+	28	40,100
96,900	147,700	21,919.00+	31	96,900
147,700	263,750	37,667.00+	36	147,700
263,750		79,445.00+	39.6	263,750

Once the income tax liability has been calculated based on the taxpayer's taxable income, he or she may be able to reduce the tax owed, on a dollar-for-dollar basis, by subtracting the value of any **tax credits** that are available. Examples of tax credits include the earned income credit and the child care credit. The subtraction of any tax credits yields one's final tax liability.

In addition to income taxes, this chapter examines the **unified federal gift and estate tax**. This tax is for both gift and estate tax purposes, and it is applied to the sum of one's taxable estate at death and any taxable lifetime gifts made. It is assessed on the assets owned or controlled by a decedent at his or her death before its transfer to heirs. It also may be assessed on property that the decedent gave away prior to death that exceeded the amount of the **annual gift tax exclusion**. Here one is permitted to give away as much as $10,000 in cash or other assets tax-free to each of any number of donees per year. Any gift and estate tax is paid before the property transfers to the heirs of the deceased and it is paid by the estate of the deceased person.[4] The federal gift and estate tax is a unified tax where the taxes due on gifts given prior to death are combined with the taxes due on the property transferred at death.

To calculate the federal estate tax, one begins with the **gross estate**. This includes the fair market value of everything owned at the time of death, such as bank deposits, securities, business interests, real estate, personal property, life insurance, personal pension plans, and employer-provided pensions, as well as the decedent's ownership share of everything owned jointly with others. The gross estate is reduced by estate settlement costs, income taxes that are owed, mortgages owed, the marital deduction (up to 100% of the estate, if married), and charitable bequests. The remainder is the **taxable estate** upon which the tax is calculated. The tax is reduced by application of the **unified tax credit** of $192,800 which effectively exempts any estate valued at $600,000 (the **exemption equivalent** amount), or less, from federal estate taxation. However, as each individual is allowed the $600,000 unified tax credit and individuals can only die once, forward thinking financial planning requires the maximization of the use of each individual's unified tax credit.

EXAMPLES OF MATHEMATICAL CONCEPTS RELATED TO INCOME AND ESTATE TAXES

1. Taxable Income and Tax Liability

Conceptual Idea 10.1: Federal income taxes can be calculated with three major steps. First, the taxable income is calculated by subtracting the adjustments to income, deductions (the larger of itemized or standard deduction), and personal exemptions from the gross income. Second, estimate the income tax based on the amount of taxable income. Third, calculate the tax liability by subtracting the tax credits, if any, from the estimated income tax.

▼ **Example 10.1.1:** Mikel Bolish is single and works as an interpreter in Washington D.C. Mikel has wage income of $35,000, self employment income of $9,000, and he contributed $1,500 to a qualified retirement plan for the current tax year. Mikel contributes $2,400 to his local church. Mikel rents his home and paid state income taxes of $1,200; he itemized his deductions last year. What is Mikel's taxable income?

Solution:

Gross Income:		
Wage income	$35,000	
Self-employment income	+ 9,000	
Total		$44,000
Adjustments to Income:		
IRA contributions	− 1,500	
Total adjusments		− 1,500
Adjusted Gross Income		$42,500
Deductions to income:		
(1) Itemized deduction		
Church contributions	− 2,400	
State income taxes	− 1,200	
	− 3,600	
(2) Standard deduction		− 4,000
Exemptions to Income:		
One individual		− 2,550
Taxable Income		$ 35,950
Tax Liability		$ 6,946

❖ **Interpretation:** This example illustrates how to calculate federal income taxes. Mikel's wage ($35,000) and self-employment income ($9,000) are both included as a part of his gross income ($44,000). His contribution to his individual retirement account ($1,500) is subtracted as an adjustment to income, leaving an adjusted gross income of $42,500. As Mikel's standard deduction for a single taxpayer ($4,000) is greater than his itemized deductions ($3,600, in which $2,400 in contributions and $1,200 in state income taxes), he may subtract the standard deduction amount from his adjusted gross income. Then he subtracts his single exemption amount of $2,550, which results in a taxable income of $35,950. Using the tax-rate schedule for a single return, the tax liability amounts to: $3,600 + .28 × (35,950 - $24,000) = $6,946.

▼   **Example 10.1.2:** Van is married to Helen. They live with their three children in their own home on which they paid $7,600 in mortgage interest and $780 in real estate taxes last year. Van has gross wages of $85,000. Van contributed $5,000 to his qualified pension plan at work. Last year their middle child was severely ill and required medical attention. Unfortunately, at the time of the illness Van was between jobs and the family was temporarily without medical insurance. Their medical expenses for the year totaled $18,000. Van and Helen contributed, above their membership, $1,000 to the local YMCA. They also paid $200 in interest charges on their stock investment accounts on which they also earned $1,200 in dividends and interest. Their miscellaneous deductions, subject to the 2% of adjusted gross income limitation, totaled $1,700. What is their tax due?

Solution:

Gross Income		
Van's wage income	$ 85,000	
Investment income	+ 1,200	
Total		$86,200
Adjustments to Income		
Pension contributions	− 5,000	
Total adjustments		− 5,000
Adjusted Gross Income		$81,200
Deductions		
Mortgage interest	$ 7,600	
Real estate taxes	780	
YMCA contributions	1,000	
Investment interest	200	
Medical expenses	11,910	
Miscellaneous deductions	76	
Total		−21,566
Exemptions		
Five individuals		−12,750
Taxable Income		$ 46,884
Tax Liability		$ 7,915

▼   **Interpretation:** Van wage income and their investment income of $1,200 are included as a part of gross income. Van's contribution to his pension plan ($5,000) is subtracted as an adjustment leaving an adjusted gross income of $81,200. To calculate their itemized deductions, the mortgage interest and YMCA contributions are fully deductible, as is their investment interest as it is less than their investment income of $1,200. The cost of their child's medical care, while deductible in this case, are not fully deductible. Medical expenses are deductible only to the extent the sum of medical expenses exceeds 7.5% of the household's adjusted gross income. Seven and one-half percent of $81,200 is $6,090, therefore, $11,910 ($18,000 – $6,090) is the amount of the medical expenses allowed as a deduction. Similarly, their total miscellaneous expenses were greater than 2% of their adjusted gross income ($1,624 = .02 × $81,200) by the amount of $76 ($1,700– $1,624). Itemized deductions total $21,566 which is greater than the standard deduction of $6,700, and the larger amount may be deducted from adjusted gross income. The household has five members resulting in exemptions to be subtracted equaling $12,750 as each member is allowed an exemption of $2,550. The result is a taxable income of $46,884. Using the tax-rate schedule for marrieds filing jointly, their tax liability is: $6,015 + .28 × ($46,884 – $40,100) = $7,914.52.

2. Taxable Income, Tax Liability, and Capital Gains/Losses

Conceptual Idea 10.2: Capital gains will increase one's income tax liability, but capital losses will reduce the liability.

▼ **Example 10.2:** Pam and her husband Dan recently lost $24,000 when DEF Communications (DEF) went bankrupt and their stock became worthless. Earlier in the year they had sold their stock in XYZ Corporation to provide money to purchase DEF Communications. When they sold the XYZ stock, they had a capital gain of $15,000. If Pam and Dan had gross wage income of $111,000, itemized deductions of $10,500, three children, and contributed $7,500 each in their respective 401(k) plans, what is their tax liability?

Solution:

Gross Income		
Gross income		$ 111,000
Net Capital Gain/Loss		– 3,000
Total		$ 108,000
Adjustments to Gross Income		
Pam's 401(k) contributions	– 7,500	
Dan's 401(k) contributions	– 7,500	
Total adjustments		– 15,000
Adjusted Gross Income		$ 93,000
Deductions		
Total itemized deductions		– 10,500
Exemptions		
Five individuals		– 12,750
Taxable Income		$ 69,750
Tax Liability		$ 14,317

❖ **Interpretation:** This example demonstrate the effects of capital gain/loss on income taxes. A **capital gain** is income received from the sale of a capital asset above the costs incurred to purchase and sell the asset, while a **capital loss** is income received below the costs. Net capital gain/loss should be counted into the gross income during the tax year. Pam and Dan had capital gains of $15,000 and capital losses of $24,000. Before calculating gross income, their capital losses may be subtracted from their capital gains. However, only $3,000 of losses, in excess of any gains, may be used to offset other income in a tax year. As such, their capital gain is not taxable and they may reduce the current year's wage income by $3,000. Any additional losses may be carried forward to future tax years. In this case, the additional loss of $6,000 ($24,000 total capital loss - $15,000 total capital gain - $3,000 maximum loss in excess of gain) may be carried forward and deducted in the future tax years. For this year, Pam and Dan had a gross income of $108,000 ($111,000 - $3,000). From the gross income of $108,000, their combined 401(k) contributions, $15,000 ($7,500 + $7,500) are subtracted as adjustments resulting in an adjusted gross income of $93,000. Their itemized deductions ($10,500) exceed the standard deduction ($6,700), so that they can choose to subtract the itemized deduction from their adjusted gross income ($93,000). After subtracting the allowable exemptions of $2,550 per person ($12,750 total), they have a taxable income of $69,750. Using the tax-rate schedule for marrieds filing jointly, their tax liability is: $6,015 + .28 × ($69,750 - $40,100) = $14,317.

3. Taxable Income, Tax Liability, Dependent Care Expenses

Conceptual Idea 10.3: Dependent care expenses, through tax credits or flexible spending benefits programs, will reduce income tax liabilities.

▼   **Example 10.3.1:** Bill and Mary are married with an 18 month old child. They live in their own home on which they paid $6,500 in qualified mortgage interest last year and $700 in real estate taxes. Bill has a salary income of $45,750 and Mary's wages are $25,000. Bill contributed $1,500 to his qualified pension plan and Mary choose not to participate in her retirement plan. The cost of day care for their child was $5,750, and that figure calculates (not shown) to a child care tax credit of $960. Bill and Mary contribute $1,000 per year to their church. They had $500 in dividend and interest income. Their miscellaneous deductions, subject to the 2% of adjusted gross income limitation, totaled $950. What is their taxable income and tax due—both before and after the child care tax credit is applied?

Solution:

Gross Income		
Bill's salary income	$ 45,750	
Mary's wage income	25,000	
Investment income	500	
Total		$ 71,250
Adjustments to Income		
Pension contributions	− 1,500	
Total adjustments		− 1,500
Adjusted Gross Income		$ 69,750
Deductions		
Mortgage interest	6,500	
Church contributions	1,000	
Real Estate Taxes	700	
Miscellaneous deductions	0	
Total		− 8,200
Exemptions		
Three individuals		− 7,650
Taxable Income		$53,900

Calculated Tax Liability	$ 9,879
Less Child-Care Tax Credit	– 960
Tax Liability	$ 8,919

❖ **Interpretation:** Bill's income ($45,750) and Mary's income ($25,000) and their investment income of $500 are included as a part of gross income ($71,250). Bill's contribution to his qualified pension plan ($1,500) is their only adjustment to income. This leaves an adjusted gross income of $69,750. To calculate their total of itemized deductions ($8,200), the mortgage interest ($6,500), church contributions ($1,000), and real estate taxes ($700) are fully deductible. Their total miscellaneous expenses ($950) are less than 2% of their adjusted gross income ($950 < $1,395 = .02 × $69,750), therefore, they are not deductible. Since the total itemized deductions ($8,200) are greater than the standard deduction for a married couple household ($6,700), the larger amount should be deducted from adjusted gross income. As the household has three members, the amount of exemptions to be subtracted totals $7,650 as each member is allowed an exemption of $2,550. The result is a taxable income of $53,900. Using the tax-rate schedule for marrieds filing jointly, their tax liability is: $6,015 + .28 ($53,900 - $40,100) = $9,879. The child care tax credit of $960 (calculation not shown) is subtracted form the estimated tax liability and it results in a final tax liability of $8,919.

▼ **Example 10.3.2:** Using the above example, what would be the difference in the answer had Mary participated in the flexible benefit program at her place of work and contributed $5,000 toward her day-care expenses?

Solution:

Gross Income		
Bill's salary income	$ 45,750	
Mary's wage income	25,000	
Investment income	500	
Total		$71,250
Adjustments to Income		
Pension contributions	1,500	
Child-Care Flexible Benefits	5,000	
Total adjustments		– 6,500
Adjusted Gross Income		$64,750
Deductions		
Mortgage interest	6,500	
Church contributions	1,000	
Real Estate Taxes	700	
Miscellaneous deductions	0	
Total		– 8,200
Exemptions		
Three individuals		– 7,650
Taxable Income		$48,900
Tax Liability		$ 8,479

❖   **Interpretation:** If instead of taking the child-care credit of $960, Bill and Mary contribute $5,000 to the Child-Care Flexible Benefits program at work, they may take the $5000 as an adjustment to income. This reduces their tax liability to: $6,015 + .28 × ($48,900 - $40,100) = $8,479. This compares to $8,919 when using the child-care tax credit. Thus, Bill and Mary reduce their tax liability $440 ($8,919 - $8,479) by using the flexible benefits program rather than taking the child care credit. Generally, taxpayers that pay at the 28% rate, or higher, marginal tax rate benefit more from income reducing strategies, such as flexible benefit plans, than they do from tax credits.

4. After-Tax Equivalent Yield

Formula 10.4: TEY = TY (1 - MTR)

Where: TEY = tax-exempt yield; TY = taxable yield; and MTR = marginal tax rate.

▼   **Example 10.4.1:** John is subject to the 31% federal marginal tax rate and he is considering investing in a taxable bond yielding 7.7%. What is the after-tax equivalent yield of that investment for John?

$$TEY = 7.7 \times (1 - 0.31)$$
$$= 7.7 \times 0.69$$
$$= 5.3\%$$

❖   **Interpretation:** The 7.7% bond will provide John a return of 5.3% after he pays income taxes on the interest income. When considering alternative investments, the best way to compare choices is to convert the returns into an after-tax basis. That means: What return will competing investments provide a particular investor after income taxes have been paid? In a similar way, people sometimes need to know whether a tax-exempt or taxable investment is to their advantage. To determine the correct answers to these types of questions, one must calculate the **after-tax equivalent yield**. This amount is the return to a particular taxpayer from a taxable investment after the impact of income taxes when compared with the return from a tax-exempt investment. If the investment alternatives are otherwise equal, one should select the investment with the higher after-tax equivalent yield.

▼   **Example 10.4.2:** Jane pays taxes at the 28% federal marginal tax rate and is considering two alternatives. First, there is a taxable bond paying 7.7%. Second, there is a tax-exempt bond paying 5.3%. Which investment will pay Jane a higher after-tax return?

$$TEY = 7.7 \times (1 - 0.28)$$
$$= 7.7 \times 0.72$$
$$= 5.544$$

❖ **Interpretation:** Jane will receive a higher after-tax return from the taxable bond paying 7.7% because that bond will earn her an after-tax equivalent yield of 5.54%, and that is higher than the tax-exempt bond paying 5.3%.

▼ **Example 10.4.3:** Jake pays taxes at the 28% federal marginal tax rate and is considering two alternatives. First, there is a taxable bond paying 7.4%. Second, there is a tax-exempt bond paying 5.2%. Which will pay Jake a higher after-tax return?

Solution 1:

$$5.2 = TY (1 - 0.28) = TY \, 0.72$$
$$TY = 5.2 / 0.72 = 7.222$$

Solution 2:

$$TEY = 7.4 \times (1 - 0.28)$$
$$= 7.4 \times 0.72$$
$$= 5.328$$

❖ **Interpretation:** In Solution 1, knowing the tax-exempt yield of one bond paying is 5.2% tells Jake that the 7.4% taxable bond is a better deal because the 5.2% is equivalent to a taxable return of only 7.222%. This question also can be answered using the other formula. In Solution 2, Jake calculates that the 7.4% taxable bond converts to 5.32% on an after-tax basis, therefore, the 7.4% bond provides a better after-tax return (5.328%) than the 5.2% tax-exempt bond.

5. Gifting to Children and the Kiddie Tax

Conceptual Idea 10.5: Tax savings can be calculated by comparing parent's and child's tax liabilities.

▼ **Example 10.5.1:** John and Rhonda are trying to decide whether to save their recent inheritance of $20,000 for their child's college education in their name or in the name of their 5-year old child. Assume that they expect to earn 9% on the invested funds, they pay taxes at the 31% marginal tax rate, that they do not expect to be eligible for financial aid when their child is college aged, and that the first $650 of a child's income is tax exempt. How much in income taxes will be saved if the parent's put the gift in the child's name?

Solution:

(1) Tax liability in parent's name.

Income of Parents	$1,800
Tax Rate	× .31
Total Tax Liability if Parental Ownership	$ 558

(2) Tax liability in child's name

Income of Child	$1,800	
Exempt Income	– 650	
Taxable Income	$1,150	
Amount Taxed at 15% $650= >Taxes Owed by Child	= $ 97.50	
Amount Taxed at 31% $500= >Taxes Owed by John & Rhonda	= 155.00	
Total Tax Liability if Child Ownership	$ 252.50	

(3) Tax Liability Savings

Taxes if Parental Ownership	$558.00
Taxes if Child Ownership	252.50
Tax Savings	$305.50

❖ **Interpretation:** This example indicates the situation of **kiddie tax rate**. A child under 14 pays no tax on the first $650 of unearned income and are taxed at their own rate on the next $650 of unearned income. After that level, the child's unearned income is taxed at the parent's marginal tax rate, which is known as the kiddie tax rate. The Step (2) of the above example details the calculation of kiddie taxes. John and Rhonda's $20,000 is earning $1,800 per year, given the 9% return. Last year, John and Rhonda would have paid $558 in taxes, given a 31% marginal tax rate being applied to the $1,800 of unearned income. On the other hand, they could have given the money to their child. If the child owns the money asset, then the unearned income that the money earns is partially exempt from income taxes (the first $650), partially taxed at the child's marginal tax rate of 15% (the next $650), and the remainder ($500 in this case) is taxed at the parents' marginal tax rate of 31% . The difference between parental ownership (taxes of $558) and child ownership (taxes of $252.50) is, therefore, $305.50.

▼ **Example 10.5.2:** How much in taxes would be saved had John and Rhonda's child been aged 14, or older?

Solution:

Amount to be Taxed	$1800
Tax Rate of Child	× .15
Tax Liability Owed by Child	$ 270
Tax Liability at Parent's Rate	$ 558
Less Tax Liability at Child's Rate	– 270
Tax Savings	$ 288

❖ **Interpretation:** Here the kiddie tax regulations do not apply. The income earned by children age 14 and over is taxed at the child's own tax rate, not that of his/her parents. In exchange, the first $650 of unearned income is subject to taxation .If John and Rhonda's child was 14 years of age, or older, during the year in which the unearned income is earned, the entire $1,800 would be taxed at the child's marginal tax rate, typically 15%. Then, if John and Rhonda give the money to their child, they will save $288 ($558 - $270) taxes.

6. Value of Mortgage Interest Tax Deduction

Formula 10.6: $MIC_{at} = MID - (TS_{id} - TS_{sd})$

Where: MIC_{at} = after-tax mortgage interest costs; MID = mortgage interest deduction; TS_{id} = tax savings through itemized deduction; and TS_{sd} = tax savings through standard deduction.

Note that $(TS_{id} - TS_{sd})$ represents the tax advantage of itemized deductions, given the condition that the amount of itemized deduction is greater than standard deduction.

▼ **Example 10.6:** Bill and Susan are a married couple who file their taxes jointly. They have a mortgage on which they paid $8,750 in mortgage interest with additional itemized deductions of $3,500. Bill and Susan pay taxes at the 28% federal marginal tax rate. For 1996, the standard deduction for a married couple filing jointly is $6,700. What are tax advantages of using mortgage interests as an itemized deduction, and what is the after-tax mortgage interest costs?

Solution:

Since, TS_{id} = $12,250 × .28 = $3,430, TS_{sd} = $6,700 × .28 = $1,876
Then, TS_{id} - TS_{sd} = $3,430 - $1,876 = $1,554
Then, MIC_{at} = $8,750 - $1,554 = $7,196

❖ **Interpretation:** In this case, using mortgage interest as an itemized deduction will save $1,554 more than using the standard deduction. Considering the tax savings of using mortgage interest as an itemized deduction, the after-tax cost of mortgage interests is only $7,196. The savings of $1,554 can be used to make mortgage payments instead of paying taxes. For most homeowners, the payment of mortgage interest causes the sum of their itemized deductions to be greater than the standard deduction. When this occurs, it allows the taxpayer to itemize deductions which reduces the tax liability. Note, however, that the benefit of itemized deductions exists only to the extent that the itemized deductions are greater than the standard deduction. In the case above, Bill and Susan would not have been able to itemize their deductions ($3,500) unless they had a home mortgage interest deduction, and without that interest deduction, they would have taken the $6,700 standard deduction.

7. Early Withdrawals from Qualified Retirement Plan

Formula 10.7: $AW = AN/(1 - MTR - PR)$

Where: AW = amount to withdraw; AN = amount needed; MTR = marginal tax rate; and PR = penalty rate.

▼ **Example 10.7:** Ed, age 50, has been faithfully investing $2,000 in a tax-sheltered retirement plan at the end of each year for the past 25 years. Ed has been earning 8%

on his investments, which now total more than $140,000. He needs $50,000 this year to pay for the college tuition of his children. Ed recognizes that if he withdraws the money before the age of 59 1/2 he will have to pay a 10% penalty tax in addition to his 28% marginal rate of tax during the year of the withdrawal. How much does Ed have to withdraw in order to have $50,000 and pay the taxes due?

Solution:

Since AN = $50,000, MTR = .28, and PR = .10, then
AW = $50,000/(1 - .28 - .10) = $50,000/.62 = $80,645

❖ **Interpretation:** Ed pays taxes at the 28% marginal tax rate and must pay a 10% penalty tax (called an **early withdrawal penalty**) for taking a premature distribution from a tax-sheltered retirement program. Therefore, Ed must take out sufficient funds both to pay the taxes and to have $50,000 left for his child's college education. As the product of the amount withdrawn times one minus the effective marginal tax rate must equal $50,000, by dividing the $50,000 by one minus the effective marginal tax rate one finds the amount that must be withdrawn. Ed's tax liability for withdrawing the previously untaxed $80,645 will be $30,645 ($80,645 × .38).

8. Federal Estate Taxes

Conceptual Idea 10.8: Federal estate tax equals estimated estate taxes based on the taxable gross estate less the unified estate and gift tax credit. The Unified Federal Gift and Estate Tax Rates are included in Table 10-2.

Table 10-2
Unified Federal Gift and Estate Tax Rates

(1) Taxable Estate plus Taxable Gifts	(2) Tax	(3) Plus Rate of Tax on Excess over Amount in Column 1	(4) Unified Gift and Estate Tax Credit	(5) Federal Gift and Estate Tax Liability
Under $10,000	18% of amount	—	$192,800	—
$10,000	$ 1,800	20%	192,800	—
20,000	3,800	22	192,800	—
40,000	8,200	24	192,800	—
60,000	13,000	26	192,800	—
80,000	18,200	28	192,800	—
100,000	23,800	30	192,800	—
150,000	38,800	32	192,800	—
250,000	70,800	34	192,800	—
500,000	155,800	37	192,800	—
750,000	248,300	39	192,800	$55,500
1,000,000	345,800	41	192,800	153,000
1,250,000	448,300	43	192,800	255,500
1,500,000	555,800	45	192,800	363,000
2,000,000	780,800	49	192,800	588,000
2,500,000	1,025,800	53	192,800	833,000
3,000,000	1,290,800*	55	192,800	1,098,000

(Source: Internal Revenue Service)

*Plus 5% of the cumulative transfers in excess of $10,000,000 but not exceeding $21,040,000.

▼ **Example 10.8:** Seth is dead. Seth's wife, Maryanne, jointly owned everything with Seth and had rights to survivorship, which means Seth's entire $850,000 estate passed to Maryanne. However, Maryanne died in a accident a month after Seth's death. Assuming that Maryanne had paid $10,000 for Seth's funeral, how much does her estate owe in federal estate taxes following her death?

Solution:

Since, Maryanne's taxable estate = $850,000 - $10,000 = $840,000

According to Table 10-2,
estimated estate tax = $248,300 + ($840,000 - $750,000) × .39 = $243,400
unified estate and gift tax credit = $192,800

Then, federal estate tax liability = $243,400 - $192,800 = $90,600

❖ **Interpretation:** The **unlimited gift tax marital deduction** provision of the federal gift and estate tax regulations eliminates the tax on gifts between spouses because it permits a married person to give his or her spouse an unlimited amount free of any gift tax. When Seth died, he owned everything jointly with rights of survivorship with his wife Maryanne. Assuming she did not make any changes in ownership immediately following his death, Maryanne is the owner of everything. Therefore, the entire estate ($840,000) is taxable less the cost of the funeral ($10,000). An **estimated federal estate tax** liability of $283,400 would result. However, little or no tax may be owed on the taxable portion of an estate because of the **unified gift and estate tax credit**. This dollar-for-dollar reduction in the gift and estate tax represents the amount that one may give away or bequeath free of federal estate taxes. This credit of $192,000 is equivalent to the tax on an estate valued at $600,000. Therefore, in this case, the estimated estate tax of $283,400 may be reduced by $192,800, which results in a federal estate tax liability of $90,600 ($283,400 - $192,800). Here we see that by Seth bequeathing his entire estate to Maryanne, through joint ownership, her subsequent estate is subject to federal estate taxes. The surviving family had to pay almost 11% ($90,600/$840,000) of the value of the estate to the federal government.

9. Assets in an Irrevocable Bypass Trust Reduce Estate Taxes

Conceptual Idea 10.9: Estate taxes can be reduced by using irrevocable bypass trusts to reduce taxable gross estate.

▼ **Example 10.9.1:** A few years ago, Seth's brother Ralph married Beulah and they had three children. After their children were born, Ralph and Beulah decided they wanted to minimize the estate taxes on their combined assets of $2,000,000. As such, they structured their estate plan in such a way that when the first spouse died part of the assets would pass to the surviving spouse to take advantage of the unlimited marital deduction and an exemption equivalent amount of their assets would be placed in a form of **irrevocable trust**. This is a trust used to give away assets to reduce estate taxes. Their attorney had written a **bypass trust** for them which would go into effect upon the death of one spouse. (This is sometimes called a **credit-shelter trust** or a **Qualified Terminal Interest Property [QTIP] trust**.) It was designed to transfer $400,000 in several separately titled assets to children and grandchildren while providing income to a surviving spouse. The surviving spouse, Ralph or Beulah, would receive income from the trust but retained no control or ownership over the principal (**corpus**) of the trust. They planned that certain other assets, $1,000,000, would transfer as an unlimited marital deduction. Ralph died suddenly upon learning of the death of his brother Seth. What are the estate taxes due upon Ralph's death?

Solution:

Ralph's gross estate	$2,000,000
Assets Transferred to Credit-Shelter Trust	− 400,000
Unlimited Marital Deduction	−1,000,000
Taxable Estate	$ 600,000
Estimated Estate Tax	$ 192,800
Unified Estate and Gift Tax Credit	− 192,800
Estate Tax Liability	$ 0

❖   **Interpretation:** Upon Ralph's death, $400,000 was placed into a trust designed to allow Beulah to receive the income from the trust while she is alive. Upon her death, the assets in the trust will pass to other heirs. Another $1,000,000 in assets passed directly to Beulah as an unlimited marital deduction, and that left an estate of $600,000. According to Table 10-2, the estimated estate tax should be: $155,800 + ($600,000 - $500,000) × .37 = $192,800. After subtracting the value of the unified tax credit ($192,800), the tax liability on Ralph's estate is zero.

▼   **Example 10.9.2:** Unfortunately, Beulah died only a few months following Ralph's funeral. Assuming that Beulah had paid $10,000 for Ralph's funeral, what is the estate tax liability on her estate?

Solution:

Beulah's gross estate	$1,590,000
Unlimited marital deduction	− 0
Taxable Estate	$1,590,000
Estimated Estate Tax	$ 596,300
Unified Estate and Gift Tax Credit	− 192,800
Estate Tax Liability	$ 403,500

❖   **Interpretation:** Beulah's gross estate was $1,590,000 ($1,600,00 - $10,000). She did not own the bypass trust. It is, therefore, not included in her estate. Using Table 10-2, the estimated estate tax should be: $555,800 + ($1,590,000 - $1,500,000) × .45 = $596,300. After subtracting the unified estate and gift tax credit of $192,800, the result is an estate tax due of $403,500. The above two examples indicate that the use of the bypass trust effectively reduced estate taxes. People with substantial estates often use similar legal techniques, primarily trusts, to reduce estate taxes.

INFORMATION AND COMPUTING RESOURCES

1. Popular computer software programs to help prepare income tax returns include *Kiplinger Tax Cut* (Block Financial Software), *Personal Tax Edge* (Parsons), *Simply Tax* (4Home Productions), *TaxCut* (H&R Block), and *Turbo Tax* (Intuit). Computer programs for estate planning are also available in the market, such as *WillMaker* (Nolo Press), *Home Laywer* (MECA Software), *Personal Lawyer* (ImsiSoftware), and *Quicken Family Lawyer* (Intuit).

2. Every year during the tax season, January through April, popular personal finance or economic journals and magazines, such as *Kiplinger's Personal Finance Magazine*, *Fortune*, *Money*, *Smart Money*, *Wall Street Journal*, and *Worth* will publish news, tips, and feature articles about tax preparation. These magazines also have feature articles about estate planning to avoid or reduce estate taxes.

3. The following are related web sites:

    ■ *Charitable deductions:* http://www.taxsave.com (list of prices for goods for calculation of charitable deductions, but you have to pay a fee)

    ■ *Ernst & Young:* http://www.ey.com/us/tax (publisher of tax preparation books)

    ■ *Estate planning:* http://www.wwlaw.com/fye.htm (tips on estate planning)

    ■ *Internal Revenue Service:* http://www.irs.usteas.gov (tax information and tax forms)

    ■ *Online tax preparation:* http://www.parsonstech.com (there is a fee for the service)

    ■ *State forms:* http://www.1040.com (download state forms and search for preparer in your area)

    ■ *Tax code:* http//www.tns.lcs.mit.edu/uscode/ (help search for tax information from complete U.S. tax code, but may not be totally up-to-date)

    ■ *Tax link:* http//www.best/com/~ftmexpat/html/taxsites.html (prepared by a tax preparer in San Francisco)

    ■ *Tax link:* http://www.uni.edu/schmidt/tax.html (prepared by an accounting professor at the University of Northern Iowa)

    ■ *Tax preparer:* http://www.intuit.com (maintain a database of tax preparers in your zip code)

- *Tax Prophet:* http://www.taxprophet.com (obtain tax lawyer advice on a wide rage of topics)

EXERCISE PROBLEMS

Taxable Income and Tax Liability

1. Mary and Mark Jensen work for salaries. Mary earns $44,000 and Mark earns $34,000. Mary contributed $3,500 to a qualified retirement plan for the current tax year; Mark contributed zero. The Jensens contributed $3,000 to their church. They rent their home and paid state income taxes of $4,200 last year, and they itemized deductions last year. (a) What is the Jensen's taxable income? (b) What is the Jensen's federal tax liability?

2. Susan and Bill live with their two children in their own home on which they paid $8,500 in qualified mortgage interest and $870 in real estate taxes last year. Bill has gross wages of $45,000 and Susan's wages are $60,000. Bill contributed $2,500 to his 401(k) plan and Susan contributed $4,000 to hers. Last year their oldest child was severely ill and at the time of the illness the family was temporarily without medical insurance. Their medical expenses for the year totaled $14,500. Bill and Susan contribute $10,000 per year to their church. They paid $900 in interest on a auto loan, $250 in interest on their credit cards, and $500 in interest on their investment accounts on which they had $3,500 in dividend and interest. Their miscellaneous deductions, subjcct to the 2% of adjusted gross income limitation, totaled $2,500. Calculate the taxable income and tax due.

3. Kentucky Ray has had a good year with lots of income from his job as a professional golfer, $275,000; net rental income of $85,000, speaker fees of $54,000, and taxable interest and dividend income of $5,000. He has contributed $10,500 to his Keogh plan, and $75,000 in alimony to previous wives. Ray has mortgage interest on his home of $15,500, property taxes of $2,500, charitable contributions of $1,200, and miscellaneous deductions of $3,000 that are subject to the 2% rule. Kentucky Ray's filing status is married, filing jointly. He and his wife have no dependent children. What is the family's adjusted gross income, allowable deductions, exemptions, taxable income and tax due?

Taxable Income, Tax Liability, and Capital Gains/Losses

4. Johnnie Carson, a single man, has the following income: $29,000 in wages, $100 in savings interest, $3,000 in long-term capital gains, and $2,500 in net rental income. Carson contributes $1,000 to his church, paid $6,000 in mortgage interest, had miscellaneous deductions subject to the 2% of AGI rule of $1,000, and paid real estate taxes of $2,400. (a) What is Carson's taxable income? (b) What is Carson's federal tax liability?

5. The Reimers, Jacque and Jean, are self-employed entertainers with no dependents. They were married in 1995 and own everything as joint tenants with rights of survivorship. In 1997, they earned $150,000 in entertainment income net of expenses, $75,000 in net-income from their dance school, $4,000 in dividend income, $3,500 in municipal bond interest, $1,300 in corporate bond interest, and $4,500 in net short-term capital gain income. They contributed $40,000 to their Keogh plan. Their deduction items consisted of $7,500 in mortgage interest on their residence, $3,000 in contributions to Big-Brothers of Wahoo County, unreimbursed medical expenses of $1,200, $500 in contributions to a church memorial for their friend, $2,025 in miscellaneous deductions subject to the 2% of Adjusted Gross Income floor, and $2,400 in state income taxes. What is the Reimers' taxable income? (*Hint: The value of each personal exemption is phased out when a family's income is at a certain higher level, see Endnote 2. In this example, the allowed total exemption is the total exemption less $1,683.*)

6. If the Reimers, Jacque and Jean, are an unmarried couple living together, what would be their tax liability as individuals if Jacque earned $42,000 last year and Jean earned $28,000?

7. Terry and her husband Louis recently lost $15,000 when Foster Brook Trout (FBT) went bankrupt and their stock became worthless. Earlier in the year they had sold their stock in Bullbud Ale to provide money to purchase FBT. When they sold Bullbud Ale, they had a capital gain of $2,500. If Terry and Louis had gross wage income of $67,000, itemized deductions of $8,760, three children, and contributed $2,500 each in their respective 401k plans, what is their tax liability for the 1996 tax year if their filing status is married, filing jointly?

Taxable Income, Tax Liability, and Dependent Care Expenses

8. The Funkel Family (B.J., husband; J.B., wife; and three children) has the following income: $80,000 in wages, $200 in corporate bond interest, $1,200 in corporate dividends, $3,000 in long-term capital losses, $2,500 in net-rental income, and $200 long-term capital gains. The Funkels contribute $4,000 to their church, paid $8,500 in mortgage interest, had miscellaneous deductions subject to the 2% of AGI rule of $2,250, paid state income taxes of $3,411, contributed $13,000 to their qualified retirement savings plans, and $5,000 in dependent-care flexible benefits. What is the Funkel's taxable income?

9. Smitty and Fran are married with a 3 year old child. They live in the home Smitty's father gave them and have no mortgage debt. Last year they paid $900 in real estate taxes. Smitty has self-employment income as a entertainer of $55,000 and Fran's wages as a teacher are $35,000. Smitty contributed $5,500 to his Keogh retirement plan and Fran choose to contribute $3,000 to her 403(b) retirement plan. Last year the cost of day care for their child was $5,500 which they reported and took the child care tax credit of $960 (calculation not shown; see Chapter 6, Section 8 for an example). Smitty and Fran contribute $3,000 per year to their church. They paid $800 in interest on their credit cards, and $700

in interest on their educational loans. They had $750 in dividend and interest income. Their miscellaneous deductions, subject to the 2% of adjusted gross income limitation, totaled $1150. What is their taxable income and tax due — both before and after the child care tax credit is applied?

10. In the above problem, what would be the difference in the answer had Fran participated in the flexible benefit program at her place of work and contributed the maximum amount of $5,000 toward the day-care expenses of her child?

Gifting to Children and the Kiddie Tax

11. Skip and Kathy are trying to decide whether to save their recent inheritance of $45,000 for their child's college education in their name or in the name of their child. Assume that they expect to earn 10% on the invested funds, they are in the 31% marginal tax bracket, and that they do not expect to be eligible for financial aid when their child is college aged. How much in federal taxes do they save for tax year 1996?

12. How much additional taxes would have been saved had Skip and Kathy's child been aged 14, or older?

13. Marie and Joe are trying to decide whether to put $20,000 for their child's college education in their names or in the name of their fifteen-year old child. Assume that they expect to earn 8% on the invested funds, they pay taxes at the 38% marginal tax rate, and that they do not expect to be eligible for financial aid when their child is college aged. In what way they can save taxes, and how much they can save?

After-tax Equivalent Yield

14. Janey is subject to the 39.6% federal marginal tax rate and she is considering investing in a taxable bond yielding 9.7%. What is the after-tax equivalent yield of that investment for Janey?

15. Harry pays taxes at the 28% federal marginal tax rate and is considering two alternatives. First, there is a taxable bond paying 8.7%. Second, there is a tax-exempt bond paying 6.1%. Which investment will pay Harry a higher after-tax return?

16. Lucy pays taxes at the 28% federal marginal tax rate and is considering two alternatives. First, there is a taxable bond paying 9.1%. Second, there is a tax-exempt bond paying 6.7%. Which will pay Lucy a higher after-tax return?

Value of Mortgage Interest Tax Deduction

17. John and Mary are a married couple who file their taxes jointly. They have a mortgage on which they paid $11,495 in mortgage interest with additional itemized deductions of $5,200. John and Mary are in the 28% federal marginal

tax bracket. For 1996, the standard deduction for a married couple filing jointly is $6,700. What is the after tax cost of the mortgage? (Hint: What is the marginal benefit of being a mortgagee?)

18. Phil is single and pays $5,000 in mortgage interest for the current year. He has additional itemized deductions of $2,125. He is in the 28% marginal tax bracket. For 1996, the standard deduction for a single person was $4,000. What is the after-tax cost of the mortgage?

Early Withdrawals from Qualified Retirement Plan

19. Rex, age 50, has been faithfully saving in his 401(k) plan each year for the past 20 years. Ed has been earning 9% on his deposits and now needs $75,000 to pay for his child's college education. Ed recognizes that, if he withdraws the money before the age of 59.5, he will have to pay a 10% penalty tax in addition to his 28% marginal rate of taxation. How much does he have to withdraw in order to have $75,000 after he has paid the taxes due?

Federal Estate Taxes

20. Bacchus Bob has died. Bob's wife, Betty Lou, jointly owned everything with Bob and had rights to survivorship. The entire family fortune of $1,250,000 is now Betty Lou's alone. What is Bob's gross estate and taxes due?

21. Betty Lou died shortly after Bob's death. Assuming that Betty Lou had paid $12,500 for Bob's funeral, how much does her estate owe in federal estate taxes following her death?

Assets in an Irrevocable Bypass Trust Reduce Estate Taxes

22. Bob's younger brother Buck is an estate lawyer that Bob never listened to. Several years ago, Buck suggested that Bob and Betty Lou do some estate planning. In fact, if his suggestions had been followed, they would have structured their estate plan to provide for two trusts, each with one-half of the household's assets. In this way, when the first spouse died, one-half of the assets would already belong to the surviving spouse and one half of their assets would be left as Qualified Terminal Interest Property (Q-TIP) Trust to provide income for the survivor but, at the death of the second spouse, to distribute the assets to Bob and Betty Lou's children. As such, the surviving spouse does not own the by-pass trust. What would the estate taxes have been under this scenario upon Bob's death?

23. When Betty Lou subsequently passes away, what are the estate taxes due? What are the estate tax savings compared to no planning (question #22)?

24. Mrs. Kerby thinks she needs estate planning. At this time, she owns everything as a joint tenant with rights of survivorship with her husband, and she estimates the total family estate to be worth $23,435,000. What would be the estate taxes

due upon her death, if no estate planning occurs? Assume she predeceases her husband.

25. Assuming that Mr. Kerby is able to preserve the entire family estate until his death, what would be the estate taxes due at his death if no further estate planning is done? *(Hint: If taxable estates are greater than $10,000,000, 5% of the cumulative transfers in excess of that amount should be added.)*

26. If Mr. and Mrs. Kerby would have amicably divided the estate in half prior to the death of Mrs. Kerby, what would have been the estate taxes paid and the total tax savings? *(Hint: If taxable estates are greater than $10,000,000, 5% of the cumulative transfers in excess of that amount should be added.)*

SELECTED REFERENCES

Annual publications

Bernstein, P. (ed.). *The Ernst & Young tax guide*, annual. New York: Wiley.

Bernstein, P. (ed.). *The Ernst & Young's tax-saving strategies*, annual. New York: Wiley.

Esaner, W., et al. *Consumer Report's book guide to income tax preparation*, annual. Yonkers, NY: Consumer Report Books.

J. K. Lasser's your income tax, annual. New York: Prentice-Hall.

Internal Revenue Service. *Student's guide to federal income tax*. Publication 4. Washington, DC: U.S. Government Printing Office.

Internal Revenue Service. *Federal income taxes*, annual. Publication 17. Washington, DC: U.S. Government Printing Office.

Internal Revenue Service. *Federal estate and gift taxes*. Publication 448. Washington, DC: U.S. Government Printing Office.

Other publications

Clifford, D. (1989). *Plan your estate*. Berkeley, CA: Nolo Press.

College for Financial Planning (1988). *Study guide, CFP VI: Estate planning*, College for Financial Planning.

Esperti, R. A., & Peterson, R. L. (1991). *The handbook of estate planning*. New York: McGraw-Hill.

Garman, E. T., & Forgue, R. E. (1997). *Personal finance*, (5th ed.). Boston: Houghton Mifflin Company. (Excellent taxes chapter.)

Leimberg, S. R. (1995), et al. *The tools and techniques of estate planning*. (8th ed.). Cincinnati, OH: National Underwriter.

Rainaldi, F. L. (1994). *The Kugler cases: Practical applications in estate and business planning*. Byrn Mawr, PA: Rainaldi & Associates, American Society of CLU and ChFC.

Shenkman, M. M. (1991). *Estate planning guide*. New York: John Wiley & Sons.

What you ought to know about living trusts (1992). Chicago, IL: Commerce Clearing House, Inc.

ENDNOTES

1.   There is a 3% reduction of certain itemized items if one's 1996 adjusted gross income exceeds $117,950 (or $58,975 if the taxpayer is married and files a separate return).

2.   For higher income taxpayers ($176,950 for marrieds filing jointly and $117,950 for singles), the value of each personal exemption is phased out. The effect is to increase one's marginal tax rate.

3.   Not shown are the filing status for "head of household" and "married filing separately."

4.   Some states also levy **inheritance taxes**, payable by the heirs, upon the receipt of the property.

Chapter 11
Planned Purchasing Math

▼ Marginal Utility Analysis and the Law of Diminishing Marginal Utility

▼ The Equimarginal Principle

▼ Using a Major Purchase Score Sheet

▼ Paying Cash Versus Paying on Credit

▼ Accepting a Rebate Versus Selecting a Lower Interest Rate Loan

▼ The Effect of a Trade-in on Cost

▼ The Effect of a Down Payment on Cost

▼ Buying on Credit Versus Leasing

▼ Refinancing a Major Purchase

Chapter 11
Planned Purchasing Math

Vickie L. Hampton[1]

OVERVIEW

As consumers, we make numerous buying decisions daily. Planned purchases, however, are made only infrequently. **Planned purchases** are consumer goods and services that are more costly than items purchased daily, and because such purchases are relatively expensive, the consumer is likely to go through an extensive decision-making process before making the actual purchase. Examples include cameras, computers, and vehicles.

It is critical to one's personal financial well-being to carefully consider aspects of expensive purchases. An **impulse purchase** (e.g., buying a new CD for $15 without fully considering needs and alternatives) may not be the wisest use of one's money, but it is only $15. By cutting back on a single night's entertainment or carrying lunch for a few days, one could easily cut $15 from his/her expenditures to make up for such a purchase. On the other hand if a consumer impulsively purchases a new $2,500 computer and finances it for 24 months, this impulse purchase could seriously affect one's budget for two years or longer.

There are many aspects to the process of making planned purchases. The consumer needs to be able to evaluate his/her wants. This involves decisions regarding the kind of product or service desired (e.g., television, computer) as well as decisions regarding the desired options (e.g., CD Rom, 17-inch monitor). With the large variety of products and options available, planned purchasing decisions can become very complex. And adding to that complexity are related questions: Does the purchase fit into one's budget? Should one pay cash or use credit? If financing, should he/she make a large down payment or a small one, take advantage of a rebate in lieu of a low-interest loan, and/or use a trade-in to lower costs? All of these issues make most planned purchasing decisions more complex than they may first appear.

---

[1]Vickie L. Hampton, Ph.D., CFP, CFCS, Associate Professor, Human Ecology, The University of Texas, Austin, TX 78712. v.hampton@mail.utexas.edu

However, there are ways to answer these questions for the consumer who wishes to make the best use of his/her resources. Examples follow.

Marginal utility analysis and the equimarginal principle provide a theoretical approach which helps focus on the additional satisfaction that is received from spending an additional dollar. **Utility** is the ability of a good or service to satisfy a human want, and it is measured by the amount of satisfaction received from a good or service. **Marginal utility analysis** refers to the extra utility, or satisfaction, that a consumer obtains from one additional unit of a specific product or service. For example, you might receive a certain amount of satisfaction (utility) from eating a piece of candy (utility), and you can obtain a slightly different amount of satisfaction (marginal utility) from eating a second piece of candy. This concept is important in consumer decision-making because it helps concentrate attention on the additional utility received when more and more units of a good are consumed. The **equimarginal principle** focuses on the amount of additional satisfaction received by spending an additional dollar.

A major purchase score sheet supplies a usable strategy to help focus on the importance of various characteristics of a major purchase and to compare competing products rationally. Also critical when making large purchase decisions is calculation of the relative "cost of using credit versus paying cash."

Although not exclusively related to vehicle purchases, there are additional decisions that are common when purchasing something like an automobile or truck. One may need to choose between borrowing using the dealer's low-interest financing or accepting a dealer rebate and financing with a higher-interest loan. There will often be issues on whether to trade-in an existing vehicle as well as how much down payment to make on a loan. Finally, the decision whether to buy with a typical loan or to lease is now quite common. Each of these questions is important to one's personal finances and deserves consideration. However, when actually making a vehicle purchase it sometimes may be very difficult to keep all these factors separate. Therefore, it takes an informed consumer to be able to evaluate all the important issues.

There is also a final planned purchasing decision that is important to understand after a purchase has been made. While most common in respect to housing, this decision could apply to any credit arrangement. At times when interest rates have fallen after one has entered into a long-term, fixed-rate loan, decisions regarding refinancing the loan may by necessary. **Refinancing** is simply a situation where one takes out a new, lower-interest loan to pay off an original, higher-interest loan. In doing so, it is necessary to calculate whether the costs of refinancing are actually worth the benefits received.

This chapter examines marginal utility analysis and the law of diminishing marginal utility, the equimarginal principle, using a major purchase score sheet, paying cash versus paying on credit, accepting a rebate versus selecting a lower interest rate loan, the effect of a trade-in on cost, the effect of a down payment on cost, buying on credit versus leasing, and refinancing a major purchase.

EXAMPLES OF MATHEMATICAL CONCEPTS RELATED TO PLANNED PURCHASING

1. Marginal Utility and the Law of Diminishing Marginal Utility

Formula 11.1: $MU = \dfrac{\partial U}{\partial Q}$

Where: MU = marginal utility; ∂U = change of utility; and ∂Q = change of quantity.

▼   **Example 11.1:** Tony is a hungry college student who stopped by the campus pizza parlor for the lunch buffet. After eating the first slice of pizza, Tony assigns the utility (or satisfaction) he received from eating it a score of 10 (on a 1 - 10 scale with 10 being the highest). Tony thought the first slice was great and his total utility from that first slice of pizza is rated a 10. After eating the second, third, and fourth slices, Tony raised his total utility to 19, 26, and 30, respectively, and he then decided that he was too full for another slice. What is Tony's marginal utility from each slice of pizza?

Solution: Tony's marginal utility for each slice of pizza is

First slice: $MU = \dfrac{10}{1} = 10$ Third slice: $MU = \dfrac{26 - 19}{1} = 7$

Second slice: $MU = \dfrac{19 - 10}{1} = 9$ Fourth slice: $MU = \dfrac{30 - 26}{1} = 4$

❖   **Interpretation:** While utility is the amount of satisfaction received from a good or service, **utils** are measures of utility. The marginal utility (or satisfaction) is important because it concentrates on the additional utility received when more and more units of a good are consumed. While one generally does not assign a value to the utility received from everything consumed in real life, the concept of **diminishing marginal utility** does explain the very real-life fact that as people consume more and more of any product their total utility increases but at a diminishing rate. This means that specific consumer wants can be fulfilled with succeeding fewer units of a commodity. This is true not only of food but also for clothing, vehicles, and other goods. As a result, consumers resist buying more of any one good unless the price drops. Sellers recognize the principle of diminishing marginal utility by lowering the price on a product in order to induce consumers to purchase large quantities of a product.

2. The Equimarginal Principle

Formula 11.2: $\dfrac{MU_{good\ 1}}{P_1} = \dfrac{MU_{good\ 2}}{P_2} = \ldots = \dfrac{MU_{good\ n}}{P_n} = M$ per \$ amount

Where: MU = marginal utility; P = price; and 1, 2, ... n = good 1, 2, ... n.

▼ **Example 11.2:** Suppose that Tony (from the previous example) wanted a little more variety for lunch. In addition to pizza which costs \$1.50 per slice, the pizza parlor also serves soft drinks for \$0.50 a glass, and salads for \$2.00 each. The following table summarizes the marginal utility Tony receives from these three food products. What would Tony have for lunch if his budget limit was \$2.00? What would he select if he could spend \$6.00 for lunch?

	Quantity	Total Utility	Marginal Utility	MU/Price
Pizza (\$1.50)	1	10	10	6.67
	2	19	9	6.00
	3	26	7	4.67
	4	30	4	2.67
Soft drinks (\$0.50)	1	4	4	8.00
	2	7	3	6.00
	3	8	1	2.00
Salad (\$2.00)	1	12	12	6.00
	2	18	6	3.00
	3	20	2	1.00

Solution: With \$2.00 for lunch, Tony could buy (1) four soft drinks (4 × \$0.50 = \$2) or (2) one salad (1 × \$2) or (3) one slice of pizza (1 × \$1.50) and one soft drink (1 × \$0.50). From those choices, a rational Tony wishing to maximize his choice would select one slice of pizza and one soft drink because his marginal utility for the dollars spent is the highest for the first soft drink (8.00) and second highest for the first slice of pizza (6.67). If Tony wants to spend \$6.00 for lunch, he would have one soft drink (1 × \$0.50), two slices of pizza (2 × \$1.50 = \$3), and one salad (1 × \$2). This results from choosing the products which provide the most added satisfaction per dollar spent that can be purchased for \$6.00.

❖ **Interpretation:** The equimarginal principle helps us focus on the items that generate larger amounts of additional satisfaction by spending an additional dollar. This can be useful in two situations: (1) when trying to decide among a large number of products, and (2) when deciding whether to purchase additional options on products (such as adding a fancy CD player to a new vehicle). In reality, consumers cannot exactly measure marginal utility and sometimes emotions get in the way of rational consumer behavior; however, the theory can still help people understand the decision-making process.

3. Using a Major Purchases Score Sheet

Formula 11.3: $T = W_1 \cdot R_1 + W_2 \cdot R_2 + \ldots + W_n \cdot R_n$

Where: T = total score for each product; W = weight based on importance of attribute; R = rating of each attribute; and 1, 2, ... n = attribute 1, 2, ... n.

▼ **Example 11.3:** Jose is hunting for an apartment and he decides to use a **major purchases score sheet**. This is a decision-making grid that allows one to visually and mathematically weigh the decision he/she is about to make. The first task in developing such a score sheet is to determine the various criteria for making the decision. Next each criterion is assigned a weight that reflects the importance each has in the mind of the consumer. Each alternative is then given a score that indicates how well it performs on that criterion. Jose has looked at several apartments and has narrowed his choices to three, but he can't decide which would provide the best value for his money. The characteristics that are important to Jose are sufficient square footage, proximity to work, swimming pool availability, and personal safety. Of these characteristics, safety and square footage are most important so Jose gives them a rating of 5 (on a scale of 1 - 5, with 5 being the most important). Proximity to work is weighted 4 and a swimming pool is rated 2. With his criteria weighted, Jose visits the three apartments again and rates each one on the four characteristics that are important to him. His ratings are presented in the following table.

Apartment Buying Score Sheet Table							
Attribute	**Weight**	**First Apartment** Cost = $700		**Second Apartment** Cost = $725		**Third Apartment** Cost = $735	
		Rating (1-10)	Weighted Score	Rating (1-10)	Weighted Score	Rating (1-10)	Weighted Score
Square footage	5	8	40	9	45	7	35
Proximity to work	4	6	24	8	32	8	32
Swimming pool	2	10	20	6	12	7	14
Safety	5	7	35	8	40	8	40
Total Score			119		129		121
Weighted Score/Dollar			0.17		0.18		0.16

Solution: Looking at the total weighted scores for each apartment, we see that if all these apartments are within Jose's price range he would pick the second apartment since it has the highest weighted score. Even after considering the price of each apartment, the second apartment provides the highest weighted score per dollar spent.

❖ **Interpretation:** By identifying the attributes of a purchase that are important and then assigning a weight to those attributes based on the level of importance, a consumer can simplify complex purchase decisions. The scale that one chooses for the weightings can vary. A scale of 1 - 5 was used in the example, but one might prefer a 1 - 3 or a 1 - 10 scale. Alternatively, one might want to assign a percentage of 100% to each characteristic. For example in the apartment decision, one might say that square footage and safety each comprise 30 percent of the total weighting while proximity of work makes up 25 percent and swimming pool accounts for the final 15 percent. Regardless of the weightings used, the system of using a major purchases score sheet assists in adding objectivity to the decision-making process and making more informed decisions.

4. Paying Cash Versus Purchasing on Credit

Formula 11.4: $C = (P \cdot N - CP) - CP \cdot R \cdot Y$

Where: C = cost of credit; P = credit payment; N = number of payments; CP = cash price of purchase; R = rate of return earned on savings; and Y = number of years.

▼ **Example 11.4:** Idelia and John are considering the purchase of a new camera that costs $435 including taxes. The retailer offers 12 percent, 6-month financing with monthly payments of $75.06. Idelia and John have the money to buy the camera in their savings account earning 3 percent. What is the cost of buying the camera on credit rather than using their savings to pay for the camera?

Solution: $C = (\$75.06 \times 6 - \$435) - \$435 \times 0.03 \times 0.5$
$C = (\$450.36 - \$435) - \$6.53$
$C = \$8.83$

❖ **Interpretation:** The cost of credit for Idelia and John is $8.83. The critical factors in comparing the cost of buying on credit versus the cost of paying cash are the dollar cost of credit and the opportunity cost of using cash. The **dollar cost of credit** is defined as all additional costs of using credit (e.g., interest, transaction fees, over-the-limit fees, required insurance, late payment fees) above the actual cost of paying cash for a purchase. The **opportunity cost** of using cash is the foregone interest that could be earned in savings. Note that in Formula 11.4, the opportunity cost is calculated with the simple interest method. The opportunity cost would be higher if the compounding interest method is used. The difference between those two costs is the **cost of using credit rather than cash.**

5. Accepting a Rebate Versus Selecting a Lower Interest Rate Loan

Formula 11.5: $C = (P_I \cdot N_I - R) - P_D \cdot N_D$

Where: C = cost difference; P = credit payment; N = number of payments; R = rebate; I = independent financing; and D = dealer financing.

▼ **Example 11.5:** Fred and Missy need a new vehicle. They have shopped several weeks and negotiated what they believe is a good price of $13,000. They have also shopped for vehicle loans, and the two best options are an 8.5 percent, 3-year loan with their bank ($410.38 monthly payment) or a 6.5 percent, 3-year loan through the dealership ($398.44 monthly payment). The dealership also offers a $700 rebate on this vehicle but only if the buyer does not use the dealer's low-interest financing. Considering the rebate, which of the two loans is the better deal for Fred and Missy?

Solution: C = ($410.38 × 36 - $700) - $398.44 × 36
C = ($14,774 - $700) - $14,344
C = $14,074 - $14,344
C = - $270

Fred and Missy will save $270 by using the 8.5 percent bank financing and the rebate rather than using the 6.5 percent dealer financing where they forego the rebate.

❖   **Interpretation:** The choice of accepting either a cash rebate or low-rate financing is common with vehicle purchases. Therefore, it is important for a consumer to know the cost of alternative financing sources before making the rebate/low-rate financing choice. The opportunity cost of the rebate must be considered as a reduction to the cost of independent financing (or alternatively as an additional cost of the low-rate dealer financing).

6. The Effect of a Trade-In on Cost

Formula 11.6: $C = P_1 \cdot N_1 - P_2 \cdot N_2$

Where: C = cost difference; P = payment; N = number of payments; and 1, 2 = payment method 1, 2.

▼   **Example 11.6.1:** Sally plans on paying cash for a new stereo. The model she wants costs $1,200 at each of two retailers, but one of the retailers is offering to accept used electronic equipment in trade. This retailer has offered Sally $55 for an old television that Sally hardly uses. What is the effect of the trade-in on the cost of the stereo purchase?

Solution: C = $1,200 × 1 - ($1,200 - $55) × 1
C = $1,200 - $1,145
C = $55

❖   **Interpretation:** Some cost calculations are simple to interpret, like this one. Occasionally, however, such calculations are difficult to interpret as shown in the next example.

▼   **Example 11.6.2:** Jake is negotiating the purchase of a late-model used truck. He would like to trade his current vehicle as part of the deal. Slick's Used Cars has offered him $2,000 for his current vehicle in trade for a $10,000 truck (including tax, title, and license). Second Chance Used Cars has offered Jake a generous $2,500 for his current vehicle in trade for a similar late-model truck also costing $10,000 (including tax, title, and license). Regardless of which deal Jake selects, he will finance the purchase with a 10.5 percent, 3-year loan through his credit union. This will result in a monthly payment of $260 at Slick's or $244 at Second Chance. What is the effect of Jake's trade-in on the cost of the late-model truck?

Solution: $C = \$260 \times 36 - \$244 \times 36$
$C = \$9,360 - \$8,784$
$C = \$576$

❖   **Interpretation:** The effect of a trade-in on the cost of a purchase may seem obvious, whether there is one dealer or two. However, it should be noted that when additional variables, such as financing, are involved, the impact is more difficult to determine. In this case, the impact of the financing variable is much larger that just the difference in the value of the trade-in. Additionally, in real life this effect commingles with the impact of other variables, such as differences in the price of the purchase, interest rates, rebate offers, pay-off terms, additional costs of financing, and amount of down payment. Purchasing a vehicle, in particular, is somewhat like playing in someone else's chemistry laboratory. The salesperson will want to mix all the chemicals in the beaker together so that the consumer loses track of exactly what is happening. On the other hand, it is in the best interest of the consumer to add one chemical to the beaker at a time. Only by looking at the impact of each individual variable will a consumer be able to make an informed decision.

7. The Effect of a Down Payment on Cost

Formula 11.7: $C = (D_1 + P_1 \cdot N_1 + D_1 \cdot R \cdot Y) - (D_2 + P_2 \cdot N_2 + D_2 \cdot R \cdot Y)$

Where: C = cost difference; D = down payment; P = credit payment; N = number of payments; R = rate of return earned on savings; Y = number of years; and 1, 2 = payment method 1, 2.

▼   **Example 11.7:** Kevin has always wanted a motorcycle, and now that he is out of college and has managed to save $4,000 in a money market mutual fund earning 4.5 percent he has decided to buy one. Kevin has selected a very nice bike that costs $9,000 with 2-year, 13 percent financing at his credit union. The credit union requires a 10 percent down payment, but Kevin cannot decide whether to put the minimum amount of $900 ($9,000 × .10) down (resulting in a $385 monthly payment) or to make a $4,000 down payment (resulting in a $238 monthly payment). What is the difference in the cost of the motorcycle purchase as a result of the down payment chosen?

Solution: $C = (\$900 + \$385 \times 24 + \$900 \times 0.045 \times 2)$
$\quad\quad - (\$4,000 + \$238 \times 24 + \$4,000 \times 0.045 \times 2)$
$C = (\$900 + \$9,240 + \$81) - (\$4,000 + \$5,712 + \$360)$
$C = \$10,221 + \$10,072$
$C = \$149$

Making the larger down payment would save Kevin $149 on the motorcycle purchase.

❖   **Interpretation:** The effect of a down payment on cost considers the same issues as the cost of cash versus credit decision. In the case of a down payment, the consumer is combining a cash and a credit purchase. The cost difference will depend on the differential between the interest rate that the consumer has to pay to borrow money and the rate of return the consumer can earn on investments. Note that the opportunity cost (the potential interest income) is calculated using the simple interest method. The opportunity costs would be higher if the compounding interest method is used.

8. Buying on Credit Versus Leasing

Formula 11.8: $C = (FC_B + MC_B + OC_B - R_B) - (FC_L + MC_L + OC_L)$

Where: C = cost difference; FC = front-end costs; MC = monthly costs; OC = other costs; R = residual value; B = buying on credit; L = leasing.

❖   **Example 11.8:** Chuck and Nancy have just found a beautiful bright red Chevy C1500 X-Cab with all the options they need. They have negotiated a price of $15,000 plus $900 sales tax and $125 in title and license fees. If they finance the truck, they will make a $4,000 down payment and use 9 percent financing for 36 months with a monthly payment of $350. They have also been offered a lease with a $304 monthly payment for 36 months and monthly sales tax payments of $20. The lease requires a capital cost reduction of $399 plus title and license fees. It also has a disposition fee of $250. The lease allows 12,000 miles per year, and they will be charged 15¢ per mile on miles over 12,000; however, Chuck and Nancy don't believe they will put that many miles on the truck. The **residual value** (the projected value of a leased asset at the end of the lease time period) of the truck is expected to be $8,000 at the end of three years. Assuming Chuck and Nancy can earn 4 percent on their savings, will financing or leasing the truck be less expensive? The worksheet below illustrates the calculation process.

Buying on Credit Versus Leasing Worksheet—Chevy C1500 X-Cab		
	Buying on Credit	**Leasing**
FRONT-END COSTS		
Down payment	$ 4,000	
Capital cost reduction		$ 399
Sales tax	$ 900	
Fees, license, etc.	$ 125	$ 125
Total front-end costs	**$ 5,025**	**$ 524**
MONTHLY COSTS		
Loan/lease payment	$ 350	$ 304
Sales tax		$ 20
Total monthly costs (payment + sales tax) × (number of months)	**$ 12,600**	**$11,664**
OTHER COSTS		
Lost interest (opportunity cost) (down payment or capital cost reduction) × (interest rate) × (number of years)	$ 480	$ 48
Disposition fee and/or other end-of-lease charges		$ 250
Cost at end of lease	**$18,105**	**$12,486**
Residual value	$ 8,000	
TOTAL COST	**$10,105**	**$12,486**

Solution: Buying the truck on credit will be $2,381 less expensive than leasing the truck assuming Chuck and Nancy do not exceed the annual mileage limit on the lease. The difference would be even greater if the mileage limit were exceeded.

❖ **Interpretation:** Automobile leasing is becoming more and more popular with approximately one-third of all new vehicle purchases being leases. As with all purchase arrangements, it is critical that a consumer understand all the potential costs involved. Both the down payment and the monthly payments are typically lower for a lease than for a loan for the same vehicle, thus, giving the appearance that leasing is less expensive than borrowing. However, there are additional costs of leasing that must be considered. On an **open-end lease**, the consumer has to pay the difference between the projected and the actual market value at the end of the lease if the vehicle is worth less than expected. On a **closed-end lease** (also called a **walkaway lease**), the consumer pays no charge if the end-of-lease market value of the vehicle is lower than the originally projected residual value. In this instance, there is no charge for excess depreciation, however, the consumer is charged 10 - 15¢ per mile if the vehicle has more miles on it than specified in the lease agreement. The **capitalized cost reduction** represents the moneys paid on the lease at its inception including any down payment or the value of a trade-in. Other costs that may be included in a lease are a **security deposit** (which is refundable), an **acquisition fee** (similar to a down payment, but not refundable), a **disposition fee** (assessed at the end of the lease to get the vehicle ready for sale), and/or a **termination fee** (which may be charged if one wants to get out of the lease agreement early, or when the vehicle is wrecked or stolen). At the end of any lease, the consumer can purchase the vehicle for its market value. In contrast, at the end of a loan repayment schedule the consumer already owns the vehicle.

9. Refinancing a Major Purchase

Formula 11.9: $S = 12 (PI_1 - PI_2) FVA_{R,Y} - (P + C) FV_{R,Y}$

Where: S = savings from refinancing; PI = monthly payment for principle and interest; FVA = future value of an annuity factor; P = prepayment penalties; C = closing costs; FV = future value factor; R = rate of return earned on savings; and Y = number of years expected to pay on the loan.

▼ **Example 11.9:** Marcia purchased a condominium 3 years ago and financed $75,000 with a 10 percent, 30-year mortgage and a $658 principal and interest payment. The mortgage has no prepayment penalty. Marcia read that interest rates had fallen so she shopped for mortgages and found she could qualify for an 8.5 percent, 30-year mortgage with a $577 principle and interest payment with closing costs of $2,725. Assuming Marcia expects to live in the condo 5 more years and can earn 6 percent on her investments, how much can she save by refinancing?

Solution: $S = 12 \times (\$658 - \$577) \times 5.637 - \$2,725 \times 1.338$
$S = \$5,479 - \$3,646$
$S = \$1,833$

❖ **Interpretation:** When taking out a new, lower-interest loan to pay off an existing loan, a consumer must consider the savings in monthly payments compared to the up-front costs of prepaying the existing mortgage and the cost of acquiring the new loan. While the calculation can be done ignoring the time value of money, the analysis is more accurate if the rate of return one can earn on savings is also considered. In this example, Marcia expects to save $1,833 by refinancing her condominium mortgage loan. The number of years one expects to live in the house is very important in the decision to refinance an existing mortgage. In this example, the future value of an annuity factor and the future value factor can be found in Appendix A.3 and A.1, and the approach is called table method. The problem in this example can also be solved with financial calculator, computer, or formula methods. You may try to find how by yourself.

INFORMATION AND COMPUTING RESOURCES

1. There are many excellent books available on the various aspects of planned purchasing. *Improving Your Credit and Reducing Your Debt* by G. Liberman & A. Lavine (Wiley, 1994) discusses buying versus leasing and refinancing.

2. Many personal finance and general magazines, such as *Money, Kiplinger's Personal Finance Magazine, Smart Money, Worth, Consumer Reports, Business Week, NewsWeek,* and *U.S. News & World Report*, periodically feature articles on credit use, how to purchase automobiles using credit and leasing, and mortgage refinancing. They will occasionally print wise buying articles as well.

3. Numerous materials have also been developed on planned purchasing by government agencies and are available through the Consumer Information Center. For a free *Consumer Information Catalog*, write to Consumer Information Center, Pueblo, CO 81009. In addition, the Agricultural Extension Agencies in many states have developed educational materials on these subjects. For information on what is available in your state, call your country agricultural extension office. The number will be listed in your local phone directory.

4. *Expert Lease* is IBM compatible software available through Chart Software at 800-418-8450 ($50 for the standard version; $100 for the professional version, with residuals and prices for 204 makes of cars and trucks, plus one free update). This program will complete a lease-buy analysis and will easily show how changing one factor affects the others.

5. The following web sites have information for car purchases:

    ▪ *Auto-By-Tel:* http://www.autobytel.com/ (Internet broker with links to 1,300 dealers).

    ▪ *AutoHelp:* http://thespher.com/AutoHelp/ (Offers quotes on new cars, locates any make and model of used car anywhere in the world and finds new factory parts worldwide).

- *Automobile Information Center:* http://www.autoinfocenter.com/ (A database for buying and selling cars).

- *AutoLink:* http://www.autolink.com/ (Websites of interest to the auto industry).

- *Auto Outlet:* http://205.230.55.103/auto/index.html (A used-car-sales bulletin board)

- *Dealernet:* http://www.dealernet.com/ (A compendium of dealers, leasing information and hundreds of web links).

- *Edmund Publications:* http://www.enews.com/magazines/edmunds (Automobile buyer's guide).

- *Internet AutoSource:* http://autosource-usa.com (2,500 pages of information on auto shows and events, used-car prices, and a database that compares specifications for different makes and models).

- *James Martindale's Calculators On-Line Center:* http://www-sci.lib.usi.edu/HSG/RefCalculators.html (More than 3,000 calculators that assist with a variety of financial planning calculations.)

- *The Finance Center:* http://www.financenter.com (Offers a wide variety of financial planning information including numerous financial calculators.)

EXERCISE PROBLEMS

Marginal Utility Analysis and the Law of Diminishing Marginal Utility

1. Melinda is interested in adding to her wardrobe of shoes. She has picked out three pairs that she really likes and estimates her total satisfaction from these shoes as 30 if she buys just one pair, 50 if she purchases two pairs, and 65 if she buys all three pairs. How much marginal utility will Melinda receive from each pair of shoes? Does the marginal utility she receives conform to the law of diminishing marginal utility?

2. Dale needs a new telephone for his five-room apartment. At the store the salesperson points out how convenient it would be if Dale had four phones rather than just one. Dale knows that he would receive a great deal of satisfaction from having the first phone, but he is less certain about the additional phones. Dale decides to leave the store so that he can think about his needs. Over a soda, he estimates that he would receive 20 units of satisfaction from the first phone and that his total satisfaction would rise to 38, 48, and 53 with each additional phone. What is Dale's marginal utility from each phone?

The Equimarginal Principle

3. Tim is shopping for a professional wardrobe for interviewing. He is looking at suits, shirts, and neckties. The following table summarizes the utility Tim would receive from various quantities of these items. Calculate the marginal utility and the marginal utility per dollar for each item. What would Tim purchase if he has no more than $250 to spend? What would he purchase if he has $300 to spend?

	Quantity	Total Utility	Marginal Utility	MU/Price
Suits ($150)	1	200		
	2	325		
Shirts ($30)	1	50		
	2	90		
	3	120		
Neckties ($20)	1	40		
	2	70		
	3	90		

4. Bonnie has just moved into her first apartment after graduating from college. She has budgeted $425 to furnish her kitchen, but she has so many appliances she would really like to have. The following table summarizes the utility Bonnie would receive from these items. Calculate the marginal utility and the marginal utility per dollar for each item. What would Bonnie purchase if she has no more than $425 to spend? If she decided to "break the budget" and buy just one more item, what would she purchase and by how much would she exceed her original budget limit?

	Quantity	Total Utility	Marginal Utility	MU/Price
Microwave ($200)	1	300		
	2	35		
Small television ($130)	1	150		
	2	170		
Electric mixer ($220)	1	240		
	2	250		
Dishes	3	100		
($50 for 3 place settings)	6	190		
	9	270		
	12	340		
	15	360		

Using a Major Purchase Score Sheet

5. Ricky and Rhonda have decided it's time to get in shape, and they have decided to purchase a motorized treadmill. They have weighted the characteristics they feel are most important on a scale of 1 - 5 and compared the three models listed in the table below. Assuming they are willing to spend up to $1,500 but would like to purchase the model that gives them the highest weighted score for their money, which treadmill would they buy?

Treadmill Buying Table							
Attribute	Weight	First Treadmill Cost = $1,500		Second Treadmill Cost = $900		Third Treadmill Cost = $850	
		Rating (1-10)	Weighted Score	Rating (1-10)	Weighted Score	Rating (1-10)	Weighted Score
Ergonomics	5	9		10		7	
Reliability	4	8		8		6	
Smoothness	4	10		9		9	
Noise	3	7		6		9	
Adjustments	2	10		8		6	
Total Score							
Weighted Score/Dollar							

6. Trey wants to purchase a bread maker. He has rated the various attributes that are important to him and has compared three models that are within his price range. The following table summarizes this information. Which bread maker should Trey buy if he would like to get the model within his $200 price range that has the highest score? If Trey wanted to purchase the model with the highest weighted score per dollar, which model would he purchase?

Bread Maker Buying Table							
Attribute	Weight	First Bead Maker Cost = $165		Second Bread Maker Cost = $195		Third Bread Maker Cost = $200	
		Rating (1-10)	Weighted Score	Rating (1-10)	Weighted Score	Rating (1-10)	Weighted Score
Ease of use	5	8		10		9	
Cleaning	4	9		8		10	
Noise	3	5		6		5	
Cycle time	2	10		9		8	
Total Score							
Weighted Score/Dollar							

7. *Out-of-Class Exercise* Select a product that you are interested in purchasing. Identify the characteristics of the product that are most important to you, then decide on an importance weighting for each characteristic. After completing the weightings, compare three different models rating the characteristics of each model on a scale of 1 - 10. Based on the weighted scores, which product would you purchase? Based on the weighted score per dollar, which product would you purchase?

Paying Cash Versus Purchasing on Credit

8. Jamie's auto insurance for her 1996 Grand Am costs $1,200 for the year. She can pay $1,200 in October or she can pay $107 monthly for 12 months. If Jamie has the $1,200 in savings earning 4 percent, how much is the cost of financing the insurance premium?

9. Robert has selected a very nice VCR costing $375 including taxes to complete his home entertainment center. If he pays cash, he will use funds from his 2.5 percent savings account. However, the store offers 9-month, 16 percent financing with monthly payments of $45. How much more will the VCR cost if Robert finances the VCR rather than paying cash?

10. Becky and Gary are expecting their first child so they feel they need a camcorder. The local appliance store has the model they want for $960 including taxes, and the store offers 12-month interest-free financing if all 12 monthly payments of $80 are paid on time. If they miss any of the payments, they will have to pay 21 percent on the loan resulting in monthly payments of $89. Assuming Becky and Gary have the $960 in a money market mutual fund earning 5 percent, how much can they save by making monthly payments if they make all the payments on time? How much more will the financing cost, compared to paying cash, if Becky and Gary miss any of the monthly payments?

Accepting a Rebate Versus Selecting a Lower Interest Rate Loan

11. The local auto dealership is offering 1.9 percent financing or a $1,500 rebate on the vehicle Tammy and Ralph want to finance. They plan on financing $15,000 over 4 years, and they could get a 9 percent loan from their credit union. The monthly payment on the dealer financing would be $325 while the monthly payment on the credit union financing would be $373. Which of the financing offers will save Tammy and Ralph the most money?

12. Amie is purchasing her first new vehicle. She has selected a small pickup truck and will finance $12,000 over 3 years. Her bank has offered her 10.5 percent financing ($390 monthly payment), but the dealer offers either a 2.9 percent loan ($348 monthly payment) or a $900 rebate. Amie is confused. Which deal is most cost effective for Amie?

13. *Out-of-Class Exercise* Look in a local newspaper and/or talk with auto dealers and lenders. Using information on rebate/low-interest financing offered through dealers and auto financing available through lenders, calculate which would be most cost effective for a vehicle you are interested in buying.

The Effect of a Trade-In on Cost

14. Ted and Carri are purchasing a new computer for $2,700 and financing it over 2 years with a 9 percent loan and a $123 monthly payment. However, the retailer will take their old computer in trade and reduce the loan to $2,000. This would reduce their monthly payment to $91. How much would the trade-in reduce the cost of the new computer?

15. Brooks has just negotiated the price of a new 4-wheel drive vehicle for $23,000 including taxes and licenses. He plans on making a $7,000 down payment and financing it over 4 years with an 8 percent loan. His only question is whether to trade his current car in or to sell it privately. If the dealer will give Brooks $5,000 for his trade-in, what is the cost savings over the life of the loan? The monthly payment without the trade-in would be $391 while the monthly payment with the trade-in would be $269.

The Effect of a Down Payment on Cost

16. Julia and Chad are buying a new boat for $15,000 using a 13 percent, 3-year loan. The required down payment is $1,500; however, they are considering a down payment of $4,000. If they make the $1,500 down payment, the monthly payment would be $455 while it would be only $371 if they put $4,000 down. Assuming Julia and Chad can earn 6 percent on their savings, how much would they save by making the larger down payment?

17. Eduardo is purchasing a $4,000 big-screen television. He will make at least a $100 down payment, but he is considering a $1,000 down payment. Eduardo will finance the television with a 14 percent, 18-month loan. With the $100 down payment, the monthly payment would be $241 while the payment would be $186 with a $1,000 down payment. If Eduardo can earn 5 percent on his savings, how much would he save by making the larger down payment?

Buying on Credit Versus Leasing

18. Linda is considering the purchase of a Chrysler Cirrus. She has negotiated a price of $20,000 and would pay taxes of $1,200 and fees and licenses of $150. If she finances the Cirrus, Linda would make a $10,000 down payment on an 8 percent loan and make monthly payments of $452 for 2 years. If she decides to lease this vehicle, Linda would have to make a $1,255 capital cost reduction payment and make 24 payments of $269 plus monthly tax payments of $35. The residual value at the end of two years is expected to be $13,500, and the disposition fee on the

lease is $300. Assuming Linda can earn 4 percent on her savings, what is the cost difference between buying and leasing this vehicle?

19. Geoffrey and Lori want to celebrate landing their new "power" jobs by purchasing a new Infiniti I30. They have negotiated a purchase price of $30,000 and would make a down payment of $3,000. Sales taxes on the purchase would be $1,800 and licenses and fees would add another $500 to the cost. They would finance the purchase over 3 years with an 8.5 percent loan and monthly payments of $852. They have also been offered a lease on this vehicle. The lease requires a down payment of $1,925, monthly payments of $400 and sales tax payments of $40 for 36 months, and $0.15 per mile charges on mileage in excess of 12,000 per year. The residual value at the end of the lease is expected to be $20,060. Assuming Geoffrey and Lori average 14,000 miles per year and can earn 5 percent on their savings, what is the cost difference between buying and leasing this vehicle?

20. *Out-of-Class Exercise* Look in a local newspaper or talk with a salesperson at an auto dealership to learn about the buy versus lease options available on a vehicle you are interested in. Based on this information, calculate whether it would be more cost effective for you to finance or lease the vehicle.

Refinancing a Major Purchase

21. Mickey purchased a new car last year using a 12 percent, 5-year loan with a principal of $15,000 and a monthly payment of $334. The loan has a prepayment penalty of $50. But recently Mickey's credit union has advertised 7 percent loans for members that want to refinance existing loans. Mickey has decided she would like to refinance the remaining $12,671 for the next 4 years at 7 percent if it saves her money. The new monthly payment would be $303. If Mickey earns 4 percent on her savings, how much could she save by refinancing?

22. Ernest and Carole financed their new home three years ago using a $75,000, 10.5 percent, 30-year mortgage. The loan has a monthly principal and interest payment of $686. Now interest rates have fallen and they can finance the $73,745 outstanding balance with an 8 percent 27-year mortgage. The new monthly principal and interest payment would be $556. There is no prepayment penalty on their existing mortgage, but the closing costs on the new mortgage would be $1,500 and they would pay this with funds from their savings. If Ernest and Carole expect to live in the house 10 more years and they can earn 6 percent on their savings, how much could they save by refinancing?

SELECTED REFERENCES

A loan again, naturally. (1996, April). *Smart money*, p. 106-115.

Buying vs. leasing. (1995, December). *Motor trend*, p. 44-48

Dodging the traps in a car lease. (1996, April). *Kiplinger's personal finance magazine*, p. 89-92.

Garman, E.T. (1997). *Consumer economic issues in america*. (5th ed.). Houston, TX: Dame Publications, Inc.

Garman, E.T., & Forgue, R.E. (1997). *Personal finance*. (5th ed.). Boston, MA: Houghton Mifflin.

Gitman, L.J., & Joehnk, M.D. (1996). *Personal financial planning*. (7th ed.). Fort Worth, TX: Dryden.

Hampton, V.L., Kitt, K.A., & Greninger, S.A. (1996). *Personal financial management*. Austin, TX: Texas Textbooks.

Kapor, J.R., Dlabay, L.R., & Hughes, R.J. (1996). *Personal finance*. (4th ed.). Chicago, IL: Irwin.

Liberman, G., & Lavine, A. (1994). *Improving your credit and reducing your debt*. New York, NY: John Wiley & Sons, Inc.

Samuelson, P.A., & Nordhaus, W.D. (1992). *Economics*. (14th ed.). New York, NY: McGraw-Hill, Inc.

Should You Lease? (1993, April). *Consumer Reports*, p. 204-206.

Chapter 12
Property and Casualty Insurance Mathematics

▼ Calculating the Actual Cash Value of Insured Assets
▼ The Deductible and Coinsurance Reimbursement Formula
▼ The Dwelling Loss Replacement Cost Requirement Formula
▼ Application of a Standard HO-3 Homeowner's Insurance Policy to a Loss
▼ Application of a Vehicle Insurance Policy to an Accident

Chapter 12
Property and Casualty Insurance Mathematics

Raymond E. Forgue[1]

OVERVIEW

Insurance has been described as a mechanism for transferring and reducing risk by having a large number of policyholders share in the losses of the group. **Risk** is the uncertainty of financial loss associated with the ownership of property or with behaviors which have the potential to cause losses to the policyholder or other persons for which the policyholder may be held legally responsible.

Property insurance reimburses the insured party for financial losses due to the damage, destruction, or loss of use of property owned or controlled by the insured. **Liability insurance** reimburses the insured party for property or bodily injuries suffered by others but for which the insured is legally responsible. For example, the driver of an automobile who runs a stop sign and crashes into another vehicle causing an accident will be held legally responsible for losses suffered by the other driver. These losses would be covered by liability insurance. The losses to the violator's own vehicle will be covered by property insurance. Since owning a home or vehicle carries both liability and property damage risk, vehicle and homeowners insurance policies are fashioned as packages of liability and property insurance obviating the need for separate policies. Events such as vehicle crashes, storms, vandalism, and fires result in what are called **casualty losses**, and property and liability insurance policies are designed to pay for these casualty losses.

The type of risk addressed by insurance is referred to as **pure risk** because there is no potential for gain. **Speculative risk**, such as that associated with gambling or investing, carries the potential for both gains and losses. Insurance is not designed to address situations involving speculative risk.

To ensure that insurance maintains its focus on pure risk, insurance policies contain several important provisions. One involves the **principle of indemnity** which

---

[1]Raymond E. Forgue, Ph.D., Associate Professor, Department of Family Studies, University of Kentucky, Lexington, KY 40506-0054. FAM004@ukcc.uky.edu

states that insurance will reimburse a policyholder for no more than the actual loss incurred (otherwise, there would be potential for a gain). Thus, insurance on an vehicle would cover repairs up to the actual cash value of the vehicle rather than its replacement cost. **Actual cash value** is generally thought to be the purchase price of the item less depreciation due to wear and tear or market conditions. The **replacement cost** (or **replacement value**) is the amount required to purchase a like asset to replace the one that experienced a loss. For example, if John buys an automobile for $15,000 this year, it may only be worth $10,000 two years from now because of the wear and tear associated with driving. If John were to crash the vehicle two years from now the maximum he could expect to be reimbursed would be $10,000, its actual cash value. The insurance company would not pay John its replacement value (probably more than $15,000 since inflation may have pushed the price higher). Note that this is the maximum reimbursement due to the principal of indemnity. If the policy were to provide John with the funds to buy a brand new vehicle, he would have been better off after the crash than before and would have gained financially.

Insurance policies often have other provisions that result in a maximum reimbursement somewhat below even that allowed by the principal of indemnity. Three important provisions are common (deductibles, coinsurance, and policy limits, which are examined below). Collectively, these provisions lead to the possibility that not all of a loss will be covered by insurance. Hence, it is important to be able to apply the terms of a policy to a specific loss to calculate the amount of the loss covered by insurance and the amount to be paid by the insured. The mathematics problems covered below all, in some way, relate to these calculations.

Deductibles are requirements that the insured pay an initial portion of any loss. For example, vehicle collision insurance is often written with a $200 deductible. The first $200 of loss to the vehicle must be paid by the policyholder. The insurer then pays the remainder of the loss, up to the limits of the policy. Deductibles are also included in most health and property insurance policies. They are sometimes required and sometimes optional, and one usually have a choice of deductible amounts. The higher the deductible chosen, the lower the premiums will be.

Coinsurance is a method by which insured and insurer share proportionately in the payment for a loss. For example, it is common in health insurance for the insured to pay 20 percent of a loss and the insurer to pay the remaining 80 percent. Substantial premium reductions can be realized through coinsurance, but one must be prepared to pay his or her share of losses. Homeowner's insurance policies usually contain a **replacement-cost requirement** that stipulates that a home must be insured for a minimum of 80 percent of its replacement value in order for the policy to pay full reimbursement (after payment of the deductible by the policyholder) for any losses to the dwelling. Thus, a home with a replacement value of $100,000 would need to be insured for $80,000 and that amount would be the maximum that the insurance company would be obligated to pay for any loss. However, if the insured fails to meet the replacement-cost requirement, he or she will not be fully insured because he or she will by default be using a form of coinsurance.

Policy limits set overall maximums that will be paid under a policy on a per loss, per year, or even lifetime basis. The policy limits for vehicle liability insurance are usually quoted with three figures, such as 200/500/100, with each figure representing a multiple of $1,000. The first figure signifies the maximum that will be paid for liability for *any one* person's bodily injury losses resulting from a vehicle accident, or $200,000 in our example. The middle figure signifies the overall maximum that will be paid for bodily injury liability losses to *any number* of persons resulting from a vehicle accident, or $500,000 in our example. The third figure signifies the maximum that will be paid for property damage liability losses resulting from an accident, $100,000 in our example. These liability limits may, in some policies, be stated as a single figure, such as $500,000. Under such policies, all property and bodily injury liability losses from an accident would be paid until the single limit is reached. Note that vehicle liability insurance covers the insured for losses suffered by others. Thus it cannot be used to pay for losses suffered by the driver at fault or for property damage to that driver's vehicle. Injured passengers of the at-fault driver may collect under his/her **medical payments coverage** as it pays regardless of who is at fault for an accident. If this amount is insufficient, the liability coverage may be used but usually only after those injured in other vehicles or as pedestrians are reimbursed.

This chapter examines several examples of mathematical concepts related to property and casualty insurance, including calculating the actual cash value of insured assets, the deductible and coinsurance reimbursement formula, the dwelling loss replacement cost requirement formula, application of a standard HO-3 homeowner's insurance policy to a loss, and application of a vehicle insurance policy to an accident.

EXAMPLES OF MATHEMATICAL CONCEPTS RELATED TO PROPERTY AND CASUALTY INSURANCE

1. Calculating the Actual Cash Value of Insured Assets

Formula 12.1: $ACV = P(1 - CA/LE)$

Where: P = purchase price of the property; CA = current age of the property in years; and LE = life expectancy of the property in years.

▼ **Example 12.1:** Karen Parkes had her home burglarized and her eight-year-old color television set was stolen. The TV cost $500 new and had a life expectancy of 10 years. Its actual cash value at the time it was stolen was

Solution: Since CA = 8 and LE = 10, then
             $ACV = \$500 (1 - 8/10) = \$500 (1 - 0.8) = \$500 \times 0.2 = \$100$

❖ **Interpretation:** Historically, property insurance policies paid only the **actual cash value** of an item of personal property. This is the purchase price of the property less depreciation. The actual cash value of Karen's television would be $100 representing the remaining value of the TV over its projected useful life. However, in all likelihood, Karen's insurance policy probably also contains a deductible clause and a coinsurance requirement that would further reduce the amount that insurance would reimburse, and these topics are examined in the next section.

2. The Deductible and Coinsurance Reimbursement Formula

Formula 12.2: $R = (1 - CP)(L - D)$

Where: R = reimbursement (e.g., the amount the insurance company will pay), CP = coinsurance percentage required of the insured; L = loss; and D = deductible.

▼ **Example 12.2:** James Bardo has a health insurance policy with a $200 deductible per hospital stay and a 20 percent coinsurance requirement. If his hospital bill is $1,650, for what amount will James be reimbursed?

Solution: Since CP = 20%, L = $1,650, and D = $200, then
$R = (1.00 - 0.20)(\$1,650 - \$200) = 0.80(\$1,450) = \$1,160$

❖ **Interpretation:** The **deductible and coinsurance reimbursement formula** can be used to determine the amount of an insured loss that will be reimbursed when there is a deductible and a coinsurance clause. **Deductibles** are requirements that the insured pay an initial portion of any loss. In this example, James has a $200 deductible clause. This means that he must pay the first $200 of any insured loss. The insurer pays the remainder of the loss, up to the limits of the policy. A **Coinsurance** is a method by which the insured and the insurer share proportionately in the payment for a loss. In this example, James' insurance policy has a 20 percent requirement. This means that he must pay 20 percent of a loss and the insurer will pay the remaining 80 percent. Thus, James will receive a $1,160 reimbursement from his insurance company.

The remaining $490 ($1,650 - $1,160) represents the $200 deductible and $290 coinsurance of the remaining loss (.20 × $1,450). Note that the deductible requirement is applied in the calculation before the coinsurance clause.

3. The Dwelling Loss Replacement Cost Requirement Formula

Formula 12.3: $R = (L - D)\ I/0.8RV$, if $I < 0.8RV$ or $R = L - D$, if $I \geq 0.8RV$

Where: R = reimbursement payable; L = the amount of loss; D = deductible, if any; I = amount of insurance actually carried; and RV = replacement value of the dwelling.

▼ **Example:** Kevin Carpenter owns a home with a $100,000 replacement value which he has insured for only $72,000 without a deductible. The home suffers a fire which caused $40,000 in damages.

Solution: Since L = $40,000, D = 0, I = $72,000, and RV = $100,000, then

$$R = (\$40,000 - 0) \times \frac{\$72,000}{0.8 \times \$100,000} = \$40,000 \times \frac{\$72,000}{\$80,000} = \$40,000 \times 0.90 = \$36,000$$

❖ **Interpretation:** The amount of reimbursement for any insured loss will be calculated using the **replacement-cost-requirement formula**. A **replacement-cost requirement** stipulates that a home must be insured for 80 percent of its replacement value in order for the policy to pay full reimbursement (after payment of the deductible by the policyholder) for any losses to the dwelling. This requirement exists because without it insurance companies would be forced to pay full values for underinsured losses. The logic continues that when a home is destroyed, the land upon which it was built remains, and that land is typically valued at 20 percent of the total price of the home. Moreover, insuring a home for 80 percent of its value is considered fully insured. In this example, Kevin will be reimbursed for only $36,000 of his loss. His failure to insure his house for 80 percent of its replacement cost, or $80,000 = ($100,000 × 0.80), means his loss will not be covered for 100 percent. Kevin's loss is insured for only 90 percent ($72,000/$80,000). As a result, he must pay 10 percent of the total cost of any repairs, in this case, $4,000. Note that when one has more insurance than required, more than the 80 percent, or even more than 100 percent [e.g., I/0.8RV exceeds 1], the reimbursement (R) simply equals the loss (L − D). *In this example, the deductible is 0. When a deductible exists, it usually is very small, such as $100.*

4. Application of a Standard HO-3 Homeowner's Insurance Policy to a Fire Loss

Conceptual Idea 12.4: A popular type of homeowner's insurance, **Standard HO-3 comprehensive-form homeowner's policy** provides open-perils protection (except for commonly listed perils of war, earthquake, and flood) and for four property coverages: losses to the dwelling, losses to other structures, landscaping losses, and losses generating additional living expenses, up to certain limits.

▼ **Example 12.4:** Frank and Jeannie Connor recently suffered a fire in their home. The home had a value of $105,000, and it was insured for $90,000 under a **Standard HO-3 comprehensive-form homeowner's policy**. The usual HO-3 policy provides the following coverages after a $500 deductible: detached structures up to 10 percent of the dwelling coverage, contents coverage for actual cash value up to 50 percent of the dwelling coverage, cash up to $200 and stamps up to $1,000, and up to 20 percent of the dwelling for additional living expenses. By paying an additional premium, the Connor's Standard HO-3 policy also provided for replacement cost protection.

The fire began in a crawl space at the back of the home, causing $44,000 of damage to the dwelling. The garage, valued at $4,800, was totally destroyed but did not contain a vehicle at the time. The damage to their personal property in the home and garage came to $36,500 for replacement and $21,230 for actual cash value. Also, $450 in cash and a stamp collection valued at $4,215 were destroyed. While the damage was being repaired, the Connors stayed in a motel for two weeks and spent $1,950 on food and lodging before renting a furnished apartment for another month for $900. What is the amount of reimbursement payment from the insurance company?

Solution: You must first determine whether they have adequate dwelling replacement coverage, and if not, what percentage of the necessary 80 percent coverage they do have. The resulting answer will determine the percentage of the loss to the dwelling covered, and consequently the amount to be reimbursed by the insurance company. Assuming that the deductible was applied to the damage to the dwelling, you need to calculate the amount covered by insurance and the amount paid by the Connors on the dwelling itself, the garage, the contents, the cash and stamp collection as these are treated separately, and the extra living expenses.

(1) *The damage to the dwelling.* Since the Connors did insure their home for at least 80 percent of its replacement value ($90,000/$105,000 = 86%), the damage to the dwelling would be fully covered less the deductible ($43,500 [$44,000 – $500]).

(2) *The garage.* HO-3 policies cover detached structures up to 10 percent of the dwelling coverage (in this case $9,000 [$90,000 × .10]), thus, the garage was covered for the full $4,800.

(3) *The contents.* HO-3 policies cover contents for actual cash value up to 50 percent of the dwelling coverage (in this case $45,000 [$90,000 × .50]). Thus, the contents (other than the cash and the stamp collection) were covered for the replacement value of $36,500. (Note that if the Connor's had only actual cash value protection on their contents, their reimbursement would have been $21,230.)

(4) *The cash and stamp collection.* Standard HO-3 policies cover cash up to $200 and stamps up to $1,000. Thus, the cash was covered for $200 (and the Connors will not be reimbursed for the remaining $250) and the stamps are covered for $1,000 (and the Connors will not be reimbursed for the remaining $3,215).

(5) *The additional living expenses.* Standard HO-3 policies provide up to 20 percent of the coverage on the dwelling (in this case $18,000 [$90,000 × .20]) for additional living expenses coverage, thus, the $2,850 ($1,950 + $900) for additional living expenses that they spent was fully covered.

(6) *The total amount of reimbursement payment.*

Thus, the insurance company should send them a check amounting to:

$43,500 + $4,800 + $36,500 + $200 + $1,000 + $2,850 = $88,850

❖ **Interpretation:** The above example illustrates the application Formula 12.3 and other common provisions for a homeowner's insurance policy to determine the amount of reimbursement payment.

5. Application of a Vehicle Insurance Policy to an Accident

Conceptual Idea 12.5: A typical car insurance will have following coverages with limits: liability (for both bodily injury and property damage), medical payments, and collision losses. Usually, both insurance companies of the parties involved in the accident will pay for its own policy holder's medical payment and collision coverage, but the insurance companies of non-faulty party can use **subrogation rights** to take action against the faulty party who caused a loss suffered by a policyholder of the insurance company.

▼ **Example 12.5:** In September of last year, Donna Palmer caused a serious accident when her brakes failed and she crashed into another vehicle. Donna suffered a broken arm and facial cuts resulting in medical costs of $2,490. Her passenger, Philip Compton, was seriously injured, with head and neck wounds requiring surgery, a two-week hospital stay, and rehabilitation. Philip's injuries resulted in medical costs of $26,000. The driver of the other vehicle, John Johnson, suffered serious back and internal injuries and facial burns resulting in some disfigurement. His medical care costs were $38,600. His passenger, Annette Johnson, suffered cuts and bruises requiring minor medical care at a cost of $723. Both vehicles were totally destroyed. Donna's 10-year-old Toyota was valued at $3,150. John's brand-new Buick was valued at $26,350. The force of the impact spun John's vehicle around, causing it to destroy a traffic signal control box (valued at $3,650) and catch fire. Both drivers in this example had vehicle insurance policies with liability policy limits of $20,000/$50,000/$15,000, medical payments limits of $10,000 per person, and actual cash value coverage with $100 deductible. How much will Donna's insurance company pay for the accident, how much will Donna have to pay by herself, and how much will John's insurance company will pay if his company exercises its subrogation rights?

Solution: The following lists how much who will pay for what.

Coverage	Donna's Vehicle Policy	John's Vehicle Policy
Liability (limits: $20,000/$50,000/$15,000)		
Bodily injury:		
John Johnson	$20,000	
Annette Johnson	$ 723	
Philip Compton	$16,000	
Property damage:		
John Johnson's vehicle	$15,000	
Medical payments (limits: $10,000)		
John Johnson		$10,000*
Annette Johnson		$ 723*
Donna Palmer	$ 2,490	
Philip Compton	$10,000	
Collision coverage (actual cash value, $100 deductible)		
Donna's vehicle	$ 3,050	
John's vehicle		$26,250*
Donna's out-of-pocket expenses:		
John Johnson's bodily injury	$18,600	
John Johnson's vehicle	$11,350	
Traffic signal control box	$ 3,650	
Collision insurance deductible	$ 100	

*This amount is included in Donna's column, since John's insurance company filed a claim against Donna's company thereby exercising its subrogation rights.

(1) How much John's insurance company should pay? Remember that **medical payments insurance** pays regardless of who is at fault for an accident. Therefore, John and Annette Johnson were initially reimbursed by John's policy for $10,000 (the policy limit) and $723, respectively. Under the collision coverage, John should receive a $26,250 (the actual cash value of vehicle less $100 deducible) payment from his insurance company. However, John's insurance company exercises the subrogation rights that allows it to collect the exact amount it pays to John from Donna's insurance company.

(2) How much Donna's insurance company should pay? Donna and Philip were reimbursed for their medical losses by Donna's medical payments coverage. Because Philip's losses ($26,000) exceeded Donna's medical payments policy limits, he also made a liability claim against her policy. John Johnson's policy also comes into play here. Then John made a claim against Donna's insurance company in order to be reimbursed for the remainder of his bodily injury losses. Also, John's insurer exercised its subrogation rights and made a claim against Donna's insurer in order to collect the $10,000 it had paid John and the $723 it had paid Annette. Donna's policy paid $20,000 (the per-person policy limit) toward John's injuries ($10,000 to John and $10,000 to his insurance company) and $723 for Annette's injuries. It also paid Phillip Compton $16,000 for the bodily injury losses. John's collision insurance covered his vehicle less his $100 deductible. Then John's insurance company applied its subrogation rights for the entire amount of the loss (including the deductible) against Donna's property damage liability coverage, and Donna' policy should pay the limit of property damage coverage, $15,000. Donna Palmer also collected $3,050 for her vehicle under her collision coverage, which carried a $100 deductible.

(3) How much Donna should pay? Since Donna's policy paid $20,000 (the per-person limit) for John's medical costs ($10,000 to John and $10,000 to his insurance company), the rest $18,600 should be paid by Donna out from her own pocket. Also, Donna has to pay $11,350 to cover John's car value, since her insurance has already paid $15,000 for property damage. In addition, Donna has to pay for the damage of the traffic signal control box ($3,650) and the collision insurance deductible ($100). In total, Donna had to pay $33,700 out of her own pocket, since the policy limits were exceeded by John Johnson's injuries and the property damage.

(4) Summary. Thus, Donna's insurance company has to pay $67,263, Donna has to pay $33,700, and John's insurance company needs not to pay because it exercises the subrogation rights.

❖ **Interpretation:** The example above illustrates the application of policy limits and deductible clauses in a vehicle insurance policy to determine the amount of reimbursement payment.

INFORMATION AND COMPUTING RESOURCES

Relevant web sites:

- *InsWeb:* http://www.insweb.com (a comprehensive resource for consumers and insurance professionals to get information on the insurance industry).

- *Insurance News:* http://www.insure.com/ (factual consumer information about auto, home and life insurance, as well as company ratings information from Standard & Poor's).

- *Insurance information:* http://www.insure.com (basic information and current developments about auto, home, and life insurance).

EXERCISE PROBLEMS

Calculating the Actual Cash Value of Insured Assets Problems

1. Melissa Thompson had her home burglarized and her four-year-old color television set was stolen. The TV cost $680 new and had a total life expectancy of eight years. Calculate its actual cash value.

2. Robert Hamilton had his home burglarized and his two-year-old color computer was stolen. The computer cost $3,000 new and had a total life expectancy of five years. Calculate its actual cash value.

3. Jenny Olson owned a three-year-old bass fishing boat. Recently the boat was destroyed in a fire. The boat cost $7,000 new and had a total life expectancy of 12 years. Calculate its actual cash value.

4. Katy Jenkins recently suffered an electrical system overload in her home and her one-year-old home entertainment system was destroyed. The system cost $3,300 new and had a total life expectancy of 10 years. Calculate its actual cash value.

The Deductible and Coinsurance Reimbursement Formula

5. Joan Meyers recently had a hospital stay for removal of her appendix, costing $4,600. Her hospital insurance policy has a $250 deductible per year and a coinsurance requirement that she pay 20 percent and her insurance company pay 80 percent of any loss. This event was her only hospitalization for the year.
   a.   How much of the loss was paid by her insurance company?
   b.   How much of the loss was paid by Joan?

6. Assume that Bob Smith has a health insurance policy with a $500 deductible per year and a 20 percent coinsurance requirement. If his hospital bill is $2,500, for what amount will Bob be reimbursed if this is his only hospital stay this year?

7. Assume that Pete Wilkinson has a health insurance policy with a $100 deductible per hospital stay and a 20 percent coinsurance requirement. If his hospital bill is $5,000, for what amount will Pete be reimbursed?

8. Assume that Tina Anderson has a health insurance policy with a $50 deductible per hospital stay and a 20 percent coinsurance requirement. If her hospital bill is $3,500, for what amount will Tina be reimbursed?

The Dwelling Loss Replacement Cost Requirement Formula

9. Ned Peterson has owned his home for ten years. At the time of its purchase for $68,000 he bought a $85,000 homeowners insurance policy. He still owns that policy although the replacement cost of the home is now $150,000. If Ned suffered a $30,000 fire loss to the home what dollar amount of the loss would be covered by his policy, assuming no deductible?

10. Michael Bower owns a home with a $180,000 replacement value which he has insured for $172,000. The home suffered a fire which caused $20,000 in damages. What dollar amount of the loss would be covered by his policy, assuming no deductible?

11. Branson Fuller owns a home with a $110,000 replacement value which he has insured for $69,000. The home suffered a fire which caused $40,000 in damages. What dollar amount of the loss would be covered by his policy, assuming no deductible?

12. Claudia Palmer owns a home with a $250,000 replacement value which she has insured for $150,000. The home was struck by a tornado which caused $90,000 in damages. What dollar amount of the loss would be covered by his policy, assuming no deductible?

Application of a Standard HO-3 Homeowner's Insurance Policy to a Loss

13. The home of Leanne and Don Carter was recently damaged in a windstorm causing $34,000 of damage to the dwelling. The garage, valued at $10,700, was totally destroyed but did not contain a vehicle at the time. The damage to their personal property in the home and garage came to $15,500 for replacement and $7,600 actual cash value. Also, a stamp collection valued at $4,763 was destroyed. While the damage was being repaired, the Carter's stayed in a motel for one week and spent $1,950 on food and lodging. The home had a value of $125,000, and was insured for $95,000 under an HO-3 comprehensive-form homeowner's policy with a $1,000 deductible and contents actual-cash-value protection. *(Hint: If the ratio, home insurance/10.8 × home value, is less than 100%, the insurance company will reimburse all losses based on this ratio instead of 100%.)*
    a. Assuming that the deductible was applied to the damage to the dwelling, calculate the amount covered by insurance and the amount paid by the

Carter's for each loss listed: the dwelling itself, the garage, the contents, the stamp collection, and the extra living expenses.
b.   What amount and percentage of the total loss was paid by the Carter's?

Application of a Vehicle Insurance Policy to an Accident

14.   Regina Miller drives a Plymouth valued at $4,600. She has a 50/100/25 automobile policy with $25,000 per person medical payments coverage and both collision ($250 deductible) and comprehensive coverage. Ryan Smith drives a Chevrolet Lumina valued at $8,250. He has a 25/50/15 automobile policy with $30,000 in medical payments coverage and both collision ($200 deductible) and comprehensive. Late one evening, while he was driving back from a party, Ryan's vehicle crossed the center line, striking Regina's vehicle and forcing it into the ditch. Ryan's vehicle also left the road and did extensive damage to several signs. The following table outlines the damages and the dollar amounts of each:

Item	Dollar Amount
Bodily injuries suffered by Regina	$ 8,800
Bodily injuries suffered by Gayle, a passenger in Regina's vehicle	23,634
Regina's vehicle	4,600
Bodily injuries suffered by Ryan	3,500
Bodily injuries suffered by Pam, a passenger in Ryan's vehicle	15,835
Ryan's vehicle	8,250
Damage to the signs	10,400

Complete the chart below and use the information to answer the following questions:
a.   How much will Regina's policy pay Regina and Gayle for their medical bills?
b.   Will subrogation rights come into play? How?
c.   How much will Ryan's bodily injury liability protection pay?
d.   To whom and how much will Ryan's property damage liability protection pay?
e.   To whom and how much will Ryan's medical protection pay?
f.   How much reimbursement will Ryan receive for his vehicle?
g.   How much will Ryan be required to pay out of his own pocket?

REGINA MILLER'S ACCIDENT: WHO PAYS WHAT?

Coverage	Ryan's Policy	Regina's Policy
Liability Coverage(limits)	_____	_____
Bodily injury		
Regina	_____	_____
Gayle	_____	_____
Pam	_____	_____
Property damage		
Regina's vehicle	_____	_____
Road signs	_____	_____

Medical payments (limits)		
Ryan	_____	_____
Pam	_____	_____
Regina	_____	_____
Gayle	_____	_____
Collision coverage (limits)		
Ryan's vehicle	_____	_____
Regina's vehicle	_____	_____
Ryan's out-of-pocket expenses		
Excess bodily injury losses	_____	_____
Excess property damage losses	_____	_____
Collision insurance deductible	_____	_____

SELECTED REFERENCES

Garman, E. T., & Forgue, R. E. (1997). *Personal finance* (5th ed.). Chapter 11: Risk management and property/liability insurance (pp. 326-364). Boston: Houghton Mifflin.

Chapter 13
Health Plan Mathematics

▼ **Deductibles Reduce Reimbursements**
▼ **Coinsurance**
▼ **Applying Both the Deductible and Coinsurance Clauses**
▼ **Copayments**
▼ **Application of Policy Limits**

Chapter 13
Health Plan Mathematics

Gong-Soog Hong and Sugato Chakravaraty[1]

OVERVIEW

Health care spending in the U.S. has increased rapidly in recent years. It was over $800 billion in 1993, almost $1 trillion in 1996, and is expected to reach $1.7 trillion in the year 2000. At that time, health care expenditures are expected to consume approximately 18% of the gross domestic product (GDP). Health care services in the U.S. are financed by three major parties: government, private health insurance, and individuals. About 70% of the expenditures are covered by the government and private health insurance programs, and the remaining 30% are out-of-pocket expenditures of individuals. This latter figure has been rising in recent years.

Approximately 85 percent of Americans are covered by some form of **health care** (or simply **health**) **plan**. This is health insurance or another plan that pays for or provides reimbursement for health care expenditures and/or losses. Those with higher incomes and education had health care coverage more than those with lower incomes and education. Younger persons made up a disproportionate share of the uninsured.

Health care plans—like private insurance, managed care plans, preferred provider organizations, health maintenance organizations, and government health care programs (Medicare and Medicaid)—offer protection to alleviate financial burdens resulting from illness, injury, or disability. Health care plans can be written to cover an individual, a family, or a group. The **policyholder** is the qualified participant in a health care plan that may or may not covered other family members.

Insurance of any kind—be it health, disability, life, long-term care, or automobile—is inherently based on the notion of risk sharing. The central idea is to collect small sums (the essence of a premium) from many policyholders and pay out

---

[1]Gong-Soog Hong, Ph.D., Assistant Professor, Consumer and Family Economics, Purdue University, West Lafayette, IN 47907-1262. honggs@purdue.edu; and Sugato Chakravaraty, Ph.D., Assistant Professor, Consumer Economics, Purdue University, West Lafayette, IN 47907-1262. sugato@purdue.edu

relatively few large sums in medical claims. **Insurance** and similar health care plans transfer and reduce risk by having a large number of policyholders share in the losses of the group. The insurance **premium** actually includes the individual's share of the group's losses, insurance company reserves set aside to pay future losses, a proportional share of the expenses of administering the insurance plan, and, when the plan is administered by a profit-seeking company, an allowance for profit. All types of health care plans operate on the same principle as insurance—sharing the risk.

A simple example illustrates the notion of risk sharing in health care. Assume a fictitious island in the South Pacific with 100 families. Over the years the village elders have noticed that every year an average of two families fall ill for which they are required to be transferred to the mainland in helicopters and treated in the big hospital there. The cost to each family is around $50,000. The island has no available insurance company, so the village elders decide to start a non-profit health care plan of their own. Since they anticipate a total loss of $100,000 annually, they compute the annual premium for each family to be $1,000 (100,000/100). Now any unlucky family can take money from the village "pot" to pay their medical bills should anyone fall ill during the course of the year.

This chapter illustrates typical examples of mathematical concepts related to health care plans: deductibles reduce reimbursements, coinsurance, applying both the deductible and coinsurance clauses, copayments, and an application of policy limits.

EXAMPLES OF MATHEMATICAL CONCEPTS RELATED TO HEALTH CARE PLANS

1. Deductibles Reduce Reimbursements

Formula 13.1: $R = ME - D$

Where: R = Reimbursement (the total amount that the health care plan will pay the policyholder and/or service providers); ME = medical expense; and D = deductible.

▼   **Example 13.1:** Jean bell bought a health care plan with a deductible of $100 per hospital stay and a $500 yearly deductible. Last week Jean went to the emergency room for what turned out to be a sprained ankle, and the bill for the out-patient medical services was $800. After applying the deductible, how much does the health care plan reimburse Jean and/or the hospital?

Solution: $R = \$800 - \$100 = \$700$

❖   **Interpretation:** A **deductible** provision of an health care plan requires the policyholder to pay an initial portion of any loss, such as medical expenses, before receiving reimbursement. Medical care plan provisions often have *two* deductibles, one amount per incident and one amount for the year. For example, popular deductible provision in health care plans is $500 annually; some deductibles are $1,000 or $2,000 per year. Further, most health care plan have a deductible of $100 or $200 per medical incident. In this example, since Jean's health care plan has a $100 per incident deductible clause, she is responsible for $100. In this simple example, the remaining portion of the hospital bill, $700, will be covered by the provisions of her health care plan. In the real world, this portion may not be fully covered because of other restrictions of health care plans, which will be introduced in the following sections.

2. Coinsurance

Formula 13.2: R = ME (1 − CP)

Where: R = Reimbursement (the amount the health care plan will pay the policyholder and/or service providers); ME = medical expenses incurred; and CP = coinsurance percentage required of the policyholder.

▼ **Example 13.2:** Jane Green has a health care plan with a 80/20 coinsurance clause that requires her to pay 20 percent of her medical expenses while the plan pays 80 percent. Jane had a recent medical bill totaling $5,000. How much does the health care provider reimburse using Formula 13.2, and how much money is Jane responsible for?

Solution: R = $5,000 (1 − .20) = $4,000

❖ **Interpretation:** Jane's health care plan will reimburse her and/or those that provided her health care services $4,000 under the coinsurance clause. Therefore, Jane is responsible for $1,000 ($5,000 − $4,000) of the total medical bill. **Coinsurance** is a method by which the health care plan and the policyholder share proportionately in the payment of medical expenses. A popular coinsurance share is 80/20 with the policyholder paying 20 percent.

3. Applying Both the Deductible and Coinsurance Clauses

Formula 13.3: R = (1 − CP)(ME − D)

Where: R = Reimbursement (the amount the health care plan will pay the policyholder and/or service providers); CP = coinsurance percentage required of the policyholder; ME = medical expenses incurred; and D = deductible.

▼ **Example 13.3:** Sharon Johnson recently spent 10 days in a hospital following an automobile accident. The hospital room cost $600 per day. In addition, she incurred physician's fees of $2,000 and laboratory charges of $1,000. Sharon has a health care plan with a $250 deductible per incident and an 80/20 coinsurance clause. After applying the deductible, how much does Sharon owe the hospital, and how much does the health care plan pay?

Solution:

Since, CP = .2, D = $250, and ME = $6,000 + $2,000 + $1,000 = $9,000
Then, R = (1 − .2) ($9,000 − $250) = .8 × $8,750 = $7,000
And Sharon has to pay: $9,000 − $7,000 = $2,000

❖ **Interpretation:** After applying the $250 deductible to the medical bill of $9,000, Sharon is responsible for a 20% coinsurance payment of $1,750, and her health care plan will be responsible for an 80% coinsurance payment of $7,000. Money out of Sharon's pocket totals $2,000 ($250 deductible plus $1,750 coinsurance payment).

4. Copayment

Formula 13.4: $R = ME - \sum CP_i \cdot n_i$

Where: R = Reimbursement (the amount the health care plan will pay the policyholder and/or service providers); ME = medical expenses incurred; CP_i = copayment required per medical incident for service i; and N = number of medical incidents for service i.

▼ **Example 13.4:** John Watt has a health care plan with a copayment clause, $10 per X-ray and $5 for each prescription. During the past year, John had several other medical expenses: 7 visits to his family physician ($40 each), 15 drug prescriptions (totaling $520 [none cost less than $10]), and 2 X-rays of his fractured wrist (totaling $90). How much is John's total copayment amount, and how much does the health care plan reimburse John and/or other medical service providers?

Solution:

Step 1: Compute the total medical bill.

7 physician visits @ $40 each	$280
15 drug prescriptions	520
2 X-rays	90
Total	$890

Step 2: Compute the policyholder's total copayment amount.

7 physician visits @ $20 each	$140
15 drug prescriptions @ $10 each	150
2 X-rays	40
Total	$330

Step 3: Compute the health care plan's reimbursement amount.

R = $890 − $330 = $560

❖ **Interpretation:** In this example, Joe is responsible for total copayment amount of $330 and the health care plan's reimbursement amount is $890. A **copayment clause** requires the policyholder to pay a particular dollar amount for each specific covered medical expense. Copayments are a variation of a deductible clause. Copayments are a form of cost sharing designed in part to discourage excessive use of medical services by making the policyholder partially responsible for expenses incurred. Copayments are often required for physician visits, prescription drugs, and X-rays. A copayment differs from a deductible in that a deductible might require that the policyholder pay the first $100 of X-ray expenses during a year, while a copayment might require the policyholder to pay the first $20 of *each* X-ray.

5. Application of Policy Limits

Conceptual Idea 13.5: Health care plans do not reimburse the policyholder and/or service provider for every dollar spent on associated services. In addition to deductibles, coinsurance, and copayments, health care plans also have **policy limits**. These are set overall maximums that will be paid under a health care plan on a per loss (medical utilization), per year, or even lifetime basis. The poorest amount of health care protection is provided through **hospital and surgical indemnity insurance** policies because they provide only a cash payment of a specific amounts per day of hospitalization and for certain surgical events. (This is illustrated in Examples 13.5.1 and 13.5.2.) No attempt is made to match the payment to real cost of a specific item of medical expense. Better health care coverage is available with plans that offer reimbursement on a **usual, customary and reasonable (ucr)** basis where charges for surgical and hospital related charges are based upon what most service providers charge for similar services with a specific geographic area (as illustrated in Example 13.5.3).

▼ **Example 13.5.1:** Sujoy Misra's health care plan (a typical hospital and surgical indemnity insurance policy) has hospital expense coverage with daily policy limits of $250 for no more than 30 days per year. In addition, the hospital expense coverage promises to reimburse a maximum of $50 per day for miscellaneous hospital expenses for no more than 30 days per year. This inexpensive employer-provided health care plan has a maximum lifetime limit of $100,000. It also has a deductible of $100 per hospital stay with a $500 yearly deductible, a copayment requirement of $20 per physician visit, and a 80/20 coinsurance clause that requires him to pay 20 percent of his medical expenses while the plan pays 80 percent.

Sujoy has been in failing health in recent years, and he has been hospitalized several times. Over the years, he has run up bills amounting to $90,000 on his health care plan. This year, unfortunately, started out poorly for Sujoy as he suffered a stroke that required neurosurgery and expensive intensive care hospitalization and rehabilitation. His medical bills are listed below.

Physician's and surgeon's fees (20 visits)	$12,000
Hospital room (60 days at $600/day)	36,000
Miscellaneous hospital expenses (60 days at $55/day)	3,300
Total medical bill	$51,300

According to the information given, how much would Sujoy's plan pay for this incident, and how much would Sujoy pay?

Solution:

Step 1: Allowed costs by the health plan

Physician and surgeon bills $12,000
20 visits at $20 . . . . <u>−   400</u>
Allowed physician and surgeon bills $11,600

Actual hospital room (60 days at $600/day) $36,000
Policy limit (30 days at $250/day) . . . . $ 7,500

Actual miscellaneous hospital expenses (60 days at $55/day) . . . $ 3,300
Policy limit (30 days at $50/day) . . . . $ 1,500

Total allowed expenses $20,600

Step 2: Estimated health plan coinsurance payment.

Since, total allowed expenses = $20,600, health plan coinsurance percentage = .8. Then, estimated health plan coinsurance payment = $20,600 × .8 = $16,480

Step 3: Apply the lifetime maximum lifetime policy limit.

The maximum lifetime limit of the health care plan is $100,000, and the amounts previously paid by plan totaled 90,000. Thus, the balance of policy limits available equals $10,000, which is the amount that will be paid by the health plan.

Step 4: Determine total amount owed by policyholder.

Since the total bill equals $51,300, and the reimbursed by health care plan equals $10,000, then the net amount owed by policyholder is $51,300 less $10,000, or $41,300

❖ **Interpretation:** Sujoy owes $41,300 in medical expenses after applying the deductibles, coinsurance, and lifetime policy limits of his health care plan. Note that the deductible of this case is ignored in the calculation, since Sujoy's actual expenses greatly exceeded the policy limits, thus the deducible is automatically included in the amount that should be paid by Sujoy. The total amount of reimbursement that the health care plan paid to the health service providers was $10,000. The health expense coverage of a health care plan typically has policy limits. The **hospital expense coverage** of a health care plan pays for medical expenses incurred while in hospital. Standard hospital expense coverage provides two basic benefits: (1) an amount for daily hospital charges for room and board, and (2) an amount for miscellaneous hospital expenses. Coverage typically pays stated amounts for each day in the hospital up to some maximum number of days.

▼   **Continuing example 13.5.2:** If Sujoy's health care plan had a maximum lifetime policy limit of $250,000, how much would the health plan pay for his bill, and how much would he owe for the medical event?

Solution:

Steps 1 and 2 will be the same as in Example 13.5.1, and the coinsurance payment by the health plan remains $16,480. The difference starts from Step 3.

Step 3: Apply the lifetime maximum lifetime policy limit.

Since the maximum lifetime limit of the health care plan equals $250,000, and the amounts previously paid by plan equals 90,000, the balance of policy limit available equals $160,000, which is far more enough to reimburse this year's expenses of $16,480.

Step 4: Determine total amount owed by policyholder.

Since the total bill equals $51,300, and the reimbursed amount by health care plan equals $16,480, then the net amount owed by policyholder is $51,300 less $16,480, or $34,820.

❖   **Interpretation:** Sujoy owes $35,300 in medical expenses after applying the coinsurance of his health care plan. For the same reason as in Example 13.5.1, the deductible is ignored in the calculation. The total amount of reimbursement that the health care plan paid to the health service providers was $16,000. Clearly, it is wise to buy health care plan coverage with sufficiently high policy limits, such as $250,000 to $1,000,000, although, of course, the premiums would be somewhat higher.

▼   **Continuing example 13.5.3:** If in addition to not having a maximum lifetime limit, Sujoy's health care plan paid for usual, customary and reasonable (UCR) services, how much would he owe for the medical event? Here reimbursement for charges for surgical and hospital related expenses are based upon what most service providers charge for similar services with a specific geographic area. In the example below, assume that the hospital and miscellaneous hospital expenses are within the UCR guidelines.

Solution:

Step 1: Allowed costs by the health plan

Physician and surgeon bills	$12,000
20 visits at $20	− 400
Allowed physician and surgeon bills	$11,600
Actual hospital room (60 days at $600/day)	$36,000
Actual miscellaneous hospital expenses (60 days at $55/day) . . .	$ 3,300
Total allowed expenses	$50,900

Step 2: Estimated health plan coinsurance payment.

Since the total allowed expenses equals $20,600, the health plan coinsurance percentage equals .8, the deductible for one incident equals $100, then the estimated health plan coinsurance payment equals $50,900 less $100 multiplied times .8 equals $40,640.

Step 3: Apply the lifetime maximum policy limit.

Since there is no lifetime maximum limit, the health plan will pay $40,640.

Step 4: Determine total amount owed by policyholder.

Since the total bill equals $51,300, and the reimbursement by the health care plan equals $40,640, then the net amount owed by policyholder equals $51,300 less $40,640, or $10,660.

❖ **Interpretation:** Sujoy owes $10,660 in medical expenses after applying the deductibles, copayments, and coinsurance of his health care plan. The total amount of reimbursement that the health care plan paid to the health service providers was $40,640. Clearly, it is wise to buy health care plan coverage with a usual, customary and reasonable provision, although, of course, the premiums would be somewhat higher.

6. Estimating Social Security Disability Benefits

Conceptual Idea 13.6: When an insured worker becomes disabled, Social Security will pay benefits to the worker, dependent children, and a spouse. The amount depends upon the eligibility of the disabled worker.

▼ **Example 13.6:** Oracle J. Simpson had a serious automobile accident that left him disabled and unable to work. He also cannot play golf anymore. Oracle is age 50, married, but has no children, and his earned income last year was $36,000. Estimate the amount of the monthly disability benefit Oracle would receive from the Social Security Administration.

Solution: Using the appropriate table in Appendix B, Oracle's estimated disability benefit would total $1,667 a month ($1,118 for his benefit and $559 for his wife's benefit).

❖ **Interpretation:** The exact figure for one's disability benefits is calculated by the Social Security Administration. Oracle's and his wife's $1,667 disability benefit amounts to $20,124 ($1,667 × 12) annually.

INFORMATION AND COMPUTING RESOURCES

1. *Health Online* (Addison-Wesley), authored by Tom Ferguson, a physician, is a guide to destinations on the information superhighway. Another book to check

out is *NetPractice: A Beginners' Guide to Healthcare Networking on the Internet,* by Mary Frances Miller (Opus Communications).

2. Three major online services, American Online (800-827-6364), CompuServe (800-848-8199), and Prodigy (800-776-3449), offer medical references, support groups and access to the Internet with its links to health information worldwide. Go to: *health* on CompuServe and you can find 200,000 articles from consumer and health magazines in "Health Database Plus." "Paper Chase" has access to medical data bases, including the National Library of Medicine's Medline data base. Go to *handicapped* and you will find "Handicapped User's Database," which lists resources for disabled people. On America Online, you may click on "Search Health Forum" in the Better health & Medical Forum (keyword: *better health*) and download news articles in the Health Channel (keyword: *health*). You also have direct access to the Medline data base (keyword: *medline*). Prodigy offers articles and news releases on healthcare (go to: *health news*).

3. Some useful home pages.

    ■ *ADA Online:* http://www.ada.org (For dental professionals, but also gives consumer information on subjects ranging from sealants to insurance benefits.)

    ■ *HMO SmartPages:* http://www.buysmart.com (Contains information on 160 HMOs, with more to come. Listings include details on the number of board-certified physicians, the types of coverage available, and how doctors are compensated.)

    ■ *Natural Medicine:* http://www.amrta.org/~amrta (A site for information on everything from acupuncture to yoga with links to internal medicine and health resources, professional journals, and recommended books and magazines.)

    ■ *Patient Advocacy List:* http://infonet.welch.jhu.edu/advocacy.html (Toll-free numbers for patient-advocacy organizations are compiled by Johns Hopkins Medical Institutions Information Network.)

    ■ *PharmInfoNet:* http://pharminfo.com/pin_hp.html (Plenty of drug-related topics.)

    ■ *Psych Central:* http://www.coil.com/~grohol (Lets you check out symptoms for a range of mental disorders and gives links to related Web pages, consumer articles, and a book list.)

EXERCISE PROBLEMS

Deductibles Reduce Reimbursements

1. Joan had three medical bills in a year that totaled $3,500. After applying the $500 deductible, how much does the health care plan reimburse Joan and/or the medical care providers, assuming that her health plan would cover the rest?

2. Mark's medical bill last year was $1,340. He has a health plan that requires a $2,000 deductible. How much will the plan reimburse for his medical bill, and how much will Mark have to pay?

Coinsurance

3. Grace has a health plan which requires her to pay 25% of her medical expenses. Last year, her medical expenses totaled $2,340. How much would her plan reimburse her?

4. Jerry received $2,340 reimbursement from his health plan for his medical bills amounting to $2,925 last year. What is Jerry's percentage of the coinsurance payment?

Applying Both the Deductible and Coinsurance Clauses

5. Julia Ford bought a health plan with a $500 deductible per hospital stay and a 20% coinsurance requirement. Julia's hospital bill for a recent illness was $4,200. What will be the amount that the health care plan pay for this incident, and what amount will be Julia's responsibility?

6. Frank has a 75/25 coinsurance health plan with a $800 deductible annually. His health plan sent him an reimbursement check of $3,360 for last year's medical expenses. What was the total amount of his medical bills last year?

Copayments

7. Joe Walden's health care plan has a number of copayment requirements: $20 for each visit to a physician, $10 for each prescription, and $20 for each X-ray. While recovering from a fractured wrist, Joe had to visit his orthopedic physician three times for checkups at $50 per visit. How much is Joe's total copayment amount, and how much does the health care plan reimburse Joe and/or the physician?

8. Wanda paid $60 copayments for three X-rays last year and received a reimbursement check of $240 from her health plan. What is the copayment for each visit and what is the total amount of medical bills?

Application of Policy Limits

9. Sean's health care plan has hospital expense coverage with daily policy limits of $200 for no more than 30 days per year. In addition, the hospital expense coverage promises to reimburse a maximum of $60 per day for miscellaneous hospital expenses for no more than 30 days per year. The employer-provided health care plan has a maximum lifetime limit of $120,000. It also has a deductible of $150 per hospital stay with a $600 yearly deductible, a copayment requirement of $25 per physician visit, and a 75/25 coinsurance clause that requires him to pay 25 percent of his medical expenses while the plan pays 75 percent.

Sean has been in failing health in recent years, and he has been hospitalized several times. Over the years, he has run up bills amounting to $108,000 on his health care plan. The following is Sean's medical bills last year.

Physician's and surgeon's fees (20 visits)	$13,000
Hospital room (60 days at $650/day)	39,000
Miscellaneous hospital expenses (60 days at $50/day)	3,000
Total medical bill	$55,000

According to the information given, how much would Sean's plan pay for this year's medical expenses, and how much would Sean pay by himself?

10. If Sean's health care plan had a maximum lifetime policy limit of $150,000, how much would the health plan pay for his bill, and how much would he owe for the medical event?

11. If in addition to not having a maximum lifetime limit, Sean's health care plan paid for usual, customary and reasonable (UCR) services, how much would he owe for the medical event?

Estimating Social Security Disability Benefits

12. Julie is 35 years old and single. She is disabled and unable to work because of a recent ski accident. If she earned $24,000 last year and is qualified for Social Security benefits for her disability, what is the amount she will receive annually from the Social Security Administration?

SELECTED REFERENCES

Bender, D., & Leone, B. (1995). *Health care in America: Opposing viewpoints.* San Diego, CA: Greenhaven Press, Inc.

Davis, K. (1995). Health insurance and the size and shape of the problem, *Inquiry, 32,* 196-203.

Fuchs, V. R. (1991). National health insurance revisited. *Health Affairs, 10,* 7-17.

Grossman, W. (1993). Comparing the options for universal coverage, *Health Affairs, 11,* 283-287.

Pauly, M., Danson, P., & Hoff, J. (1991). A plan for responsible health insurance, *Health Affairs, 10,* 5-25.

Posey, G. (1995). *Health insurance* (Current Population Reports, Series P23-189). Washington, DC.: US Government Printing Office.

Schieber, G., Poullier, P., & Greenwald, L. (1992). US Health expenditure performance, *Health Care Financing Review, 13,* 1-87.

Chapter 14
Life Insurance Math

▼ Estimating Social Security Survivor's Benefits
▼ Using the Multiple-of-Earnings Approach to Estimate Life Insurance Needs
▼ Using the Needs Approach to Estimate Life Insurance Needs
▼ Income Tax Implications of Life Insurance
▼ Commission Loads
▼ Using the Net Cost Method to Compare Policy Costs
▼ Using the Interest-Adjusted Cost Method to Compare Policy Costs

Chapter 14
Life Insurance Math

Ronald W. Gibbs, E. Thomas Garman and Jing J. Xiao[1]

OVERVIEW

Life insurance is probably one of the most talked about and misunderstood topics in the financial marketplace. It is not like any other purchase a person is going to make. Most people are unfamiliar with much of the terminology and the confusing numbers of life insurance. It can be bewildering.

Life insurance is an insurance contract that protects against financial losses resulting from death. Life insurance can allow the survivors and heirs of the deceased to continue with their lives free from the financial burdens that death can bring. Proceeds from a life insurance policy are often used to provide for the basic needs of survivors, maintain housing, permit a surviving parent to remain at home rather than work for money income, pay for college expenses, and provide retirement income for survivors. Approximately 25 percent of today's adults will die during their working years.

Key to making a good purchasing decision is to select the proper amount of life insurance coverage. This is best accomplished using the **needs approach** which is a method of estimating life insurance needs considering all of the factors that might affect the level of need, especially the time value of money.

There are a number of important income tax implications in life insurance that should be considered when making decisions in personal finance. For example, the death benefit of a life insurance policy is generally not subject to federal and state income taxes for the beneficiary, the insured, or the owner of the policy. In addition, the cash-value accumulations within certain life insurance policies in excess of premiums paid are not taxable as they are earned, but will be taxed if the policy is cashed in prior to the death of the insured. This is an example of a **tax-sheltered benefit** meaning that the life insurance policy owner avoids paying current income

[1]Ronald W. Gibbs, MBA, Adjunct Instructor, College of Human Resources and Education, Virginia Tech, Blacksburg, VA 24060. Senior Associate, r. **bowen** international, York, PA, gibbsr@bev.net; E. Thomas Garman and Jing J. Xiao.

taxes on the value of the benefits received, e.g., the income accumulating within the policy. Because of this special treatment in income tax law, cash-value insurance is often used as an investment vehicle.[1] **Insurance dividends** are defined legally by the Internal Revenue Service as a return of a portion of the premium paid for a life insurance policy; they are not considered taxable income.

Another factor that affects the cost of a life insurance policy is the **load**. This is a cost that reflects the life insurance company agent's commission as well as the company's marketing and overhead costs. **Low-load** life insurance does not involve payment of a commission by the insurer to an insurance agent.

While in reality there are only two types of life insurance policies (term and cash-value), many people are confused by the variety of policies offered by the industry. **Term life insurance** offers "pure protection" because it pays benefits only if the insured person dies within the time period of the policy. The policy must, therefore, be renewed if coverage is desired for another time period. **Cash-value life insurance** pays benefits at death and includes a savings/investment element that can provide benefits to the policyholder while still alive. The presence of a cash value makes cost comparisons difficult, and various methods are available to make contrast polices.

This chapter overviews mathematical concepts related to life insurance in the following areas: using multiple-of-earnings approach to estimating life insurance needs, using the needs approach to estimate life insurance needs, income tax implications, commission loads, using the net cost method to compare policy costs, and using the interest-adjusted cost method to compare policy costs.

EXAMPLES OF MATHEMATICAL CONCEPTS RELATED TO LIFE INSURANCE

1. Estimating Social Security Survivor's Benefits

Conceptual Idea 14.1: When an insured worker dies, Social Security will pay benefits to the surviving children, to a surviving spouse caring for the children, and a surviving spouse. There are eligibility requirements. The amount of the benefit depends upon the eligibility of the deceased worker.

▼ **Example 14.1:** Reggie Jackson died recently. Reggie was 60 years of age and his spouse was also age 60 when he passed away. His earned income last year was $48,000. Estimate the amount of the monthly survivor's benefit Reggie's wife would receive from the Social Security Administration.

Solution: Using the appropriate table in Appendix B, Reggie's wife's estimated survivor's benefit would total $850 a month.

❖ **Interpretation:** The exact figure for a survivor's benefit is calculated by the Social Security Administration. Reggie's wife's estimated monthly survivor's benefit of $850 amounts to $10,200 ($850 × 12) annually.

2. Using the Multiple-of-Earnings Approach to Estimate Life Insurance Needs

Formula 14.2: $L = 0.75 \, PVA_I - L_c$

Where: L = insurance needed using the multiple-of-earnings approach; PVA_I = present value of an annuity (a series of income replacement needs which equals to the annual take home income of the policy holder); and L_c = current life insurance.

▼ **Example 14.2.1:** Joel Raymond is 35, married to Marie (age 35), a computer programmer, and they have two children, Kate (age 3) and Paul (age 2). As a shift foreman at a local computer assembly plant, his annual gross income is $40,000, his take-home pay (after deductions for insurance, taxes and other items) is about $36,000. Joel assumes that the historic inflation rate has been about 4 percent. Joel wants to replace his income for 25 years, at which time his spouse would no longer need to support her children financially and she would be eligible for Social Security survivor's benefits at age 60. Joel currently has employer provided term life insurance in the amount of twice his annual salary. What amount of life insurance will Joel need using the multiple-of-earnings approach?

Solution: Note that I is a present value of an annuity, a series of payments (annual take home income) of $36,000 for 25 years with a 4% inflation rate, the factor will be 15.6 using Appendix Table A.4, then, I = $36,000 × 15.6 = 561,600 (you may also use the financial calculator to get a similar answer); and L_c = 2 × $40,000 = $80,000, then L = 0.75 × $561,600 - $80,000 = $421,200 - $80,000 = $341,200.

❖ **Interpretation**: Joel needs a policy amount to $341,200. Note that several assumptions are made in this example. Joel assumes that his spouse needs 25 year support, his family needs 75% of his take home income after his death, the inflation rate will be 4% for each year, and the proceeds received will be invested to have at least 4% return rate besides the funds used for current living expenses.[2] This example illustrates the multiple-of-earnings approach to estimate life insurance needs. The approach calculates the dollar amount of loss by multiplying a portion of the annual after-tax income of the person involved (the **insured**) by an interest factor based on the number of years income will be needed. A figure of 75 percent of after-tax income is often used because approximately one quarter of a worker's take-home pay is typically spent on his or her own personal needs and taxes, and such needs end at death. An interest factor is used because the life insurance proceeds which are received after the insured's death can be invested and earn a favorable return.

While the multiple-of-earnings approach is an improvement upon the **human life approach** to estimating insurance needs (which estimates the dollar value on the life to be insured based on the notion of the psychological loss that would be felt by survivors, rather the earnings potential of the insured,)[3] it is still inadequate because it addresses only one of the factors affecting the need for life insurance—the necessity to replace income. It does not take into consideration such factors as age, family situation, and losses other than income (such as government benefits) than can occur when someone dies. While the multiple-of-earnings approach does provide a rough guideline for life insurance needs, it is simplistic and should only be used as a crude estimate. While the multiple-of-earnings approach is an imprecise (although relatively easy-to-use) method for determining life insurance needs, a superior and more accurate method is the **needs approach**, which is described next.

3. Using the Needs Approach to Estimate Life Insurance Needs

Formula 14.3: $L = I + F + R + P + D + O - G - L_c$

Where: L = life insurance required using the needs approach; I = income replacement needs fund; F = final expense needs; R = readjustment-period needs; P = post-secondary school expense needs; D = debt-repayment needs; O = other special needs; G = present value of a series of government benefits; and L_c = current life insurance.

▼ **Example 14.3:** Using the information in Example 14.2, if Joel considers more factors besides his income replacement and current life insurance policy after his death, he may need a policy with a greater face value. Joel may consider that he needs to provide a $10,000 fund to pay bills after death, such as expenses for medical, funeral, burial, travel, attorney, and taxes. His wife may need extra funds, around $19,000, to cover employment interruptions, dependent care, an emergency fund, and possible education expenses. He may also desire to have a $75,000 fund for his children's post-secondary education, and $10,000 for the repayment of installment debt and/or education loans. To save insurance costs, Social Security survivor's benefits should also be included when the life insurance needs are calculated. If considering all these factors, what is the face value of a life insurance policy he should purchase?

Solution: Since, I = $341,200, L_c = $80,000 (use the results from Example 14.1), F = $10,000, R = $19,000, P = $75,000, D = $10,000, O = 0. Since his children will receive Social Security benefits for 15 years (until the younger one turns 18 years old) the monthly benefits will be $1,958 or $23,496 annually according to the Appendix B "Estimating Social Security Benefits," and the inflation rate will be 4%, the inflation factor will be 11.118 using Appendix A.4, and the present value of the benefits is (you may also use the financial calculator to get a similar answer): $23,496 × 11.118 = $261,229. Then, L = $341,200 + $10,000 + $19,000 + $75,000 + $10,000 - $80,000 - $261,229 = $113,971.

❖ **Interpretation:** Although the needs approach takes longer to calculate an estimate of life insurance requirements, it is more complete than any other method. Note that many assumptions are made when the various factors are considered and calculated. The assumptions used in the projections need to be as accurate as possible to get a good estimate.

4. Income Tax Implications of Life Insurance

Conceptual Idea 14.4: Some of the advantages of life insurance policies are that cash dividends, the cash surrender value, and growth in the cash value are free of current income taxes.

▼ **Example 14.4.1:** Rebecca Smithfield purchased a $50,000 cash-value life insurance policy 20 years ago which now has $14,808 in accumulated cash-surrender value built up. **Cash-surrender value** is the value of the investment in a life insurance policy that belongs to the owner of the policy while still alive that can be borrowed from the company or obtained by surrendering and canceling the policy. The annual statement Rebecca received from her life insurance company shows that the cash value grew $800 from last year ($14,008) to this year ($14,808). What is Rebecca's after-tax return on her life insurance cash value, assuming that her combined marginal income tax rate is 33 percent (28% federal and 5% state)? What would be Rebecca's after-tax return on $800 if that amount was a dividend from an investment in a mutual fund?

Solution: Since the $800 growth in cash value is tax free, the return rate will be:
$800/$14,008 = 5.7%;
If Rebecca invested the funds in a mutual fund, the after-tax return rate would be:
($800/$14,008) × (1 – 33%) = 5.7% × 67% = 3.8%; and
Rebecca would collect an after-tax return of $800 (1 – 33%) = $536.

❖ **Interpretation:** This example indicates that Rebecca had tax savings of $264 because she used cash value life insurance instead of other investment instruments. Note that Rebecca may get a higher return from other investments. Also, you may consider your needs and costs of cash value life insurance policies when comparing the returns of different investment instruments.

▼ **Example 14.4.2:** Jane Marywood listened to a sales presentation by a life insurance salesperson who showed her an illustration demonstrating the tax-free growth within a cash-value policy. Assuming that a portion of her annual insurance premium, $600, grows free of income taxes at a rate of 4 percent, what will it amount to after 20 years? If instead of growing free of income taxes within a life insurance policy, the $600 a year income was from interest on a savings account, what would be the future value sum after taxes in 20 years growing at a rate of 4 percent assuming that her combined marginal income tax rate is 33 percent (28% federal and 5% state)?

Solution:

(1) *Cash-value policy.*

Calculate the future value of a series of payments ($600 here) for 20 years with an interest rate of 4% using the financial calculator (see Chapter 1 for specific steps) reveals:
FVA = $17,866.85

(2) *Savings account.*

If the money is put into a savings account, the $600 return will be taxed at a rate of 33%, and the annual after-tax return will be: $600 (1 – 0.33) = $402. Then the

payment = $402, n = 20 years, and r = 4%, using the financial calculator (see Chapter 1 for specific steps),
FVA = $11,970.79

❖ **Interpretation:** If Jane pays a combined income tax rate of 33 percent on the $600 in savings income, she will only have $402 after taxes that will grow at a rate of 4 percent. Thus, her return will be only $11,970.79, considerably less, $5,896.06 ($17,866.85 – $11,970.79) than the $17,866.85 within the cash-value life insurance policy. This example illustrates the benefit of using life insurance as a tax-advantaged investment. Favorable tax treatment exists on the growth of value within a life insurance policy. The funds inside a life insurance policy grow tax-free while funds invested outside a life insurance policy are subject to annual income taxes. This treatment makes life insurance a tax-sheltered investment.

5. Commission Loads

Conceptual Idea 14.5: Most policies have a commission load that is related to the premium size and number of years of the policy.

▼ **Example 14.5:** Joel Raymond contacts Sammy Sales to discuss the purchase of a cash-value life insurance policy with a face amount of $237,000. The annual premium has been calculated at $1,800. Sammy Sales will receive a commission from the sale of this policy in accordance with his company's commission schedule. His company pays a commission of 40% of the 1st year premiums plus 5% on years 2 outward. Using the premium above, what will be the total commission Sammy can expect from this sale if Joel Raymond continues to pay the premium until age 65?

Solution: First year commission = 0.40 × $1,800 = $720
The projected 29 years of commissions = 0.05 × $1,800 × 29 = $2,610
Total commission = $720 + $2,610 = 3,330

❖ **Interpretation:** Commission fees are the agent's earnings derived from working with the client. The agent provides guidance for the client to come to a decision about life insurance. Because most people know they need life insurance but don't want to talk about their own death, selling life insurance is considered one of the hardest products to sell to consumers. Why? A life insurance agent is selling an intangible to someone who generally is not going to personally benefit from the proceeds—his or her survivors are. Knowing this fact, most companies pay a higher front-load commission than one would expect to receive from selling other products. Most policies have a commission load unless they are purchased through a no-load insurance offering. Even then there often are various fees added to the premium, usually ranging from $50 to $100.

6. Using the Net Cost Method to Compare Policy Costs[4]

Formula 14.6: $NC = (P \cdot Y - CV - D)/0.001F \cdot Y$

Where: NC = net cost; P = premiums paid for a designated time period; Y = years to pay premium; CV = cash value of the policy at surrender; D = accrued dividends if any; and F = face value of the policy.

▼ **Example 14.6**: Joel Raymond's policy for $237,000 costs him $150 per month, or $1,800 per year. If he decides to surrender the policy after 10 years, what is his net cost assuming the cash value of his policy is $14,591 after 10 years? There are no accrued dividends.

Solution: Since P = $1,800, Y = 10, CV = $14,591, D = 0, F = $237,000,
                then NC = ($1,800 × 10 – $14,591 – 0)/0.001 × $237,000 × 10 = $3,409/2,370 = 1.44

❖ **Interpretation**: By making this calculation with several similar policies, an insured can determine the policy with the lowest number, and using false logic, assume that it has the lowest cost. However, there are three main problems with this cost calculation. First, it assumes the policyholder will have the policy for exactly 10 years, where in fact, the averages will be different for other time periods, such as a 20-year period. Second, cash value and dividends are only assumptions, and if they are higher or lower than predicted, cost averages will be affected. Third, the comparison does not take into account when premiums and benefits are paid, which ignores the time value of money. The following section will present a formula to compare the genuine cost of life insurance policies taking account of the time value of money.

7. Using the Interest-Adjusted Cost Method to Compare Policy Costs[5]

Formula 14.7: IAC = (P · FVAD – D – CV)/0.001F · FVAD

Where: IAC = interest-adjusted cost; P = annual premium payment; FVAD = the factor of future value of annuity due; D = dividends; CV = cash value; and F = face value of the policy.

▼ **Example 14.7:** Using all the same numbers from Example 14.5, what is the interest-adjusted cost index assuming 4% and 10 years?

Solution: Since P = $1,800, FVAD (n = 10, r = 4%) = 12.49, D = 0, CV = $14,591, F = $237,000, then
                IAC = ($1,800 × 12.49 – 0 – $14,591)/0.001 × $237,000 × 12.49 = $7,891/$2,960 = 2.67

Note that FVAD can be figured out with both the calculator and the table method. If using a calculator, the mode should be set to calculate annuity due. If using table method, the FVAD should be calculated as follows: The value 13.49 is the value for 11 years at 4% in Appendix A.3, which should be deducted by 1 to get 12.49, since the deposit is made at the beginning of the year and not at the end of the year.

❖ **Interpretation**: Under the guidelines established by the Association of Insurance Commissioners, the interest-adjusted cost index is required to be calculated for each insurance illustration presented to the consumer. Even with this method, however, comparison of policy costs is still inexact, partially because coverages provided may differ slightly among similar policies. Also, the cash value and dividend amounts are assumptions only. No policy is cost-effective for an insured if it does not meet that individual's needs. Before purchasing any life insurance policy, one should be aware of the financial ratings established for each life insurance company by independent ratings services, as these offer guidance as the each company's ability to pay its obligations.

INFORMATION AND COMPUTING RESOURCES

1. The following sources provide ratings of life and health insurance companies:

   - *Insurance Forum*, P. O. Box 245-J, Ellettsville, IN 47429, publishes a summary of ratings (available for a fee of $15) from various insurance rating organizations on more than 1,000 life and health insurance companies.

   - *A. M. Best Company* (900-555-BEST; $2.95 per call) rates the financial strength of companies on a 15-point scale from A++ to F.

   - *Standard & Poor's* (212-208-1527) for up to five free ratings.

   - *Moody's* (212-553-0377) for up to three free ratings.

   - *Duff & Phelps* (312-629-3833 for up to five free ratings, or $25 for a mailed rating that includes strengths and weaknesses of a company.

   - *Weiss* (800-289-9222; $15 per telephone rating, or $25 for a mailed rating that includes strengths and weaknesses of a company.

2. You may save a substantial amount on term life insurance premium by using a **premium quote service**, an independent life insurance agent or group of agents who concentrate on one thing—low rates. Although they provide price information for policies, such services may offer no assistance in figuring how much life insurance one needs or what type of policy should be purchased. The services that do not charge a fee but do receive a commission if you buy from a recommended company include Master Quote (800-337-5433), LifeRates of America (800-457-2837), TermQuote (800-444-8376), Quotesmith (800-431-1147), SelectQuote (800-343-1985), and Insurance Quote Service (800-972-1104).

3. You may search web sites for information relevant to life insurance purchases. Some on-line premium quote services will help consumers estimate term life insurance needs, compare policy costs, and search for the companies with the lowest prices. See, for example, InstantQuote (www.instantquote.com) and

Quotesmith (quotesmith.com). You may also go to the web sites of different life insurance companies to review their policies for comparison, such as Life Insurance Company of Virginia (www.lifeofvirginia.com) or Prudential Insurance Company at (www.prudential.com).

EXERCISES PROBLEMS

Estimating Social Security Survivor's Benefits

1. Ronald is the surviving spouse of Amy who died recently at age 45. If Amy's earnings last year were $67,000 and if they have three young children, what is the maximum annual family benefit Ronald will receive from the Social Security Administration?

Using the Multiple-of-Earnings Approach to Estimate Life Insurance Needs

2. Steven Luo is 40, married to Sharon Young (age 30), an accountant. As an electronic engineer at an international company, his take home salary is about $60,000. Even his company provides a term insurance policy of $150,000, he still considers to buy another one to fully support his wife until she reaches age 60 to be eligible for Social Security survivor's benefits in case of his death. What is his life insurance need if the multiple-of-earnings approach is used and the inflation rate is assumed as 3%?

3. John Shaw is an assistant professor of immunology at a state university and single currently. He lives with his widow mother. He is considering to buy a term life insurance policy for her mother for 20 years. If his take home salary is about $45,000, and his university provides a life insurance of $100,000, how much else does he need with the multiple-of-earnings approach if the inflation rate is assumed to be 4%?

Using the Needs Approach to Estimate Life Insurance Needs

4. Peter Quincy is a computer programmer working for a local company and has an annual earning of $48,000 which equals to about $36,000 take home pay. His wife Lily is an interior designer with a take home pay about $40,000. The couple's ages are both 45 years old. They have two children, Alicia at age 13 and Kerri at age 10. Peter considers to buy a life insurance policy to support his family until his wife is 60 years old. He also considers to use the proceeds to pay for the two children's college education which is estimated to be $100,000. In case of Peter's death, the monthly Social Security benefits, $2,195, will be received until Kerri turns 18. If the final expenses are estimated as $10,000, the readjustment-period needs are $20,000, and the debt-repayment needs are $20,000, how much is the face value of the policy Peter should purchase if the inflation rate is 3% and the needs approach is used?

5. Amenda Yates is a single mother (age 30) with her son Jonathan (age 8). Amenda works as a daycare center teacher with an annual pay of $30,000 or take home pay about $24,000. She hope she will pay for her son's college education which may be $50,000 ten years later, which means she would like to support her son until he turns 22. To calculate her life insurance needs, she has checked the local funeral services costs and her own financial papers. She finds that her final expenses are about $8,000, and debt-repayment needs are $9,000. If she dies suddenly, the federal government will pay her son $635 monthly through the Social Security survivor's benefits until he turns 18. How much Amenda should buy for a life insurance policy if the needs approach is used and the inflation rate is 4%.

Tax Implications of Life Insurance

6. Marty Johnson purchased a $50,000 cash-value life insurance policy 18 years ago for which he has been paying a $700 annual premium. This year he received $1,000 cash dividend check from his insurance company. What is Marty's after-tax return on the $1,000 assuming that his combined marginal income tax rate is 33 percent (28% federal and 5% state)? What would be Marty's after-tax return if the $1,000 income was a dividend from an investment in a stock or mutual fund?

7. Jean Wood listened to a sales presentation by a life insurance salesperson who showed her an illustration demonstrating the tax-free growth within a cash-value policy. Assuming that a portion of her annual insurance premium, $400, grows free of income taxes at a rate of 3 percent, what will it amount to after 15 years? If instead of growing free of income taxes within a life insurance policy, the $400 a year income was from interest on a savings account, what would be the future value sum after taxes in 15 years growing at a rate of 3 percent assuming that her combined marginal income tax rate is 33 percent (28% federal and 5% state)?

Commission Loads

8. Mark Horn contacts Tom Carr to discuss the purchasing of an cash-value life insurance policy with a face amount of $300,000. The annual premium has been calculated at $2,000. Tom Carr will receive a commission from the sale of this policy in accordance with his company's commission schedule. His company pays a commission of 40% of the 1st year premiums plus 4% on years 2 outward. Using the premium above, what will be the total commission Tom Carr expect from this sale if Mark Horn continues to pay the premium for 20 years?

9. Patrick Hurrington earned $3,500 commission for serving a clients for 30 years. If the annual premium is $1,900, and the first year's percentage of premium for commission is 45%, what is the average percentage of premium for commissions for the rest of the years?

Using Net Cost Method to Compare Policy Costs

10. Jim Abbit's policy for $300,000 costs him $2,000 per year. If he decides to surrender the policy after 15 years, what is his net cost assuming the cash value of his policy is $25,483 after 15 years? There are no accrued dividends and the net cost method is used.

11. Use the net cost method to calculate the cost of a policy with face value of $500,000 and annual premium of $3,000, assume the cash value at the surrendering date is $35,323 after 20 years?

Using the Interest-Adjusted Cost Method to Compare Policy Costs

12. Use the interest-adjusted cost method to do Exercise 9, assume that the inflation rate is 3%.

13. Use the interest-adjusted cost method to do Exercise 10, assume that the inflation rate is 3%.

SELECTED REFERENCES

Black, K. Jr., & Skipper, H. D. Jr. (1994). *Life insurance* (12th ed.). Englewood Cliffs, NJ: Prentice Hall.

Financial needs analysis (1995). Vernon, CN: Vernon Publishing Company.

Longo, T. (January, 1996). How to get a great rate fast. *Kiplinger's Personal Finance Magazine*, pp. 67-72.

Leimberg, S. R., & McFadden, J. J. (1995). *The tools and techniques of employee benefit and retirement planning*, (4th ed.). Cincinnati, OH: The National Underwriter.

Longo, T. (October, 1995). The is no free insurance. *Kiplinger's Personal Finance Magazine*, pp. 97-101.

When it is time to buy life insurance, Part I (July, 1993). *Consumer Reports*, pp. 431-442.

When it is time to buy life insurance, Part I (August 1993). *Consumer Reports*, pp. 523-539.

ENDNOTES

1. Note that the additional benefit of tax deductibility of payments into a cash-value life insurance investment—available for IRS-qualified retirement savings programs—is not permitted for life insurance. Before one considers using life insurance as a tax shelter for cash value accumulations, he or she should consider many factors. It is possible to fund tax deferred retirement plans and non-tax deferred insurance plans, such as cash value insurance, if one uses proper planning and guidance. While retirement plans provide for retirement income, life insurance plans can provide financial protection for survivors should the primary income producer

die unexpectedly. One should take into account the many advantages and disadvantages of each.

2.   When estimating, a fair approximation is to multiply initial annual needs for life insurance by the number of years, because one can assume that the return earned on life insurance death benefits is balanced by inflation and income taxes.

3.   The human life approach (also called the **value-of-life approach**) to estimating life insurance needs was developed in the 1920s by Dr. S. S. Huebner founder of The American College, Bryn Mawr, Pennsylvania. It was based on the concept that when a working person dies or loses his or her ability to produce income or support a family, the true value cannot be placed on the life itself. In this illustration, for example, Joel might guess that his life is worth $1 million despite that there is no rhyme or reason for his logic. If Joel purchased $1 million in life insurance coverage, he might be overinsured or underinsured. This approach to estimating life insurance needs is particularly hazardous because it carries so much potential for error. It should not be used. A variation of the value-of-life approach is to convert future earnings to a present value. For example, to replace Joel's $27,000 after-tax income for 25 years assuming a 4 percent annual return would require a sum of $421,797 (using Appendix Table A-3).

4.   A more sophisticated formula can be found in Black and Skipper (1994, p.273).

5.   A more sophisticated formula can be found in Black and Skipper (1994, p. 273).

Chapter 15
Stock Mathematics

Chapter 15
Stock Mathematics

Jing J. Xiao and E. Thomas Garman[1]

OVERVIEW

Stocks are shares of ownership in the assets and earnings of a business corporation. **Common stock** is the most basic form of ownership of a corporation. The owner of stock, called a **shareholder** or **stockholder**, has a claim on the assets and earnings of the firm. Stockholders expect that the corporation will be profitable enough to pay **dividends** (a share of profits distributed in cash), and that there will be an increase in the **market value** (or **market price**). For individual investors, they hope the market prices of the stocks they hold will increase from the original prices they paid, which indicate the increase of their wealth.

As an investment tool, stocks have the highest potential rate of return. For example, the rate of return on common stocks has substantially exceeded the rate of inflation, providing a real return of nearly 8% during the period of 1802 to 1993. For comparison, the rate of return on Treasury bills exceeded the rate of inflation by over 3% in the same period.[1] The difference between the real rate on stocks and bonds is called **equity premium**.[2] Investment in stocks will help achieve many long-term household financial goals, such as income for retirement. However, only 18 percent of American households owned stocks, and median value of holdings among stockholders was $10,000.[3]

Based on different assumptions, there are different approaches to investing in stocks. The **fundamental approach** assumes that each particular stock has an intrinsic, or true, value based on its expected future earnings; therefore, some stocks can be identified that will outperform others. A stock's price movement is assumed to be determined by current and future earnings trends, industry outlook, and management's expertise. The **technical approach** is an attempt to assess the possible effect of current market action on future supply and demand for securities and

---

[1]Jing J. Xiao and E. Thomas Garman.

individual issues and then make buying and selling decisions accordingly. Technical analysts carefully plot price movements in conjunction with various market indexes and other technical data and use mathematical models to predict best time for buying and selling. The **random-walk approach** holds that price movements are unpredictable and that as a result investment analysis will not help predict future behavior. The market is assumed to react swiftly to all unexpected information from news accounts, brokerage analysts, and disclosure documents filed with the Securities and Exchange Commission and properly prices each stock. Luck is the most important factor considered by the random-walk approach believers.

To choose stocks for specific investment goals, besides other determinants, several financial factors should be considered, such as rate of return, yield, earnings per share, price/earnings ratio, cash dividend payout ratio, price/sale ratio, price/book ratio, and beta. Calculations and interpretations of these factors will be detailed in the next section.

Purchases of stocks will depend on a person's or family's needs, financial capacities, and investment goals. Many costs of purchasing stocks should be considered, such as stock prices, opportunity costs, costs related to information search, and commission fees. Timing is also an important factor. The stock market has several empirical regularities, such as January effect, weekend effect, and holiday effect, which could be considered by individual investors when buying or selling stocks. For example, January has been approximately 3 percent higher than the average monthly returns in February through December, Monday was found to be much lower than the average return on any other day of the week, and average stock returns on trading days immediately before federal holidays are 9 to 14 times higher than the average daily returns during the rest of the year.[4]

EXAMPLES OF MATHEMATICAL CONCEPTS RELATED TO STOCKS

1. Financial Ratios Relevant to Stocks

The most frequently cited financial ratios relevant to stocks are (1) earning per shares (EPS), (2) price/earning ratio (P/E), (3) price/sale ratio (P/S), (4) price/book ratio (P/B), (5) dividend yield (Y), and (6) Dividend Payout Ratio (DP).

Formula 15.1.1: $EPS = \dfrac{NP}{n}$

Where: EPS = earnings per share; NP = net profits; and n = number of shares of the stock.

Formula 15.1.2: $P/E = \dfrac{p}{EPS}$

Where: P/E = price/earning ratio; p = price per share of stock; and EPS = earning per share.

Formula 15.1.3: $P/S = \dfrac{P}{R}$

Where: P/S = price/sale ratio; P = total stock price; and R = total revenue.

Formula 15.1.4: $P/B = \dfrac{p}{b}$

Where: P/B = price/book ratio, p = price per share of stock, b = book value per share.

Formula 15.1.5: $Y = \dfrac{d}{p}$

Where: Y = dividend yield; d = dividends per share; and p = price per share.

Formula 15.1.6: $DP = \dfrac{D}{E}$

Where: DP = dividend payout ratio; D = total dividends; and E = total earnings.

▼ **Example 15.1:** A small dog food company has a revenue of $660,000 and a net profit of $45,000. The company has 30,000 shares of the stock outstanding with a market price of $26 per share. The net worth of the company is $340,000 and the cash dividends per share of the stock is $.66. What are (1) EPS, (2) P/E, (3) P/S, (4) P/B, (5) Y, and (6) DP?

Solution for (1): $EPS = \dfrac{\$45,000}{30,000} = \$1.50$

❖ **Interpretation: Earnings per share (EPS)** indicates the amount of income a company has, on a per share basis, to pay dividends and reinvest in itself as retained earnings. The EPS is a dollar figure determined by dividing the corporation's total after-tax annual earnings (before common stock cash dividends but after payment of dividends to preferred stockholders) by the total number of shares of common stock held by investors. It is a useful measure of the profitability of a firm on a common-stock per-share basis because investors can use it to compare the financial conditions of companies. The higher value of EPS indicates the company is more profitable.

Solution for (2): $P/E = \dfrac{\$26}{\$1.50} = 17.3$

❖ **Interpretation:** The **P/E ratio** is a useful way to compare stocks selling at different prices. It is a ratio of the current market value (price) of a common stock to its earnings per share (EPS), and indicates how many times a stock's selling price is greater than its earnings per share. The P/E shows in ratio form how the market is valuing the stock because it describes the amount of money investors are willing to pay for each dollar of a company's earnings. Further, it is a measure of investor confidence in a stock's future over the next five years or so. P/E ratios can be used to divide companies into different types, such as financial successful (P/E = 7 – 10), rapid growing (P/E = 15 – 25), and speculative companies (P/E = 40 – 50).

Solution for (3): $P/S = \dfrac{\$26 \times 30,000}{\$660,000} = 1.18$

❖ **Interpretation:** The **price/sale ratio (P/S)** is a ratio obtained by dividing the total current market value of a stock (current market price multiplied by the number of shares outstanding) by the total corporate revenues (sales) over the past year. The ratio is a measure of how good a buy a particular stock is at its current market price. The lower the P/S ratio, the better the marketability of the stock. Market analysts generally suggest that investors avoid companies with a ratio greater than 1.5 and stay with those that have P/S of less than 0.75.

Solution for (4):

First figure out the book value per share: $\dfrac{\$340,000}{30,000} = \$11.30$

Then, $P/B = \dfrac{\$36}{\$11.30} = 1.9$

❖ **Interpretation:** The **book value per share** is the book value of a company (determined by subtracting total liabilities from total assets, and also called **shareholder's equity**) divided by the number of shares of common stock outstanding. Often there is little relationship between the book value of a company and its earnings or the market price of its stock. However, the market price for a company's common stock is usually higher than its book value per share because stockholders anticipate earnings and dividends in the future and expect the market price to rise. When the value of the assets per share exceeds the price per share, the stock may truly be underpriced.

The **P/B ratio** is a ratio of the **market value** (**current price**) of a common stock to its book value per share. Simply take the company's book value per share and divide it into price per share. The current P/B ratio for most stocks is between 2.1 and 1.0. The lower the ratio, the less highly a company's assets have been valued, indicating that the stock may be currently underpriced. If the ratio is less than one, something is wrong with the usefulness of the assets, and in such cases, an underperforming and undervalued company may become the target of a corporate takeover.

Solution for (5): $Y = \dfrac{\$0.66}{\$26} = 0.025 = 2.5\%$

❖ **Interpretation:** The **dividend yield** is the cash dividend return to an investor expressed as a percentage of the value of a security. Thus, it is a percentage calculation on a per share basis of the cash dividends paid in cash to holders of stock divided by the price of the stock. Financially successful companies generally have relatively high dividend yields, while growth and speculative companies usually have low or zero dividend yields because they choose to retain such earnings within the company to finance future endeavors.

Solution for (6): $DP = \dfrac{\$.66 \times 30,000}{\$45,000} = .44 = 44\%$

❖ **Interpretation:** The **dividend payout ratio** is a measure of the percentage of total earnings paid out to stockholders as cash dividends. Newer companies usually retain most if not all of their profits to facilitate growth; companies with a stable cash flow, such as utilities, usually have a high payout ratio. An investor interested in growth may want to invest in a company with a low payout ratio.

2. Using Beta to Calculate an Estimated Rate

Formula 15.2: $r = r_T + \beta \sum r_m$

Where: r = estimated rate of return; r_T = T-bill rate; ß = beta; and r_m = market risk rate.

▼ **Example 15.2:** If betas for three companies, A, B, C, are 2, 0.5, and -1, respectively, the stock prices of the three companies are expected to change by different amounts. This example assumes that the T-bill rate is 5 percent and the market risk is 8 percent.

Solution:

Company A's stock price is likely to increase by
   $5 + (2 \times 8) = 21\%$

Company B's stock price is likely to increase less by
   $5 + (1 \times 8) = 13\%$

And Company C's stock price is likely to decrease by
   $5 + (-1 \times 8) = -3\%$

❖ **Interpretation:** Using beta to calculate an estimated rate of return is a method of projecting the rate of return of a stock in the future based upon the relative risk of a particular investment compared the market return for all investments. **Beta** has to do with statistically estimating the relative risk of a particular investment compared with the market risk for all investments by using historical data. A beta figure shows how responsive the price of an individual investment has been to overall market fluctuations. As such, it is a measure of the price volatility of an investment, such as a stock, relative to the market for other similar investments, such as stocks, as a whole. Higher betas mean greater risk relative to the market. The average for all stocks in the market is always 1 and most stocks have positive betas of between 0.5 and 2.0. However, betas also can be negative.

Beta can be used to categorize stock types. For example, betas of income stocks are less than 1.0, betas of growth stocks are from 1.5 to 2.0, and speculative stocks have betas greater than 2.0. If betas are positive and above 1, the stocks are called **cyclical** because they go up and down with the market. A **countercyclical stock** has a beta of less than one, and as such it exhibits price movements that are contrary to downward movements in the business cycle (such as cigarette and utility companies).

One can obtain the betas for specific stocks from a brokerage firm, mutual fund company, realtor, library reference book, as well as from magazines that write about investments. You may also estimate betas by yourself using regression models with historical data. Once a beta for a particular investment is known, you can begin to calculate your total estimated rate of return on an investment. To complete the calculation, you also will need estimates of both the current Treasury-bill rate and the market risk, information that is readily available.

3. Calculating a Projected Rate of Return

Formula 15.3: $r = p_f - p_p + d$

Where: r = projected rate of return; p_f = future price per share; p_p = present price per share, and d = dividends per share.

▼ **Example 15.3:** A person has stocks in a cat food company priced at $40 per share. The last 12-month earnings amounted to $3.50 and the cash dividend for the same period was $0.77 per share. Assuming that the dividend growth rate will be 14 percent and P/E ratio will remain the same, what is the return in the fifth year?

Solution:

In the fifth year, the earnings will be:
$3.50 \times (1 + 0.14)^5 = $6.74

P/E ratio is:
$40.00/3.5 = 11.4

The stock price in the fifth year will be:
$6.74 \times 11.4 = $76.84

The dividends for five years will be:
($.77 \times 1.14) + ($.77 \times 1.14^2) + ($.77 \times 1.14^3) + ($.77 \times 1.14^4) + ($.77 \times 1.14^5) = $5.80

The return for the fifth year will be:
($76.84 - $40.00) + $5.80 = $42.64

❖ **Interpretation:** The **projected rate of return** for a stock over a period of years can be determined by adding anticipated income (from dividends, interest, rents, or whatever) to the future value of the investment less its original cost. In the case of stocks, the potential return is influenced by a number of factors, including the original stock price, the dividend, its future price, the company's rate of growth, and the length of time period. The rates of return of several stocks can be compared to identify those with the best potential.

4. Approximate Compound Yield (ACY)

Formula 15.4:

$$ACY = \frac{d + \dfrac{p_f - p_p}{n}}{\dfrac{p_f - p_p}{2}}$$

Where: ACY = approximate compound yield; d = average annual dividend; p_f = future price per share; p_p = present price per share; and n = number of years projected.

▼ **Example 15.4:** Using the figures in Example 15.3, what is the approximate compound yield?

Solution:

Since the average annual dividends will be:

$5.80/5 = $1.16

Then:

$$ACY = \frac{\$1.16 + (\$76.84 - \$40.00)/5}{(\$76.84 + \$40.00)/2} = \$8.528/\$58.42 = .146 = 14.6\%$$

❖ **Interpretation:** The **ACY** formula is a measure of the annualized compound growth of any long-term investment, such as a stock. Note that the calculation requires an *annual average dividend* to be used rather than the specific projected dividends. Once the ACY has been calculated, it can be compared to the yields of other investment alternatives, such as stocks, bonds, and mutual funds.

5. Growth Rate of Stock Prices

Formula 15.5 (Same as **Formula 4.3**): $FV = PV (1 + r)^n$

Where: FV = future price per share; PV = present price per share; r = annual growth rate; and n = number of years estimated.

▼ **Example 15.5:** An oil company's stock is worth $55 now and thirty years ago it was priced at $61. The stock has split 2 for 1 on two different occasions. What was the annual rate of changes in market value of the stock on a compound interest basis?

Solution 1: Using the time value table in Appendix A.

To solve this problem, three steps are needed.

(1) *Calculate the current price of the stock.*

Since the stock has split 2 for 1 for two times, the original one share is now four shares. The original price of one share is worth:

$4 \times \$55 = \$220$

(2) *Calculate the factor of future value.*

The factor of future value can be calculated by substituting numbers into the formula, $\$61 \times (1 + r)^{30} = \$220$. Then,

Factor of FV $= (1 + r)^{30} = \$220/\$61 = 3.606$

(3) *Estimate the change rate.*

From Appendix 1A (FV Sum Table), the closest value of FV factor for 30 year period is 3.243, which corresponds to a rate of 4 percent, implying the change rate of the stock is between 4 to 5 percent. To estimate the change rate, the approach of comparing two ratios is used.

Since, $(1 + 4\%)^{30} = 3.243$, and $(1 + r)^{30} = 3.606$

Then, $r/4 = 3.606/3.243 = 1.1119$

And, $r = 1.1119 \times 4 = 4.45$

The change rate of the stock price is approximately 4.45 percent.

Solution 2: Using the financial calculator.

First calculate the current price of the stock in the same way discussed in Solution 1. Then identify that in this question the following factors are given: present value ($61), future value ($220), and time period (30 years). The annual rate of change (equivalent to interest rate) can be gained by hitting following keys:

Input/Result	EL-733A	HP-10B	BA-II Plus
Present value	61 [+/-][PV]	61 [+/-][PV]	61 [+/-][PV]
Future value	220 [FV]	220 [FV]	220 [FV]
Time periods: year	30 [n]	30 [N]	30 [N]
Result: Interest rate	[COMP] [i] 4.37	[I/YR] 4.37	[CPT] [I/Y] 4.37

The change rate of the stock price is 4.37 percent. The result from the financial calculator is more accurate than the result from using the time value of money table.

❖   **Interpretation:** For the purpose of wealth accumulation, the higher growth rate will be more desirable. The change rate of the stock price is also positively related to the return of the stock. The rates of price changes of different stocks can be compared with historical data in order to buy stocks with comparatively higher growth rates, as well as to sell stocks with lower or negative growth rates.

INFORMATION AND COMPUTING RESOURCES

1.   National newspapers, such as *The Wall Street Journal* and *Barron's*, as well as big city newspapers, such as *U.S.A. Today*, *The Washington Post*, *New York Times*, *Boston Globe*, *Los Angeles Times*, and *Miami Herald*, regularly carry up-to-date stock indexes for Dow Jones Industrial Average, Standard & Poor's 500, New York Stock Exchange Composite, American Stock Exchange, and NASDAQ composite. Current P/E values, prices, dividends, and yields of hundreds of stocks can be found in these newspapers.

2.   Many financial or general magazines, such as *Money*, *Kiplinger's Personal Finance Magazine*, *Smart Money*, *Worth*, *Business Week*, *Fortune*, *U.S. News & World Report*, carry analyses of the financial markets, and current situations of many companies. Some of these magazines also report historical data of stocks and provide analyses by financial experts.

3.   Publications about industries include *Industry Surveys*, *The Outlook*, *Value Line Investment Surveys*, *Monthly Economic Letter*, and *Industrial Manual*. Many publications by trade associations also provide information on individual industries.

4.   Information regarding individual companies can be obtained from annual reports and prospectuses of the companies. Publications rating individual company performance are provided by Standard & Poor's, Moody's, Value Line, Trendline, Securities Research, and other ratings publishing companies. Research reports regarding stock performance are available from many big financial service companies and banks. Companies registered with the Securities and Exchange Commission must report many financial particulars to the SEC by filing a 10-K report annually, and the 10-K reports are available to the public. Information on profits, revenues, book values, and other financial information of individual companies can be found in these publications.

5.   Historical data on thousands of stocks can be gained through on-line computer network. Many commercial networks, such as American Online, CompuServe, and Prodigy, provide such services for a fee. To access to present data of stock transactions on-line, an additional fee typically is charged. There are also resources available for free in the computer network.[5]

- *Security and Exchange Commission:* http://www.sec.gov (10-K reports on companies can be acquired through EDGAR programs.)

- *Historical data:* http://nearnet.gnn.com/gnn/meta /finance/index.html (Historical data on a variety of government and equity series.)

- *Cambridge Interactive:* http://www.al.mit.edu/stocks.html (Data on individual stocks from Cam-bridge Interactive.)

- *MIT Database:* http://www.money.com (Data on individual stocks from MIT Experimental Database.)

- *Direct Investor:* http://www.netstockdirect.com (A daily list of companies with direct stock purchase plans.)

- *Dow Jones Business Information Services:* http://bis.dowjones.com/index.html (News and information for investors, investment counselors, and students.)

- *Internet brokers:*
  Accutrade: http://www.accutrade.com
  American Express: http://www.americanexpress.com/direct
  Aufauser: http://www.aufhauser.com
  Ceres Securities: http://www.ceres.com
  Datek: http://www.datek.com
  eBroker: http://www.ebroker.com
  *E*Trade:* http://www.etrade.com
  Lombard: http://www.lombard.com
  National Discount Broker: http://www.pawws.com/ndb
  Net Investor: http://www.netinvestor.com
  PCFN: http://www.pcfn.com
  Quick & Reilly: http://www.quick-reilly.com
  Schwab: http://www.eschawb.com
  Waterhouse: http://www.waterhouse. com
  JackWhite: http://www.pawws.com/jackwhite

- *Investing for kids:* http://tqd.advanced.org:80/3096/index.htm (Show kids, step by step, how to pick, buy, and monitor stocks.)

- *Stock exchanges:*
  Chicago Mercantile Exchange: http://www.cme.com/
  New York Stock Exchange: http://www.nyse.com
  American Stock Exchange: http://www.amex. com/
  Stock Exchange Markets: http://www.qualisteam.com/acct.html

- *Stock market simulation:* http://www.finalbell.com ("Play" the stock market, sponsored by USA Today.)

- *Stock quote:* http://www.pcquote.com (Practically real time quotes of stocks supplied by PC Quote Inc.)

- *Technology stocks:* http://www.techstocks.com (Focused on technology stocks created by the Silicon Investor.)

- *Wall Street Research Net:* http://www.wsrn.com/ (Over 65,000 links for researching companies, markets, and the economy.)

EXERCISE PROBLEMS

Financial Ratios Relevant to Stocks

1. A company had net profits of $84,000 and 40,000 shares of stock outstanding last year. What is its EPS?

2. A company's stock price is $15 per share. Last year, its earnings were $105,000 with 50,000 shares of stock outstanding. What is its P/E?

3. Last year, a company's revenue was $280,000 with 20,000 shares of stock at price of $10 per share. What is its P/S?

4. If a company's stock price is $41 per share with 320,000 shares of stock outstanding, and the net worth is $8,700,000, what is its P/B?

5. A company gives cash dividends amount to $1.09 per share and its stock price $51 is per share. What is its Y?

6. If a company's earnings were $130,000, and the cash dividends were $.87 per share with 45,000 shares of stock outstanding last year, what is its DP?

7. The following table is stock information from a recent date. Fill in the blank cells of the table.

	Closing Price	Dividend	Earnings	Yield (%)	P/E
AT&T		1.32		2.2	26
BellAtl	63.750		3.984	4.4	
Exxon	75.750	3.00			15
GnMotr	45.000	1.20			6
IBM	95.375	1.00	9.538		
Nynex		2.36		4.9	24
PacGE	30.125		2.739	6.5	
PacTel	29.750	2.18			12
Sears	36.000	.92			8
Uswst	47.000	2.14	2.938		

8. A small company has 40,000 shares of stocks outstanding. The company earned $34,000 and paid a cash dividend of $31,000 to the stockholders. The revenue over the past year is $950,000 and net worth of the company is $450,000. The current price of the stock per share is $33, what are the EPS, P/E, yield, dividend payout ratio, price/sale ratio, and price/book ratio?

9. *Out-of-Class Exercise* Choose a company and find its stock's current price, yield, dividend, P/E, dividend payout ratio, price/sale ratio, and price/book ratio. Write an endnote to indicate what sources are used to get the data.

10. *Out-of-Class Exercise* Pick ten companies, and compare their P/Es, dividends, prices, dividend payout ratios, price/sale ratios, and price/book ratios. Write an endnote to indicate data sources. Discuss what are the characteristics of these companies in terms of the financial ratios collected.

11. *Out-of-Class Exercise* Get access to financial data bases in on-line financial services, and find the information required by Question 9. Download the information and print it out.

Using Beta to Calculate an Estimated Rate of Return

12. Assume that T-bill rate is zero. If a person buys a stock with a market price of $45 and a beta value of 1.6, what would be the likely value of her $4,500 investment after one year if the general market for stocks rose 15 percent? And what is the investment worth if the general market for stocks dropped 15 percent?

13. Assume the T-bill rate is 4% and market risk is 7%. If a company's beta is 1.5, what is the estimated rate of return when beta is used?

14. If using beta to estimate the rate of return of a company and find it is -4%, given that the T-bill rate is 5% and the market risk is 8%, what is the beta of the company?

15. Assume that the market change is 30%, and betas of a series of stocks ranged from -5 to 5 with the interval of .5, what are the price changes of these stocks. You may observe the patterns of the changes. Use spreadsheet and its graphing function to do the exercise.

16. *Out-of-Class Exercise* Use beta as a measure to identify three companies in the real world, and each of them belongs to income, growth, and speculative company, respectively. Report what sources are used to find betas.

Calculating a Projected Rate of Return

17. If a company's stock price is $60 now, and will be $76 at the end of the third year in future, and the cash dividends are $3.4 per share now and will increase at a rate of 12%, what is the projected return of the stock?

18. It is projected that the cash dividends of a company will be $6.10 per share over next four years. If the P/E ratio will be the same, which is 12.3 now, and the EPS now is $3.5 and at the fourth year will be $4.1, what is the projected rate of return of the stock?

19. A company's stock is currently priced $25 per share, and cash dividend is $.26. Assume the growth rate of the company is 18%, and the cash dividend growth rate is 8%, what is the rate of return in the fourth year?

20. *Out-of-Class Exercise* Find a company's current stock price, the price 5 years ago, and its average dividends over the five years. Calculate the projected rate of return of the stock, and report information sources used.

Approximate Compound Yield

21. A company's stock price is $15 now and was $9 five years ago. The cash dividend has been increased to $.89 at a rate of 10%. What is the ACY?

22. Ten years ago, a company's stock price was $20. The price has been gone up at a rate of 11% over past ten years. The annual cash dividend, on average, was $.72. What is the ACY?

23. The current price of a company's stock is $60, and the stock price four years ago was $35, and the average annual dividend over the four years is $2.10, what is the approximate compound yield?

24. A company's current stock price is $40, and it is predicted to increase in a compound annual rate 10% in five years. The current dividend per share is $.81, and it will be increased in a rate of 12%. What is the approximate compound yield in the end of fifth year?

25. *Out-of-Class Exercise* Choose a company, locate needed information, and calculate its approximate compound yield from last 5, 10, 15, and 20 years. Report the information sources used.

Change Rate of Stock Prices

26. A company's stock was worth $30 in 1980, and in 1997 is worth $45, what is the annual rate of change in the stock price?

27. If a company's current stock price is $75, and its average change rate over past 12 years is 6%, what is the price twelve years ago?

28. A company's stock price is $4 now, and it expects that the price will be $20 in ten years, what is the change rate of the stock price over next ten years?

29. A company's stock is worth $66 in 1997 and $72 in 1974. The stock has split 2 for 1 on three different occasions. What was the annual rate of changes in market value of the stock on a compound interest basis?

30. *Out-of-Class Exercise* Choose a company, and find its current stock price and the price 10 years ago. Calculate the annual rate of changes in market value of the stock and report the information sources used.

SELECTED REFERENCES

AAII. (1996). *The individual investor's guide to computerized investing.* Chicago, IL: American Association of Individual Investors.

Abel, A. B. (1991). The equity premium puzzle. *Federal Reserve Bank of Philadelphia Business Review.* (September-October), 3-14.

Benartzi, S., & Thaler, R. H. (1995). Myopic loss aversion and the equity premium puzzle. *Quarterly Journal of Economics*, 73-92.

Haliassos, M., & Bertaut, C. C. (1995). Why do so few hold stocks? *The Economic Journal.*

Kennickell, A. B., & Starr-McCluer, M. (1994). Changes in family finances from 1989 to 1992: Evidence from the survey of consumer finances. *Federal Reserve Bulletin*, (October), 861-82.

Mehra, R., & Prescott, E. C. (1985). The equity premium puzzle. *Journal of Monetary Economics*, *15*, 145-61.

Poterba, J. M., & Samwick, A. A. (1995) Stock ownership patterns, stock market fluctuations, and consumption. *Brookings Papers on Economic Activity, 2,* 295-372.

Sharpe, W. F., Alexander, G. J., & Bailey, J. V. (1995). *Investments.* (5th ed.). Englewood Cliffs, NJ: Prentice Hall.

Siegel, J. J. (1992). The equity premium: Stock and bond returns since 1802. *Financial Analysts Journal, 48*, 28-38.

Zhong, L. X., & Xiao, J. J. (1995). Determinants of household stock and bond holdings. *Financial Counseling and Planning, 6*, 107-14.

ENDNOTES

1. The comparison between real returns of stocks and bonds has been made by Abel (1991), Mehra and Prescott (1985), and Siegel (1992).

2. The empirical fact that stocks have outperformed bonds over the last century by a surprisingly large margin is called the **equity premium puzzle**. Studies related to the possible explanations of equity premium puzzle are discussed in Benartzi and Thaler (1995).

3. See Kennickell and Starr-McCluer (1994) for descriptive statistics of stock ownership and median holdings by several demographic factors. Several recent studies investigated consumer behavior in stock holdings, such as reasons why so

few consumers own stocks (Haliassos & Bertaut, 1995), stock ownership patterns (Poterba & Samwick, 1995), and determinants of household stock holdings (Zhong & Xiao, 1995).

4.   See Sharpe, Alexander, and Bailey (1995, pp. 548-556) for a detailed discussion of empirical regularities in the stock market and related studies.

5.   Fees, ratings, qualities of services, and other information regarding the computer on-line services are discussed in AAII (1996).

Chapter 16
The Mathematics of Bonds

▼　Coupon Yield

▼　Current Yield

▼　Approximate Yield to Call

▼　Yield to Maturity

▼　Estimating the Selling Price of a Bond

▼　Discount Yield

▼　Municipal Bonds and After-Tax Equivalent Yield

▼　Zero-Coupon Bonds

▼　Inflation-Linked Treasury Bonds

▼　Duration of a Bond

Chapter 16
The Mathematics of Bonds

Kenneth Huggins, Ramon Griffin, E. Thomas Garman and Jing J. Xiao[1]

OVERVIEW

A **bond** is a written legal agreement between a group of bondholders (representing each investing bondholder) and the debtor (a company or government) that describes the terms of the debt by setting forth the maturity date, interest rate, and other factors.

When a bond is first issued, it is sold in one of three ways: (1) at its **face value**, or **par value** (the amount specified on the bond certificate that the issuer is legally obligated to pay upon redemption at the maturity date, usually $1,000, (2) at a **discount** below its face value, or (3) at a **premium** above its face value. Most bonds are sold through stockbrokers at par value, rather than at a premium or at a discount. The **maturity date** (or **maturity**) is when the face amount of a bond is due to be paid off or retired.

The interest rates on newly issued bonds changes over time. Because the face value interest rate on the bond remains fixed, over time the price of a bond changes to provide a competitive effective rate of return with comparable investments. Thus, some $1,000 face value bonds issued a few years ago may sell today for less than $1,000 (at a discount) while others may sell today for more than $1,000 (at a premium).

A bond's **value** (its price on any given day) is affected by its type, coupon rate, availability in the marketplace, demand for the bond, prices for similar bonds, the underlying credit quality of the issuer, the number of years that must elapse before its maturity, and fluctuations in current market interest rates. **Current market interest rates** are the current long- and short-term interest rates paid on various types of corporate and government debts that carry similar levels of risk. These rates are

[1]Kenneth Huggins, CFP, Chair, Finance Department, Metropolitan State College, P.O. Box 173362, Denver, CO 80217-3362, hugginsk@mscd.edu; Ramon Griffin, Associate Professor, Finance Department, Metropolitan State College, Denver, CO 80217. griffinr@mscd.edu; E. Thomas Garman and Jing J. Xiao.

largely set by investors in the bond market, primarily based upon their expectations of future inflation. If investors expect inflation to rise, they will demand higher interest rates on bonds for that risk. When market interest rates increase, interest rates paid on newly issued bonds will rise and the price of existing bonds will fall. This action occurs so that the existing bonds and the new bonds offer investors approximately the same yield. Bond prices move toward the face value as the security approaches maturity or at maturity; therefore, the change in bond prices and yields are related to the maturity time of the security.

There are three types of income situations with regard to bonds. First, bonds issued by corporations are considered **taxable bonds** because the interest income on such bonds is subject to federal, state and local income taxes. Second, bonds issued by the federal government are exempt from state and local income taxes, although they are taxable at the state and local levels if the investor lives in a place where such taxes are imposed. Third, bonds issued by municipalities (see below) are exempt from federal income taxes. Any bond sold for more than its purchase price is subject to income taxes (because of the long-term or short-term gain), unless the exchange occurs within a tax-sheltered retirement plan.

Municipal bonds (also called **munnies**) are long-term debts issued by local governments (cities, states, and various districts and political subdivisions) and their agencies that are used to finance public improvement projects, such as roads, bridges, and parks, or to pay for ongoing expenses. The U.S. Constitution requires that municipal bond interest be exempt from federal income tax. Thus, municipal bonds are also known as **tax-free bonds** or **tax-exempt bonds**. An investor in a municipal bond who also lives in the state which issued the bond will also be exempt from any state and local income taxes. Since municipal bonds are exempt from federal taxation, the stated yield is almost always lower than for other bonds.

This chapter examines mathematical examples associated with bonds, including coupon yield, current yield, approximate yield to call, yield to maturity, estimating the selling price of a bond, discount yield, municipal bonds and after-tax equivalent yield, zero-coupon bonds, inflation-linked Treasury bonds, and duration of a bond.

EXAMPLES OF MATHEMATICAL CONCEPTS RELATED TO BONDS

1. Coupon Yield

Formula 16.1: $Y = CI / P$

Where: Y = coupon yield; CI = current annual interest income in dollars; and P = par value of bond.

▼ **Example 16.1:** Bert Lancaster paid $1,000 to his stockbroker for a newly issued $1,000 bond that is to pay interest of $35 semi-annually for 20 years. What is the coupon yield of Bert's bond?

Solution: $Y = \$70/\$1,000 = 7\%$

❖ **Interpretation:** Bert paid the par value of $1,000 for the bond which pays $70 annually ($35 × 2), and that calculates to a 7% coupon yield.

2. Current Yield

Formula 16.2: CY = CI/CP

Where: CBY = current bond yield; CI = current annual interest income in dollars; and CP = current market price.

▼ **Example 16.2:** Martin Johnson paid $940 to his stockbroker for a previously issued $1,000, 20-year bond which has just over 19 years of interest payments of $70 per year in cash dividends ($35 semi-annually) remaining. What is the current yield on Martin's bond?

Solution: CY = $70/$940 = 7.45%

❖ **Interpretation:** Martin's current yield is calculated to be 7.45%. The **current yield** is a measure of the current annual income (the total of both semiannual interest payments in dollars) expressed as a percentage when divided by a bond's current market price. The current yield on a bond will be the same as the coupon yield when the bond is purchased at par value.

3. Approximate Yield to Call

Formula 16.3: $AYC = \dfrac{I + (P - MP)/n}{(P + MP)/2}$

Where: AYC = approximate yield to call; I = annual interest income in dollars; P = par value of bond; MP = market price of bond; and Y = number of years to call.

▼ **Example 16.3.1:** Sally Bowen paid $920 to her stockbroker for a previously issued $1,000, 20-year bond which has 16 years of interest payments of $70 per year in cash dividends ($35 semi-annually) remaining. The bond is callable 5 years after the original date of issue. What is the current yield on Sally's bond?

Solution: Since, I = $70, P = $1,000, MP = $920, n = 4, then

$$AYC = \frac{\$70 + (\$1,000 - \$920)/4}{(\$920 + \$1,000)/2}$$

$$= \frac{\$70 + \$80/4}{\$1,920/2}$$

$$= \$90/\$875$$

$$= 10.28\%$$

❖ **Interpretation:** The approximate yield to call on Sally's bond is 10.28%. Thus, the yield to Sally will be 10.28% for the next four years. At any point after that, 5 total years after original date of issue, the debtor has the right (but may or may not exercise it) to call in the bond by giving Sally $1,000. Sally's bond, like most bonds issued today, is **callable**. This is a legally binding clause that requires that the security may be bought back from the investor by the issuer before the maturity date. Most callable bonds have a **call protection period** during which the bond may not be called. In Sally's case, the 20-year bond has a 5-year call protection period after which it may be called. Issuers often issue callable bonds so that they can save money by calling in high interest bonds. If funds are needed by the issuer, the company or agency may sell new securities to raise the money (perhaps by issuing new bonds with a lower interest rate or selling new shares of common stock). If an investor, like Sally, owns a bond that is callable, he or she may have to reinvest the proceeds earlier than the expected maturity date, most likely at a lower interest rate. If such a bond was purchased at a premium, a bondholder could suffer a significant loss. Sally bought her bond at a discount, $920.

4. Yield to Maturity

Formula 16.4: $\text{AYC} = \dfrac{I + (P - MP)/N}{(P + MP)/2}$

Where: YTM = yield to maturity; I = annual interest income in dollars; P = par value of bond; MP = market price of bond; and N = number of years until maturity.

▼ **Example 16.4:** Juanita Morales bought a 20-year bond with a coupon rate of 7% and a par value of $1,000 at a discount for $940. What is Juanita's yield to maturity?

Solution: Since, I = $70, P = $1,000, MP = $940, N = 20, then

$$\text{AYC} = \frac{\$70 + (\$1,000 - \$940)/20}{(\$1,000 + \$940)/2}$$

$$= \frac{\$70 + \$60/20}{\$1,940/2}$$

$$= \$73/\$970$$

$$= 7.53\%$$

❖ **Interpretation:** The yield to maturity on Juanita's bond is 7.53%. **Yield to maturity (YTM)** is the total annual effective rate of return earned by a bondholder on a bond when it is held to maturity. It reflects *both* the current income *and* any difference if the bond was purchased at a price other than face value spread over the life of the bond. The market price of a bond equals the present value of its future interest payments and the present value of its face value when the bond matures. The YTM factors in the approximate appreciation when a bond is bought at a discount or at a premium.

5. Estimating the Selling Price of a Bond

Formula 16.5: $P_e = DI/MI$

Where: P_e = estimated selling price of a bond (assuming it is more than a few years from maturity); DI = annual dividend income in dollars; and MI = market interest rates on comparable bonds.

▼ **Example 16.5.1:** Margaret Swenson paid $1,000 for a 20-year, 7% bond and because she needed money she was forced to sell it after interest rates on comparable bonds had increased to 9%. Estimate how much Margaret's bond would (1) sell for if she had to sell the bond today, (2) how much of a financial loss she would suffer as a result, and (3) how much her bond might sell for if, instead, market interest rates dropped to 5.5%.

Solution:

(1) P_e = $70/.09 = $777.78

(2) $1,000 − $777.78 = $222.18

(3) P_e = $70/.055 = $1,272.72

❖ **Interpretation:** The estimated selling price of Margaret's bond would be $777.78, and she would lose approximately $222.18 if she had to sell. (Of course, if Margaret keeps her bond until maturity the issuer is obligated to redeem it for $1,0000.) If market interest rates decline to 5.5%, Margaret's bond has an estimated selling price of $1,272.72. Note that Formula 16.5 is a simplified way to estimate the bond price. A more accurate way to estimate the bond price should consider the lengths of the maturity and coupon rate besides the interest rate changes. In general, rising interest rates reduce bond prices, and falling rates increase bond prices. The longer the time until maturity of a bond, the more sensitive the price to changes in interest rates. In addition, the percentage change in a bond's price owing to a change in its yield will be smaller if its coupon rate is higher.[1]

6. Discount Yield

Formula 16.6: $DY = (P - MP)/MP$

Where: DY = discount yield on a bond; P = par value of bond; and MP = market price of the bond.

▼ **Example 16.6.1:** Lonnie Reynolds bought a 52-week, $10,000 Treasury bill from a Federal Reserve bank at a discount price of $9,500. Which is the discount yield on Lonnie's bond?

Solution: $DY = (\$10,000 - \$9,500)/\$9,500 = 5.26\%$

❖ **Interpretation:** The Treasury bill Lonnie purchased will pay a discount yield of 5.26%. A **discount yield** is the effective yield earned on a bond investment that is purchased at a discount from the bond's face value. **Treasury bills** (also known as **T-bills**) are one type of security issued by the United States Treasury. (Other Treasury securities are notes and bonds.) T-bills do not pay current interest income because they are sold at a discount from face value, where the difference between the bond's selling price and the T-bill's value at maturity—the gain—represents the interest. T-bills mature in one year or less, such as in 13, 26, or 52 weeks. Individuals buy new issues of T-bills on a noncompetitive bid basis by submitting a certified or cashier's check for the face amount along with the proper form. A few days later, the government will electronically wire the investor a refund that represents the difference between the face value of the bill and the purchase price. Once that exact amount is known, the investor can accurately calculate the discount yield.

7. Municipal Bonds and After-Tax Equivalent Yield[2]

Formula 16.7.1 (same as Formula 10.4): $TEY = TY (1 - MTR)$

Formula 16.7.2: $TY = TEY/(1 - MTR)$

Where: TEY = tax-exempt yield; TY = taxable yield; and MTR = marginal tax rate.

▼ **Example 16.7.1:** Jose is subject to the 31% federal marginal tax rate and he is considering investing in a taxable corporate bond yielding 8.7%. What is the after-tax equivalent yield of that investment for Jose?

Solution: $TEY = 8.7\% \times (1 - 0.31) = 8.7\% \times 0.69 = 6.003\%$

---

[2]This section was written by Robert O. Weagley, Ph.D., CFP, Associate Professor, Department of Consumer and Family Economics, University of Missouri-Columbia, Columbia, MO 65211. Robert_O._Weagley@muccmail.missouri.edu

❖   **Interpretation:** The 8.7% bond will provide Jose a return of 6.003% after he pays income taxes on the interest income. When considering alternative investments, the best way to equalize choices is to convert the returns into an after-tax basis. That means what return will various investments provide a particular investor after income taxes have been paid. In a similar way, people sometimes need to know whether a tax-exempt or taxable investment is to their advantage. To determine the correct answers to these types of questions, one must calculate the **after-tax equivalent yield**. This amount is the return to a particular taxpayer from a taxable investment after the impact of income taxes when compared with the return from a tax-exempt investment. If the investment alternatives are otherwise equal, one should select the investment with the higher after-tax equivalent yield. Formula 16.7.2 is used when one knows the taxable yield and needs to calculate the after-tax-equivalent yield. Formula 16.7.2 (a rearrangement of Formula 16.7.1) is used when one knows the tax-equivalent yield and needs to calculate the taxable yield.

▼   **Example 16.7.2:** Mary pays taxes at the 28% federal marginal tax rate and is considering two alternatives. First, there is a taxable bond paying 9.1%. Second, there is a tax-exempt municipal bond paying 6.9%. Which investment will pay Mary a higher after-tax return?

Solution: TEY = 9.1% × (1 − 0.28) = 9.1% × 0.72 = 6.55%

❖   **Interpretation:** Mary will receive a higher after-tax return from the tax-exempt municipal bond paying 6.9% because that return is higher than the after-tax return of 6.55% on the taxable bond paying 9.1%.

▼   **Example 16.7.3:** Charlie pays taxes at the 28% federal marginal tax rate and is considering two alternatives. First, there is a taxable bond paying 7.4%. Second, there is a tax-exempt bond paying 5.2%. Which will pay Charlie a higher after-tax return?

Solution: Since, 5.2% = TY (1 − 0.28) = TY 0.72, then
TY = 5.2%/0.72 = 7.22%

❖   **Interpretation:** Knowing the tax-exempt yield of one bond paying is 5.2% tells Charlie that the 7.4% taxable bond is a better deal because the 5.2% is equivalent to a taxable return of only 7.22%.

8. Zero-Coupon Bonds

Formula 16.8: $PV = P (1 + r/2)^{-2N}$

Where: PV = present value (or price) of a zero-coupon bond; P = par value of the zero-coupon bond; r = annual interest rate of the zero-coupon bond; and N = the maturity of the zero-coupon bond.

▼ **Example 16.8.1:** Johnny Carsoni is considering investing in a new $1,000 zero-coupon bond with a coupon rate of 7% that is scheduled to be redeemed by the U.S. government 20 years from now. What is the price Johnny should expect to pay for that bond?

Solution: Since, P = $1,000, r = 7% = .07 , N = 20, then
$$PV = \$1,000 \ (1 + .07/2)^{-2 \times 20} = \$252.57$$

▼ **Interpretation:** The price for the new zero-coupon bond available to Johnny likely is priced at $252.57. **Zero-coupon bonds** (also called **zeros** or **deep discount bonds**) are municipal, corporate, and Treasury securities that pay no annual interest. They are sold to investors at sharp discounts from their face value, and then redeemed at full value upon maturity. The interest, which is usually compounded semiannually, accumulates within the bond itself. The return to the investor comes from redeeming the bond at its stated face value at maturity. Thus, zeros operate much like Series EE savings bonds (examined in Chapter 5) and T-bills. Zeros pay **"phantom interest"** (income earned but not received) and, although no interest money is received every year, the owner must pay income taxes on the interest unless the securities are held in a qualified tax-sheltered retirement plan, such as an **IRA** (individual retirement account) or 401(k) plan (both examined in Chapter 20). The price paid for zero-coupon bond is the present value of the maturity value of the bond.

Continuing example 16.8.2: Alternatively, Johnny is considering investing in an existing $1,000 zero-coupon bond with a coupon rate of 8% that is scheduled to be redeemed by the U.S. government 17 years from now. What is the price Johnny should expect to pay for that bond?

Solution: Since, P = $1,000, r = 8% = .08, N = 17, then
$$PV = \$1,000 \ (1 + .08/2)^{-2 \times 17} = \$263.55$$

❖ **Interpretation:** The price for the existing zero-coupon bond available to Johnny likely is priced at $263.55. Like all **fixed-income investments** (where the face value interest rate remains the same over time), zero-coupon bonds vary in value because they were originally sold at a discount below face value. The current price of a zeros, especially those with a duration of many years, can vary dramatically over time so that they provide a competitive effective rate of return with comparable investments.

▼ **Continuing example 16.8.3:** Two years later, Johnny is considering selling his zero-coupon bond to help pay for a planned vacation to Disney World. However, interest rates in the economy have increased in response to fears about inflation. What would be the likely selling price of Johnny's zero-coupon bond if interest rates today at 2% higher than when he purchased it?

Solution: Since, P = $1,000, r = 10% = .1, N = 15, then
$$PV = \$1,000 \ (1 + .1/2)^{-2 \times 15} = \$231.38$$

❖ **Interpretation:** The price for the existing zero-coupon bond available to Johnny likely is priced at $231.38. Bonds with a long duration decline in price substantially when interest rates increase, although the loss can be avoided by not selling the investment.

▼ **Continuing example 16.8.4:** Assume instead that over the past two years, interest rates had declined 2% because the economy had slowed down significantly. In this scenario, what would be the likely selling price of Johnny's zero-coupon bond?

Solution: Since, P = $1,000, r = 6% = .06, N = 15, then
$$PV = \$1,000 \, (1 + .06/2)^{-2 \times 15} = \$411.99$$

❖ **Interpretation:** The price for the existing zero-coupon bond available to Johnny likely is priced at $411.99. Bonds with long duration appreciate in price substantially when interest rates decline, although the gain cannot be realized unless the investor sells the asset. Such capital gains, when realized, are taxable income to the investor unless the securities are held in a qualified tax-sheltered retirement plan.

9. Inflation-Linked Treasury Bonds

Formula 16.9.1: $P = P' \, (1 + CPI)^n$

Where: P = par value of the bond in this period; P′ = the initial par value of the bond; CPI = consumer price index change between this and last period; and n = number of the period. Note that Formula 16.9.1 can be applied only when the annual CPI changes are the same in the whole life of the bond.

Formula 16.9.2: $I = P \cdot r$

Where: I = interest earned in the bond; and r = interest rate for the period.

▼ **Example 16.9.1:** In January, James Nuggent buys a 10-year, $1,000 U.S. inflation-linked Treasury bond carrying a "real" interest rate of 3% plus the CPI bonus. What is the par value of James' bond after six months if the CPI rose 1% during the first 6 months?

Solution: Since P′ = $1,000, CPI = 1% = .01, n = 1, then using Formula 16.9.1
$$P = \$1,000 \, (1 + .01)^1 = \$1,000 \times 1.01 = \$1,010$$

❖ **Interpretation:** The value of James' bond principal rises to $1,010. **Inflation-linked Treasury bonds (ILTBs)** in the United States are an innovation that began in 1997 with the first issues by the U.S. Treasury Department. ILTBs are U.S. Treasury bonds with returns adjusted to the consumer price index (CPI) twice a year.[2] The Treasury Department will credit an investor with the increase in principal every six months (if the CPI rises), but the amount will not be paid until the note matures. However, each year's increase in principal must be treated as current income for income tax purposes ("phantom interest"), thus bond holders must pay taxes on the interest every year unless the securities are held in a qualified tax-sheltered retirement plan, such as an IRA (individual retirement account) or 401(k) plan (both examined in Chapter 20)[1] ILTBs are expected to be popular with individual investors because inflation is offset for the investor. For example, if inflation jumps to 6% (as it did in 1991), a 3% ILTB bond will earn a return of 9%; recall, too, that ILTB interest is exempt from state and local income taxes. In addition, the long-term safety of ILTBs is expected to do well balancing the riskier portions of individuals' investment portfolios, which may enable them to accept more risk (and likely subsequent growth as well) with their other investments.

▼ **Continuing example 16.9.2:** What will be the first semi-annual interest payment James will receive on the ILTB?

Solution: Since, P = $1,010, r = .03/2 = .015, then using Formula 16.9.2
           I = $1,010 × 0.015 = $15.15

❖ **Interpretation:** James will receive $15.15 as his first semiannual interest payment because the principal upon which the interest is calculated in an inflation-adjusted Treasury bond increases with inflation.

▼ **Continuing example 16.9.3:** What would the semi-annual interest payment be if James had instead purchased a regular 3% Treasury bond, which is not indexed to inflation?

Solution: Since, P = $1,000, r = .03/2 = .015, then using Formula 16.9.2
           I = $1,000 × .015 = $15.00

❖ **Interpretation:** Comparing Examples 16.9.2 and 16.9.3 reveals that if the Treasury bond is not indexed to inflation, the interest rate in six month will be $.15 ($15.15 – $15) less than the bond that is indexed to inflation. The difference of earned interests will be greater if the maturity of the bond is longer.

▼ **Continuing example 16.9.4:** If inflation accelerated so that it reached 3 percent for the full year, what would be the par value of James' bond and the interest earned in six months?

Solution:

(1) Par value
       Since P' = $1,000, r = .03/2=.015, n = 1, then using Formula 16.9.1
       P = $1,000 (1 + .015)^1 = $1,000 × 1.015 = $1,015

(2) Interest
       Since P = $1,015, r = .03/2 =.015, then using Formula 16.9.2
       I = $1,015 × .015 = $15.23

▼   **Continuing example 16.9.5:** Assuming the annual inflation will be 3%, what would be (1) the total of the interest payments to James, and (2) the par value of the bond at maturity?

Solution: This can be easily calculated by using a spreadsheet program. The following are results from Excel. Note that for the "Principal" column, we used Formula 16.9.1, and for the "Interest" column, we used Formula 16.9.2. The "P + I" is the sum of "Principal" and "Interest." Also note that since the bond is compounded semiannually, then CPI = .03/2 = .015, and r = .03/2 = .015, and the total number of periods = 2 × 10 = 20.

(1)   The calculation for Period 1 is the same as one in Example 16.9.4.

(2)   For Period 2, since $P' = \$1,000$, CPI = .015, n = 2, then using Formula 16.9.1
       $P = \$1,000 (1 + .015)^2 = \$1,030.23$;

(3)   Since P = \$1,030.23, r = .015, then using Formula 16.9.2
       $I = \$1,030.23 \times .015 = \$15.45$ (see Column "Interest" and Period 2).

(4)   The numbers for other periods are calculated in a similar way.

n	Principal	Interest	P + I
0	$1,000		
1	$1,015.00	15.225	1030.23
2	$1,030.23	15.453	1045.68
3	$1,045.68	15.685	1061.36
4	$1,061.36	15.920	1077.28
5	$1,077.28	16.159	1093.44
6	$1,093.44	16.402	1109.84
7	$1,109.84	16.648	1126.49
8	$1,126.49	16.897	1143.39
9	$1,143.39	17.151	1160.54
10	$1,160.54	17.408	1177.95
11	$1,177.95	17.669	1195.62
12	$1,195.62	17.934	1213.55
13	$1,213.55	18.203	1231.76
14	$1,231.76	18.476	1250.23
15	$1,250.23	18.753	1268.99
16	$1,268.99	19.035	1288.02
17	$1,288.02	19.320	1307.34
18	$1,307.34	19.610	1326.95
19	$1,326.95	19.904	1346.86
20	$1,346.86	20.203	1367.06
Total		352.06	

❖   **Interpretation:** The total interest paid will be $352.06. The par value (principal) at maturity will be $1,346.86.

10. Duration of a Bond

Conceptual Idea 16.10: Duration is defined as the number of years to fully recover the purchase price of a bond, given the present value of its cash flow.

▼ **Example 16.10:** What is the duration if you purchase a $1,000 bond that has an 8% interest rate and 5 years until maturity? Assume that you will receive $40 interest payment every six months.

Solution:

This can be easily done with a spreadsheet program as follows.

Year	Cash Flow	PV	PV*Year/1000
0.5	40	$38.49	0.01925
1	40	$37.04	0.03704
1.5	40	$35.64	0.05346
2	40	$34.29	0.06859
2.5	40	$33.00	0.08250
3	40	$31.75	0.09526
3.5	40	$34.87	0.12204
4	40	$29.40	0.11760
4.5	40	$28.29	0.12731
5	1040	$707.81	3.53903
Duration			4.26208

Thus, the duration is 4.26 in this case.

❖ **Interpretation:** Duration is a method of measuring the entire pattern of cash flow over the life of a bond. For a zero coupon bond, duration is equal the maturity date. For coupon payment bonds, the duration will always be less than the number of years.

INFORMATION AND COMPUTING RESOURCES

1. To open a *Treasury Direct account*, which enables one to purchase government securities, like T-bills, write your nearest Federal Reserve Bank and ask for Form PD 5182. The form is also available from the Treasury Department, Division of Customer Services, Washington, DC 20239 (1-800-874-4000).

2. Some relevant web sites:

    ■ *Gruntal & Company:* http://www.gruntal.com/investments/wms.html (provides rates of 6-month CD and Treasury instruments for the current and previous weeks.)

- *Holt's Market Report:* http://turnpike.net/metro/holt/index.html (current rates for the Federal Funds rates, the Prime rate, and rates of Treasury Bills, Notes, and Bonds.)

- *QuoteCom:* http://www.quote.com/ (charges a monthly fee and provides a maximum of 50 real time quotes a day from 500 debt securities with different maturities and coupons.)

- *T-Bill Direct*: http://www.netfactory.com/mondenet/tbdira1.html (provides background information to buy Treasury securities.)

- *Wall Street Direct:* http://www.cts.com:80/~wallst/ (information on books that allow one to learn more about analyzing fixed-income securities.)

EXERCISE PROBLEMS

Coupon Yield

1. Betsy paid $1,000 to her stockbroker for a newly issued $1,000 bond that is to pay interest of $30 semi-annually for 10 years. What is the coupon yield of Betsy's bond?

2. If a bond's coupon yield is 6.5%, what is the interest paid every six month if the par value of the bond is $1,000?

Current Yield

3. Megan paid $890 to her stockbroker for a previously issued $1,000, 20-year bond which has just over 19 years of interest payments of $80 per year in cash dividends ($80 semi-annually) remaining. What is the current yield on Megan's bond?

4. If Margaret bought a bond with a current yield of 8% by spending $920, what is the interest paid for the year?

Approximate Yield to Call

5. Sam paid $940 to his stockbroker for a previously issued $1,000, 20-year bond which has 14 years of interest payments of $60 per year in cash dividends ($30 semi-annually) remaining. The bond is callable 5 years after the original date of issue. What is the approximate yield to call on Sam's bond?

6. Mark paid $900 to his stockbroker for a previously issued $1,000, 15-year bond which has 10 years of interest payments of $70 per year in cash dividends ($35 semi-annually) remaining. The bond is callable 5 years after the original date of issue. What is the current yield on Sam's bond?

Yield to Maturity

7. Julie bought a 20-year bond with a coupon rate of 8% and a par value of $1,000 at a discount for $960. What is the bond's yield to maturity?

8. Joe bought a 10-year bond with a coupon rate of 6% and a par value of $1,000 at a discount for $920. What is the bond's yield to maturity?

Estimating the Selling Price of a Bond

9. Bobby paid $1,000 for a 10-year, 8% bond and was forced to sell it after interest rates on comparable bonds had increased to 9.5%. Estimate how much Bobby's bond would (1) sell for if he had to sell the bond today, (2) how much of a financial loss he would suffer as a result, and (3) how much his bond might sell for if, instead, market interest rates dropped to 6%.

10. Tammy paid $1,000 for a 10-year, 7.5% bond and was forced to sell it after interest rates on comparable bonds had increased to 9%. How much of a financial loss would she suffer as a result?

Discount Yield

11. Loren bought a 52-week, $10,000 Treasury bill from a Federal Reserve bank at a discount price of $9,300. Which is the discount yield on Loren's bond?

12. If a bond's discount yield is 6.5% and the par value is $1,000, what is the discount price?

Municipal Bonds and After-Tax Equivalent Yield

13. Jian is subject to the 28% federal marginal tax rate and he is considering investing in a taxable corporate bond yielding 8.2%. What is the after-tax equivalent yield of that investment for Jian?

14. Courtney pays taxes at the 15% federal marginal tax rate and is considering two alternatives. First, there is a taxable bond paying 8.9%. Second, there is a tax-exempt municipal bond paying 7.2%. Which investment will pay Courtney a higher after-tax return?

Zero-Coupon Bonds

15. Jessica is considering investing in a new $1,500 zero-coupon bond with a coupon rate of 6% that is scheduled to be redeemed by the U.S. government 15 years from now. What is the price Johnny should expect to pay for that bond?

16. If Gale spent $556.45 to buy a zero-coupon bond with a coupon rate of 6.5% that will be redeemed by the U.S. government 20 years from now, what is the par value of the bond?

Inflation-Linked Treasury Bonds

17. Joan bought a 10-year, $1,500 U. S. inflation-linked Treasury bond carrying a "real" interest rate of 2.5% plus the CPI adjustments. The bond is compounded semi-annually. If the annual CPI is 2%, what is the par value of the bond, and what is the interest earned by Joan at the second half of the first year?

18. Using the information in the above question. What is the par value of the bond at the maturity, and what is the total interest Joan will earn?

Duration of a Bond

19. What is the duration if you purchase a $1,000 bond at 7% interest rate and 5 years to maturity? Assume that you will receive $30 interest payment every six months.

20. What is the duration if you purchase a $1,000 bond at 9% interest rate and 5 years to maturity? Assume that there is no interest payment every six months.

SELECTED REFERENCES

Fister, M. (1995). *A pocket tour of money on the internet.* San Francisco: Sybex.

Garman, E. T. & Forgue, R. E. (1997). *Personal finance.* (5th ed.) Boston: Houghton Mifflin.

Sharpe, W. F., Alexander, G. J., & Bailey, J. V. (1995). *Investments* (5th ed.). Englewood Cliffs, NJ: Prentice Hall.

ENDNOTES

1. For more discussion of bond price estimation, see Sharpe, Alexander, and Baily (1995, pp. 465-468).

2. The Treasury Department is expected to have a *Savings Bond* version of inflation-adjusted Treasury bonds available in 1998.

Chapter 17
Mutual Fund Mathematics

▼ Net Asset Value, Loads and Share Prices
▼ Cost Measurements
▼ Measuring Mutual Fund Risk
▼ Measuring Fund Returns
▼ Computation of Tax Basis for Shares Sold
▼ Measuring Portfolio Diversification
▼ Dollar Cost Averaging and Value Averaging

Chapter 17
Mutual Fund Mathematics

Paul Camp and Jessie X. Fan[1]

OVERVIEW

An **investment company** is a corporation, trust, or partnership in which investors with similar financial goals pool their money to utilize professional management and to diversify their investments in securities and other investments. The most popular form of investment company is the mutual fund. A **mutual fund** is an open-end investment company that combines the funds of investors who have purchased shares of ownership in the investment company and then invests that money in a diversified portfolio of securities issued by various corporations and/or governments. Shares generally are offered for sale on a continuous basis, with the fund standing ready to buy back shares on demand. Today, there are more mutual funds in existence (over 8,000) than there are companies listed on the New York Stock Exchange and the American Stock Exchange combined.

There are two types of returns a mutual fund investor can expect from owning shares in a mutual fund. The first return is from **distributions**, which includes both dividend distributions and capital gains distributions. **Dividend distributions** come from the interest and dividend income received from securities owned by the fund. **Capital gains distributions** represent the net gains (capital gains minus capital losses) that a fund realizes on its sale of securities from its portfolio during the year. Capital gains distributions are usually made on an annual basis, often in the month of December.[1] The second type of return from mutual funds comes from **share price appreciation**. The investor hopes that, over time, the **market price** of the fund's shares (or **share price**), and the **net asset value (NAV)** will increase.

Mutual funds are often classified according to one of four broad investment objectives. A mutual fund with an **income** objective has a primary purpose to earn

[1]Paul Camp, Ph.D. candidate, CMFC, Consumer Science and Retailing, Purdue University, West Lafayette, IN 47907. pcamp@cm.cc.purdue.edu; and Jessie X. Fan, Ph.D., Assistant Professor, Family and Consumer Studies, University of Utah, Salt Lake City, UT 84112. fan@fcs.utah.edu

a high level of current interest and dividends from the investments in its portfolio without exposing investors to undue risk. A mutual fund with a **growth** objective focuses on long-term growth in the value of the securities (price appreciation) held in its portfolio rather than a flow of dividends, thus they invest primarily in securities with projections of steadily increasing earnings. Funds with a **growth and income** objective aim for an above-average return by investing in securities that are expected to provide some income from dividends as well as the potential for long-term price appreciation. Funds with a **balanced** objective typically emphasize preservation of invested capital along with moderate growth and income, thus they usually invest in a mix of bonds, preferred stocks, and common stocks.

Mutual funds try to accomplish their investment objectives in a variety of ways, often by investing in various types of securities. As a result, mutual funds are frequently classified and described on the basis of their portfolio holdings. Accordingly, there are dozens of labels for mutual funds. **Common stock funds**, for example, invest primarily in common stocks. Likewise, a **small company fund** would specializes in investing in lesser-known common stocks that pay little, if any, dividends but offer strong growth potential. **Specialty funds** are created for more narrowly defined investment needs. Examples include precious metal and gold funds, mortgage funds, and socially conscious funds. Finally, **money market funds (MMFs)**, which are also called **money market mutual funds (MMMFs)**, restrict their investments to short-term interest-bearing securities issued by corporations and governments, which, by law must have maturities of less than 1 year, and the portfolio's average maturity must be less than 90 days.

Mutual funds may be classified as to whether or not they have a **sales charge**, which is also called a **commission** or **load**. Mutual funds that assesses a sales charge are called **load funds.** Load funds sold to the public by a broker, banker, or financial planner require payment of a sales commission on the amount invested at the time of purchase. The commission, often ranging from 5.5 to 8.5 percent, is called a **front-end load** since it is paid at the time of each purchase. Funds that have only a 1 to 3 percent sales charge are called **low-load funds**.

A mutual fund that does not assess a sales charge at the time of the investment is called a **no-load fund**, and such companies allow people to directly invest with them, without the services of a broker, banker, or financial planner.

Many mutual funds, both load and no-load, assess a **back-end load** (also called a **contingent deferred sales charge**). Here a commission is assessed on the sale of shares (not purchase). A charge is paid at the time of redemption if an investor redeems shares within a specified number of years after purchase, often 5 or 6 years. Typically the fee begins at 5 or 6 percent and then declines 1 percentage point for each year the investor owns the fund. Some mutual funds have both front-end and back-end loads.

People with a long-term investment perspective use two common approaches when investing in mutual funds: dollar cost averaging and value averaging. **Dollar cost averaging** is a technique in which equal dollar amounts are invested periodically. Because these dollars purchase more shares when the price is low and fewer when it is high, the investor's average price per share is minimized. **Value averaging** is a technique by which the investor invests whatever funds are necessary to keep the account balance growing according to a pre-determined schedule. This approach forces the investor to invest more than under the dollar-cost-averaging approach when the share price drops exceptionally low and to sell shares when the share price is high. Value averaging will tend to perform better compared to dollar cost averaging when share prices are exceptionally volatile. Value averaging is more complex than dollar cost averaging, requiring more time and effort to be employed successfully.

Once the investor has developed a long-term investment program, some periodic maintenance of his or her portfolio may be required. One recurring task is rebalancing. Over time, some investments will perform better than others. The result is that some investments may come to dominate the portfolio and, in so doing, may expose the investor to unacceptably high levels of risk. **Rebalancing** the portfolio means bringing your asset allocation back to your original target. Since the original asset allocation was determined by the risk one was willing to accept and the potential rewards a particular allocation offered, it makes sense to hold the allocation relatively constant unless those considerations change. Through regular monitoring of the portfolio's asset allocation and fund mix, investors can ensure that their portfolios are kept closely aligned with their own investment objectives.

An often neglected issue associated with investing in mutual funds is the tax treatment of purchases and sales of fund shares. While a steadily increasing per-share price is a welcome occurrence for the investor, it creates a tax liability when the shares are eventually sold, unless the securities are held in a qualified tax-sheltered retirement plan, such as an IRA or 401(k). In that instance, income taxes are deferred until the funds are withdrawn. (The uses of tax-sheltered investments for retirement planning are discussed in Chapter 20.)

A **capital gain** is income received from the sale of a capital asset above its purchase price; this gain is normally taxable. A **capital loss** results when the sale of a capital asset brings less income than its purchase cost. Capital losses may be used to offset capital gains on other investments. Because investors may buy and sell securities at a variety of prices over time, it can become difficult to accurately determine the exact cost of certain assets. As a result, the Internal Revenue Service recognizes three different methods of computing the **tax basis** (or cost) of securities purchased, such as stocks and mutual funds. Each method results in different estimates of the per share purchase price, and therefore results in different tax liabilities.

This chapter examines several mathematical concepts associated with mutual funds: net asset value, loads and share prices; cost measurements; measuring mutual fund risk; measuring fund returns; comparison of basis methods in identifying mutual fund shares sold; measuring mutual fund portfolio diversification; and dollar cost averaging and value averaging.

EXAMPLES OF MATHEMATICAL CONCEPTS RELATED TO MUTUAL FUNDS

1. Net Asset Value, Loads and Share Prices

Formula 17.1.1: $NAV = \dfrac{MV + C - L}{n}$

Where: NAV = net asset value per share; MV = market value of a fund's invested assets; C = cash on hand; L = liabilities, including fund expenses; and n = number of outstanding shares.

Formula 17.1.2: $OP = \dfrac{NAV}{(1 - FEL)}$

Where: OP = offering price; NAV = net asset value per share; and FEL = front-end load (also called a sales load).

Formula 17.1.3: $SP = NAV \times (1 - BEL)$

Where: SP = selling price; NAV = net asset value per share; and BEL = back-end load (also called a redemption charge).

▼ **Example 17.1:** Concept Mutual Fund owns the following securities: 100,000 shares of Ford, 200,000 shares of Micron Technology, and 300,000 shares of P&G. The fund also has $100,000 cash on hand and $30,000 in liabilities. Assume on a particular day that the market values of these stocks are: $20 per share for Ford, $10 per share for Micron Technology, and $5 per share for P&G. On that day, Concept Mutual fund has 100,000 shares outstanding. Suppose the fund's front-end load is 5 percent and the back-end load is 3 percent. Compute (1) the mutual fund's NAV, (2) offering price (OP), and (3) selling price (SP).

Solution:

First, calculate the market value of invested assets:

$$MV = (\$20 \times 100{,}000) + (\$10 \times 200{,}000) + (\$5 \times 300{,}000) = \$5{,}500{,}000$$

Second, compute the net asset value per share, as well as the offering and selling prices:

(1) $NAV = \dfrac{\$5{,}500{,}000 + \$100{,}000 - \$30{,}000}{100{,}000} = \$55.70$

(2) $OP = \dfrac{\$55.70}{1 - 5\%} = \dfrac{\$55.70}{.95} = \$58.632$

(3) $SP = \$55.70 \times (1 - 3\%) = \dfrac{\$55.70}{.97} = \$54.029$

❖ **Interpretation:** A mutual fund's net assets are defined as the current **market value** of all assets held by the fund, plus cash and any accrued dividend or interest income, less liabilities. The market value of a fund is needed in order to calculate its net asset value per share. The **net asset value per share** is determined by dividing the total number of shares outstanding into a fund's net assets. A mutual fund's share price is measured by its net asset value per share (NAV). In this example, the market value of the mutual fund is $5,500,000, and after applying Formula 17.1.1, the NAV calculates to $55.70.

A fund's **offering price (OP)** is the price per share one pays when purchasing shares of a fund; it is determined by dividing the NAV by 1 minus any front-end load. A fund's **selling price (SP)** is the price per share one receives when shares are redeemed (sold); it is determined by multiplying the NAV by 1 minus any back-end load. Applying Formulas 17.1.2 and 17.1.3 reveal a offering price of $58.63 and a selling price of $54.03.

The impact of sales loads can be seen in both the offering and selling prices. Suppose you buy 100 shares of Concept Mutual Fund. On that day, you will pay $5,863.20 with a total front-end load of $293.16 ($5,863.20 × .05) paid to the mutual fund as commission. Alternatively, if you sell 100 shares of Concept Mutual Fund, you will receive only $5,402.90 because of the imposition of a back-end redemption fee of $167.10 ($5,570 × .03). There are many no-load mutual funds that do not impose either frond-end sales loads or back-end redemption fees. For no-load funds, its NAV is also its offering and selling price per share. While the existence of sales loads should not be the only criterion used to select mutual funds, they certainly have a negative impact on fund performance. Information on NAV, offering and selling prices are available in the business section of most big city daily newspapers. Information on front-end and back-end sales loads and other transaction charges are also presented in a mutual fund's prospectus.

2. Cost Measurements

Formula 17.2.1: $$ER = \frac{AE}{\left(\dfrac{A1 + A2}{2} \right)}$$

Where: ER = expense ratio; AE = annual expenses; A1 = assets at the beginning of the year; and A2 = assets at the end of the year.

Formula 17.2.2: $$ATE = \frac{FEL}{n} + ER + \frac{BEL}{n}$$

Where: ATE = estimated annual total investment expense; FEL = front-end sales load; ER = total expense ratio; BEL = back-end load (or redemption charge); and n = holding period (in years).

Formula 17.2.3: $$TR = \frac{\min (AP, AS)}{MANA}$$

Where: TR = turnover ratio; AS = annual sales of securities; AP = annual purchase of securities; "min" means minimum or choose the smaller number; and MANA = monthly average net assets.

▼ **Example 17.2.1:** Concept Mutual Fund had $5,000,000 net assets at the beginning of the year. By the end of the year, its net assets increased to $5,800,000. During that year, the fund's total operating expenses were $50,000. What is Concept Mutual Fund's expense ratio?

Solution: Since AE = $50,000, A1 = $5,500,000, and A2 = $5,800,000, using Formula 17.2.1:

$$ER = \frac{\$50,000}{\left(\dfrac{\$5,500,000 + \$5,800,000}{2}\right)} = 0.88\%$$

❖ **Interpretation:** Mutual funds have a variety of fee structures, however, three measures are helpful to investors when assessing a mutual fund's costs: (1) expense ratio (ER), (2) estimated annual total investment expense (ATE), and (3) turnover ratio (TR). The **expense ratio** presents the fund's operating expenses as a percentage of average net assets. As a shareholder, you should be willing to pay for reasonable costs of management and administration, which usually include management expenses, investment advisory fees, shareholder accounting costs, 12b-1 fees, and other expenses. You should keep in mind that the fund's operating expenses directly reduce the returns on your investment. That is, everything else being equal, a fund with a lower expense ratio will give you a higher total return than a fund with a higher expense ratio. While expense ratios vary with a fund's investment objective and the costs of operation, most range from .35% to 1.50%. In general, you should think twice about investing in a fund that has an expense ratio of greater than the mean for funds with similar objectives. A fund's expense ratio is published in the prospectus. In this example, Concept Mutual Fund's expense ratio is 0.88%.

▼ **Example 17.2.2:** As noted above, Concept Mutual Fund's front-end sales charge is 5 percent and its back-end redemption charge is 3 percent. In addition, its expense ratio is 0.88%. Suppose your holding period for Concept Mutual Fund is 4 years. What is your estimate of annual total investment expense (ATE)?

Solution: Since FEL = 5%, n = 4, ER = .88%, and BEL = 3%, using Formula 17.2.2:

$$ATE = \frac{5\%}{4} + 0.88\% + \frac{3\%}{4} = 2.88\%$$

❖ **Interpretation:** For no-load funds, the expense ratio is sufficient for comparing investment expenses. However, if the fund is a load fund, then any comparison among funds becomes more difficult since the expense ratio does not take into account the effects of sales loads. The **estimated annual total investment expense (ATE)** provides a simplified means for approximating the effects of sales loads. If front-end and back-end loads are divided by the holding period, the annual effects of these sales and redemption loads can be estimated. In this example, the annual cost of front-end and back-end loads is 2%, and when that figure is added to the expense ratio, the estimate of annual total investment expense (ATE) is 2.88%.

▼ **Example 17.2.3:** Last year, Concept Mutual Fund's annual sales of securities was $500,000 and annual purchases of securities totaled $800,000. Assuming its monthly average net assets for that year was $5,600,000, what was Concept Mutual Fund's portfolio turnover ratio?

Solution: Since AP = $500,000, AS = $800,000, and MANA = $5,600,000, using Formula 17.2.3:

$$TR = \frac{\min(\$500,000,\ \$800,000)}{\$5,600,000} = \frac{\$500,000}{\$5,600,000} = 8.93\%$$

❖ **Interpretation:** The **turnover rate** of a portfolio is a measure of how frequently the mutual fund manager trades the securities held in the portfolio. It is calculated by dividing the lesser of the fund's annual purchases or sales (exclusive of purchases or sales of securities with maturities of less than one year) by the monthly average value of the securities owned by the fund during the year. The higher the turnover rate, the more brokerage commissions the fund is paying. This reduces an investor's total return. Excessive market trading can also lead to higher tax liabilities. One should think twice about investing in a mutual fund with an expense ratio and/or a turnover ratio higher than the average for mutual funds with similar investment objectives. In this example, the turnover ratio was a relatively low 8.93%.

3. Measuring Mutual Fund Risk

Formula 17.3.1: $\sigma = \sqrt{\dfrac{\Sigma(x_i - \bar{x})^2}{n - 1}}$

Where: x_i = return for period i; $\bar{x}$ = mean periodic return; and n = number of periods.

Formula 17.3.2: $\beta = \displaystyle\sum_{i=1}^{n} \beta_i W_i$

Where: β = the beta coefficient of a mutual fund; β_i = the beta coefficient for each individual stock the mutual fund holds; and W_i = market value weight for each individual stock.

▼ **Example 17.3.1:** Assume that a hypothetical fund has annual total return figures as shown in column one. The standard deviations for this fund are calculated as follows:

Year	x_i	$\bar{x}$	$x_i - \bar{x}$	$(x_i - \bar{x})^2$
1	10.00%	7.00%	3.00%	0.0009
2	5.00%	7.00%	-2.00%	0.0004
3	-9.00%	7.00%	-16.00%	0.0256
4	17.00%	7.00%	10.00%	0.0100
5	12.00%	7.00%	5.00%	0.0025
				Sum = 0.0394

$$\sigma = \sqrt{\frac{0.0394}{5 - 1}} = 9.92\%$$

❖ **Interpretation:** A mutual fund's risk can be measured using standard deviations and the fund's beta coefficient. **Standard deviation** is a method of describing how closely observed returns cluster around the mean. If we make the simplifying assumption that these five years are typical of all past returns, then the knowledge of the mean return together with the standard deviation allows us to draw some important conclusions. About two-thirds of all observations fall within a range of ±1 standard deviations from the mean. In this example, annual return is 7%, and the standard deviation is 9.92%. Therefore, we can expect about two-thirds of this fund's previous annual returns to fall between -2.92% and 16.92%.

Note that the size of the standard deviation can be an effective proxy for total risk exposure. Consider another fund, also with a mean annual return of 7%. If this fund had a standard deviation of 5%, then two-thirds of its previous returns could be expected to fall within a range of 2% and 12% per year. The more narrow range of returns for the second fund suggests less uncertainty in the level of returns, and hence less risk. The important lesson is that smaller standard deviations of returns generally imply less risky mutual funds.

▼ **Example 17.3.2:** Suppose a mutual fund held stock in only 3 companies and in the proportions listed below. What is the total beta for the fund? The weights are calculated by dividing each company's market value by the total portfolio value. As displayed in the table, each weight is multiplied by the company's beta, then the individual totals are added to determine the beta for the entire fund.

Security	Mkt Value	W_i	β_i	$\beta_i W_i$
ABC Corp.	$100,000	0.2	1.3	0.26
XYZ Inc.	$250,000	0.5	1.1	0.55
ZXY Industries	$150,000	0.3	0.7	0.21
Sum	$500,000	1		$\beta_t = 1.01$

❖ **Interpretation:** While a fund's standard deviation measures total risk, the beta (β) coefficient measures a fund's exposure to **systematic risk**. This is also known as **market risk** or **non-diversifiable risk**. This is the risk associated with the impact of the overall economy on securities markets; it is the risk associated with just being in the stock market. Systematic risk cannot be diversified away, no matter how many stocks are included in the portfolio. Systematic risk may cause the market price of a particular stock, bond or mutual fund to change, even though nothing has changed in the underlying fundamental values of the security. Calculating a beta coefficient for a mutual fund is simply a matter of calculating a weighted average of the betas of the individual securities held in the portfolio. To do so, we use the ratio of the security's market value to total portfolio value as the weight. In this example, the fund's 30% position in ZXY Industries is used to offset the greater systematic risk exposure of the more aggressive ABC Corporation and XYZ Incorporated holdings. The end result is that the fund's beta coefficient is essentially equal to the market beta of 1.00, despite the fact that 70% of the fund is invested in relatively aggressive securities (as measured by beta). This illustrates that it is possible for a mutual fund with a beta of 1 to have the majority of its assets invested quite aggressively relative to the broader market. Thus, it is important to consider the nature of the security holdings disclosed in the prospectus as well as any aggregate risk measures such as beta.

4. Measuring Fund Returns

Formula 17.4.1:
$$R = \frac{(\Delta P + D + CG) \times S}{I}$$

Where: R = total return; ΔP = change in price per share; D = dividends received per share; CG = capital gain distributions per share; S = number of shares owned; and I = amount invested.

Formula 17.4.2:
$$T = \frac{R_i - R_f}{\beta}$$

Where: T = Treynor measure; R_i = the rate of return generated by the fund over the period in question; R_f = the risk-free rate of return (usually measured by the 91-day Treasury rate); and β = the fund's beta coefficient.

Formula 17.4.3:
$$S = \frac{R_i - R_f}{\sigma}$$

Where: S = Sharpe ratio; R_i = the rate of return generated by the fund over the period in question; R_f = the risk-free rate of return (usually measured by the 91-day Treasury rate); and σ_i = the fund's standard deviation of returns.

Formula 17.4.4: $\quad \alpha = R_i - [R_f + \beta (R_m - R_f)]$

Where: $\quad \alpha$ = alpha coefficient; R_i = the actual rate of return provided by the fund during the period; R_f = the "risk free" rate of return; R_m = the rate of return observed in the stock market during the period; and β = the fund's beta coefficient.

▼ **Example 17.4.1:** There are two general ways to measure a fund's return, using total return and any of three risk-adjusted methods. **Total return (R)** is a measure of a fund's return but it is not adjusted for risk. The Treynor measure, the Sharpe ratio, and alpha are risk-adjusted methods. Let's assume that you invested $1,000 in a hypothetical mutual fund in January when shares were priced at $10 each. To keep matters simple, we'll assume you made no additional investments throughout the remainder of the year. By the end of December, the fund's per share price has increased to $10.90. In December, the fund's management paid dividends of $.10 per share and distributed $.20 per share in capital gains. Assume this mutual fund had a beta of 1.01 and a standard deviation of returns of 9.92 during that time. Also assume the risk-free rate of return during the same period was 4% and that the rate of return in the broader market was 10%. Compute the fund's (1) total return, (2) Treynor measure, (3) Sharpe ratio, and (4) alpha.

Solution:

(1) *Total return.*

Since $\Delta P = \$10.90 - \$10 = \$.90$, D = $.20, CG = $.10, S = 100, I = $1,000, then using Formula 17.4.1:

$$R = \frac{[(\$10.90 - \$10) + \$0.20 + \$0.10] \times 100}{\$1,000} = \frac{\$120}{\$1,000} = 12\%$$

❖ **Interpretation:** A fund's **total return** is the sum of dividends received and any capital gains received, expressed as a percentage of the amount initially invested. It represents the change in shareholder's wealth resulting from investment in a mutual fund. In this example, you have earned a 12% total return on your initial investment over the year.

A more difficult question for an investor is whether this is an acceptable rate of return. At a minimum, one's return should be high enough to provide positive returns after the negative impacts of income taxes and inflation are taken into account. For example, if you assume that one has a combined state and federal income tax rate of 30% while the long-term average annual inflation is 3%, the after-tax real total return for this hypothetical fund is only 5.24% [(12% × 70% - 3%) / (1 + 3%)]. Remember, too, that high dividend distributions do not imply high total returns. Falling share prices can reduce or eliminate the positive returns generated by dividends received. For that reason, always consider total return figures when evaluating mutual funds, not just dividend yields.

Solution:

(2) *Treynor measure.*

Since $R_i = 12\%$, $R_f = 4\%$, $\beta_i = 1.01$, then using Formula 17.4.2:

$$T = \frac{12\% - 4\%}{1.01} = 7.92\%$$

❖ **Interpretation:** What if two mutual funds each have earned a 12% total return during a given period? Does this mean they have performed equally well? The answer is "no" if they exposed themselves to different levels of risk along the way. The **Treynor measure** relates **excess return** (return in excess of the "risk-free" rate) to the amount of systematic risk taken by the fund, as measured by the fund's beta. A higher ratio value is preferable since high values suggest greater returns are being provided for each unit of risk exposure. In this example, calculation indicates that a fund provided 7.92% return over and above the risk-free rate for every unit of systematic risk to which it was exposed, with the market average risk defined as one unit of systematic risk. We have just used beta to "adjust" our fund's return for the level of risk to which we have been exposed as shareholders. Now, we can use this figure to compare against other funds with similar investment objectives to see how we fared relative to the competition. Our fund's Treynor measure of 7.92% would indicate superior risk-adjusted performance when compared to a fund with a figure of 6.51%, yet would be considered inferior to a fund with a Treynor measure of 8.50%. Thus, the Treynor measure can be used to rank funds in order of their risk-adjusted performance.

Solution:

(3) *Sharpe ratio.*

Since $R_i = 12\%$, $R_f = 4\%$, $\delta_i = 9.92\%$, then using Formula 17.4.3:

$$S = \frac{12\% - 4\%}{9.92\%} = 0.81$$

❖ **Interpretation:** If you don't have access to the fund's beta coefficient, the Sharpe ratio performs a similar role using the fund's standard deviation of returns. The **Sharpe ratio** relates excess return to the amount of total risk taken by the fund. (This is in contrast to the Treynor measure's focus only on systematic risk. However Treynor's narrow focus is not problematic with a mutual fund since, with a well diversified mutual fund, any non-systematic risk will have almost always been diversified away). Here again, high ratio values are preferable since they suggest greater returns are being provided for each unit of total risk exposure. In this example, calculation indicates that our fund provided 0.81% return beyond the risk-free rate for every unit of total risk to which it was exposed, with a standard deviation of 1% defined a one unit of total risk. As with the Treynor measure, we can use this figure to rank order funds in terms of their risk-adjusted performance. Warning: The

Sharpe ratio and Treynor measures may be used interchangeably when comparing mutual fund performance. Both will yield identical rankings since well diversified mutual funds, company-specific risk will have been diversified away to nearly zero. Thus, for funds *only*, systematic risk equals total risk. For individual securities and non-diversified portfolios, this is clearly not the case. Some degree of non-systematic risk will still be present in the investment. To rank order these investments, you *must* use the Sharpe ratio.

Solution:

(4) *Alpha coefficient.*

Since $R_i = 12\%$, $R_f = 4\%$, $\beta = 1.01$, $R_m = 10\%$, then using Formula 17.4.4:

$$\alpha = 12\% - [4\% + 1.01 \ (10\% - 4\%)] = 1.94\%$$

❖ **Interpretation:** A fund's **alpha coefficient** (α) is another commonly accepted method of measuring risk-adjusted performance. **Alpha** is the difference between the fund's actual total return and the return we would have expected the fund to provide, given its beta. Note first in Formula 17.4.1 that the bracketed part of the formula represents the rate of return we would expect given the fund's beta of 1.01. We would expect to get the risk-free rate of 4% *plus* some additional return as compensation for bearing the additional risk of investing in the stock market. In this example, that risk premium turns out to be 6.06% so that our *expected* return during this period is 10.06%. In this example, the fund's alpha, 1.94%, is merely the difference between the actual and predicted rates of return.

Speaking in general terms, a positive alpha is desirable because it indicates that the fund provided a greater return than would have been expected given the riskiness of the overall portfolio. The same logic dictates that larger alphas are preferred over smaller alphas. Conversely, negative alphas are a worrisome sign in that they indicate that the fund provided a total return less than what would have been expected given its risk level. In this case, our fund's alpha of 1.94% indicates that we have received (1) the risk-free rate of return, (2) full compensation for the systematic risk we have taken (measured by beta), and, in addition, (3) we have earned a "bonus" return of 1.94%. As with the Treynor measure, alpha coefficients can be used to rank order funds in terms of their risk-adjusted performance.

5. Computation of Tax Basis for Shares Sold

Conceptual Idea 17.5.1: When an investor instructs a mutual fund company to redeem all or part of his/her shares, that investor has transacted a sale subject to capital gain or loss rules. Calculating gains or losses depends on knowing the cost, or **tax basis**, of the shares sold.

The tax basis can be calculated in different ways, and each method can have a significant effect on the computation of capital gains and losses. A **basis method** is a procedure approved by the Internal Revenue Service to figure gain or loss on a sale depending upon identification of which mutual fund shares have been sold. The difference between the proceeds of mutual fund sales and their original purchase prices is called a **capital gain** or a **capital loss**. Gains are taxable unless the securities are held in a qualified tax-sheltered retirement plan, such as an IRA or 401(k). One's precise income tax liability on capital gains varies depending upon which one of the three basis methods is utilized: (1) specific identification, (2) first-in, first-out, and (3) average basis.

▼ **Example 17.5.1:** Consider the investments in a no-load fund shown in the following table.

Purchase Date	Shares	Price
January 15	100	$15.00
March 27	50	$16.50
May 17	50	$15.25
July 28	25	$15.75

Now, on September 1, assume that the investor sells 175 shares at the market price on that date, $16.25 per share. Total sales proceeds are $2,843.75 (175 × $16.25). Calculate the tax basis and determine any capital gains using each of the three calculation methods: (1) specific identification, (2) FIFO (first in-first out), and (3) average basis.

Solution:

(1) *Specific identification method.*

$$CG = \$2,843.75 - [(\$16.50 \times 50) + (\$15.75 \times 25) + (\$15.25 \times 50) + (\$15.00 \times 50)]$$

$$= \$2,843.75 - [\$825.00 + \$393.75 + \$762.50 + \$750.00]$$

$$= \$112.50$$

Interpretation: The **specific identification method** allows the investor to instruct the fund to sell specific shares that were bought on a particular day and at a particular price. This means that the investor can fix profit or loss on the sale, depending upon the cost of the shares selected. The investor should request that the fund provide written confirmation that acknowledges the instruction since IRS regulations require such documentation. This method obviously allows the shareholder the greatest control over the tax consequences associated with the sale. Depending upon one's situation, an investor may want to maximize or minimize the gain or loss on a sale. In general, the highest cost shares should be sold since this minimizes the realized capital gains associated with the trade. In this example, the 175 highest cost shares include 50 shares bought at $16.50 (cost $825), 25 shares at $15.75 (cost of $393.75), 50 shares at $15.25 (cost of $762.50), and 50 of the 100 shares previously bought at $15.00 (cost of $750). Thus, the total cost of the shares for income tax purposes was $2,731.25. Total sales proceeds are $2,843.75 (175 × $16.25). Therefore, the capital gain using this basis method is $112.50 ($2,843.75 − $2,731.25).

Solution:

(2) *FIFO (First-in, first-out) method.*

CG = $2,843.75 − [($15.00 × 100) + ($16.50 × 50) + ($15.25 × 25)]

    = $2,843.75 − [$1,500.00 + $825.00 + $381.25]

    = $137.50

Interpretation: The **FIFO (first-in, first-out) method** assumes that the investor compute gain or loss as if shares were sold in the order in which they were acquired. In this example, the 175 shares to be sold would be comprised of the 100 shares acquired on January 15 (cost of $1,500), 50 shares acquired on March 27 (cost of $825), 25 of the 50 shares acquired on May 17 (cost of $381.25). Thus, the total cost of the shares for income tax purposes was $2,706.25 ($1,500 + $825 + $381.25). Total sales proceeds are $2,843.75 (175 × $16.25). Therefore, the capital gain using this basis method is $137.50 ($2,843.75 − $2,706.25).

Solution:

(3) *Average basis method.*

First, the average purchase price per mutual fund share is computed:

$$AP = \frac{[(\$15.00 \times 100) + (\$16.50 \times 50) + (\$15.25 \times 50) + (\$15.75 \times 25)]}{(100 + 50 + 50 + 25)} = \$15.47$$

Then the capital gain can be computed:

CG = $2,843.75 − $15.47 × 175 = $136.11

❖ **Interpretation:** The **average basis method** allows the taxpayer to average the cost of shares acquired at different times and prices by dividing the total basis for all shares in the account by the number of shares owned. The investor still needs records of the total basis, but averaging avoids the difficult task of identifying the exact shares being sold. Some mutual funds ease the recordkeeping task by providing shareholders who have redeemed shares a statement showing their average cost basis. Calculating the basis using the average basis method requires determining the mean price per share of the shares currently owned, and subtracting this total from the sale proceeds. In this example, the average purchase price is $15.47. Total sales proceeds are $2,843.75 (175 × $16.25). Therefore, the capital gain using this basis method is $137.50 ($2,843.75 − $2,707.25 [$15.47 × 175]). The IRS assumes any shares sold to be identified on a first-in, first-out basis, so that in this case the 100 shares purchased on January 15, the 50 shares purchased on March 27, and 25 of the 50 shares purchased on May 17 would be considered sold.

Note further that for any subsequent sales, the IRS requires that a new tax basis must be computed for the shares remaining in the account. A new tax basis can be calculated as follows:

$$AP = \frac{[(\$15.25 \times 25) + (\$15.75 \times 25)]}{(25 + 25)} = \$15.50$$

6. Measuring Portfolio Diversification

Formula 17.6: $r = \dfrac{COV_{ab}}{\sigma_a \, \sigma_b} = \dfrac{\dfrac{\sum (a_i - \bar{a})(b_i - \bar{b})}{n-1}}{\sigma_a \, \sigma_b}$

Where: r = Pearson's r (correlation coefficient); COV_{ab} = covariance of returns for fund A and fund B; σ_a = standard deviation of returns for fund A; σ_b = standard deviation of returns for fund B; a_i = the return for fund A for period i; b_i = the return for fund B for period i; $\bar{a}$ = mean return for fund A; and $\bar{b}$ = mean return for fund B.

▼ **Example 17.6.1:** If you are investing in more than one mutual fund, Pearson's r (also called the correlation coefficient) may be useful for assessing your portfolio's diversification. For example, assume we have the following five years of performance data for mutual funds A and B. Our first task is to calculate the covariance using the formula above. (Note that all return figures are percentages or percentages squared, whenever appropriate.)

Year	a_i	$\bar{a}$	$a_i - \bar{a}$	$(a_i - \bar{a})^2$	b_i	$\bar{b}$	$b_i - \bar{b}$	$(b_i - \bar{b})^2$	$(a_i - \bar{a})(b_i - \bar{b})$
1	10	7	3	9	13	7	6	36	18
2	5	7	-2	4	-2	7	-9	81	18
3	-9	7	-16	256	-7	7	-14	196	224
4	17	7	10	100	15	7	8	64	80
5	12	7	5	25	16	7	9	81	45

Solution: From the table, we have:

$\sigma_a = 9.92$, $\sigma_b = 10.70$, $COV_{ab} = 385/4 = 96.25$

$r = \dfrac{96.25}{9.92 \times 10.70} = 0.907$

❖ **Interpretation: Pearson's r coefficient** is a statistic used to measure the nature of the relationship between two variables. A correlation coefficient can range from a low of -1 to a high of $+1$, and tells us two very important things. First, the sign of the coefficient tells us about how the variables tend to move relative to each other. A negative sign suggests they tend to move in opposite directions while a positive sign tells us they tend to move in the same direction. Second, the magnitude of the coefficient tells us a great deal about the strength or consistency of the relationship. A number very close to +1 or -1 suggests the relationship is very dependable, while numbers closer to zero suggest a weaker, less dependable relationship. In the rare case when the coefficient exactly equals 1 or -1, this suggests that the movement is perfectly dependable and the variables *always* move in the same (+1) or opposite (-1) directions.

In this example, the coefficient calculated (.907) tells us two things. First, the positive sign tells us that the returns generated by the two funds tend to move in the same direction, with the funds tending to have good years and bad years simultaneously. The fact that the coefficient is so near to 1.0 suggests that this relationship is quite dependable, nearly always occurring (at least, in the years for which we have data).

Pearson's r is an important means of measuring the **diversification** of an investor's overall portfolio. Remember that the point of diversifying among funds is in order that poor performances suffered by one or more investments may be offset with the good performances enjoyed by others. In this particular example, however, the high positive correlation between fund A and fund B suggests that these funds tend to have good years and bad years simultaneously. Therefore, there would be almost no diversification benefit to be gained by constructing a portfolio consisting of fund A and fund B. When pairing two funds together in a portfolio, remember that more diversification benefits are captured by combining funds with the lowest possible correlation coefficients. Adding more funds by itself does not necessarily mean greater diversification in your portfolio.

7. Dollar Cost Averaging and Value Averaging

Formula 17.7.1: $ASC = \dfrac{A_D \times n}{\sum N_i}$

Where: ASC = average share cost; A_D = fixed amount of investment for every period with dollar cost averaging; n = number of periods; and N_i = number of shares purchased for ith investment.

Formula 17.7.2: $\bar{P} = \dfrac{\sum P_i}{n}$

Where: $\bar{P}$ = average offering price or purchasing price; P_i = offering price for the ith investment; and n = number of periods.

Formula 17.7.3: $A_v = \Delta V + (P_p - P_c)\,n_p$

Where: A_v = the amount of money invested each period; ΔV = the fixed amount that the mutual fund account is expected to grow each period; P_p = price per share for the previous period; P_c = price per share for the current period; and n_p = number of shares owned in the previous period.

▼ **Example 17.7.1:** Assume that the investor purchases $100 in shares of the ABC Fund every month, which is a no-load fund. The prices paid are as follows:

Month	Price (P)	N
1	$10.00	10.000
2	$9.00	11.111
3	$8.00	12.500
4	$9.00	11.111
5	$9.50	10.526
6	$10.00	10.000

(1) What is the unit cost of investment over this six-month period, (2) What is the average offering price of this mutual fund over this six-month period, and (3) What is the amount of money invested each period?

Solution:

(**1**) *Use Formula 17.7.1 to calculate the average share cost:*

$$\text{ASC} = \frac{\$100 \times 6}{10 + 11.111 + 12.5 + 11.111 + 10.526 + 10} = \frac{\$600}{65.248} = \$9.196$$

(**2**) *Use Formula 17.7.2 to calculate average offering price:*

$$\bar{P} = \frac{\$10 + \$9 + \$8 + \$9 + \$9.5 + \$10}{6} = \$9.25$$

❖ **Interpretation:** Two of the most popular approaches to investing in mutual funds are dollar cost averaging and value averaging. The **dollar-cost averaging** approach is a systematic program of investing equal sums of money at regular intervals regardless of the price of the investment. Because an equal number of dollars will purchase more mutual fund shares when the price is low and less when it is high, the investor's average per share *cost* is lower than it might be otherwise.

Two formulas are relevant with dollar cost averaging: (1) the average share cost of mutual fund shares, and (2) the average offering price ($\bar{P}$). The **average share cost (ASC)** of a mutual fund investment is the average cost basis of the investment to the investor, and it may be used for income tax purposes. It is calculated by dividing the total amount invested by the total shares purchased. In this example, the average share cost is $9.196. The **average offering price** ($\bar{P}$) is a simple calculation that divides the share price total by the number of investment periods. In this example, the average offering price is $9.25.

In order for dollar-cost averaging to work, the investor must have the discipline to continue buying shares, even during bear markets. If the investor stops buying during markets when prices are depressed, the purpose of dollar-cost averaging is defeated. While dollar-cost averaging does not guarantee a profit, the approach does reduce the average cost of shares purchased. This will increase one's return over the long haul.

▼   **Example 17.7.2:** Assume that you want your ABC mutual fund account balance to grow by $500 each quarter (every three months). You begin by buying 50 shares at $10 each. Suppose, in the subsequent quarter, the share prices are (1) $8, (2) $9, (3) $11, and (4) $21. To make your account worth $1,000, use Formula 17.7.3 to calculate the amount of money to invest under each situation. For simplicity, assume the mutual fund is a no-load fund.

Solution: Using Formula 17.7.3 to calculate the investment amount:

(1) A_v = $500 + ($10 – $8) × 50 = $500 + $100 = $600

(2) A_v = $500 + ($10 – $9) × 50 = $500 + $50 = $550

(3) A_v = $500 + ($10 – $11) × 50 = $500 – $50 = $450

(4) A_v = $500 + ($10 – $21) × 50 = $500 – $550 = –$50

❖   **Interpretation:** Using the **value averaging approach**, one invests the amount needed to increase the value of the account by a fixed target amount. With value averaging, computing the amount to invest (A_V) for every period is very important. This approach forces the investor to invest more than when using the dollar-cost averaging approach. Under the first two scenarios in this example, since the price per share has dropped, you will invest more money ($600 and $550). If the price per share has increased, as has occurred during the third quarter, then you will need to invest less money into this fund ($450). Furthermore, if the price per share has increased dramatically, as in scenario 4, you actually sell shares. The more extreme the moves in share prices, the better the value averaging approach performs in comparison with dollar-cost-averaging. However, value averaging requires more time and effort to employ successfully. You must calculate and invest the correct amount each period to maintain your account balance according to your investment schedule. Also, when you sell shares, you may incur brokerage charges and capital gains taxes, both of which will reduce your return.

INFORMATION AND COMPUTING RESOURCES

1.   Newspapers: Your daily newspaper is an excellent tool for tracking the progress of a mutual fund portfolio. Most papers carry in their financial pages the closing share prices for many mutual funds. In addition, most major papers devote editorial coverage to mutual funds. Some of the more prominent national publications, such as *The Wall Street Journal* and *USA Today*, devote considerable attention to mutual funds.

2.   Magazines: Magazines that emphasize mutual funds include *Money*, *Kiplinger's Personal Finance Magazine*, and *Mutual Fund Magazine*. Other publications,

such as *Business Week, Forbes, Fortune, Worth, Barron's,* and *Smart Money,* also cover mutual funds regularly. In addition, most of these publications produce special editions on mutual funds that feature comprehensive fund rankings and articles geared to interest mutual fund investors. *Forbes,* for instance, publishes an annual guide in late August that features its "Honor Roll" funds and "Best Buy" selections. *Money* usually publishes "mutual fund" editions in February and August. *Consumer Reports* magazine provides a similar listing.

3. Newsletters: There are scores of newsletters dedicated to covering mutual funds and, in some cases, the funds of a single mutual fund family. Among the many publications, only a small number offer timely and useful information, accurate fund data, and prudent advice. When it comes to newsletter subscription, "Look carefully before you subscribe."

4. Rating Services: *Morningstar Mutual Funds,* published by Chicago-based Morningstar, Inc., is one of the leading sources of information on funds. This publication reports a considerable amount of data about a fund, including long-term performance results, portfolio holdings, investment manager and tenure, expenses, and portfolio turnover rates. The report also includes a brief commentary on the fund and its strategy by a Morningstar analyst. *Value Line,* a New York-based firm, offers a similar publication. These publications are available for purchase or may be found in most local libraries.

5. Books: There are a growing number of books on the subject of mutual funds. See the reference list for more information.

6. Trade Group Information: The *Investment Company Institute,* the mutual fund industry's largest trade organization, publishes an annual fund publication called the "Directory of Mutual Funds." The *Mutual Fund Education Alliance,* a Kansas City-based mutual fund industry trade group, offers a semi-annual fund guide—"The Investor's Guide to Low-Cost Mutual Funds."

7. Historical mutual fund data can also be obtained on-line. Many commercial networks, such as America Online, CompuServe, and Prodigy, provide such services for a monthly fee. There are also resources available for free on the Internet. Mutual fund magazine (www.mfmag.com) maintains an extensive on-line database of fund performance data. Most mutual fund companies now have their home pages on the World Wide Web, such as the Vanguard Mutual Fund home page.

8. Relevant web sites.

    ■   *Fidelity:* http://www.fid-inv.com/ (online access for account holders and prospective clients to its product information.)

- *Mutual Funds Home Page:* http://ultranet.com/~marla/funds.html
  (interactive services and timely information for mutual fund investing.)

- *Mutual Fund Information:*
  http://www.researchmag.com/investor/mutual.htm (information, data, and
  investment advice on mutual funds compiled by *Research* magazine.)

- *Mutual Funds Online:* http://www.mfmag.com (an online magazine and
  database focused on the mutual funds industry.)

- *NETworth:* http://networth.galt.com/ (the most comprehensive financial
  information service on mutual funds.)

EXERCISE PROBLEMS

Net Asset Value, Loads and Share Prices

1. ABC Mutual Fund owns the following: 150,000 shares of American Express,
   100,000 shares of Guess jeans and 20,000 shares of GTE. The fund also has
   $100,000 cash on hand, and $30,000 liabilities. Assume on a particular day, the
   market values of these stocks are: $45/share for American Express, $15/share for
   Guess, and $40/share for GTE. On that day, ABC Mutual fund has 100,000
   outstanding shares. Suppose the fund's front-end load is 3%, and back-end load
   is 1%. Compute (1) the fund's NAV; (2) the offering price (OP); and (3) the
   selling price (SP).

2. Suppose you are investing $10,000 in Content Mutual Fund. The fund has a
   front-end sales load of 1.5%. It's NAV on that particular day is $20. How many
   shares can you purchase?

3. You are selling 100 shares of User Mutual Fund. The fund has a back-end
   redemption charge of 0.7%. The fund has a NAV of $50 on that particular day.
   How much money will you receive in exchange for your 100 shares?

Cost Measurements

4. ABC Mutual Fund had $10,000,000 net assets at the beginning of the year. At
   the end of the year, its net assets increased to $11,000,000. During that year, the
   fund's total operating expense was $70,000. What's ABC Mutual Fund's
   expense ratio (ER)?

5. Suppose Future Mutual Fund has an expense ratio (ER) of 1.77%. In a particular
   year, the average annual net assets for Future Mutual Fund were $1 million.
   What is the fund's total operating expense that year?

6. Definition Mutual Fund's front-end sales charge is 4%, back-end redemption
   charge is 1%, and it's total expense ratio is 0.35%. Suppose your holding period

for Definition Mutual Fund is 4 years. What is your estimate of annual total investment expense (ATE)?

7. Fund A has a front-end sales charge of 0.3%, and a back-end redemption charge of 0.5%. It's expense ratio is 0.50%. Fund B is a no-load fund with an expense ratio of 0.85%. Suppose your holding period is 5 years. Which fund has a lower total cost to you? What if your holding period is only 1 year?

8. Last year, Definition Mutual Fund's annual sales of securities were $800,000, annual purchases of securities were $780,000. Assuming its monthly average net assets for that year were $7,600,000, what was Definition Mutual Fund's portfolio turnover ratio last year?

Measuring Mutual Fund Risk

9. You currently hold shares in four mutual funds as described below:

	Shares	Current Price	Beta
Fund A	50	$11.00	1.05
Fund B	200	$22.50	.90
Fund C	50	$15.00	1.15
Fund D	200	$18.00	.90

   a. What is the weighted average beta of your portfolio?
   b. How does that average compare with the market beta of 1.00. What can you conclude about the risk level of your portfolio relative to that of the market?
   c. If you felt that having a portfolio 5% riskier than the market would be more appropriate (given your personal circumstances) than the level calculated in 'b' above, what specific changes could you make in your holdings to achieve this goal?

Measuring Fund Returns

10. On January 2, you invested $2,500 in a mutual fund at a per share price of $16.50. You held these shares all year, and on December 20, the fund's management announces a dividend distribution of $.15 per share together with capital gain distributions of $.75 per shares based on the December 31 closing price. On December 31, the fund closes at $18.20 per share.
   a. What is your total return for the year?
   b. How much of this return survives after taxes and inflation if your combined federal and state tax bracket is 35% and inflation was 3% during the year.
   c. How does the return calculated in 'a' above compare with a second fund that experienced a total return of 12.4%? Which performed better? Explain.

11. Over the last 10 years, the average annual total return provided by XYZ fund was 14.4%. Over that same period, the stock market as a whole was up 12.3%

annually. During this time, the fund's average beta was 1.10 and its standard deviation of returns was 9.8%.

  a.   Calculate this fund's Treynor measure for the ten year period.
  b.   What was the fund's Sharpe ratio for the period?
  c.   Consider the ABC fund with an average annual total return of 13.8% and a beta of .95 during the same period. Which fund performed better?
  d.   Now consider, in addition, the common stock of Widgets, Inc., which experienced average annual total returns of 15.2% over the ten years and has a beta of 1.25. How do these three investments compare in terms of their risk adjusted returns?
  e.   What if Widgets, Inc. stock showed a standard deviation of returns of 9.5%? How might this effect your answer to 'd' above?

12. During the year just ended, Fund A generated a 14.5% total return for its shareholders. During this time, the risk-free rate of interest was 4%, the fund's beta was 1.1, and the return generated by the S&P 500 was 11.3%.

  a.   Calculate Fund A's alpha coefficient for the year just ended
  b.   What rate of return would we have expected the fund to generate, given the risk level to which it was exposed?
  c.   How did the fund perform relative to those expectations?
  d.   What if you were considering another fund (Fund B) with an alpha coefficient of 6.3 over the same period. Which performed better on a risk adjusted basis.?

Comparison of Tax Basis for Shares Sold

13. Use the following information to answer this question:

Purchase Date	Purchase Amount	Share Price	Share Purchased	Shares Owned
January 2	$1,000	$16.50	60.606	60.606
February 15	$500	$15.75	31.746	92.352
March 20	$250	$16.00	15.625	107.977
May 20	$600	$17.00	35.294	143.271
August 1	$500	$17.50	28.571	171.842

Assume that on September 1, with shares in the fund selling for $17.25, you place an order to sell $2,000 worth of your holdings.

  a.   Calculate the tax basis of the shares sold using each of the three methods discussed in the chapter.
  b.   Calculate the resulting capital gain liability resulting from the sales using each of the three inventory valuation methods discussed in the chapter.
  c.   What is the tax basis of the shares remaining in your account after the sale if you use the average-basis method for determining tax basis of shares sold?

Measuring Portfolio Diversification

14. Consider the following annual total returns for the mutual funds listed.

	Fund A	Fund B	Fund C
1991	24.3%	16.8%	19.2%
1992	14.6%	17.1%	10.9%
1993	15.1%	6.4%	16.8%
1994	4.2%	3.8%	8.7%
1995	13.5%	9.1%	12.8%

    Now, assume that you currently own shares in Fund A and you are considering adding either Fund B or Fund C to your personal portfolio of funds in search of greater diversification. Based solely on the annual performance data above, which fund would make the most sense to pair with your original fund (Fund A)? Why?

Dollar Cost Averaging and Value Averaging

15. Assume that you use dollar cost averaging approach and invest $500 every month to buy ABC Fund, which is a no-load fund. The offering prices are as follows:

Month	Price (P)
1	$50
2	$46
3	$48
4	$52
5	$50
6	$44

    a. What is your unit cost of investment over this six-month period?
    b. What is the average offering price of this mutual fund over this six-month period?

16. Assume that you want your XYZ mutual fund account to grow $1,000 each quarter. You begin by buying 50 shares at $20 each. Suppose, in the second quarter, the share price is (1) $15, (2) $18, (3) $25, and (4) $50. To make your account worth $2,000, how much money do you have to invest under each situation?

SELECTED REFERENCES

AAII journal. Chicago, IL: American Association of Individual Investors. (Written for a lay audience, this publication frequently carries articles concerning mutual fund performance as well as a host of other personal finance issues)

Dorf, R. (1991). *The new mutual fund investment adviser*. Chicago: Probus.

Lefkowitz, K. (1994). *Mutual fund primer for investors*. Great Barrington, MA: American Institute for Economic Research.

Malkiel, B. (1996). *A random walk down wall street*. New York: W. W. Norton. (An excellent investment primer for individual investors, and includes a section geared toward helping investors evaluate and select mutual funds)

ENDNOTES

1. Investors should avoid investing in a mutual fund immediately before the fund pays dividends or capital gains distributions. Such distributions are taxable income even when not realized (unless the securities are held in a qualified tax-sheltered retirement plan). For example, on September 28 Ronnie puts $5,000 into XYZ Mutual Fund at an NAV of $21.38, which purchased 234 shares. The next day, XYZ declared $5.55 per share in distributions. This adds to about $1,300 in Ronnie's 234 shares. Accordingly, XYZ NAV per share drops by $5.55 from $21.38 to $15.83. Ronnie had signed an agreement to reinvest dividends, so he received 82 new shares. The result is that Ronnie owned 316 shares (234 + 82) that are still worth $5,000. However, the Internal Revenue Service considers the $1,300 in distributions as taxable income. At a 28 percent federal income tax rate, Ronnie would owe over $364 to the IRS. Beware: Before buying a mutual fund, find out the date the capital distributions. Because Ronnie did not wait until after the distribution date to invest, he had to pay over 7 percent of his investment in taxes.

Chapter 18
Options Mathematics

Chapter 18
Options Mathematics

Jonathan Fox and Dorit Samuel[1]

OVERVIEW

Options are standardized legal contracts which give the holder the right (not the obligation) to buy or sell a specific asset at a fixed price for a stated term, usually less than a year. Markets exist for options related to common stocks, debt instruments, foreign currencies, stock indexes, and even unleaded gasoline. Options are examples of **derivatives**, a financial instrument that is based on the values of other financial instruments (such as index rates, foreign exchange rates, commodity prices, or stock market indexes. Option trading occurs throughout the world.[1]

The most common are **stock options**, which are contracts giving the holder the right to buy or sell a specific number of shares (normally 100) of a certain stock at a specified price (called the **exercise price** or **strike price**). Options are created by an **option writer**, one who issues through a stock broker an option contract promising either to buy or to sell a specified asset for a fixed strike price; in return, the option writer receives an **option premium** (the price of the option itself) for standing ready to buy or sell the asset at the wishes of the option purchaser. The **option holder** is the person who actually owns the option contract. The original option writer always remains responsible for buying or selling the asset if requested by the holder of the option contract.

The price at which the option itself is traded depends on the price of the underlying security and the expected price changes in the underlying asset for the life of the option. This chapter covers two types of options: calls and puts. A **call option** gives its holder the right to purchase an asset for a specified price on or before the expiration date. A **put option** gives its holder the right to sell an asset for a specified price on or before expiration. The holder of the option is not required to exercise the option, but can do so at any time before the expiration of the contract. The length of

---

[1]Jonathan Fox, Ph.D., Assistant Professor, Department of Consumer and Textile Sciences, The Ohio State University, Columbus, OH 43210. fox.99@osu.edu. Dorit Samuel, Ph.D. Candidate, Department of Finance, The Ohio State University, Columbus, OH 43210. dsamuel@postbox.acs.ohio-state.edu.

option contracts usually range from one to nine months.[2] An **option contract** is created when the original buyer pays a premium to the option writer for granting the option. During the life of the option, the trading is done at market determined prices, that change continuously. The buyer of an option is said to be **long** in the option, while the writer of the option is **short** in the option.

A call option is **"in the money"** when the market price is greater than the exercise price. A put option is "in the money" when the market price is less than the exercise price. Exercising an option in both instances would produce a profit. An option is **"at the money"** when the exercise price equals the stock price where exercising your option produces no profit (an actual loss will occur due to the fees involved in the transaction). A call option is **"out of the money"** when the market price is less than the exercise price. A put option is "out of the money" when the market price is greater than the exercise price. Exercising your option in both instances would be unprofitable.

Options do not give one any of the rights a shareholder has, but the value of an option is adjusted for stock splits and dividends. In exercising an option two things can happen. First, the owner can select to take physical delivery of the asset (**call**) or deliver the asset (**put**). Second, the owner can settle the option where a cash payment is credited (debited) based on the difference between the underlying value of the asset and the exercise price of the option.

There are two situations of option trading. The **naked positions** occur when the option writer does not own the underlying asset although trades are made with the asset or the option, but not both; this is a speculative form of investing in options. While many naked trades are made, options are more frequently made by investors with covered positions. **Covered positions** occur when the option writer has an ownership position in the underlying asset. Here option and assets may be combined in a conservative manner to hedge against market risk and create unique return patterns. A **hedge** is achieved when ownership of an asset or option protects the owner from losses in other assets or options. Three such examples are spreads, straddles, and combinations. A **spread** combines an option (a call or a put) on the same underlying asset that is bought or written with different expirations or strike prices. Common spreads are the vertical spread, horizontal spread, and butterfly spread. A **vertical spread** occurs when an option is bought and sold on the same asset with the same expiration date but different strike prices. A **horizontal spread** is the result of buying and selling an option on the same asset with the same strike prices but different expiration dates. The most renowned spread is the **butterfly** spread, where several options are either bought or written at different strike prices. A **straddle** is a combination strategy that involves the same number of puts and calls on the same underlying security with the same striking price and expiration date. These option combinations allow the investor to take advantage of special situations where holding an uncovered or naked position is considered too risky or otherwise undesirable.

The length of option contracts usually range from one to nine months. Maturity months fall on one of three cycles: January-April-July-October, February-May-August-November, or March-June-September-December. At any time, options are available to the investor for the next three month cycle. An **American option** allows its holder to exercise it on or before the expiration date, while an **European option** allows its holder to exercise it only at expiration date. The **Option Clearing**

Corporation (OCC) is jointly owned by the exchanges in which stock options are traded. The OCC is the "middleman" among the traders. All private investors trade in options through a broker who clears the trade through the OCC. The OCC tracks the trades, matches buyers and sellers, and guarantees contract performance. The Chicago Board Options Exchange, the American Stock Exchange, the Philadelphia Stock Exchange, New York Stock Exchange, and the Pacific Stock Exchanges provide the market for most listed options in the United States. Conventional options are traded in the over-the-counter market. Options on assets other than stocks are also available, such as index options, foreign currency options, futures options, and interest rate options.

Options are very flexible instruments that can be used in combination with other options and/or underlying assets to create patterns of returns that are not available by holding traditional investments alone. While options are perceived by many investors as risky instruments, certain combined option strategies can successfully be used as a hedge against downside market risk. Some investors may actually prefer options given the benefits provided by financial leverage with limited liability for the term of the option. In the mathematical examples that follow, many of the benefits of using options to balance risk and return in an individual's portfolio are demonstrated. These benefits of options available to the individual investor include: a pattern of returns that cannot be achieved by trading in stocks only, patterns of returns that mimic borrowing and lending at more favorable rates, tax advantages unavailable when holding stocks or bonds, lower transaction costs, opportunity to hedge against unanticipated or anticipated changes in stock volatility, and perhaps most useful of all, insurance against sudden drops in stock prices. This chapter illustrates typical examples of mathematical concepts related to options: understanding options; intrinsic value of a call option; intrinsic value of a put option; time value of options; combinations of puts, calls, and direct asset ownership; impact of leverage on option returns; and market valuation of option contracts.

EXAMPLES OF MATHEMATICAL CONCEPTS RELATED TO OPTIONS

1. Understanding Options[3]

Formula 18.1.1: $NV_o = \text{Max} \{P - X, 0\} - f$

Where: NV_o = net value of obtaining the right to buy an asset; P = asset price; X = strike price; and f = fee.

Formula 18.1.2: $NV_g = \text{Min} \{X - P, 0\} - f$

Where: NV_g = net value of granting the right to buy an asset; P = asset price; X = strike price; and f = fee.

▼   **Example 18.1:** Option contracts can be written on any asset. As an example, consider an option to buy a house. A creative buyer becomes aware of a house that just came up on the market and would like to purchase the property with money that will be received from an inheritance. However, as a result of poor estate planning by his grandparents, the potential buyer does not know exactly how much money he will collect or exactly when the money will be received. Committing to buy the house immediately would be impossible should he not receive enough money to cover the cost of the purchase. One solution for the perspective buyer is to acquire an option to buy the house for an agreed price. This will insulate the potential buyer from economic changes in the real estate market during the time necessary for the inherited estate to work its way through probate. The buyer figures that within three months he will be able to work out the finances. Should he receive the money required during that period, he could exercise the option and buy the house. In the event that problems arise in probate and the inheritance is delayed or that the amount is smaller than needed, he has the option not to exercise the contract and walk away from the deal. To convince the seller to wait for the potential buyer for three months the buyer needs to pay a fee. The potential buyer and the seller agreed to a price of $150,000 for the house. Since the buyer may need three months for funds to clear the probate court, a contractual agreement is made with the seller that entitles the buyer to buy the house within the next three months for an agreed price of $150,000. For agreeing to sell the house at a later date, the seller receives a non-refundable fee of $500. What are values of the contract to the buyer and seller if (1) the real estate market skyrockets and the market value of the house goes to $200,000, (2) the real estate market drops and the market value of the house goes to $100,000, and (3) there is little change in the housing market and the buyer obtains the money in a timely manner and executes the deal?

Solution:

(1) Use Formula 18.1.1 to calculate the value of obtaining the right to buy the house.

Since f = $500, X = $150,000, if P = $200,000, then

NV_o = Max {$200,000 − $150,000, 0} − $500 = $50,000 − $500 = $49,500

Use Formula 17.1.2 to calculate the value of granting the right to buy the house.

Since f = $500, X = $150,000, if P = $200,000, then

NV_g = Min {$150,000 − $200,000, 0} + $500 = 0 + $500 = $500

The results imply that if the house price increases by $200,000, the contract to the buyer will be worth $49,500 as net profit. The net value of the contract to the seller will be $500. In this case, the house option is favorable to the buyer.

(2) If P = $100,000, then

NV_o = Max {$100,000 − $150,000, 0} − $500 = 0 − $500 = −$500

NV_g = Min {$150,000 − $100,000, 0} + $500 = 0 + $500 = $500

If the real estate market drops and the price of the house goes to $100,000, the contract held by the buyer entitles him to walk away from the purchase contract. Thus, he avoids loosing $50,000. The would-be buyer is out only the $500 fee to the seller for the contract. The net value of granting the contract for the seller is only $500.

(3) If P = $150,000, then

$$NV_o = \text{Max } \{\$150,000 - \$150,000, 0\} - \$500 = 0 - \$500 = -\$500$$

$$NV_g = \text{Min } \{\$150,000 - \$150,000, 0\} + \$500 = 0 + \$500 = \$500$$

If the buyer received adequate funds to purchase the house and the present market value of the house warrants the deal, then the buyer would go ahead with the purchase. Should the buyer not receive the funds he could walk away form the deal incurring only the $500 cost of the fee. In this case, the only difference of the contract values for the buyer and seller is the non-refundable fee.

❖   **Interpretation:** This problem describes a call option where the underlying asset is a house. The owner of the house (the writer of the call) is willing, for a non-refundable fee of $500, to wait an agreed time period for the potential buyer to buy the house. While the seller is taking the risk of market value changes during this waiting period, the seller is also securing the price at which the house may be sold. The buyer secures the purchase price and pays the seller a non-refundable fee of $500 for the option to change his mind over the next three months.

2. Intrinsic Value of a Call Option

Formula 18.2.1: $V_c(B) = \text{Max } \{P_s - X, 0\}$

Where: $V_c(B)$ = value of the call to the buyer; P_s = price of the stock; and X = strike price.

Formula 18.2.2: $V_c(W) = \text{Min } \{X - P_s, 0\}$

Where: $V_c(W)$ = value of the call to the writer; P_s = price of the stock; and X = strike price.

▼   **Example 18.2.1:** The market price of AT&T stock is $60 and the strike price of the call option is $50. What is the value of the call to (1) the buyer and (2) the writer or option maker?

Solution:

(1) *Value of the call to the buyer.*

Since X = $50, P = $60, then, using Formula 18.2.1

$$V_c(B)_{AT\&T} = Max\{\$60-\$50, 0\} = \$10$$

Thus, the value of the call for the buyer is $10.

❖   **Interpretation:** The intrinsic value of a call increases on a one-for-one basis with the price of the underlying asset once it is above the exercise price. The intrinsic value of the call to the buyer will change dollar-for-dollar with the price of the stock. If the price of AT&T drops to $55 then the intrinsic value of the call will be $5. The call buyer exercises the option to buy at $50 and resells at the market price of $55 for a profit of $5, not accounting for the option premium. If the price of AT&T rises to $65 then the intrinsic value of the call will be $15. The buyer of the call benefits from price increases while not incurring looses when the price of AT&T falls. For a graphical interpretation of the changes in the value of a purchased call given increases in the price of the underlying asset see the first panel of the call payoff diagram (Figure 18-1). This strategy requires also that a fee is to be paid to the call writer which reduces the potential gain from purchasing a call option. The dotted line in the diagram reflects this cost.

FIGURE 18-1
Call Payoff Diagram

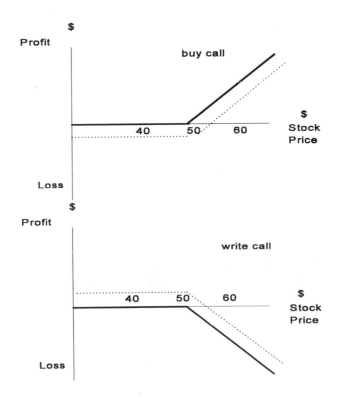

(2) *Value of the call to the writer.*

Since X = $50, P = $60, then, using Formula 18.2.2

$$V_c(W)_{AT\&T} = Min\{\$50-\$60,0\} = -\$10$$

Thus, the value of the call for the writer is -$10.

❖ **Interpretation:** The intrinsic value of the call to the option writer becomes negative as the price of the stock rises above the strike price. The call option writer needs to deliver the stock to the buyer, hence the writer may need to purchase the stock for $60 (market price) and receive only $50 (agreed price) from the buyer upon delivery. For every dollar increase in the price of AT&T the call writer looses an additional dollar. The second panel of the call payoff diagram (Figure 18-1) shows a one-for-one drop in the value of the call given increases in the price of the stock. The money earned by the call writer in fees are reflected by the dotted line in the call payoff diagram.

▼ **Example 18.2.2:** The market price of AT&T is $40 and the strike price of the option is $50. What is the value of the call to (1) the buyer and (2) the writer or option maker?

Solution:

(1) *Value of the call to the buyer.*

Since X = $50, P = $40, then, using Formula 18.2.1

$$V_c(B)_{AT\&T} = Max\{\$40 - \$50, 0\} = \$0$$

Thus, the value of the call for the buyer is 0.

❖ **Interpretation:** While the strike price exceeds the price of the stock, the call contract has no value for the buyer. The buyer would not exercise the contract to buy the stock at a price that is above market price. The call payoff diagram (Figure 18-1) for buying a call shows this are of $0 profit when the stock price is below $50. The actual loss on the deal is reflected by the dotted line that accounts for contract fees paid by the buyer.

(2) *Value of the call to the writer.*

Since X = $50, P = $40, then, using Formula 18.2.2

$$V_c(W)_{AT\&T} = Min\{\$50 - \$40, 0\} = \$0$$

Thus, the value of the call for the writer is 0.

❖ **Interpretation:** The intrinsic value of the call to the option writer is $0 so long as the market price remains below the strike price. This is the ideal position for the option writer in that the entire premium paid for the option can be retained as profit should the call option expire out of the money. The call payoff diagram (Figure 18-1) for writing a call shows this $0 loss on the stock price movement and the profit of the fee shown by the dotted line.

3. Intrinsic Value of a Put Option

Formula 18.3.1: $V_p(B) = \text{Max } \{X - P_s, 0\}$

Where: $V_p(B)$ = value of the put the buyer; X = strike price; and P_s = price of the stock.

Formula 18.3.2: $V_p(W) = \text{Min } \{P_s - X, 0\}$

Where: $V_p(W)$ = value of the put the writer; X = strike price; and P_s = price of the stock.

▼ **Example 18.3.1:** The market price of AT&T is $50 and the strike price of the put option is $60. What is the value of the put to (1) the buyer and (2) the writer of the put option?

Solution:

(1) *Value of the put to the buyer.*

Since P_s = $50, X = $60, then using Formula 18.3.1

$V_p(B)_{AT\&T} = \text{Max}\{\$60 - \$50, 0\} = \$10$

Thus, the value of the put for the buyer is $10.

❖ **Interpretation:** The intrinsic value of a put rises on a one-to-one basis with decreases in the price of the underlying asset below the strike price. The intrinsic value of the put to the buyer will change dollar-for-dollar with the price of the stock. If the price of AT&T drops to $45 then the intrinsic value of a single put will be $15. The put option writer committed to buy the stock from the put option buyer for $60 (strike price), hence the put buyer purchases the stock for $45 (market price) and receives $60 upon delivery for a $15 profit not accounting for fees paid. The buyer of the put benefits from price drops only. The put payoff diagram (Figure 18-2) shows these higher profits coming with lower underlying asset prices.

(2) *Value of the put to the writer.*

Since P_s = $50, X = $60, then using Formula 18.3.2

FIGURE 18-2
Put Payoff Diagram

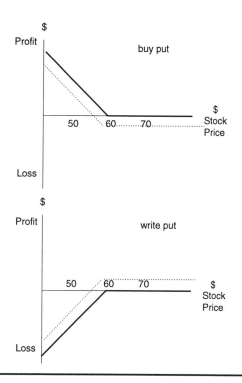

$$V_p(W)_{AT\&T} = Min\{\$50 - \$60, 0\} = -\$10$$

Thus, the value of the put for the writer is $-\$10$.

❖   **Interpretation:** The intrinsic value of the put to the option writer becomes negative as the price falls below the strike price. For every dollar decrease in the price of AT&T the put writer looses an *additional* dollar. The loss can be offset if it is small enough to be covered by the fee received for writing the put. This "break-even point" is shown by the intersection of the dotted line and the x-axis in the second panel of the put payoff diagram (Figure 18-2).

▼   **Example 18.3.2:** The market price of AT&T is $60 and the strike price of the option is $55. What is the value of the put to (1) the buyer and (2) the writer or option maker?

Solution:

(1)   *Value of the put to the buyer.*

Since $P_s = \$60$, $X = \$55$, then using Formula 18.3.1

$$V_p(B)_{AT\&T} = Max\{\$55 - \$60, 0\} = \$0$$

Thus, the value of the put for the buyer is 0.

❖ **Interpretation:** While the strike price is less than the price of the stock there is no value of the put to the buyer. The buyer would not exercise the contract to sell the stock and force the buyer to buy it at a price that is above the strike price. If the option expires while the stock price is above the exercise price then the loss to the investor is the amount paid for the option shown by the dotted line in the top panel of the put payoff diagram (Figure 18-2).

(2) *Value of the put to the writer.*

Since $P_s = \$60$, $X = \$55$, then using Formula 18.3.2

$$V_p(W)_{AT\&T} = Min\{\$60 - \$55, 0\} = \$0$$

Thus, the value of the put for the writer is 0.

❖ **Interpretation:** The intrinsic value of the put to the option maker is $0 so long as the market price remains above the strike price. This is the ideal position for the put option writer so that the entire premium paid for the option can be retained as profit should the put option expire out of the money (see Figure 18-2).

4. Time Value of Options

Formula 18.4: $P_o = V_I + V_t$

Where: P_o = price of the option; V_I = intrinsic value of the option; and V_t = time value of the option.

▼ **Example 18.4:** A call option for AT&T is priced at $5 (most likely costing the call option buyer $500 as contracts are usually written for blocks of 100 shares). The strike price is $60 per share and the current price of AT&T is $62. (1) What is the intrinsic value of the call? (2) What is the time value or speculative value of the call?

Solution:

(1) *Value of the call to the buyer.*

Since $P = \$62$, $X = \$60$, then using Formula 18.2.1

$$V_{I,c,AT\&T} = Max\{\$62 - \$60, 0\} = \$2$$

❖ **Interpretation:** The value of the call to the buyer is $2. As the value of the underlying asset exceeds the strike price the intrinsic value of the call option rises dollar for dollar with the price of the asset.

(**2**) *Time value of the call.*

Since $P_o = \$5$, $Vi = \$2$, then using Formula 18.4

$\$5 = \$2 + V_t$

$V_t = \$5 - \$2 = \$3$

❖ **Interpretation:** The time value of the call is $3. Option prices are not based only on their intrinsic value. Options also attract a speculative premium, or time value, that must be added to the intrinsic value to get the total value of the option, or the option price. Therefore, the observed market price of an option will not exactly match the calculated intrinsic value of the option. The difference is called **time value**. The time value is derived from factors such as variability in the price of the asset, forecasted prices, contract expiration dates, leverage, and expected dividends of underlying assets. The speculative or time value of the option is the difference between the option price and the intrinsic value of the option. Changes in the expectations for future prices or dividends would lead to changes in the speculative value of the option and thus changes in the option price.

5. Combinations of Puts, Calls, and Direct Asset Ownership

Conceptual Idea 18.5: Combinations of options and assets, different option types (call/put), different strike prices, or different expiration dates may help investors hedge against market risk and create unique return patterns.

▼ **Example 18.5.1:** An investor is expecting the price of a favorite stock, currently priced at $40, to remain very stable for the coming months and is thus considering the following combination of options: writing two puts with a strike price $40 and buying one put with a strike price $30 and one put with strike price $50. Calculate the intrinsic value of this combination of contracts if the stock price is (1) $30, (2) $40, and (3) $50.

Solutions:

Use Formula 18.3.2 to calculate the value of the writer, and use Formula 18.3.1 to calculate the value of the buyer.

(**1**) When the stock price is $30 the value of the combined position is:

2 puts (min $\{30 - 40, 0\}$) + 1 put (max $\{30-30, 0\}$) + 1 put ($\{$max $50-30, 0\}$)
$= -\$20 + 0 + \$20 = \$0$

(**2**) When the stock price is $40 the value of the combined position is:

2 puts (min $\{40 - 40, 0\}$) + 1 put (max $\{30-40, 0\}$) + 1 put (max $\{50-40,0\}$)
$= 0 + 0 + \$10 = \$10$

(3) When the stock price is $50 the value of the combined position is:

2 puts (min {50 – 40, 0}) + 1 put (max {30–50, 0}) + 1 put (max {50–50, 0})
= 0 + 0 + 0 = 0

❖ **Interpretation:** This example demonstrates a **butterfly spread** in which several options are either bought or written at different strike prices. An investor can take advantage of stagnant stock prices by holding a butterfly combination of options. The butterfly payoff diagram (Figure 18-3) shows how an individual investor can benefit from expectations of little price movement in the underlying asset of an option. The downside of this strategy is that the further the price of the stock moves from $40 during the life of the option, the less the combined position is worth (see the second panel of Figure 18-3).

FIGURE 18-3
Butterfly Payoff Diagram

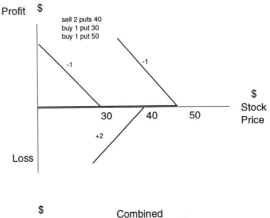

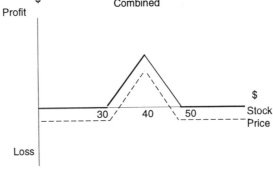

▼ **Example 18.5.2:** A drug company announces that it is awaiting approval by the U.S. Food and Drug Administration (FDA) on a very important and marketable drug. The decision is expected in about one month. If the drug receives FDA approval for sale, the stock price will go to at least $40; should the FDA not approve the drug, the stock value will probably go down to $20, or below. The stock trades today for $30. Evaluate the intrinsic value of the following combined position for the buyer of a call with strike price $30 and a put with strike price $30 if (1) the stock price goes to $20, (2) the stock price rises to $40 and (3) the stock price is $30.

Solution:

Use Formula 18.2.1 for calculating the value of the call, and Formula 18.3.1 for the value of the put.

(1) If FDA does not approve the drug and the stock price falls to $20, then
call (max $\{20-30, 0\}$) + put (max $\{30-20,0\}$) = $10

(2) If FDA approves the drug and the stock price goes up to $40, then
call (max $\{40-30, 0\}$) + put (max $\{30-40,0\}$) = $10

(3) If FDA delays it's decision and the stock price stays at $30, then
call (max $\{0-30, 0\}$) + put (max $\{30-30,0\}$) = $0

❖ **Interpretation:** Whether or not FDA approves the drug, the value of the combined options would be worth $10. But the combination would be worthless if the FDA delays the decision. This example illustrates a straddled position that results from buying both a call and put option. If expectations are for great volatility in the price of a stock then this would be the appropriate strategy. The straddle payoff diagram (Figure 18-4) shows how the buyer of the contracts benefits as the stock price moves away from the strike price. Purchasing the company's stock outright might lead to either great profits or losses. However, an option straddle allows the investor not to care about which way the stock moves as long as it moves substantially. One point of concern is the timing; the movement must occur before the options expire. If the FDA decides to delay its decision then the investor could lose all the money spent on the contracts. This strategy is known as a **vertical straddle**, defined by holding the same number of puts and calls on the same underlying security with same striking price and expiration date.

▼ **Example 18.5.3:** A loyal employee has ignored her financial planner's recommendations and amassed a portfolio weighted heavily towards her employing company's stock. (Smart investors typically diversify their holdings.) To protect herself from significant drops in the stock price, she is considering the use of options. To illustrate a risk hedging option for the loyal employee, calculate the value of the combined position when owning a stock and a put with strike price $30 when the stock price is: (1) $40, (2) $30, and (3) $20.

FIGURE 18-4
Straddle Payoff Diagram

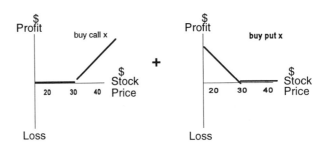

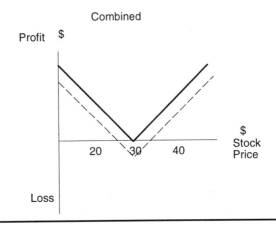

Solution:

Use Formula 18.3.1 to calculate the value of the put for the buyer.

(1) When the stock price is $40 the value of the combined position is

stock(40) + put (max {30−40,0}) = $40

(2) When the stock price is $30 the value of the combined position is

stock(30) + put (max {30−30,0}) = $30

(3) When the stock price is $20 the value of the combined position is

stock(20) + put (max {30−20,0}) = $30

❖ **Interpretation:** In this example, when the stock price goes down to $20, the value of the combination is still $30. This covered position is called a **protective put** as it entails owning both the underlying asset or stock together with a put option, and this hedges against losses. This may be a reasonable strategy for the loyal employee who prefers investing in the company for which they work. A protective put is purchased to hedge against down side risk when holding a significant position in an individual stock. This is not an uncommon position for individual investors who have compensation packages that include stock. The protective put payoff diagram (Figure 18-5) shows how combining stock ownership with a put on the same stock protect the investor from price drops below the strike price of the put option.

FIGURE 18-5
Protective Put Payoff Diagram

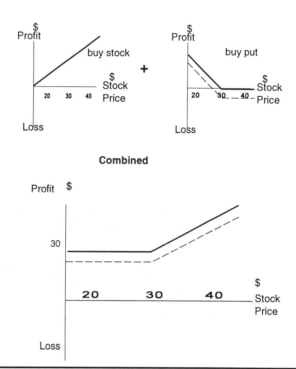

▼ **Example 18.5.4:** A conservative investor is contemplating what to do with a $25,000 year-end bonus. A favorite stock is priced at $125 and a call on this stock is currently valued at $10 with exercise price $135 and 6 months to maturity. The T-bill return is 10% annually (5% semiannually). Calculate the value of each of the three strategies listed below if the stock price is (1) $100, (2) $110, (3) $120, (4) $130, and (5) $140, (6) $150, (7) $160, and (8) $170.

Strategies:

Strategy	Shares of Stock	Number of Options	$ in T-Bills	$ Cost
A	200			$25,000
B		2500		$25,000
C		500	$20,000	$25,000

Solution:

If the stock price is $100, the values for the three strategies would be:

(1) The value of 200 shares of stocks at price of $100 is

$100 × 200 = $ 20,000

(2) Since X = $135, P = $100, then use Formula 18.2.1, the value of one call is

max {$100 – $135, 0} = 0

Then, the value of 2,500 calls is 2,500 × 0 = 0

(3) After 6 months, the $20,000 in T-bills is worth $21,000 = 1.05 × $20,000, the value of a call is 0 as calculated in B, then the value of the combination is

$21,000 + 500 × 0 = $21,000

Using the same steps as above, the values for other stock prices can be calculated, and the following are the results:

$Price of stock ▶	$100	$110	$120	$130	$140	$150	$160	$170
Strategy ▼								
$ value of A	$20,000	$22,000	$24,000	$26,000	$28,000	$30,000	$32,000	$34,000
$ value of B	$0	$0	$0	$0	$12,500	$37,500	$62,500	$87,500
$ value of C	$21,000	$21,000	$21,000	$21,000	$23,500	$33,500	$33,500	$38,500

❖ **Interpretation:** Again the combined position provides an opportunity for the individual investor. Strategy C, which is made up of a call option and T-bill investments, proves to be far less volatile than Strategy B with greater potential for gain than that of owning only the stock (strategy A). The clear advantage is seen on the downside. While the option may become worthless if the price of the stock drops below $135, the loss is limited to the $5,000 spent on the contract in Strategy C. This is not the case with Strategies A or B. This example indicates by combining bond ownership with options one may be able to take a position in a stock that is more favorable (less volatile and less susceptible to falling stock prices). In addition, option contracts may offer lower transaction costs as obtaining a position in 100 stock options is usually cheaper than purchasing 100 stocks.

6. The Impact of Leverage on Option Returns

Conceptual Idea 18.6: Many investors try to enhance the potential return on their investments by using **leverage** (using borrowed funds), and, depending upon the directions of market prices, the use of leverage in options can result in great profits as readily as substantial losses.

▼ **Example 18.6:** An individual has $10,000 to invest. If the price of a stock is $100 and a call option is valued at $5 with strike price $105 maturing in one year, then what will be the return if the stock price rises to $120 with the entire amount invested in stock or call options (assume the stock pays no dividends)? What will happen if the stock price drops to $80?

Solution:

(1) If the stock price rises to $120, then, the return rate of the stock investment is

($120 – $100)/$110 = 18.2%

In the case of call investment, since 2,000 calls ($10,000 / $5) are bought, and the value of a call is

max {$120 – $105, 0) = $ 15,

Total value of the calls is

$15 × 2,000 = $30,000

Then, the return rate of call investment is

($30,000 – $10,000)/$10,000 = 200%

(2) If the stock price drops to $80, the return rate of the stock investment is

($80 – $100)/$100 = –20%

In the case of call investment, the value of a call is

max {$80 – $100, 0} = 0

The total value of the calls will be

0 × 2,000 = 0

The return rate of the call investment is

(0 – $10,000)/$10,000 = –100%

❖ **Interpretation:** The leveraged position taken by those investing in options provide the opportunity for enormous returns. However, had the contract not been in the money the investor would have suffered a 100% loss, or the total forfeiture of the $10,000 premium paid for the options.

7. Market Valuation of Option Contracts

Formula 18.7.1: $C = (S - De^{-rT}) N(d_1) - X e^{-rT} N(d_2)$

in which, $d_1 = [\ln (S/X) + (r + .5\sigma 2)T]/ \sigma\sqrt{T}$, $d_2 = d_1 - \sigma\sqrt{T}$

Where: C = call price; S = stock price; $N(d)$ = the probability that a random draw from a standard normal distribution will be less than d (This equals the area under the normal curve up to d)[4]; X = exercise price; e = the base of natural log – 2.71828; r = risk-free interest rate with the same maturity as the option expiration; T = Time to maturity in years; and σ = standard deviation of the annualized continuously compounded rate of return of the stock.

Formula 18.7.2 $P = C + X e^{-rT} - S - D e^{-rT}$

Where: P = put price; C = call price; S = stock price; X = exercise price; e = the base of natural log – 2.71828; r = risk-free interest rate with the same maturity as the option expiration; and T = Time to maturity in years.

▼   **Example 18.7.1:** What is the value of an European call option with an exercise price of $40 and a maturity date 6 months from now if the stock price is $28, σ = .5 and r_f = 6%? Given the same conditions, what is the price of a put option?

Solution:

(1)   The call price.

Using Formula 18.7.1, first solve for d_1 and d_2. Since S = $28, X = $40, r=.06, σ = .5, D=0, then

$d_1 = [\ln (28/40) + (.06 +.5\times.5^2).5]/.5\sqrt{.5} = (-.3567+.0925)/.3536=-.7472$
and $N(d_1)$= .2266
$d_2 = -.7472 - .5\sqrt{.5} = -.7472-.3536=-1.10$ and $N(d_2)$= .1357

Note that the values of N(d) are found from the standard normal distribution table which is not included in this book (see endnote 4). Also, the N(d) value can be calculated easily in popular spreadsheet programs, such as Excel and Lotus. Then,

$C = 28 \times .2266 - 40 e^{-.06} \times.5 \times .1357 = 6.3448 - 5.2676 = \$1.08$

(2)   The put price.

Using Formula 18.7.2, since C = $2.52, X = $40, r = .06, T = .05, S = $28, D=0, then

$P = 1.08 + 40 e^{-.06} \times.5 - 28 = \$11.90$

❖   **Interpretation:** The most complicated part of option trading is option pricing. However difficult it may be, it is important for the individual investor to understand, at least conceptually if not mathematically, what will impact the price of options before they consider adding these contracts to their portfolios. The market prices of options are impacted by changes in: the current price of the underlying asset, the length of time to maturity, the volatility of the underlying asset, the exercise price, the risk-free rate of return, and dividends paid on the underlying assets. The most widely used formula in valuing a call option given the stock price, exercise price, the risk-free interest rate, time to maturity, and estimated volatility of the stock is the **Black-Scholes Formula**, originally put forth in 1973. Variants of this formula have been developed to deal with some of its limitations. Formula 18.7.1 is one of the variants that improve the precision of the call price estimation by adding the dividend factor. The formula to valuate a put option is based on the **put-call parity theorem.** Formula 18.7.2 is deducted based on this theorem.[5] Black-Scholes formula and the put-call parity theorem help investors understand the reasons behind price changes in options. In the valuing a call it makes sense to obtain a low price ($2.52) given the fact that the exercise price is well above the current price, volatility is not excessive (s = .5), and the time to maturity is short (six months). On the other hand, it is not surprising that the put option is valued at a price well above the call given the fact that the price is already well below the exercise price and volatility is not excessive with little time to maturity. Changes in the factors which impact the value of options in this example are summarized in the following table.

Variable increases	Value of call option	Value of put option
Stock Price (S_0)	up	down
Exercise price (X)	down	up
Stock volatility (s)	up	up
Time to maturity (T)	up	up
Risk-free rate (r)	up	down
Dividends (D)	down	up

INFORMATION AND COMPUTING RESOURCES

1. National newspapers, such as *The Wall Street Journal* and *Barron's*, or big city newspapers, such as *The Washington Post, New York Times, Boston Globe, Los Angeles Times*, and *Miami Herald*, carry up-to-date information on listed options quotations. In these listings you can find the available options enumerated by strike price, expiration month, and price for both calls and puts. Following the prices of options for a favorite stock is an excellent way to asses market expectations for stock price movements.

2. Each of the organized exchanges will provide on request extensive information on the process of options investing. Packages summarizing option strategies and regulations are available from all of the following:

- American Stock Exchange, Derivative Securities, 86 Trinity Place, New York, NY 10006 (800-843-2639).

- Chicago Board Options Exchange, LaSalle at Van Buren, Chicago, IL 60605 (800-678-4667).

- New York Stock Exchange, Options and Index Products, 11 Wall Street, New York, NY 1005 (800-692-6973).

- Pacific Stock Exchange, Options Marketing, 115 Sansome Street, 7th Floor, San Francisco, CA 94104 (800-825-5773).

- Philadelphia Stock Exchange, 1900 Market Street, Philadelphia, PA 19103 (800-843-7445).

3. Many World Wide Web sites exist that provide educational and proprietary information on options:

- *Wall Street Discount Corporation:* http://www.wsdc.com./options.html (provides background and trading information.)

- *Duke University:* http://www.duke.edu/~whaley/forcinfo.htm (The Futures and Options Research Center at Duke University presents information to promote "greater understanding of the uses and applications of these new financial contracts as well the functioning of the markets in which they trade.)

- *Futures and Options Reserach:*
  http://www.gopher.ag.uiuc.edu/ace/ofor/aboutofor.html (The University of Illinois at Urbana-Champaign's Office for Futures and Options Research provides links to a working paper series, options research on the WWW, and extensive reading lists on options related topics.)

- *Finance Watch:* http://www .finance.wat.ch/ (allows for some interactive learning about options in it's guided tour to finance on the Internet.)

- *Futures and Options Trading:* http://www.teleport.com/~futures (online information and services for futures and options traders.)

- *Futures Web:* http://trade-futures.com (educational and skill-building materials for success in trading commodities futures.)

EXERCISE PROBLEMS

Understanding Options

1. Harold sees a pair of the hottest selling shoes in a chic boutique on Melrose Avenue. He wants the shoes but does not have the money. The store has a layaway policy which will allow Harold to pay 10% of the $200 cost of the shoes to hold the shoes for one month. What is the value of this contract to both Harold and the store owners if: (A) Michael Jordan starts wearing the same shoes and the market price jumps to $300, (B) Bob Dole starts wearing the same shoes and the market price drops to $50, and (C) there is little price change in the market for these shoes and the buyer obtains the money in a timely manner and executes the deal?

2. *Out-of-Class Exercise* Describe other common consumer expenditures that are, or could be purchased, with option like contracts.

3. *Out-of-Class Exercise* In what way has the establishment of the organized exchanges been instrumental in the development of the option market?

Intrinsic Value of a Call Option

4. If the market price of the Limited stock today is $40 and the strike price of the option on the stock is $30, what is the value of the option to a call buyer or the value of the option to a call writer? What are the values of the call option for both the buyer and writer if the price goes up to $50, or down to $25?

5. Dan has a few days to decide weather to exercise 2 call contracts on AT&T with strike price of $30. The option contracts were purchased for $400 six month ago ($2 premium on each option). What is the minimum value of the stock for which Dan will exercise the option?

Intrinsic Value of a Put Option

6. If the market price of the Limited stock today is $40 and the strike price of the option on the stock is $30, what is the value of the option to a put buyer or the value of the option to a put writer? What are the values of the put option for both the buyer and writer if the price goes up to $50, or down to $25?

7. If you believe the stock of the Limited company will go up, do you buy calls or puts?

8. If you believe the stock of the Limited company will go down, do you buy calls or puts?

Time Value of Options

9. IBM stock is currently priced at $110 and you are considering to buy an option with a strike price of $105 which expires in 3 months. The price of the call is $9 and the price of the put is $2. What is the time or speculative value of each option?

10. *Out-of-Class Exercise* Describe market expectations in August for General Electric if the stock price is $84 and an October option has a strike price of $85 with the call valued at $3 and the put valued at $1.

11. *Out-of-Class Exercise* Explain why the speculative value on Value Jet Airlines options was so high following the crash of a Value Jet airplane in the Florida Everglades and subsequent Federal Aviation Administration (FAA) investigation.

Combinations of Puts, Calls, and Direct Asset Ownership

12. Evaluate the intrinsic value of the following strategy: buy 1 call with strike price $40, and buy 1 put with strike price $40 if the stock price (A) goes down to $35, (B) rises to $45, and (C) keeps the same. What is the name of the strategy and under what economic scenario will you choose this strategy?

13. Evaluate the intrinsic value of this strategy: purchase a stock and a put with strike price $20 if the stock price (A) goes down to $15, (B) goes up to $25, and (C) keeps the same. What is the name of the strategy and under what economic scenario will you choose this strategy?

14. Evaluate the intrinsic value of the following strategy: buy 1 put with strike price $20; 1 put with strike price $40; sell 2 puts with strike price $30, if the stock price is (A) $20, (B) $30, and (C) $40. What is the name of the strategy and under what economic scenario you will choose this strategy?

15. A conservative investor is contemplating what to do with a $14,000 year end bonus. A favorite stock is priced at $140 and a call on this stock is currently valued at $14 with exercise price $135 with 6 months to maturity. The T-bill return is 10% annually (5% semiannually). Calculate the value of each of the three strategies listed below if the stock price is (A) $120, (B) $130, (C)$140, (C) $150, and (E) $160.

Strategy	Shares of Stock	Number of Options	$ in T-Bills	$ Cost
A	100			$14,000
B		1000		$14,000
C		100	$12,600	$14,000

The Impact of Leverage on Option Returns

16. Compare the returns on an investment of $12,000 in (A) Boeing stock purchased for $80 and sold one year later for $90 and (B) a six month call option on Boeing stock with strike price 85 and current price $90 (a $3 premium was paid for the option).

Market Valuation of Option Contracts

17. What is the price of a European call if the price of the underlying common stock is $20, the exercise price is $20, the risk-free rate is 8%. the variance of the stock is .36, and the option expires six months from now? What is the put price?

18. Using the information given bellow calculate the price on a three month European call option. Stock price $47, strike price $45, risk-free rate .05, standard deviation .4. What is the price of the put?

SELECTED REFERENCES

Black, F., & Scholes, M. (1973). The pricing of options and corporate liabilities, *Journal of political economy, 81*, 637-654.

Cheng, S. S. (1996). A real-option approach to evaluating human capital investment: The case of college education. In J. K. Lewis (ed.). *The proceedings of association of financial counseling and planning.*

Cox, J. C., & Rubinstein, M. (1985). *Options market.* Englewood Cliffs, NJ: Prentice Hall, Inc.

Francis, J. C. (1991). *Investments analysis and management.* (5th ed.). Hightstown, NJ: McGraw-Hill.

Hull, J. (1989). *Options futures and other derivative securities.* Englewood Cliffs, NJ: Prentice Hall, Inc.

Miller, S. E. (1995). Economics of automobile leasing: The call option value. *Journal of consumer affairs, 29* (1), 199-218.

Sharpe, W. F., Alexander, G. J., & Bailey, J. V. (1995). *Investments* (5th ed.). Englewood Cliffs, NJ: Prentice Hall.

ENDNOTES

1. Options trading on an organized exchange started in 1973 in Chicago. The most difficult aspect of option trading is pricing the contract correctly. In 1973 Fischer Black and Myron Scholes developed a relatively easy to use model for pricing options which led to tremendous growth in options trading in organized markets. Within three years options were traded on four different exchanges in the U.S. and are now traded on exchanges throughout the world. Since the option market is standardized, only certain contracts are offered. Most of the calls and puts are written on widely traded stocks and with an exercise price close to the trading price.

2.   A new, longer-term option called **long-term equity anticipation securities (LEAPS)** is available for more than 150 stocks, which have lives as long as two and one-half years.

3.   Miller (1995) evaluates the value of a call option on an automobile lease. Cheng (1996) used the option approach to evaluate the human capital investment. Other applications of the option approach are also reviewed by Cheng (1996).

4.   To obtain the probability that a random draw from a standard normal distribution will be less than d it is necessary use tables in the appendix of any business statistics, statistics, or econometrics textbook. Some investment books include a table of d and N(d) (Sharpe, Alexander, & Bailey, 1995).

5.   The deduction of Formula 18.7.2 is as follows. The formula to evaluate a put option is based on the **put-call parity theorem**. The theorem states that if we live in a world of **"no arbitrage"** (where there are no opportunities for risk-free profits), then the payoff of a call option with exercise price X and T years to maturity combined with a risk-free bond that pays X at maturity (present value = $X\,e^{-rT}$) should equal the payoff of a put option with exercise price X and T years to maturity combined with the underlying security. Using the same notation as above, the put-call parity principle can be expressed as:

$$P + S_o = C + X\,e^{-rT}$$

where P is the price of the put; and C is still the price of the call, and other terms are defined the same as in Formula 18.7.1. This formula can be rearranged to solve for the price of the put:

$$P = C + X\,e^{-rT} - S_o$$

Dividends (D) can be accounted for as follows:

$$P = C + X\,e^{-rT} - S - D\,e^{-rT}$$

Chapter 19
Housing and Real Estate Mathematics

Chapter 19
Housing and Real Estate Mathematics

Y. Lakshmi Malroutu[1]

[1]Y. Lakshmi Malroutu, Ph.D., Assistant Professor, Department of Family, Nutrition, and Exercise Sciences, Queens College, CUNY, Flushing, NY 11367. malroutu@qcvaxa.acc.qc.edu

OVERVIEW

The American dream for many people is to own a home. This often is a family's single biggest investment. Throughout the 1970s and early 1980s, real estate was considered to be a reliable way to accumulate wealth. Several factors contributed to startling gains in home prices during that period, including a national housing shortage, an increased number of baby boomers entering the real estate market, generous tax advantages, and high inflation expectations. However, the scenario changed in the mid-1980s and into the 1990s, as by this time most housing markets were over built, fewer baby boomers could afford homes, tax breaks were reduced, and inflation decreased. Today's real estate market is variable and remains complicated, particularly for those desiring to purchase a home for investment purposes.

Because the price of a home is large relative to family income most homes are purchased with borrowed money. An amount loaned to a borrower (**mortgagor**) by a lender (**mortgagee**) for the purchase of a home and collateralized by the home is called a **mortgage** (or **mortgage loan**). A mortgagee has the right to foreclose on a home if the mortgagor defaults on the loan. The process of gradually paying off a mortgage loan through a series of periodic payments that includes not only an amount for interest, but also for principal repayment, is called **amortization**. The payment schedule requires the complete amortization of the loan by the time the last payment is made, that is, by the end of the **mortgage term**. Mortgages are usually provided for 20, 25, or 30 years, sometimes for fewer years. The basic types of mortgages are: (1) fixed rate, fixed payment, (2) variable rate, variable payment, (3) fixed rate, variable payment, and (4) variable rate, fixed payment.

The first question one must ask in deciding where to live is whether to buy or rent. The advantages of buying and renting should be considered carefully to help in the decision-making process. The financial advantages of buying include creation of equity, capital appreciation, hedge against inflation, tax deductions, and a source of cash in the future in the form of a second mortgage, home equity loan, or reverse-annuity mortgage. At any point in time, the amount that has been paid off (including the down payment) plus any appreciation in the value of a home represents the homeowner's **equity** (the current market value of a home in excess of the amount owed on it).

There also are some advantages in renting. First, the money saved by renting can be invested in other investment options that may rise in value faster than home prices. Second, the initial costs of rent are typically less than for home ownership. Depending upon the region of the country and local factors, the median price for a existing home could be $125,000, or even $250,000. The prices on new homes are even higher. There are other advantages as well.

If you decide to buy a home, it is important to determine what kind of home you can afford by making two basic personal finance calculations: (1) How much cash will you have to spend for the initial costs of the purchase (e.g., down payment, closing costs, and points)?, and (2) How much can you afford to pay each month for the long-term expenses of owning a home (e.g., mortgage payments, maintenance and operating costs, insurance, and property taxes)?

When purchasing a home, most buyers are initially concerned with the amount of **down payment** required. For example, for a $125,000 home a buyer should have anywhere between $12,500 to $25,000 (10 to 20 percent) for the down payment, $3,750 to $7,500 (3 to 6 percent) for **closing costs**, and perhaps $2,500 for contingencies. Thus, at the time of purchase the buyer will need perhaps $18,750 to $35,000 in available funds.

Many lenders use well established guidelines, or rules of thumb, to determine a potential borrower's ability to afford a home, including: (1) thirty-five percent rule, (2) multiple of gross income rule, (3) monthly gross income rule, and (4) gross income to debt payment rule. These will be examined in this chapter.

This chapter also will examine three different types of mortgages: (1) fixed rate, fixed payment, (2) variable rate, variable payment, and (3) fixed rate, variable payment. Most people are familiar with eh **fixed rate, fixed payment** mortgage because it is the traditional method of financing a home. This is a fully amortized mortgage that calls for a specified number of uniform-sized periodic payments to be made at regular intervals, which are usually made monthly. There are personal finance pluses and minuses associated with alternative mortgage plans.

In addition, other important aspects of housing are examined in this chapter, including how points raise the effective interest rate, how to calculate when it is to one's advantage to refinance an existing mortgage, reverse-annuity mortgages, and real estate as an investment.

EXAMPLES OF MATHEMATICAL CONCEPTS RELATED TO HOUSING AND REAL ESTATE

1. Buying Versus Renting

Formula 19.1.1: $TCR = RC + RI - IDC$

Where: TRC = total cost of renting; RC = rental cost; RI = rental insurance; and IDC = interest on down payment and closing costs.

Formula 19.1.2: TCB = M + T + I + IDC − PR + ITS + PTS + HVA

Where: TCB = total cost of buying; M = mortgage payments; T = property tax; I = home owner's insurance; IDC = interest on down payment and closing costs (in this case, this refers to interest loss); PR = principle reduction in loan balance; ITS = income tax savings; PTS = property tax savings; and HVA = home value appreciation.

▼ **Example 19.1:** The Smiths are comparing the costs of renting versus buying a home. Jane and John Smith have compiled the relevant costs of each option. Costs relevant to renting include monthly rent of $875 plus $725 annually for renter's insurance. Costs and figures relevant to buying include the purchase price of the home they like, $125,000, which would have a monthly mortgage payment of $978.83, plus homeowner's insurance of $800 annually, real estate property taxes of $3,500.00, principal reduction in the loan balance of $1,746, annual interest (for year 1) of $10,000, their marginal tax rate of 28 percent, an expected appreciation in the value of home of 3 percent, down payment and closing costs of $25,000, and an estimated after-tax rate of return of 5 percent. Compare the costs of each option and recommend whether the Smiths should rent or buy their home for the first year.

Solution:

(1) *Annual Cost of Renting*

Since, annual RC = $875 × 12 = $10,500.00, annual RI = $725.00, ICS = $25,000 × 5% = $1,250,

Then, using Formula 19.1.1,
   TCR = $10,500 + $725 − $1,250 = $9,975

(2) *Annual Cost of Buying*

Since, M = $978.83 × 12 = $11,745.96 = $11,746, T = $3,500, I = $800, IL = $25,000 × 5% = $1,250, PR = $1,746, ITS = $10,000 × 28% = $2,800, PTS = $3,500 × 28% = $980, HVA = $3,750,

then using Formula 19.1.2
   TCB = $11,746 + $3,500 + $800 + $1,250 − $1,746 − $2,800 − $3,500 − $980 − $3,750 = $8,020

❖ **Interpretation:** Buying the home would be a better option for the Smith family because they could save $1955 the first year ($9,975 − $8,020). Note that the interest on down payment and closing costs are considered differently in the calculation of the costs of buying and renting. The interest decreases the total cost of renting, but increases of the cost of buying. This example, even though it does not consider every mathematical aspects of buying versus renting, does demonstrate what factors should be considered when the costs of renting and buying a home are compared.

2. Housing Affordability

Conceptual Idea 19.2: Several well established guidelines, or rules of thumb, are used in the credit industry to estimate housing affordability for borrowers: (19.2.1) affordable monthly mortgage payment should be equal or less than 35% of monthly take-home income or 25% of gross monthly income; (19.2.2) affordable home price should be 2.5 times of the annual gross income or less; (19.2.3) affordable total monthly debt payments, including payments on other loans, should be equal or less than 36% of monthly gross income; and (19.2.4) affordable home price (present value of an annuity) can be estimated when the affordable monthly payment, interest rate, and number of payments are given. Note that these rules are only rough estimates and they are not internally consistent, since different assumptions about property taxes, interest rates, and number of payments will result in different conclusions.

▼ **Example 19.2.1:** John Brock's annual gross income is $40,000 and his take-home pay is $2,500 per month. (1) What is the affordable monthly mortgage payment for him? (2) What is the maximum home price he could afford, assuming an interest rate of 10% and a 20-year term, (3) If John has a monthly debt load of $350 or less, what is his affordable mortgage payment and how much could he borrow for a home?

Solution:

(1) *Affordable mortgage repayment amount.*

Using Conceptual Idea 19.2.1 and John's monthly gross income of $40,000, his affordable monthly mortgage debt repayment amount is $833.33 ($40,000/12 × .25). Also using Conceptual Idea 19.2.1 and John's take-home pay of $2,500, his affordable mortgage repayment amount is $875 ($2,500 × .35).

(2) *Affordable home price.*

There are two ways to estimate an affordable home price for John. First, using Conceptual Idea 19.2.2, John's affordable home price is $100,000 ($40,000 gross income × 2.5). Second, using Conceptual Idea 19.2.4, we can use the information about affordable monthly payment, interest rate, and number of payments to estimate an affordable home price. If we assume John's affordable monthly payment is $875 (from Step 1 above), an interest rate is 10%, and the number of payments is 240 (20 years × 12 monthly payments), then the question is to solve the present value of an annuity (for details, see Chapter 4). This can be easily solved by using financial calculator. Following are the key strokes of the HP 10B.

Purpose	Key Stroke
Set payment frequency	12 ☐ [P/YR]
Time period: month	20 ☐ [XP/YR]
Interest rate	10 [I/YR]
Each payment	875 [+/-] [PMT]
Result: present value	90,671.54

Thus, John's affordable home price is about $90,672.

(3) *Affordable total monthly debt payments, including payments on other loans.*

Using Conceptual Idea 19.2.3, since John's affordable total monthly debt payments amount based on gross income is $1,200 ($3,333.33 × .36), and his other monthly debt payments amount to $350, then his affordable mortgage payment is $850 ($1,200 – $350). Following are the key strokes of the HP 10B to calculate affordable home price.

Purpose	Key Stroke
Set payment frequency	12 ☐ [P/YR]
Time period: month	20 ☐ [XP/YR]
Interest rate	10 [I/YR]
Each payment	850 [+/-] [PMT]
Result: present value	88,080.92

Thus, John's affordable home price is about $88,081.

❖ **Interpretation:** This example illustrate the use of rules of thumb to estimate the affordable monthly mortgage payment and home price. Note that the answers on affordability for John ranged from $88,081 to $100,000, depending upon which formula was used. In the real world, various lenders and housing agencies use different guidelines. For example, to qualify for a Federal Housing Administration (FHA) or Veterans Administration (VA) mortgage, the monthly mortgage payment, property taxes, and homeowner's insurance is not allowed to exceed 35% of the family's monthly gross income, or 50% of the gross income. Also note that because of the differing assumptions a lender may make about property taxes, interest rate, and number of payments, estimates using different methods will be similar, but not exactly the same.

3. Fixed Rate, Fixed Payment Mortgage

Conceptual Idea 19.3: The mathematical problem of the fixed rate, fixed payment mortgage is to determine the present value of an annuity (see Chapter 4), in which payment is to be solved when the interest rate (r), number of payment (n), and present value of mortgage (PV) are given.

▼ **Example 19.3:** Mary Beth was offered an annual or monthly payment plan on a mortgage loan amount of $100,000 for a mortgage term of 20 years at a 10% interest rate. Calculate the (1) annual debt service and (2) monthly debt service. Compare the two payment plans to determine which one would be cheaper.

Solution:

(1) *Annual payment plan.*

Since r = 10%, n = 20, PV = $100,000, then using the financial calculator (HP 10B),

Purpose	Key Stroke
Set payment frequency	1 □ [P/YR]
Time period: month	20 [N]
Interest rate	10 [I/YR]
PV of mortgage	100,000 [PV]
Result: present value	[PMT] –11,745.96

Paying annually, Mary Beth's payment would be $11,745.96.

(2) *Monthly payment plan.*

Since r = 10%, n = 20 = 240, PV = $100,000, then using the financial calculator (HP 10B),

Purpose	Key Stroke
Set payment frequency	12 □ [P/YR]
Time period: month	20 □ [xP/YR]
Interest rate	10 [I/YR]
PV of mortgage	100,000 [PV]
Result: present value	[PMT] –965.02

If instead of paying annually, Mary Beth made a monthly payment of $965.02, it would mean that her annual payment would be $11,580.24 ($965.02 × 12).

❖ **Interpretation:** Comparing the two plans, the monthly payment plan can save Mary Beth $165.72 ($11,745.96 – $11,580.24). This example illustrates how to calculate mortgage payments when the mortgage size, interest rate, and number of payments are given. The following example demonstrates how to create a amortization schedule.

▼ **Example 19.3.2:** Sean's mortgage loan amount is $100,000 and the term is 20 years with an interest rate of 10% and annual debt service of $11,746. (1) What would be the annual amortization schedule for the loan having level payments, and (2) how much will he pay in debt service and interest payments after 20 years?

Solution: Following is an amortization schedule created by Excel.

Year	Debt Service	Interest Payment	Principal Payment	Principal Balance
				$100,000.00
1	$ 11,745.96	10000	$ 1,745.96	$ 98,254.04
2	$ 11,745.96	9825.403752	$ 1,920.56	$ 96,333.48
3	$ 11,745.96	9633.34788	$ 2,112.61	$ 94,220.86
4	$ 11,745.96	9422.08642	$ 2,323.88	$ 91,896.99
5	$ 11,745.96	9189.698814	$ 2,556.26	$ 89,340.72
6	$ 11,745.96	8934.072448	$ 2,811.89	$ 86,528.83
7	$ 11,745.96	8652.883445	$ 3,093.08	$ 83,435.76
8	$ 11,745.96	8343.575542	$ 3,402.39	$ 80,033.37
9	$ 11,745.96	8003.336848	$ 3,742.63	$ 76,290.74
10	$ 11,745.96	7629.074285	$ 4,116.89	$ 72,173.85
11	$ 11,745.96	7217.385466	$ 4,528.58	$ 67,645.28
12	$ 11,745.96	6764.527765	$ 4,981.43	$ 62,663.84
13	$ 11,745.96	6266.384294	$ 5,479.58	$ 57,184.26
14	$ 11,745.96	5718.426476	$ 6,027.54	$ 51,156.73
15	$ 11,745.96	5115.672875	$ 6,630.29	$ 44,526.44
16	$ 11,745.96	4452.643915	$ 7,293.32	$ 37,233.12
17	$ 11,745.96	3723.312059	$ 8,022.65	$ 29,210.47
18	$ 11,745.96	2921.047017	$ 8,824.92	$ 20,385.55
19	$ 11,745.96	2038.555471	$ 9,707.41	$ 10,678.15
20	$ 11,745.96	1067.814771	$ 10,678.15	$ 0.00
Total	$234,919.25	$134,919.25	$100,000.00	

The calculation for Year 1 is as follows.

Use the function PMT to calculate annual debt service = $11,745.96
Interest payment = $100,000 * .10 = $10,000
Principal payment = $11,746 – $10,000 = $1,745.96
Principal balance = $100,000 – $1,746 = $98,254.04

Other years can be calculated in a similar way. From the bottom line you can see that Sean will pay $234,919.25 in debt service and $134,919.25 in interest payments for the 20 year term.

❖ **Interpretation:** An **amortization schedule** shows the interest and principal components of each individual mortgage payment and the amount of the loan balance outstanding after each scheduled payment. It is useful for the borrower because the interest expense figures for each year are required information for income tax deductions. With each successive mortgage payment, the interest portion decreases as the outstanding balance is reduced while the principal portion increases as a percentage of each total payment. The result is that one has a declining share of each year's cash payment for debt service that is tax deductible. Many real estate investors, therefore, consider refinancing an investment at some point by replacing the existing mortgage with a new mortgage, in order to obtain additional investment funds and to secure larger interest deductions.

Sean is scheduled to pay $134,919.25 in interest over 20 years. When faced with this high cost, Sean may assume that by satisfying a loan as soon as possible, or by paying the total cost in cash, he can save a large amount of interest. However, he should take into account the opportunity cost of such a decision. If Sean had $100,000 to buy the home outright, this amount is probably invested elsewhere earning a favorable return. If Sean was currently earning 12% on his $100,000, then the withdrawal of that money to buy the home would result in the loss of $240,000 in interest for 20 years, which is more than the interest he may pay for the mortgage. If Sean reinvests the $12,000 annual interest, the $100,000 compounded at the rate of 12% each year, will grow to $964,629.31 in 20 years. Thus, the opportunity cost incurred by paying cash for the home is nearly a million dollars.

4. Variable Rate, Variable Payment Mortgage

Conceptual Idea 19.4: Payment for a variable rate, variable payment mortgage has to be calculated year by year.

▼ **Example 19.4:** Bertha has a variable rate mortgage loan of $100,000 for a term of 20 years at 10% interest rate for the first year with a monthly debt service of $965.02. The interest rate increased by 2% the second year. What is Bertha's monthly debt service payment for the second year?

Solution:

(1) The amortization schedule for the first year is created by Excel as follows.

Month	Debt Service	Interest Payment	Principal Payment	Principal Balance
				$100,000.00
1	$ 965.02	833.33	$ 131.69	$ 99,868.31
2	$ 965.02	832.24	$ 132.79	$ 99,735.53
3	$ 965.02	831.13	$ 133.89	$ 99,601.63
4	$ 965.02	830.01	$ 135.01	$ 99,466.63
5	$ 965.02	828.89	$ 136.13	$ 99,330.49
6	$ 965.02	827.75	$ 137.27	$ 99,193.23
7	$ 965.02	826.61	$ 138.41	$ 99,054.81
8	$ 965.02	825.46	$ 139.56	$ 98,915.25
9	$ 965.02	824.29	$ 140.73	$ 98,774.52
10	$ 965.02	823.12	$ 141.90	$ 98,632.62
11	$ 965.02	821.94	$ 143.08	$ 98,489.54
12	$ 965.02	820.75	$ 144.28	$ 98,345.26
Total	$11,580.26	$9,925.52	$1,654.74	

(2) Based on the above schedule, the principal balance outstanding after the first year is $98,345.26. Note that the interest rate for the second year is 12% and the number of payments remaining on the mortgage is 228 (19 × 12), thus the monthly payment can be calculated using the financial calculator HP 10B as follows.

Purpose	Key Stroke
Set payment frequency	12 ☐ **[P/YR]**
Time period: month	19 ☐ **[xP/YR]**
Interest rate	12 **[I/YR]**
PV of mortgage	98,345.26 **[PV]**
Result: present value	**[PMT]** 1,096.93

Thus, the monthly payment for the second year is $1,096.93.

❖ **Interpretation: Variable-rate, variable payment mortgages**, also called **adjustable rate mortgages**, allow for periodic adjustments in the loan's interest rate in response to market interest rate changes. The size of the mortgage payment varies from period to period as a result of the interest rate adjustments, and in some cases the total number of payments to maturity might be altered. In this example, Bertha's monthly debt service payment for the second year has increased to $1,096.93 because the interest rate went up at the end of the first year. The variable rate mortgage effectively shifts the risk of unanticipated inflation from the lender to the borrower. Typically, the interest rate can change according to four commonly used indices: prime interest rate, short term Treasury Securities, National Average Mortgage Contract, and Federal Reserve District Cost of Funds.

5. Fixed Rate, Variable Payment Mortgage

Formula 19.5: $PMT = PB \cdot r + L/n$

Where: PMT = periodic amortization payment; PB = loan balance; r = interest rate; L = loan amount; and n = mortgage term. Note that L/n is principal payment that is constant through the whole term.

▼ **Example 19.5:** Jack has a mortgage loan amount of $100,000 at a 10% interest rate. The mortgage term is 20 years with annual payments using the variable payment plan. What is the amortization schedule for Jack's loan?

Solution: Given L = $100,000, n = 20, r = .1.

At the first year, since PB = $100,000, then
$PMT_1 = \$100,000 \times .01 + \$100,000/20 = \$10,000 + \$5,000 = \$15,000$

At the second year, since PB = $100,000 - $5,000 = $95,000, then
$PMT_2 = \$95,000 \times .01 + \$100,000/20 = \$9,500 + \$5,000 = \$14,500$

The payment for other years can be calculated in a similar way. Then we have the following schedule.

Annual Amortization Schedule for a $100,000 Fixed rate, Variable payment Mortgage

Year	Debt Service	Interest Payment	Principal Payment	Principal Balance
				$100,000
1	$ 15,000	$ 10,000	$ 5,000	$ 95,000
2	$ 14,500	$ 9,500	$ 5,000	$ 90,000
3	$ 14,000	$ 9,000	$ 5,000	$ 85,000
4	$ 13,500	$ 8,500	$ 5,000	$ 80,000
5	$ 13,000	$ 8,000	$ 5,000	$ 75,000
⋮	⋮	⋮	⋮	⋮
10	$ 10,500	$ 5,500	$ 5,000	$ 50,000
⋮	⋮	⋮	⋮	⋮
15	$ 8,000	$ 3,000	$ 5,000	$ 25,000
⋮	⋮	⋮	⋮	⋮
20	$ 5,500	$ 500	$ 5,000	0
Totals	$205,000	$105,000	$100,000	

❖ **Interpretation:** In the **fixed rate, variable payment mortgage**, the interest rate remains the same but each periodic payment is a different amount. The principal is repaid in equal periodic payments over the life of the loan. The interest portion of each succeeding payment declines as the unpaid balance is reduced. Jack's interest payment for the 20 years is $105,000, which is significantly less than the $134,919.25 paid as interest for the fixed rate, fixed payment plan described previously. The total interest payment is lower because of the faster "pay-out" of the loan principal in the early years.

6. Market Value of a Mortgage

Formula 19.6: $PVA = PMT \cdot PVIFA$

Where: PVA = loan amount; PMT = debt service payment; and PVIFA = present value interest factor.

▼ **Example 19.6:** James has a $100,000 mortgage loan at 10% for 20 years. He wants to sell the loan at the end of the second year, just after the second annual payment is made. The annual debt service payment is $11,746.00. What would be the selling price, or market value, of the loan if the interest rate is (1) 10%, (2) 8%, and (3) 12%?

Solution:

From Appendix Table A.4, the values of PVIFA for 18 years at 10% is 8.2014, for 8% is 9.3719, and for 12% it is 7.2497. Then

(1) when r = 8%, PVA = $11,746 × 8.2014 = $96,333.64

(2) when r = 10%, PVA = $11,746 × 9.3719 = $110,082.34

(3) when r = 12%, PVA = $11,746 × 7.2497 = $85,154.98

Note that this question can also be easily solved by using the financial calculator, since this is a present value of annuity type of question.

❖ **Interpretation:** If James sells his mortgage at the end of the second year for the same interest rate (10%) as the original interest rate, then the selling price would be equal to the outstanding balance indicated in the mortgage amortization schedule of $96,333.64 (see annual amortization schedule for $100,000 mortgage described above). If, on the other hand, the interest rate at the end of two years for the mortgage is only 8%, then the market value of the mortgage loan would be $110,082.34. It would sell at a premium of $13,748.69 above the outstanding loan amount of $96,333.64. If the mortgage is sold to yield 12%, a discount of $11,178.66 would result and it would sell for $85,154.98. The mortgage offering only 10% in a 12% market would have to sell at a discount.

7. Points Raise the Effective Interest Rate

Conceptual Idea 19.7: The net proceeds of a loan equals the loan amount less the points (a point is 1% of the loan amount), and the points charged increases the effective interest rate for the borrower.

▼ **Example 19.7:** The Smiths have a mortgage loan amount of $100,000 at an interest rate of 10% for 20 years with monthly payments. Their monthly debt service payment is $965.02 and the discount points are 4. Find the effective interest rate for the loan.

Solution:

Since four points equals $4,000 (4% × $100,000) the net proceeds of the loan amounts to $96,000 ($100,000 − $4,000). To calculate the effective interest rate, $96,000 can be viewed as the loan size, and r = 10%, n = 20 × 12 = 240, PMT = $965.02, then using the financial calculator (HP 10B),

Purpose	Key Stroke
Set payment frequency	12 ☐ [P/YR]
Time period: month	20 ☐ [xP/YR]
PV of mortgage	96,000 [PV]
Payment	965.02 [+/-] [PMT]
Result: interest rate	[I/YR] 10.60

Thus, the effective interest rate is 10.6%.

❖ **Interpretation:** Lenders use **points** to earn interest in excess of the stated annual interest rate for the loan. For each point charge of the lender, the borrower pays 1% of the amount of the total loan obligation as "extra" interest that is paid in advance. Because this form of interest charge is referred to as **discounting**, the points are often called **discount points**. The amount charged as points is simply deducted from the proceeds of the loan at the time the mortgage is given. If the Smiths pay four points on a $100,000 loan, they would receive only 96% of the loan, or $96,000, and the $4,000 would be an immediate, "up-front," interest charge. This additional interest amount raises the effective rate of interest for the borrower, 10.63% in this case for the Smiths. The effective interest rate can be found quickly and accurately using the calculator as the net proceeds, the debt service payment, and the number of payment periods would be input values, and the effective interest rate would be the output. Also, the conventional mortgage annuity tables can be used, however, it requires a time-consuming trial and error approach with interpolation.

8. Refinancing

Conceptual Idea 19.8: People considering refinancing must consider the following factors: (1) the monthly payment for the new loan; (2) the monthly savings between the new and old monthly payment; (3) the total refinancing costs, including closing costs and points; and (4) the recovery period that is calculated by dividing total refinancing costs by monthly savings.

▼ **Example 19.8:** The Holmes want to refinance their home. Their current loan amount is for $100,000 for 30 years at a 12% interest rate. Their monthly payments are $1,028.61. They would like to refinance their loan amount of $100,000 for 30 years at a 10% interest rate. Their refinancing costs include closing costs of $1,400 and 3 points. Calculate their (1) new monthly payments, (2) monthly savings, (3) total refinancing costs, and (4) recovery period.

Solution:

(**1**) *Monthly payment for the new loan.*

Since PV of loan = $100,000, n = 30 × 12 = 360, r = 10, then the monthly payment can be computed by the financial calculator (HP 10B).

Purpose	Key Stroke
Set payment frequency	12 □ [P/YR]
Time period: month	30 □ [xP/YR]
PV of mortgage	100,000 [PV]
Interest rate	10 □ [I/YR]
Result: monthly payment	[PMT] –877.57

Thus, the new monthly payment will be $877.57.

(2) *Monthly savings.*

Since the old payment is $1,028.61 and the new payment is $877.57, then monthly savings equals $151.04 ($1,028.61 – $877.57).

(3) *Total refinancing costs.*

Since the closing costs equals $1,400 and 3 points $3,000 (3% × $100,000), then the total refinancing costs equal $4,400 ($1,400 + $3,000).

(4) *Recovery period.*

Since the total refinancing costs are $4,400 and monthly savings are $151.04, then recovery period equals 29.13 ($4,400/$151.04) months. Thus, the refinancing costs will be covered by the monthly savings in about 30 months.

❖ **Interpretation: Refinancing** is the process by which a person takes out a new loan to replace an existing loan and the proceeds of the new loan are used to pay off the balance outstanding on the existing loan. Since the new loan has a different interest rate, principal, and/or mortgage term, the monthly debt service payment will change. The loan may be refinanced through the original lender or a different lender. Often a homeowner can borrow more money than is owed on the home because the owner's equity may have grown larger. A popular rule of thumb for refinancing is that the new mortgage should be at least 2% points less than the existing mortgage. However, refinancing can pay off with an even slimmer difference depending on closing costs and length of stay in the home. Closing costs and points are charged by the lender while refinancing, and in this case for the Holmes it amounted to $4,400. It would take the Holmes 30 months of lower payments of $877.57 to recover the $4,400 in refinancing costs. Therefore, the Holmes will need to stay in their home for 30 months after refinancing to break even. After the Holmes refinance, they will pay less interest on their new loan, and while that will save them money it will mean smaller mortgage interest deductions on their income tax returns.

9. Reverse-Annuity Mortgage

Conceptual Idea 19.9: The reverse-annuity mortgage can be viewed as a future value of annuity type question.

▼ **Example 19.9:** Sixty-five year old Donald Frump has $100,000 equity accumulated in his home. A lender is willing to make a reverse-annuity mortgage for $50,000 on the home at 11% for the next ten years. Determine the monthly annuity that the lender would be paying Mr. Frump.

Solution:

The reverse-annuity mortgage can be viewed as a question of future value of annuity. In this case, FV of loan = $50,000, r = 11%, n = 120 (10 × 12), using the financial calculator (HP 10B),

Purpose	Key Stroke
Set payment frequency	12 □ [P/YR]
Time period: month	10 □ [xP/YR]
FV of mortgage	50,000 [FV]
Interest rate	11 □ [I/YR]
Result: monthly payment	[PMT] –230.42

Thus, the lender will pay them $230.42 monthly for this reverse-annuity mortgage.

❖   **Interpretation:** A way to draw upon the equity of the home, particularly when one is retired and owns the home free and clear, is to assume a **reverse-annuity mortgage (RAM)**. This allows a borrower over age 61 to borrow against the equity in a home that is fully paid for and to receive the proceeds in a series of monthly payments, often over a period of 5 to 15 years or for life. Here instead of borrowing against the equity and paying interest, one can convert some of the equity to cash while retaining ownership and continuing to live in the home. This is also known as a **home-equity conversion loan.** These are called reverse-annuity mortgages because they are the opposite of traditional mortgages—the lender makes payments to the homeowner. With reverse-annuity mortgages the proceeds may be taken in a lump sum amount, in monthly checks, or through a line of credit that can be utilized when needed. The amount one can borrow depends on the owner's age, the value of the equity in the home, and the interest rate charged by the lender. Costs associated with a reserve-annuity mortgage include closing costs, insurance premiums, and sometimes a monthly service fee. Reverse-annuity mortgages increase the amount of interest owed every month. Over time, the interest owed can become considerable, and the equity in a home can shrink dramatically. However, a reverse-annuity mortgage can be a good way to use the equity in a person's home if he or she does not mind leaving heirs a far smaller estate upon death. All payments received from reverse-annuity mortgages are considered cash withdrawals, or nontaxable income. Therefore, reverse-annuity proceeds do not lower one's Social Security or Medicare benefits. In the Donald Frump example, the lender is paying a RAM of $50,000, meaning that the sum of $230.42 would be disbursed to Mr. Frump each month for ten years. The reverse-annuity mortgage comes due when a person dies, sells the home, or moves permanently. At that point, the homeowner, or the homeowner's estate, must repay the lender the total amount borrowed.

10. Real Estate Investment

Four techniques are commonly used by investors to determine the price to pay for real estate property: (1) gross income multiplier, (2) net income multiplier, (3) capitalization rate, and (4) discounted cash-flow method.

Formula 19.10.1:   GIM = P/GRY

Where: GIM = gross income multiplier; P = purchase price, or asking price; and GRY = gross rental income.

Formula 19.10.2:   NIM = P/NOI

Where: NIM = net income multiplier; P = purchase price, or asking price; and NOI = net operating income.

Formula 19.10.3: CR = NOI/P

Where: CR = capitalization rate; NOI = net operating income; and P = purchase price, or asking price.

Formula 19.10.4:   PVP = Σ ATC $\cdot$ PVF

Where: PVP = present value of property; ATC = after-tax cash flow; and PVF = present value factor.

Example 19.10.1: Ron Smith is considering investing in an apartment complex. The asking price of the building is $250,000, the projected annual rental income is $45,000, and the annual operating expenses are anticipated to be $8,775. What is the (1) gross income multiplier, (2) net income multiplier, and (3) capitalization rate?

Solution (1):   Since P = $250,000 and GRY = $45,000, then using Formula 19.10.1 GIM = $250,000/$45,000 = 5.555

Interpretation: The **gross income multiplier (GIM)** provides an indication of the investment value of a certain class of income-producing property, usually within a particular neighborhood. It divides the asking price, or market value, of the property by the current annual gross rental income. It is a subjective number and real estate publications and local real estate brokers can indicate the going GIM rate for various types of properties classified by age and neighborhood. An investment with a GIM greater than 8 probably pays too low a return to be profitable. The apartment complex Ron Smith is considering has a GIM rate of 5.56, which might be somewhat profitable for him. If the GIM rate and rental income for a neighborhood are known, the purchase price or the asking price of the property can be estimated.

Soluton (2):   Since P = $250,000, NOI = $36,225, then using Formula 19.10.2 NIM = $250,000/$36,225 = 6.901

❖ **Interpretation:** Net operating income is the gross rental income less allowances for vacancies and operating expenses, except depreciation and debt payments. Different properties have different operating expenses which must be taken into account when determining the value of property. The **net income multiplier (NIM)** is an estimate of the value of an income-producing real estate investment using net operating income as a variable in the calculation. It is only a rough measure, however, because the actual net operating income can be determined in different ways for comparable investment properties.

Solution (3): Since NOI = \$36,225 and P = \$250,000, then using Formula 19.10.3 CR = 14.49% (\$36,225/\$250,000 = .1449)

❖ **Interpretation:** The **capitalization rate (CR)** is often used to determine an initial rate of return on an income-producing real estate investment purchased entirely with cash. Also known as the **income yield**, this rate is calculated by dividing the projected net operating income for the first year of ownership by the total investment. The capitalization rate is a popular method of determining the rate of return because comparable data can be obtained for other properties as well as alternative investments. The capitalization rates and property prices are inversely proportional, thus, the higher the capitalization rate, the lower the price, and vice versa. A high capitalization rate reflects a riskier investment, perhaps one with less unstable rental prospects, than an investment with an equivalent cash flow, all other things being equal. An investor would, therefore, reject a property with a high capitalization rate or demand a lower selling price from the seller. Capitalization rates on good quality real estate investment usually range from 6 to 9%, the best properties may have a rate of 4 or 5%. Riskier investment properties may have a capitalization rate of 10 to 12%. This example suggests that Ron Smith would have a 14.49% yield the first year, assuming that the apartment complex is not financed.

▼ **Example 19.10.2:** Ron Smith requires a rate of return of 10% on a piece of property advertised for sale at \$100,000. It is estimated that rents can be increased each year for 5 years. Mr. Smith expects that after all expenses he would have an after-tax cash flow of \$4,500, \$4,750, \$5,000, \$5,250, \$5,500 for each of the following years. He also expects that this property can sell for \$120,000 at the end of the fifth year. How much should Mr. Smith be willing to pay for this property?

Solution:

The present value factors utilized in the following table can be found in Appendix Table A.2.

Year	After-tax cash flow	Present value factor at 10%	Present value of after-tax cash flow
1	$ 4,500	0.909	$ 4,090.50
2	$ 4,750	0.826	$ 3,923.50
3	$ 5,000	0.751	$ 3,755.00
4	$ 5,250	0.683	$ 3,585.75
5	$ 5,500	0.621	$ 3,415.50
Sell property	$120,000	0.621	$74,250.00
Present value of property			$93,290.25

Ron Smith should be willing to pay $93,290.25 for the property. Note that this problem can also be easily solved with a financial calculator (see Example 6.1.2 in Chapter 6).

❖   **Interpretation:** The **discounted cash flow method** is an effective technique to estimate the value or the purchase price of a real estate investment. It is better than the other three methods described above. The discounted cash flow method emphasizes after-tax cash flow and the return on the invested dollars discounted over time to reflect a discounted yield. In this example, the advertised price of $100,000 is too high for Ron Smith to earn an after-tax return of 10%. Mr. Smith's choices are to negotiate the price down to $93,290.25, accept a return of less than 10%, or consider another investment. The discounted cash-flow method provides an effective and widely used way of estimating real estate values because it takes into account the selling price of the property, the effect of income taxes, and the time value of money.

INFORMATION AND COMPUTING RESOURCES

1.   Magazines such as *Creative Real Estate Magazine* and *Financial Freedom Report Quarterly* cover topics on mortgages, tax aspects of real estate, single-family homes, and real estate investing. Popular magazines such as *Money, Kiplinger's Personal Finance Magazine*, and *Consumer Reports* have articles on homes, mortgages, property taxes, and refinancing.

2.   *Real Estate Weekly* is the only weekly real estate newspaper in the United States. *National Mortgage News* covers the mortgage market and mortgage lenders. Newspapers such as *The New York Times, The Washington Post*, and *Boston Globe* have real estate sections in their Sunday editions.

3.   Trade Associations such as *American Society of Home Inspectors, Mortgage Bankers Association of America, National Association of Home Builders, National Association of Realtors, National Center for Home Equity Conversion*, and *National Real Estate Investors Association* have publications that help in various aspects of buying and investing in real estate.

4. Federal Government Regulatory agencies include *Department of Housing and Urban Development, Federal National Mortgage Association, Federal Reserve Board, Federal Trade Commission*, and *Office of Thrift Supervision*. They have brochures and pamphlets highlighting topics in real estate and mortgage financing.

5. Computer software can help when calculating the financial trade-offs of real estate. Real estate software packages, such as *Buying Your Home and Mastering Your Mortgage, Buy or Rent, or Mortgage Analyzer*, can help in understanding the value of income tax benefits, the realistic costs of buying and maintaining a home, the alternative returns on money if you rent, the number of years one must stay in a home for it to pay off, amortization tables, closing costs, and other aspects of mortgage finance.

6. Online computer services and Internet: The resources available through the online computer service and the Internet can help people make better decisions when buying or selling a home. Information can be obtained on the strengths of the housing market, buying and selling strategies, applying for a mortgage, and even chatting with other homeowners. Some useful websites are

   ■ *ACCNET:* http://accnet.com/homes/index.html (a listing service and catalog of real estate properties.)

   ■ *ERA Online:* http://www.teamera.com (listings of brokers, home listing services, buying services, and financial protection for home buyers and sellers.)

   ■ *Fannie Mae:* http://www.fanniemae.com

   ■ *Homebuyer's FairFractal:* http://www.homefair.com/homepage.html

   ■ *HomeOwners Finance Center:*
   http://www.internet-is.com/homeowners/index.html

   ■ *HSH Associates:* http://www.hsh.com

   ■ *Money Personal Finance Center:* http://www.pathfinder.com

   ■ *National Association of Realtors:* http://www.realtor.net/ (home page of NAR.)

   ■ *Net Real Estate Server:* http://www.fractals.com/realestate.html

   You can also get free advice on most any home-related topic through on-line bulletin boards such as *America Online Homeowners Forum* (keyword: home), *Prodigy* (type the jump word: home), and *Compuserve* (after you type the "go word" Finforum, select the Investors + Forum to the find the real estate topic).

EXERCISE PROBLEMS

Buying Versus Renting

1. Jason Banks is being transferred for to Iowa City and is faced with the decision of whether to buy or rent a home. A quick survey of the housing market in Iowa City indicates that he can purchase a home for $70,000 with a 10% down payment on a 30 year mortgage at 10% interest rate. The closing costs would be about $3,600. Housing in the area is appreciating at 5% per year. Property taxes would be about $1,500 per year, and it is estimated that the maintenance cost would be an additional $800 per year. An alternative would be to rent a similar dwelling at $500/month and to invest the difference between the purchase cost and rent at 6.5%. Jason's personal income tax rate is 25% Federal and 5% State. Which alternative is more financially attractive?

Housing Affordability

2. Assume you have a gross monthly income of $3,000. What price can you afford for a home at 12% annual interest rate for 30 years with 15% Down payment?

3. Ryan Jensen's monthly take-home pay is $3,500. What loan amount can he apply for at 9% interest rate for 25 years?

4. Jenny's gross annual income is $35,000. What is the maximum home price she could afford?

5. Jake's gross annual income is $50,000 and his monthly debt load is $275. How much could he borrow for a home at 10% for 30 years?

6. The Hirshs have located a home that can be either rented or bought. The rent is $350 per month and the renter's insurance would be $9 per month. The home can be bought for $42,000. A bank is willing to provide an 80% loan at 12% interest for 30 years. Monthly mortgage payments are $345.61 of which $336 is for interest. Real estate taxes on the home are $720 per year and homeowners' insurance is $300 per year. Maintenance expenses are $50 per month. The Hirshs' income tax rate is 25%. The home is expected to increase in value by $150 per month on an after-tax basis. If the Hirshs do not buy the home, they will invest the down payment at 8% before taxes. Calculate the cost of renting and buying. Which is better financially?

Fixed Rate, Fixed Payment Mortgage

7. Find the monthly debt service payment needed to amortize the loan and pay taxes and insurance for the following:

Size of loan	Interest rate	Term (Years)	Annual Taxes & Insurance
a. $125,000	9%	30	$4,900
b. $139,000	8%	25	$5,700
c. $75,000	8%	25	$3,600
d. $70,000	10%	15	$3,000
e. $65,000	12%	20	$2,500

8. Bill and Karen would like to determine their monthly mortgage payment if they paid 20% down on the $150,000 home they are considering. A lender is offering a 30 year, 9% fixed rate mortgage. Calculate the monthly debt service payments for this mortgage using a calculator.

9. The same lender also offers 15 year fixed rate mortgages. Because the maturity is shorter, the lender will charge 8.0%. If Bill and Karen wanted to evaluate this mortgage, how would they calculate their monthly debt service payments using a calculator?

10. Tim Reade has taken out a 25 year, $34,000 mortgage for the purchase of a condominium. The lender charges interest at an annual rate of 12%. If Tim makes every monthly mortgage payment for the first year, what is his mortgage balance at the end of the first year?

11. Brenda Brown is buying a home for $125,000. She will make a 20% Down payment and will get a 30 year mortgage at 9%. If she plans to make monthly payments to amortize the mortgage,
    a. How much is she borrowing?
    b. How much are the monthly payments?
    c. What would be the total interest paid for the 30 year period?

Variable Rate, Variable Payment Mortgage

12. You have a $100,000 loan, with a 20 year, 10% adjustable rate mortgage. The lender will increase the interest rate by 1% in the second year. The ITA for 19 years at 11% is .010475. What is your monthly debt service payment for the second year?

13. Sally has a $25,000 mortgage at 8% for 30 years. Her monthly debt service payment is $183.44. In the second year, the lender will increase the interest rate by 2 points. The ITA for 29 years at 10% is .008825. What is Sally's monthly debt service payment in the second year?

14. Jenny's loan amount is $100,000 for 15 years at 7% interest rate and the annual debt service payment is $10,979.50. If the interest rate goes up to 8% in the second year, what is her annual debt service payment for that year?

Fixed Rate, Variable Payment Mortgage

15. Leona has a mortgage of $120,000 at 9% fixed interest rate. The mortgage term is 25 years with annual payments using the variable payment plan. What are the a) principal payment, b) interest payment, and c) debt service payment for the first year?

16. From the above example, calculate Leona's annual interest payment and debt service payment for the second year.

Market Value of a Mortgage

17. Harry has a $50,000 mortgage at 10% for 25 years. He wants to sell the mortgage at the end of the fifth year. The annual debt service payment is $5,508.40. The PVIFA for 20 years at 7% is 10.5940. What would be the market value of the mortgage is the interest rate is 7%?

18. In the above example, Harry wants to sell the mortgage after three years. The annual debt service payment is $5,508.40. The PVIFA for 22 years at 11% is 8.1757. What market value would Harry get for the mortgage if the interest rate is 11%?

Points Raise the Effective Interest Rate

19. A lender is offering two mortgages: one for $90,000 at 8% for 25 years with 3 points, and the other for 9% with no points for 25 years. Which one is better?

20. A lender is offering a 9% fixed rate mortgage, and requires a down payment of 10% of the purchase price. The lender estimates that closing costs should be equal to 2 points in loan origination and $1000. What would be the closing cost on a $150,000 home?

Refinancing

21. Becky is refinancing a $70,000 mortgage. The mortgage is for 30 years at 14%. The new interest rate is 10% and the closing costs are $3,500. What are her monthly savings and how long would it take to recover the total financing cost of $3,500?

22. If Becky was refinancing at 12%, what would be her monthly savings and how long would it take to recover the closing costs of $3,500?

Reverse-annuity Mortgage

23. A lender will give Tamara a reverse-annuity mortgage for $75,000 at 12% for the next five years. The monthly sinking fund factor is .012244. What is the monthly annuity Tamara will receive?

24. Jeanette will receive a $100,000 reverse-annuity mortgage at 10% for the next ten years. The monthly sinking fund factor is .004882. What is her monthly annuity?

Real Estate Investment

25. The net operating income (NOI) is $35,000 on an office building with a total investment of $250,000. What is the capitalization rate?

26. Tony and Glenda are comparing two residential income properties as investments. Given the financial data on two properties:

	Triplex A	Triplex B
Gross rental income	$25,000	$20,000
Net operating income	$15,000	$14,000
Asking price	$180,000	$160,000

   a. Calculate the GIM for both properties.
   b. Which one should they buy, given that the GIM for comparable properties in their area is 7.5?

27. For the above example, calculate the net income multiplier for both properties.

28. Don Minkler is considering buying an apartment complex as an investment. The gross rentals are $25,000 a year. The gross income, less allowances for vacancies and expenses (except depreciation and mortgage payments), is $18,000 a year. The asking price is $160,000.
   a. What is the gross income multiplier?
   b. What is the capitalization rate?

29. You are considering the purchase of a duplex which is expected to generate the following after-tax cash flow in each of the next 5 years:

Years	After-Tax Cash Flow
1	$2,800
2	$3,100
3	$3,400
4	$3,700
5	$4,000

The expected selling price of the property will be $150,000 in 5 years. You would like to get an after-tax return of 10%.

a. What is the present worth of this property?

b. The seller is asking for $140,000. Should you buy this property?

30. Len Svenson is considering the purchase of an apartment complex which has a current annual gross rental income of $41,500 as an investment. The GIM for similar properties in the neighborhood is about 7. What is a likely value of the apartment complex?

SELECTED REFERENCES

Garman, E.T., & Forgue, R. E. (1997). *Personal finance* (5th ed.). Chapters 10 and 18. Boston: Houghton Mifflin.

Lyons, S.A. (1995). *Home buyer: The book and software home buying kit.* Berkeley, CA: Stratosphere Publishing.

Chapter 20
Retirement Planning Mathematics

▼ Estimating Annual Retirement Needs Using Guidelines for Income Replacement
▼ Estimating Social Security Retirement Benefits
▼ Estimating Needed Retirement Savings with Net Rate of Return
▼ Determining the Gap in Savings and Investments for Retirement
▼ Calculating an After-inflation, After-tax Rate of Return
▼ Income Taxes and Retirement Planning

Chapter 20
Retirement Planning
Mathematics

Joan Gray Anderson, Jing J. Xiao and E. Thomas Garman[1]

OVERVIEW

Retirement planning has become a major concern for many Americans in recent years. People are wondering if they will have enough money to live comfortably during their retirement years. They think about questions such as: "Will my pension be sufficient to live on?" "Which costs will increase, and by how much?" "How will inflation affect me?" "Will Social Security benefits be available to me?" "In what types of investments—fixed return or equities—should I invest my retirement funds?" "Does it really make a difference if I invest more now with pre-tax dollars?" "What percentage of my current income should I be saving?"

This chapter will examine some of these questions, particularly the mathematical aspects. You should realize that the most important question in retirement planning is to determine the **gap**, if any, between one's combined current and projected savings and investments for retirement and the estimated amount required. To calculate the answer, one must know how much is required for retirement living expenses (**retirement needs**) and how much is projected in **retirement savings and investments**. If one's retirement needs are greater than what one's retirement savings and investments will generate in income, there is a gap in retirement savings and investments. With this knowledge, one can take actions to change the situation.

Retirement needs usually are expressed in annual terms and estimated as the percentage of a household's current income level. Retirement needs are different for people with different income levels. For example, a person with annual income of $15,000 may need 85% of their current income at retirement, yet another person with income of $80,000 may only need 55% of that amount for retirement. The funds utilized during retirement typically come from three major sources: (1) Social Security retirement benefits, (2) pension plans, and (3) personal savings and investments.

---

[1]Joan Gray Anderson, Ph.D., Professor, Consumer Affairs Program, College of Human Science and Services, The University of Rhode Island, Kingston, RI 02881; Jing J. Xiao and E. Thomas Garman.

Funding for Social Security benefits comes from a compulsory payroll tax split equally between employee and employer. Wage earners pay Social Security taxes, called **FICA taxes**, which is shorthand for the Federal Insurance Contributions Act, on wage income up to the **maximum taxable yearly earnings**. This is the maximum amount to which the full Social Security tax rate is applied. The maximum amount is adjusted annually for inflation, and it was $62,700 in a recent year. The total Social Security tax has been 7.65 percent, consisting of a 6.2 percent FICA tax and a 1.45 percent Medicare tax. Higher income taxpayers pay the 1.45 percent Medicare tax on all their earned income. To illustrate, a person earning $30,000 pays a Social Security tax of $2,295 ($30,000 × .0765) while a person earning $90,000 pays $5,192.40 ($62,700 × .062 + $90,000 × .0145). Employers pay taxes for every employee that must match each of these amounts. Self-employed people pay both the employee and the employer portions. One can make an estimate of their monthly Social Security retirement benefits by using the tables in Appendix B. A more accurate estimate may be obtained from the Social Security Administration. (See the "Information and Computing Resources" section at the end of the chapter.)

There are various types of pension plans. Some are established by employers for their workers (e.g., defined-benefit pension plans, defined-contribution pension plans, after-tax salary-reduction plans, nonqualified deferred-compensation plans, employee stock ownership plans [ESOPs], profit-sharing plans, and stock bonus plans); others are personal pension plans established by workers themselves (e.g., individual retirement accounts [IRAs], simplified employee pension plan-individual retirement accounts [SEP-IRAs], Keogh plans, and annuities).

There are two general types of employer-sponsored retirement plans: (1) defined-benefit pension plans, and (2) defined-contribution pension plans. A **defined-benefit pension plan** is described by the level of "benefits" received by an employee who has retired. Those benefits are usually linked to the number of years of employment and to the worker's income. One such defined benefit plan might promise a defined annual retirement benefit of 2 percent for each year of service and multiplied by the average annual income during the last 3 years of employment. For example, a worker with 25 years' service and an average income of $40,000 over the last 3 years of work would have an annual benefit of $20,000 ($40,000 × .02 × 25). The employer-sponsored plan may provide annual cost-of-living increases in the pension. If you have a defined-benefit pension plan, you may find the amount of your estimated retirement benefits by contacting the personnel office. Because of the potential high cost of offering defined-benefit pension plans, more and more employers today have replaced their defined-benefit plans with defined-contribution pension plans.

A **defined-contribution pension plan** is described by the amount of money, the "contribution," set aside and accumulated in each person's individual account through savings and investments.[1] The balance in such a plan consists of the contributions plus any income, expenses, gains, and losses within the account. For example, a worker might have contributed $3,000 a year to his or her account for 25 years and invested it in mutual funds which are now worth $220,000. In this defined-contribution plan, the worker must carefully make withdrawals so as to take out enough for living expenses without exhausting the funds before death. If you have a defined-contribution pension plan, you may estimate the amount available for potential retirement by performing some time value of money calculations, which will be explained in this chapter.

Many pension plans are classified as **tax-sheltered retirement plans** (also called **qualified retirement plans**). These retirement plans have been approved by the Internal Revenue Service as tax-sheltered vehicles, and they offer tax advantages that can reduce current income taxes and increase eventual retirement benefits.

Tax-sheltering may—but does not always—occur in two ways. First, money put into such retirement plans may reduce current taxable income because the tax liability does not have to be paid until the funds are eventually withdrawn, probably some years in the future. Thus, the money saved in taxes can be used to partially fund a larger contribution, which creates even larger returns. Second, interest, dividends, and capital gains in qualified plans accumulate free of income taxes. Thus, tax-deferred growth enhances earnings. Moreover, contributing money to pension plans allow the funds to grow free of income taxes, and the contributions may qualify as an income tax deduction in the current year.

The process of workers making contributions to their employer-sponsored defined-contribution pension plan is called **salary-reduction**. The employee requests the employer to withhold a specified amount of income each pay period to set aside for the retirement account. Popular versions of these pension plans include the **401(k)**, **403(b)**, **404(c)**, and **457** plans, which are named after sections of the IRS tax code. Each plan is restricted to a certain type of worker. When the employing organization has 100 or fewer workers, the retirement plan is known as a **savings incentive match plan for employees** (or **SIMPLE**). In 1996, the SIMPLE plan limits employee contributions to $3,000 annually; the other plans listed above are limited to a maximum employee contribution of $9,500 annually.

To calculate the gap between retirement income needs and retirement savings and investments available to meet those needs, use the following time line to help visualize the calculation.

current age   initial retirement age   death age

The time line shows three different points in time. The value of a dollar amount at any of the three points will be different. The magnitude of the difference will depend on assumptions made regarding the rate of inflation and the rate of investment return. For example, assume that one needs $20,000 in today's dollars to pay for annual retirement expenses beginning in 20 years. The $20,000 amount is a present value at one's current age and it is a future value at the initial retirement age. If an assumption is made that the inflation rate is zero, the buying power of $20,000 at the current age will be the same at the initial retirement age. Since reality about inflation suggests differently, it may be unwise to use a **zero inflation approach** to retirement planning.

Consider the same example again, but using a **non-zero inflation approach**. If an inflation rate of 2 percent is assumed, the $20,000 at the current age will lose buying power by the time of the initial retirement age. Simply to keep pace with an inflation rate of 2 percent, today's $20,000 must grow to $29,718 (using Appendix A, multiply the future value factor of 1.4859 times $20,000) at the initial retirement age.

When one believes that the rate of return on retirement savings and investments will be greater than the rate of inflation, he or she may use the difference between the projected rate of return and the inflation rate as the **net rate of return**. This technique treats the inflation rate as zero, which greatly simplifies the calculation. This method is widely recommended in books and articles on personal finance. Reality further suggests that one's projected rate of return on retirement savings and investments may well exceed the inflation rate. Here the calculations become a bit more complicated, but the results are more accurate.

After making several calculations and projections, many people determine that there may not be enough income coming in during retirement from Social Security retirement benefits and pension plans. In such instances, the only way to assure a comfortable retirement is by increasing personal savings and investments. Depending upon how one goes about increasing savings and investments for retirement, there are significant income tax implications.

This chapter examines several mathematical examples related to retirement planning, including estimating annual retirement needs using guidelines for income replacement rate; estimating Social Security retirement benefits; calculating an after-inflation, after-tax rate of return; estimating needed retirement savings and investments using zero inflation; estimating needed retirement savings and investments using a non-zero inflation rate; and income taxes and retirement planning.

EXAMPLES OF MATHEMATICAL CONCEPTS RELATED TO RETIREMENT PLANNING

1. Estimating Annual Retirement Needs Using Guidelines for Income Replacement

Conceptual Idea 20.1: A relatively simply way to estimate annual retirement needs is to use a well-accepted guideline on income replacement in conjunction with the fundamental future value of money formula.

▼ **Example 20.1:** Ted is 45 years old, has a current income of $35,000, and he plans to retire in 20 years. He expects that his income will increase 2 percent per year above the rate of inflation. What is Ted's retirement need at the time of his retirement age?

Solution: To solve this problem, two steps are needed.

(1) If Ted's income increase 2 percent after inflation for the next 20 years, his income at his last working retirement year will be $52,008. Using future value Formula 4.3.1,

$$\$35,000 \, (1 + 0.02)^{20} = \$52,008$$

(2)   Use the income ranges below to determine the Ted's income replacement rate.[2]

Income Range	Income Replacement Percentage
<$18,000	86%
$18,000-29,999	78
$30,000-35,999	71
$36,000-53,999	66
$54,000-94,999	60
≥$95,000	55

Since Ted's income at retirement is projected to be $52,008, the income replacement rate is 66 percent. This means Ted's retirement need is likely to be $34,325 ($52,008 × .66).

❖   **Interpretation:** People generally do not need 100 percent of their pre-retirement income for living expenses after retirement. This is because a number of expenses typically decrease, such as money spent on housing, transportation, life insurance, and clothing. In addition, surveys show that higher income households do not need to replace nearly as much of their pre-retirement income as do households with lower incomes. The percentage of the pre-retirement income that needs to be replaced at retirement ranges from 55% to 86%, depending on income level before retirement. The **income replacement rate** is a ratio to estimate one's retirement need for income during the first year of retirement. In this example, Ted estimates his retirement need to be $34,325 during the first year of his retirement. Of course, this method is only an estimate. Some people prefer to project a higher income replacement rate than provided in the guidelines above.

2. Estimating Social Security Retirement Benefits

Conceptual Idea 20.2: Annual retirement needs may be reduced when one qualifies for Social Security retirement benefits.

▼   **Example 20.2.1:** Jane is a single woman, age 55 and earns $36,000. Assuming Jane qualifies for Social Security benefits, use Appendix B.1 to estimate Jane's monthly and yearly Social Security retirement benefits.

Solution: The table in Appendix B.1 reveals that a person who has current annual earnings of $36,000 is projected to receive a monthly benefit of $1,077, or $12,924 ($1,077 × 12 months) at age 65.

❖ **Interpretation:** To be eligible to receive Social Security retirement benefits, a worker born after 1928 must have earned 40 credits, and a worker earns 1 credit for each three month time period. Dependent children, spouses caring for dependent children, and spouses who retired at age 62 (including surviving divorced spouses who did not remarry if the marriage lasted at least 10 years) may be eligible to collect benefits based upon the eligibility of the retired worker. In this example, Jane estimates that she is eligible for $12,924 a year in Social Security benefits.

Continuing example 20.2.2: Jane anticipates that her retirement need will be $30,000 a year. How much is the gap in income between her projected Social Security retirement benefits and her retirement need?

Solution: $30,000 − $12,924 = $17,076.

❖ **Interpretation:** Since Jane's Social Security benefits are estimated at $12,924, she projects a gap of $17,076. To have a comfortable retirement at the level of living that she projected ($30,000), Jane must save and invest to develop funds that she can draw upon to have the additional money needed during retirement, $17,076. Jane may be able to create such a fund by contributing to an employer-sponsored retirement plan and/or by making after-tax investments.

3. Estimating Needed Retirement Savings with Net Rate of Return

Conceptual Idea 20.3: The savings and investments retirement need can be estimated based on **net rate of return** which is the difference between the nominal investment rate of return and the inflation rate.

▼ **Example 20.3.1:** Chris just determined that he needs $40,000 for annual retirement living expenses. He knows that at retirement he can get $20,000 a year from his employer's pension plan and Social Security, but he presently has no additional money saved for retirement. Therefore, he needs to save and invest an amount that would provide an extra $20,000 for every retirement year. Chris is now 35 and he expects to retire at 65 years old. Chris figures that he can invest his money for retirement to earn a rate of return 3 percent higher than the inflation rate. Chris estimates that he will live 20 years after retirement. Therefore, how much Chris should save annually so that he has enough money to live 20 years past the first day of his retirement?

Solution: To solve this problem, two steps are needed.

(1) *Determine the total sum required to provide the additional income during retirement.*

Note that the inflation rate is assumed to be zero because it is exactly offset with a similar nominal rate of return. For example, if inflation is 4% and the return on investment is 7%, the net rate of return is 3%. Therefore, it is simple, in these types of calculations, to assume inflation is zero given a net rate of return above zero, in this case 3%. Here the extra $20,000 Chris needs will have the same buying power on the first day of his retirement as it does today. If Chris needs the additional $20,000 annually during his 20 retirement years earning a net rate of return of 3 percent, this becomes a present value of annuity type of question. (See Chapter 4.) The question is what is the amount of money Chris needs on the first day of his retirement if the funds are to earn a rate of net return of 3 percent and provide withdrawals of $20,000 annually?

Since r = 3%, n = 20, and A = $20,000, from Appendix Table A.4 the corresponding factor of present value of annuity is 14.8775, then

PV = $20,000 × 14.8775 = $297,550

Thus, Chris needs $297,550 in additional funds on the first day of his retirement. Note that the sum needed is in Chris' first retirement year, not in today's value.

(2) *Determine the annual extra savings and investments needed to create the total sum required.*

Now this becomes a future value of an annuity type of problem. (See Chapter 4.) Given that the future value of a lump sum is $297,550), the net rate of return is 3 percent, and the number of years to save and invest is 30 (from age 35 to age 65), and the future value factor from Appendix A.3 is 47.5754, then

$297,550 = A × 47.5754
A = $297,550/47.5754 = $6,254

Thus, Chris needs to save $6,254 annually to achieve his retirement savings and investments goal.

❖ **Interpretation:** This example demonstrates how to calculate the needed extra annual savings and investment sum when the computation is based on a net rate of return. This approach is simple and straightforward, which is why it is used in many popular personal financial magazines and textbooks. The tricky part of this example is to realize that when you calculate the total sum required to provide the additional income during retirement you are dealing with a present value of annuity question, yet when you try to determine the annual extra savings and investments needed to create the total sum required it becomes a future value of an annuity type of question. In this example, the $297,550 in the first step is a present value of annuity and it becomes a future value of annuity question in the second step. This situation is common in retirement planning calculations since you are always dealing with situations with different dates, such as today's date and the first day of retirement date. The calculations are a bit more complicated if the net rate of return method is not used.

▼ **Example 20.3.2:** Using the information in example 20.5.1 and adding the fact that Chris currently has $5,000 in savings and investments, determine the amount of extra savings and investments Chris needs for retirement.

Solution: Three steps are needed for this question.

(1) *Total extra retirement needs.*

This is the same as one in Example 20.3.1, in which the total retirement needs = $297,550.

(2) *The value of current savings at the first year of retirement.*

Since the real rate of return = 3%, present value = $5,000, years to retire = 30, and the future value factor from Table A.1 = 2.4273, then

Future value = $5,000 × 2.4273 = $12,137

(3) *Extra annual savings and investments needed.*

At the beginning of the first year of retirement, total extra retirement needs amounts to $297,550 and private savings amount to $12,137. This leaves a gap of $285,413 ($297,550 − $12,137). Since future value = $285,413, years to retire = 30, real rate of return = 3%, and the future value factor in Table A.3 = 47.5754, then

$285,413 = A × 47.5754
A = $285,413/47.5754 = $5,999

❖ **Interpretation:** If Chris has $5,000 now in savings and investments, he needs to save and invest an extra $5,999 annually for the next 30 years for his retirement. The extra $5,000 in current savings reduce his needed annual savings by $255 ($6,254 − $5,999).

4. Determining the Gap in Savings and Investments for Retirement

Conceptual Idea 20.4: A key question in retirement planning is to determine the **gap**, if any, between one's combined current and projected savings and investments for retirement and the estimated amount that must be set aside now to provide that support. To calculate the answer, you must know how much is required for retirement living expenses and how much is projected from all retirement savings and investments. If your retirement needs are greater than your income from retirement savings and investments, there is a gap that needs resolution. With this knowledge, one can take actions to change the situation.

▼ **Example 20.4.1:** Bill Smith, age 35, is married, will retire at age 62, has a current income of $30,000, currently saves and invests about $2,000 per year, contributes nothing to the company's new 401(k) savings/investment program, anticipates needing a retirement income of $24,000 a year assuming a spending lifestyle at 80 percent of pre-retirement income ($30,000 × .80), and will live an additional 20 years beyond retirement. This example assumes a net rate of return that will be three percent after inflation, a fair estimate for a typical portfolio. Bill anticipates an employer pension of $7,000 annually and he already has $12,000 in other retirement savings.

Solution Worksheet:

		Example	Your Numbers
1.	**Annual income needed at retirement in today's dollars** (Use carefully estimated numbers or a certain percentage, such as 70% or 80%.)	$ 24,000	_____
2.	**Estimated Social Security retirement benefit in today's dollars** (Use Appendix B, "Estimating Social Security Benefits," or telephone the Social Security Administration at 1-800-772-1213 for a projection of your benefits.)	$ 6,048	_____
3.	**Estimated employer pension benefit in today's dollars** (Ask your retirement benefit advisor to make an estimate of your future pension, assuming you remain in the same job at the same salary, or make a conservative estimate yourself.)	$ 7,000	_____
4.	**Total estimated retirement income from Social Security and employer pension in today's dollars** (lines 2 + 3)	$ 13,048	_____
5.	**Additional income needed at retirement in today's dollars** (lines 1 – 4)	$ 10,952	_____
6.	**Amount you must have at retirement in today's dollars to receive additional annual income in retirement** (line 5) for 20 years (from Appendix A.4, assuming a 3 percent return over 20 years, 14.878 × $10,952)	$162,944	_____
7.	**Amount already available as savings/investments in today's dollars** (add lines 7-A through 7-D and record total on line 7-E):		
	A.　Employer savings plans, such as a 401(k), SEP or profit-sharing plan	$　　0	_____
	B.　IRAs and Keoghs	$ 4,000	_____
	C.　Other investments, such as mutual funds, stocks, bonds, real estate and other assets available for retirement	$ 8,000	_____
	D.　If you wish to include a portion of the equity in your home as savings (and this is optional), enter its present value minus the cost of another home in retirement	$　　0	_____
	E.　Total retirement savings (add lines A through D)	$ 12,000	_____
8.	**Future value of current savings/investments at time of retirement** (Using Appendix A.1 and a growth rate of 3 percent over 27 years, the factor is 2.221, thus 2.221 × $12,000)	$ 26,652	_____
9.	**Additional retirement savings/investments needed at time of retirement** (line 6 – line 8)	$136,292	_____
10.	**Annual savings needed (to reach amount in line 9) before retirement** (Using Appendix A.3 and a growth rate of 3 percent over 27 years, the factor is 40.71, thus, $136,292/40.71)	$ 3,348	_____
11.	**Current annual contribution to savings/investment plans**	$ 2,000	_____
12.	**Additional amount of annual savings that you need to set aside in today's dollars to achieve retirement goal (in line 1)** (line 10 – line 11)	$ 1,348	_____

❖ **Interpretation:** Bill needs to set aside an additional $1,348 in *current* dollars. He could take steps to catch up by contributing an additional $1,348 per year into the company 401(k) plan, that is almost 4 1/2 percent of his salary. For a margin of safety, and if the rules of his employer's pension plan permit, he could save an additional 1 to 1 1/2 percent of his salary. Also, it is possible that his employer will match some or all of Bill's 401(k) contributions. Note that these figures are based upon the assumption that the growth of Bill's investments will be 3 percent beyond inflation, a reasonable assumption. Bill's financial needs would be different if the inflation rate is greater than zero, but in that case, the growth rate of the investments would be greater than 3 percent. The net rate of return approach simplifies the calculations and puts the numbers to estimate retirement needs into today's dollars.

You may use this worksheet to help calculate the annual amount you need to set aside in today's dollars so you will have enough money during your retirement. Keep in mind that a person reaching age 65 has a life expectancy of 17 or more years.

5. Calculating an After-inflation, After-tax Rate of Return

Formula 20.5: $AARR = IR/(1 - MTR)$

Where: AARR = after-inflation, after-tax rate of return; IR = inflation rate; and MTR = marginal tax rate.

▼ **Example 20.5:** If Tammy's marginal tax rate is 15% and the average inflation rate is projected to be 3 percent, what is the after-inflation, after-tax rate of return Tammy should look for if she decides to invest her retirement money?

Solution:

Since IR = 3%, MTR = 15%, then
$AARR = .03/(1 - .15) = .03/.85 = 3.53\%$

❖ **Interpretation:** The **after-inflation, after-tax rate of return** can be viewed as a minimum projected rate of return for any investment, and especially for funds invested for retirement. If your rate of return is lower than this rate, you actually are not making a positive return on the investment. In this example, Tammy should seek an investment that is projected to generate at least 3.53% return. This will permit Tammy's retirement funds to retain the same purchasing power over time when the effects of inflation and income taxes are considered.

6. Income Taxes and Retirement Planning

Formula 20.6: $RR_{at} = (1 - MTR)RR$

Where: RR_{at} = after-tax rate of return; RR = before-tax rate of return; and MTR = marginal tax rate.

▼ **Example 20.6.1:** Bruce's marginal tax rate is 15 percent. If a bank account pays 5 percent on a certificate of deposit (CD), what will be Bruce's after-tax rate of return, and, alternatively, if Bruce puts the money into a tax-deferred account, such as in an individual retirement account (IRA), what will be that rate of return?

Solution:

(**1**) *After-tax rate of return in a regular account.*

Since RR = .05, MTR = .15, then
$RR_{at} = (1 - .15) \times .05 = .85 \times .05 = .0425$

Thus, when considering the effect of income taxes, the net after-tax rate of return is 4.25%.

(**2**) *After-tax rate of return in a tax-deferred account.*

Since the investment in a tax-deferred account is not currently taxable (the income tax liability exists when the funds are withdrawn), then MTR = 0, then

$RR_{at} = (1 - 0) \times .05 = 1 \times .05 = .05$

The after-tax rate of return is 5%.

❖ **Interpretation: Tax deferred investments** for retirement means that the dollars earned in interest, dividends, and capital gains are not taxed until they are withdrawn from the account. By taking advantage of income tax regulations which permit certain kinds of retirement income to be tax deferred, one's money can grow more rapidly than when placed in a taxable investment account. In addition, some retirement plans permit the money placed into a tax-deferred investment, such as a 401(k) plan or IRA, to be a tax deduction, and this reduces current income taxes. In this example, Bruce pays fifteen cents of every dollar earned to the federal government in taxes. Due to income taxes, Bruce earns a net 4.25% on his funds deposited at the bank where they earn a 5% rate of return. If, instead, the money is put into a tax-deferred account, Bruce can earn 5%. Over time, money in a tax-deferred account can grow substantially faster than those in a taxable account.

▼ **Example 20.6.2:** The **rule of 72** states that the value of an investment will double in 72/100r years, where **r** is the rate of return. Assuming a 10 percent pre-tax rate of return, 28 percent marginal tax bracket, and a $10,000 investment, compare the after-tax values of the investments at the end of 30 years using the following three investment alternatives for retirement savings. Also calculate the values of the three investments after 30 years.

Investment 1   Principal dollars invested are taxed and interest earned is taxed (this investment is made with after-tax dollars).

Investment 2   Principal dollars invested are taxed and interest earned is tax-deferred (this investment qualifies as tax-deferred, such as an annuity or non-qualified IRA).

Investment 3   Principal dollars invested are tax-deferred and interest earned is tax-deferred (this investment fully qualifies for pension contributions).

Solution:

(1) For Investment 1, since both principal and interest are taxable, RR = 10%, and MTR = .28, the after-tax rate will be

$$Rr_{at} = (1 - .28) \times .10 = .72 \times .10 = .072 = 7.2\%$$

which means that according to the rule of 72 that the investment will be double every (72/7.2 =) 10 years.

(2) For Investment 2, since only the principal is taxable and the interest is tax-deferred, the after-tax rate of return will be still 10%, which means the investment will double every (72/10 =) 7.2 years.

(3) For Investment 3, since both the principal and interest are tax deferred and the after-tax rate of return is 10%, this means the investment will double every (72/10 =) 7.2 years. Note that the difference between Investment 2 and 3 is that the two initial investment values are different because the principal is taxed in Investment 2 and untaxed in Investment 3.

(4) The following are the values of the three investments after 30 years.

Year	Investment 1 Fully Taxed	Investment 2 Interest Untaxed	Investment 3 Principal and Interest Untaxed
0	$ 7,200	$ 7,200	$ 10,000
7.2		$ 14,400	$ 20,000
10	$14,400		
14.4		$ 28,800	$ 40,000
20	$28,800		
21.6		$ 57,600	$ 80,000
28.8		$115,200	$160,000
30	$57,600	>$115,200	>$160,000

Now we compare the results of after-tax return at the end of the 30th year.

(5) Investment 1. Since the investment value $57,600 is calculated based on the after-tax rate of return, no extra income taxes need to be considered.

(6) Investment 2. Since the principal has been taxed at the beginning of the first year, only the interest is taxed at the end of 28.8 years. Since the interest = $106,400 ($113,600 – $7,200),taxes on the interest = $29,792 ($106,400 × .28), then the after-tax value of the investment = $83,808 ($113,600 – $29,792).

Note that we assume at the end of 28.8 years that the marginal tax rate is still 28%. For many people, the marginal tax rate may be lower, such as 15%, because of a decrease in income after retirement. If that is the case, the after-tax values of the investments will be higher. Also note that $83,808 is a value at the end of 28.8 years. It would be reasonable to expect that the value will be greater than $83,808 at the end of 30 years, which means that Investment 2 has a greater after-tax return than Investment 1.

(7) Investment 3. Since both the principal and interest are tax deferred, and assuming the marginal tax rate is 28%, and the fact that deferred taxes have to be paid at the end of 28.8 years, then the income taxes due = $44,800 ($160,000 × .28), and, the after-tax return = $115,200 ($160,000 – $44,800). Thus, the after-tax return at the end of 28.8 years is $115,200, which implies that the after-tax return at the end of 30 years will be greater than this value.

❖   **Interpretation:** A comparison of three types of accounts—one fully taxable, one in which principal is taxed before investing but interest is tax deferred, and a third where the amount is invested and grows tax-deferred—clearly demonstrates that after 30 years, the fully tax-deferred investment will be worth at least twice as much as the taxed alternative even after income taxes have been paid. This example illustrates the wisdom of taking advantage of tax-deferred retirement savings and investments plans.

▼   **Example 20.6.3:** Use the information given in Example 20.6.2 to compare the after-tax returns of the three investment alternatives using a spreadsheet program.

Solution:

Year	Investment 1 Fully Taxed	Investment 2 Interest Taxed	Investment 3 Principal and Interest Taxed
0	$7,200.00	$7,200.00	$10,000.00
1	$7,718.40	$7,920.00	$11,000.00
2	$8,274.12	$8,712.00	$12,100.00
3	$8,869.86	$9,583.20	$13,310.00
4	$9,508.49	$10,541.52	$14,641.00
5	$10,193.10	$11,595.67	$16,105.10
6	$10,927.01	$12,755.24	$17,715.61
7	$11,713.75	$14,030.76	$19,487.17
8	$12,557.14	$15,433.84	$21,435.89
9	$13,461.26	$16,977.22	$23,579.48
10	$14,430.47	$18,674.95	$25,937.42
11	$15,469.46	$20,542.44	$28,531.17
12	$16,583.26	$22,596.68	$31,384.28
13	$17,777.26	$24,856.35	$34,522.71
14	$19,057.22	$27,341.99	$37,974.98
15	$20,429.34	$30,076.19	$41,772.48
16	$21,900.25	$33,083.81	$45,949.73
17	$23,477.07	$36,392.19	$50,544.70
18	$25,167.42	$40,031.40	$55,599.17
19	$26,979.47	$44,034.55	$61,159.09
20	$28,921.99	$48,438.00	$67,275.00
21	$31,004.38	$53,281.80	$74,002.50
22	$33,236.69	$58,609.98	$81,402.75
23	$35,629.73	$64,470.98	$89,543.02
24	$38,195.07	$70,918.08	$98,497.33
25	$40,945.12	$78,009.88	$108,347.06
26	$43,893.17	$85,810.87	$119,181.77
27	$47,053.47	$94,391.96	$131,099.94
28	$50,441.33	$103,831.15	$144,209.94
29	$54,073.10	$114,214.27	$158,630.93
30	$57,966.36	$125,635.70	$174,494.02
After-tax return	$57,966.36	$92,473.70	$125,635.70

The above results are from Excel, a spreadsheet program. The return for each year is based on the future value function. The after-tax returns at the bottom line are calculated using the same approach as in Example 20.6.2, and the results are more accurate than the ones in Example 20.6.2.

❖ **Interpretation:** This example illustrates the use of spreadsheet program that can be used to generate year-by-year comparisons of retirement investment alternatives easily and accurately.

INFORMATION AND COMPUTING RESOURCES

1. Top-rated retirement planning computer software programs (ranging in price from $15 to $100) include Vanguard's Retirement Planner (800-876-1840), Retire ASAP (800-225-8246), Fidelity's Retirement Planning Software (800-554-8888), Dow Jones' Plan Ahead (800-522-3567), Intuit's Quicken Financial Planner (800-624-8742), Price Waterhouse's Retire Secure (800-752-6234), and T. Row Price Retirement Planning Kit (800-541-1472).

2. To find out your estimated Social Security retirement benefits, you may call the Social Administration at 800-772-1213 or write the SSA at Box 56, Baltimore, MD 21203. The SSA will provide a free **personal earnings and benefit estimate statement (PEBES)** from the Social Security Administration. This is the SSA's record of your lifetime taxable earnings covered under Social Security regulations, the estimated taxes paid on those earnings, and estimates of your monthly Social Security benefits if you retire at age 62, 65, or 70. It also shows the monthly amount that your survivors would receive if you died in the current year and the monthly disability benefit you and your family would receive if you became unable to work.

   If you have a personal computer, you can estimate your benefits using the SSA's computer software program called "ANYPIA." It is available on the Internet from the SSA at http://www.ssa.gov, or on diskette from the National Technical Information Service (5285 Port Royal Road, Springfield, VA 22161; 703-487-4650.

3. Related web sites.

   ■ *AARP:* http://www.aarp.org/ (disseminating information about the American Association of Retired Persons).

   ■ *Canadian retirement information:* http://www.retireweb.com/ (comprehensive retirement planning information in Canada).

   ■ *Eldercare Web:* http://www.ice.net/~kstevens/FINANCE.HTM (financial healthcare resources).

   ■ *ITT Hartford:* http://webmaster.itthartford.com:80/retire/ (information and education on making sound investments and planning for retirement).

   ■ *Kiplinger:* http://www.bookpageweb.com/kiplinger/ (a retirement planning calendar to use as you approach retirement).

- *Principles of retirement planning:*
  http://www.dtonline.com/prptoc/prptoc.htm (teaching materials with comprehensive retirement planning information; can be used as references when developing retirement planning courses).

- *Retirement articles:* http://www.insworld.com/Newsletter/ (articles about retirement planning and other related topics; a free electronic newsletter).

- *Retirement calculators:* http://safetynet.doleta.go/finance.htm (created by several Federal agency employees, includes several calculators, such as life expectancy, retirement needs, and retirement savings and investments; also has information on other financial planning topics).

- *Retirement information:* http://www.investorguide.com/Retirement.htm (compiled retirement planning information from various sources).

- *Retirement questions and answers:*
  http://www.centcon.com/~billman/faqindex.html (practical information regarding retirement planning and other financial planning topics).

- *Retirement survey:* http://www.merrill-lynch.ml.com/new/emprel1.html (summary of a recent survey of retirement planning).

- *Social Security benefits:*
  http://www.ssa.gov/programs/retirement/publications/retirement.html (a booklet about Social Security benefits prepared by Social Security Administration)

EXERCISE PROBLEMS

Estimating Annual Retirement Needs Using Guidelines for Income Replacement

1. Naomi is 35 years old and plans to retire in 30 years. Her current income is $30,000 and that amount is expected to increase 3% per year after the inflation rate is considered. What is Naomi's retirement need at first year of retirement?

2. Nancy is in her 50s and doesn't think her income will increase in a rate more than the inflation rate. If her current income is $40,000, what are Nancy's retirement needs?

3. *Out-of-Class Exercise* Estimate your retirement needs using the guidelines for income replacement.

Estimating Social Security Retirement Benefits

4. Janet is a single woman, age 50, and earns $48,000. Use Appendix B.1 to estimate the monthly and yearly Social Security retirement benefits for Janet.

Estimating Needed Retirement Savings with Net Rate of Return

5. Katie just found out that she needs $30,000 for annual retirement living expenses. She knows she can get $18,000 annually from her company's pension benefits and Social Security benefits after the retirement, but she has no savings for retirement. She needs to save extra $12,000 for every retirement year. Katie is 40 and expects to retire at 65 years of age. If Katie can invest her money with a rate of return 2% higher than the inflation rate, and if she plans to live 25 more years after retirement, how much she should save annually so that she has enough money on the first day of her retirement?

6. If Katie currently has $10,000 in savings and investments for retirement, what is the extra savings and investment amount she needs for retirement?

Determining the Gap in Savings and Investments for Retirement

7. James Jones, age 45, is married, will retire at age 65, has a current income of $48,000, currently saves and invests about $2,000 per year, gives zero to the company's new 401(k) savings/investment program, anticipates needing a retirement income of $38,400 a year assuming a spending lifestyle at 80 percent of current income ($48,000 × .80), and will live an additional 20 years beyond retirement. James will receive $7,000 annually from employer pension plans, has $4,000 in IRAs and $8,000 in other investments. This example assumes that investment returns will be three percent after inflation, a fair estimate for a typical portfolio.

Calculating an After-inflation, After-tax Rate of Return

8. If Oskar's marginal tax rate is 28% and the inflation rate is going to average 4%, what is the after-inflation, after-tax rate of return Oskar should look for if he decides to invest for retirement savings?

9. Yuko's marginal tax rate is 31% and the inflation rate is projected to be 3.5%. If Yuko wants to save for her retirement purposes, what is the rate of return she should look for?

10. *Out-of-Class Exercise*   Given a marginal tax rate, describe the relationship between the inflation rate and the after-tax, after-inflation rate of return. Also, if given the inflation rate, what is the relationship between marginal tax rate and the after-tax, after-inflation rate of return?

Income Taxes and Retirement Planning

11. Alonzo's marginal tax rate is 28 percent. If a bank account pays 4.7 percent on a certificate of deposit, what will be his after-tax rate of return? Instead, if Alonzo puts the money into a tax-deferred account, what is the after-tax rate of return?

12. a. Assume a 7.2 percent pre-tax rate of return, 31 percent MTR, and a $10,000 investment, then use the rule of 72 to compare the after-tax values of the investments at the end of 30 years for the following three investment alternatives for retirement savings and investments:
    (1) Principal dollars invested are taxed; interest earned is taxed.
    (2) Principal dollars invested are taxed; interest earned is tax-deferred.
    (3) Principal dollars invested are tax-deferred; interest earned is tax-deferred.
    b. Use the information given in Exercise 9 to compare the after-tax returns of the three investment alternatives using a spreadsheet program.

SELECTED REFERENCES

Andrews, E. S. (1992) The growth and distribution of 401(k) plans. In J. A. Turner and D. J. Beller (eds.). *Trends in pensions 1992*, (pp. 149-176). Washington, DC: U.S. Department of Labor, Pension and Welfare Benefits Administration.

Garman, E. T., & Forgue, R. E. (1997). *Personal finance* (5th ed.). Chapter 19: Retirement planning. Boston: Houghton Mifflin Company.

Kusko, A. L., Poterba, J. M., & Wilcox, D. W. (1994). Employee decisions with respect to 401(k) plans: Evidence from individual-level data. National Bureau of Economic Research Working Paper 4635.

O'Neill, B. (undated). *Saving and investing for retirement*. [Brochure, PS430]. Newton, NJ: Rutgers Cooperative Extension, Rutgers University.

Papke, L. E. (1995, Spring). Participation in and contributions to 401(k) pension plans. *Journal of Human Resources,* XXX(2), 311-325.

Poterba, J. M., Venti, S. F., & Wise, D. A. (1994). 401(k) plans and tax-deferred saving. In D. A. Wise (ed.). *Studies in the economics of aging*, (pp.105-138). Chicago: University of Chicago Press.

Walden, M. L. (1992). *Economics and consumer decisions*. Chapter 10: Retirement Planning. Englewood Cliffs, NJ: Prentice Hall.

Xiao, J. J. (1996). Factors associated with 401(k) plan contributions. In J. K. Lewis (ed.). *Proceedings of Association of Financial Counseling and Planning*, pp. 47-58. Grand Rapids, MI: AFCPE.

Yuh, Y., & DeVaney, S. A. (1996). Determinants of couple's defined contribution retirement funds. *Financial Counseling and Planning*, 7, 31-38.

ENDNOTES

1.   Consumer behavior of participation and contributions to defined contribution plans can be found in following studies: Andrews (1992), Kusko, Poterba & Wilcox (1994), Papke (1995), Poterba, Venti & Wise (1994), Xiao (1996), and Yuh & DeVaney (1996).

2.   The table was originally developed by President's Commission on Pension Policy, *Coming of age: Toward a national retirement income policy.* Report of the Commission, Washington, DC, 1981, pp. 42-43. The income range figures are inflated to 1997 dollars.

Appendix A
Present and Future Value Tables[1]

A. Present and Future Value Tables

Many problems of personal finance involve decisions about money values at different points in time. These values can be directly and fairly compared only when they are adjusted to a common point in time. Chapter 1 introduced the basic time value concepts. This appendix offers more details about the time value of money, as well as provides future and present value of $1 tables with which to make calculations.

Four assumptions must be made to eliminate unnecessary complications: (1) each planning period is 1 year long; (2) only annual interest rates are considered; (3) interest rates are the same during each of the annual periods; and (4) interest is compounded and earns in subsequent periods.

Tables of present and future values can be constructed to make these adjustments. Future values are derived from the principles of compounding the dollar values ahead in time. Present values are derived from discounting (which is the inverse of compounding) the dollar values and transferring them to an earlier point in time.

For most of us it is unnecessary to have the precision of interest at the beginning of a period instead of the end of a period, or if interest compounds daily or quarterly instead of annually. (These require even more tables.) The following present and future value tables assume that money is accumulated, received, paid, compounded, or whatever at the *end* of a period. The tables can be used to compute the mathematics of personal finance with high certainty and to confirm (or reject as inaccurate) what people tell you about financial matters.

The most significant task is to be certain that you are using the correct table. Accordingly, each table is clearly described, and illustrations of use appear on the

---

[1]*Source:* E. Thomas Garman and Raymond E. Forgue (1997), *Personal Finance*, 5th edition, Boston: Houghton Mifflin Company, Appendix A, pp. A1-A11. Appreciation is expressed to Houghton Mifflin Company for permission to use their copyrighted materials.

facing page where possible. In addition, the appropriate mathematical equation is shown that can be easily solved using a calculator.

1. You invest $500 at 15 percent for 12 years. How much will you have at the end of that 12-year period?

    The future value factor is 5.350; hence the solution is $500(5.350), or $2675.

2. Property values in your neighborhood are increasing at a rate of 5 percent per year. If your home is presently worth $90,000, what will its worth be in 7 years?

    The future value factor is 1.407; hence the solution is $90,000(1.407), or $126,630.

3. You need to amass $40,000 in the next 10 years to meet a balloon payment on your home mortgage. You have $17,000 available to invest. What annual interest rate must be earned to realize the $40,000? $40,000 ÷ $17,000 = 2.353.

    Read down the "Periods" column to 10 years and across to 2.367 (close enough), which is under the 9 percent column. Hence the $17,000 invested at 9 percent for 10 years will grow to a future value of just over $40,000.

4. An apartment building is currently valued at $160,000, and it has been appreciating at 8 percent per year. If this rate continues, in how many years will it be worth $300,000? $300,000 ÷ $160,000 = 1.875.

    Read down the 8 percent column until you reach 1.851 (close enough to 1.875). Note that this number corresponds to a period of 8 years. Hence the $160,000 property appreciating at 8 percent annually will grow to a future value of $300,000 in just over 8 years.

5. You have the choice of receiving $15,000 today as a down payment from someone who wants to purchase your rental property or a personal note for $25,000 payable in 6 years. If you could expect to earn 8 percent on such funds, which is the better choice?

    The future value factor is 1.587; hence the future value of $15,000 at 8 percent is $15,000(1.587), or $23,805. Thus, it would be better to take the note for $25,000.

6. You want to know how much an automobile now priced at $20,000 will cost in 4 years, assuming an inflation rate of 5 percent annually.

    Read down the 5 percent column and across the row for 4 years to locate the future value factor 1.216. Hence the solution is $20,000(1.216), or $24,320.

7. You want to know how big a lump-sum investment you need now to have $20,000 available in 5 years assuming a 10 percent annual rate of return.

The $20,000 future value is divided by 1.611 (10 percent at 5 years), resulting in a lump-sum investment now of $12,415.

8. You have $5000 now and need $10,000 in 9 years. What rate of return is needed to reach that goal?

    Divide the future value of $10,000 by the present value of the lump sum of $5000 to obtain a future value factor of 2.0. Look along the row for 9 years to locate the future value factor 1.999 (very close to 2.0). Read up the column to find that an 8 percent return on investment is needed.

9. You want to know how many years it will take your lump-sum investment of $10,000 to grow to $16,000 with an annual rate of return of 7 percent.

    Divide the future value of $16,000 by the present value of the $10,000 lump sum to compute a future value factor of 1.6; then look down the 7 percent column to find 1.606 (close enough). Read across the row to find that an investment period of 7 years is needed.

    An alternative approach is to use a calculator to determine the future value, *FV*, of a sum of money invested today assuming the amount is left in the investment for a specified number of time periods (usually years) and it earns a certain rate of return each period. The equation is

$$FV = PV\,(1.0 + i)^n \qquad\qquad (A.1)$$

    where   FV = the *Future Value*
    PV = the *Present Value* of the investment
    i = the *interest* rate per period
    n = the *number* or periods the *PV* is invested

Appendix A.1   Future Value of $1 at the end of n periods   (Used to compute the compounded future value of a given present value lump-sum investment)

n	1%	2%	3%	4%	5%	6%	7%	8%	9%	10%	11%	12%	13%	14%	15%	16%	17%	18%	19%	20%
1	1.0100	1.0200	1.0300	1.0400	1.0500	1.0600	1.0700	1.0800	1.0900	1.1000	1.1100	1.1200	1.1300	1.1400	1.1500	1.1600	1.1700	1.1800	1.1900	1.2000
2	1.0201	1.0404	1.0609	1.0816	1.1025	1.1236	1.1449	1.1664	1.1881	1.2100	1.2321	1.2544	1.2769	1.2996	1.3225	1.3456	1.3689	1.3924	1.4161	1.4400
3	1.0303	1.0612	1.0927	1.1249	1.1576	1.1910	1.2250	1.2597	1.2950	1.3310	1.3676	1.4049	1.4429	1.4815	1.5209	1.5609	1.6016	1.6430	1.6852	1.7280
4	1.0406	1.0824	1.1255	1.1699	1.2155	1.2625	1.3108	1.3605	1.4116	1.4641	1.5181	1.5735	1.6305	1.6890	1.7490	1.8106	1.8739	1.9388	2.0053	2.0736
5	1.0510	1.1041	1.1593	1.2167	1.2763	1.3382	1.4026	1.4693	1.5386	1.6105	1.6851	1.7623	1.8424	1.9254	2.0114	2.1003	2.1924	2.2878	2.3864	2.4883
6	1.0615	1.1262	1.1941	1.2653	1.3401	1.4185	1.5007	1.5869	1.6771	1.7716	1.8704	1.9738	2.0820	2.1950	2.3131	2.4364	2.5652	2.6996	2.8398	2.9860
7	1.0721	1.1487	1.2299	1.3159	1.4071	1.5036	1.6058	1.7138	1.8280	1.9487	2.0762	2.2107	2.3526	2.5023	2.6600	2.8262	3.0012	3.1855	3.3793	3.5832
8	1.0829	1.1717	1.2668	1.3686	1.4775	1.5938	1.7182	1.8509	1.9926	2.1436	2.3045	2.4760	2.6584	2.8526	3.0590	3.2784	3.5115	3.7589	4.0214	4.2998
9	1.0937	1.1951	1.3048	1.4233	1.5513	1.6895	1.8385	1.9990	2.1719	2.3579	2.5580	2.7731	3.0040	3.2519	3.5179	3.8030	4.1084	4.4355	4.7854	5.1598
10	1.1046	1.2190	1.3439	1.4802	1.6289	1.7908	1.9672	2.1589	2.3674	2.5937	2.8394	3.1058	3.3946	3.7072	4.0456	4.4114	4.8068	5.2338	5.6947	6.1917
11	1.1157	1.2434	1.3842	1.5395	1.7103	1.8983	2.1049	2.3316	2.5804	2.8531	3.1518	3.4785	3.8359	4.2262	4.6524	5.1173	5.6240	6.1759	6.7767	7.4301
12	1.1268	1.2682	1.4258	1.6010	1.7959	2.0122	2.2522	2.5182	2.8127	3.1384	3.4985	3.8960	4.3345	4.8179	5.3503	5.9360	6.5801	7.2876	8.0642	8.9161
13	1.1381	1.2936	1.4685	1.6651	1.8856	2.1329	2.4098	2.7196	3.0658	3.4523	3.8833	4.3635	4.8980	5.4924	6.1528	6.8858	7.6987	8.5994	9.5964	10.6993
14	1.1495	1.3195	1.5126	1.7317	1.9799	2.2609	2.5785	2.9372	3.3417	3.7975	4.3104	4.8871	5.5348	6.2613	7.0757	7.9875	9.0075	10.1472	11.4198	12.8392
15	1.1610	1.3459	1.5580	1.8009	2.0789	2.3966	2.7590	3.1722	3.6425	4.1772	4.7846	5.4736	6.2543	7.1379	8.1371	9.2655	10.5387	11.9737	13.5895	15.4070
16	1.1726	1.3728	1.6047	1.8730	2.1829	2.5404	2.9522	3.4259	3.9703	4.5950	5.3109	6.1304	7.0673	8.1372	9.3576	10.7480	12.3303	14.1290	16.1715	18.4884
17	1.1843	1.4002	1.6528	1.9479	2.2920	2.6928	3.1588	3.7000	4.3276	5.0545	5.8951	6.8660	7.9861	9.2765	10.7613	12.4677	14.4265	16.6722	19.2441	22.1861
18	1.1961	1.4282	1.7024	2.0258	2.4066	2.8543	3.3799	3.9960	4.7171	5.5599	6.5436	7.6900	9.0243	10.5752	12.3755	14.4625	16.8790	19.6733	22.9005	26.6233
19	1.2081	1.4568	1.7535	2.1068	2.5270	3.0256	3.6165	4.3157	5.1417	6.1159	7.2633	8.6128	10.1974	12.0557	14.2318	16.7765	19.7484	23.2144	27.2516	31.9480
20	1.2202	1.4859	1.8061	2.1911	2.6533	3.2071	3.8697	4.6610	5.6044	6.7275	8.0623	9.6463	11.5231	13.7435	16.3665	19.4608	23.1056	27.3930	32.4294	38.3376
21	1.2324	1.5157	1.8603	2.2788	2.7860	3.3996	4.4106	5.0338	6.1088	7.4002	8.9492	10.8038	13.0211	15.6676	18.8215	22.5745	27.0336	32.3238	38.5910	46.0051
22	1.2447	1.5460	1.9161	2.3699	2.9253	3.6035	4.4304	5.4365	6.6586	8.1403	9.9336	12.1003	14.7138	17.8610	21.6447	26.1864	31.6293	38.1421	45.9233	55.2061
23	1.2572	1.5769	1.9736	2.4647	3.0715	3.8197	4.7405	5.8715	7.2579	8.9543	11.0263	13.5523	16.6266	20.3616	24.8915	30.3762	37.0062	45.0076	54.6487	66.2474
24	1.2697	1.6084	2.0328	2.5633	3.2251	4.0489	5.0724	6.3412	7.9111	9.8497	12.2392	15.1786	18.7881	23.2122	28.6252	35.2364	43.2973	53.1090	65.0320	79.4968
25	1.2824	1.6406	2.0938	2.6658	3.3864	4.2919	5.4274	6.8485	8.6231	10.8347	13.5855	17.0001	21.2305	26.4619	32.9190	40.8742	50.6578	62.6686	77.3881	95.3962
26	1.2953	1.6734	2.1566	2.7725	3.5557	4.5494	5.8074	7.3964	9.3992	11.9182	15.0799	19.0401	23.9905	30.1666	37.8568	47.4141	59.2697	73.9490	92.0918	114.4755
27	1.3082	1.7069	2.2213	2.8834	3.7335	4.8223	6.2139	7.9881	10.2451	13.1100	16.7386	21.3249	27.1093	34.3899	43.5353	55.0004	69.3455	87.2598	109.5893	137.3706
28	1.3213	1.7410	2.2879	2.9987	3.9201	5.1117	6.6488	8.6271	11.1671	14.4210	18.5799	23.8839	30.6335	39.2045	50.0656	63.8004	81.1342	102.9666	130.4112	164.8447
29	1.3345	1.7758	2.3566	3.1187	4.1161	5.4184	7.1143	9.3173	12.1722	15.8631	20.6237	26.7499	34.6158	44.6931	57.5755	74.0085	94.9271	121.5005	155.1893	197.8136
30	1.3478	1.8114	2.4273	3.2434	4.3219	5.7435	7.6123	10.0627	13.2677	17.4494	22.8923	29.9599	39.1159	50.9502	66.2118	85.8499	111.0647	143.3706	184.6753	237.3763
40	1.4889	2.2080	3.2620	4.8010	7.0400	10.2857	14.9745	21.7245	31.4094	45.2593	65.0009	93.0510	132.7816	188.8835	267.8635	378.7212	533.8687	750.3783	1051.6680	1469.7720
50	1.6446	2.6916	4.3839	7.1067	11.4674	18.4202	29.4570	46.9016	74.3575	117.3909	184.5648	289.0022	450.7359	700.2330	1083.657	1670.704	2566.215	3927.357	5988.914	9100.438

Illustrations Using Appendix A.2—Present Value of $1

To use this table, locate the present value factor for the time period and the interest rate.

1. You want to begin a college fund for your newborn child; you want $30,000 18 years from now. If a current investment opportunity yields 7 percent, how much must you invest in a lump sum to realize the $30,000 when needed?

    The present value factor if 0.296; hence the solution is $30,000 x 0.296, or $8,800.

2. You hope to retire in 25 years and want to deposit one lump sum that will grow to $250,000 at that time. If you can now invest at 8 percent, how much must you invest to realize the $250,000 when needed?

    The present value factor is 0.146; hence the solution is $250,000 x 0.146, or $36,500. The present value of $250,000 received 25 years from now is $36,500 if the interest rate is 8 percent.

3. You have the choice of receiving $15,000 today as a down payment from someone who wants to purchase your rental property or a personal note for $25,000 payable in 6 years. If you could expect to earn 8 percent on such funds, which is the better choice?

    The present value factor if 0.630; hence the solution is $25,000 x 0.630, or $15,750. Thus, the present value of $25,000 received in 6 years is greater than $15,000 received now, and is the better choice.

4. You own a $1000 bond paying 8 percent annually until maturity in 5 years. You need to sell it now even though the market rate of interest on similar bonds has increased to 10 percent. What will be the lower discounted market price of the bond so that the buyer of your bond will earn a yield of 10 percent?

    The solution first involves computing the present value of the future interest payments of $80 per year for 5 years at 10 percent (using Appendix A.4), $80 x 3.791, or $303.28. Second, compute the present value of the future principal repayment of $1000 after 5 years at 10 percent: $1000 x 0.621, or $621.00. Hence the market price is the sum of the two present values ($303.28 + $621.00), or $924.28.

    An alternative approach is to use a calculator to determine the present value, *PV*, of a single payment received some time in the future. The equation (which is a rearrangement of future value equation A.1) is

    $$PV = \frac{FV}{(1.0 + i)^n} \qquad\qquad (A.2)$$

where PV = the *Present Value* of the investment

FV = the *Future Value*

i = the *interest* rate per period

n = the *number* or periods the PV is invested

Appendix A.2 Present Value of $1

(Used to compute the present value of some known future single payment amount)

n	1%	2%	3%	4%	5%	6%	7%	8%	9%	10%	11%	12%	13%	14%	15%	16%	17%	18%	19%	20%
1	0.9901	0.9804	0.9709	0.9615	0.9524	0.9434	0.9346	0.9259	0.9174	0.9091	0.9009	0.8929	0.8850	0.8772	0.8696	0.8621	0.8547	0.8475	0.8403	0.8333
2	0.9803	0.9612	0.9426	0.9246	0.9070	0.8900	0.8734	0.8573	0.8417	0.8264	0.8116	0.7972	0.7831	0.7695	0.7561	0.7432	0.7305	0.7182	0.7062	0.6944
3	0.9706	0.9423	0.9151	0.8890	0.8638	0.8396	0.8163	0.7938	0.7722	0.7513	0.7312	0.7118	0.6931	0.6750	0.6575	0.6407	0.6244	0.6086	0.5934	0.5787
4	0.9610	0.9238	0.8885	0.8548	0.8227	0.7921	0.7629	0.7350	0.7084	0.6830	0.6587	0.6355	0.6133	0.5921	0.5718	0.5523	0.5337	0.5158	0.4987	0.4823
5	0.9515	0.9057	0.8626	0.8219	0.7835	0.7473	0.7130	0.6806	0.6499	0.6209	0.5935	0.5674	0.5428	0.5194	0.4972	0.4761	0.4561	0.4371	0.4190	0.4019
6	0.9420	0.8880	0.8375	0.7903	0.7462	0.7050	0.6663	0.6302	0.5963	0.5645	0.5346	0.5066	0.4803	0.4556	0.4323	0.4104	0.3898	0.3704	0.3521	0.3349
7	0.9327	0.8706	0.8131	0.7599	0.7107	0.6651	0.6227	0.5835	0.5470	0.5132	0.4817	0.4523	0.4251	0.3996	0.3759	0.3538	0.3332	0.3139	0.2959	0.2791
8	0.9235	0.8535	0.7894	0.7307	0.6768	0.6274	0.5820	0.5403	0.5019	0.4665	0.4339	0.4039	0.3762	0.3506	0.3269	0.3050	0.2848	0.2660	0.2487	0.2326
9	0.9143	0.8368	0.7664	0.7026	0.6446	0.5919	0.5439	0.5002	0.4604	0.4241	0.3909	0.3606	0.3329	0.3075	0.2843	0.2630	0.2434	0.2255	0.2090	0.1938
10	0.9053	0.8203	0.7441	0.6756	0.6139	0.5584	0.5083	0.4632	0.4224	0.3855	0.3522	0.3220	0.2946	0.2697	0.2472	0.2267	0.2080	0.1911	0.1756	0.1615
11	0.8963	0.8043	0.7224	0.6496	0.5847	0.5268	0.4751	0.4289	0.3875	0.3505	0.3173	0.2875	0.2607	0.2366	0.2149	0.1954	0.1778	0.1619	0.1476	0.1346
12	0.8874	0.7885	0.7014	0.6246	0.5568	0.4970	0.4440	0.3971	0.3555	0.3186	0.2858	0.2567	0.2307	0.2076	0.1869	0.1685	0.1520	0.1372	0.1240	0.1122
13	0.8787	0.7730	0.6810	0.6006	0.5303	0.4688	0.4150	0.3677	0.3262	0.2897	0.2575	0.2292	0.2042	0.1821	0.1625	0.1452	0.1299	0.1163	0.1042	0.0935
14	0.8700	0.7579	0.6611	0.5775	0.5051	0.4423	0.3878	0.3405	0.2992	0.2633	0.2320	0.2046	0.1807	0.1597	0.1413	0.1252	0.1110	0.0985	0.0876	0.0779
15	0.8613	0.7430	0.6419	0.5553	0.4810	0.4173	0.3624	0.3152	0.2745	0.2394	0.2090	0.1827	0.1599	0.1401	0.1229	0.1079	0.0949	0.0835	0.0736	0.0649
16	0.8528	0.7284	0.6232	0.5339	0.4581	0.3936	0.3387	0.2919	0.2519	0.2176	0.1883	0.1631	0.1415	0.1229	0.1069	0.0930	0.0811	0.0708	0.0618	0.0541
17	0.8444	0.7142	0.6050	0.5134	0.4363	0.3714	0.3166	0.2703	0.2311	0.1978	0.1696	0.1456	0.1252	0.1078	0.0929	0.0802	0.0693	0.0600	0.0520	0.0451
18	0.8360	0.7002	0.5874	0.4936	0.4155	0.3503	0.2959	0.2502	0.2120	0.1799	0.1528	0.1300	0.1108	0.0946	0.0808	0.0691	0.0592	0.0508	0.0437	0.0376
19	0.8277	0.6864	0.5703	0.4746	0.3957	0.3305	0.2765	0.2317	0.1945	0.1635	0.1377	0.1161	0.0981	0.0829	0.0703	0.0596	0.0506	0.0431	0.0367	0.0313
20	0.8195	0.6730	0.5537	0.4564	0.3769	0.3118	0.2584	0.2145	0.1784	0.1486	0.1240	0.1037	0.0868	0.0728	0.0611	0.0514	0.0433	0.0365	0.0308	0.0261
21	0.8114	0.6598	0.5375	0.4388	0.3589	0.2942	0.2415	0.1987	0.1637	0.1351	0.1117	0.0926	0.0768	0.0638	0.0531	0.0443	0.0370	0.0309	0.0259	0.0217
22	0.8034	0.6468	0.5219	0.4220	0.3418	0.2775	0.2257	0.1839	0.1502	0.1228	0.1007	0.0826	0.0680	0.0560	0.0462	0.0382	0.0316	0.0262	0.0218	0.0181
23	0.7954	0.6342	0.5067	0.4057	0.3256	0.2618	0.2109	0.1703	0.1378	0.1117	0.0907	0.0738	0.0601	0.0491	0.0402	0.0329	0.0270	0.0222	0.0183	0.0151
24	0.7876	0.6217	0.4919	0.3901	0.3101	0.2470	0.1971	0.1577	0.1264	0.1015	0.0817	0.0659	0.0532	0.0431	0.0349	0.0284	0.0231	0.0188	0.0154	0.0126
25	0.7798	0.6095	0.4776	0.3751	0.2953	0.2330	0.1842	0.1460	0.1160	0.0923	0.0736	0.0588	0.0471	0.0378	0.0304	0.0245	0.0197	0.0160	0.0129	0.0105
26	0.7720	0.5976	0.4637	0.3607	0.2812	0.2198	0.1722	0.1352	0.1064	0.0839	0.0663	0.0525	0.0417	0.0331	0.0264	0.0211	0.0169	0.0135	0.0109	0.0087
27	0.7644	0.5859	0.4502	0.3468	0.2678	0.2074	0.1609	0.1252	0.0976	0.0763	0.0597	0.0469	0.0369	0.0291	0.0230	0.0182	0.0144	0.0115	0.0091	0.0073
28	0.7568	0.5744	0.4371	0.3335	0.2551	0.1956	0.1504	0.1159	0.0895	0.0693	0.0538	0.0419	0.0326	0.0255	0.0200	0.0157	0.0123	0.0097	0.0077	0.0061
29	0.7493	0.5631	0.4243	0.3207	0.2429	0.1846	0.1406	0.1073	0.0822	0.0630	0.0485	0.0374	0.0289	0.0224	0.0174	0.0135	0.0105	0.0082	0.0064	0.0051
30	0.7419	0.5521	0.4120	0.3083	0.2314	0.1741	0.1314	0.0994	0.0754	0.0573	0.0437	0.0334	0.0256	0.0196	0.0151	0.0116	0.0090	0.0070	0.0054	0.0042
40	0.6717	0.4529	0.3066	0.2083	0.1420	0.0972	0.0668	0.0460	0.0318	0.0221	0.0154	0.0107	0.0075	0.0053	0.0037	0.0026	0.0019	0.0013	0.0010	0.0007
50	0.6080	0.3715	0.2281	0.1407	0.0872	0.0543	0.0339	0.0213	0.0134	0.0085	0.0054	0.0035	0.0022	0.0014	0.0009	0.0006	0.0004	0.0003	0.0002	0.0001

Illustrations Using Appendix A.3—Future Value of an Annuity of $1 per Period

To use this table, locate the future value factor for the time period and the interest rate.

1. You plan to retire after 16 years. To provide for that retirement, you initiate a savings program of $7000 per year in an investment yielding 8 percent. What will be the value of the retirement fund at the beginning of the seventeenth year?

   Your last payment into the fund will occur at the end of the sixteenth year, so scan down the periods column for period 16, and then across until you reach the 8 percent column. The future value factor is 30.32. Hence the solution is $7000(30.32), or $212,240.

2. What will be the value of an investment if you put $2000 into a retirement plan yielding 7 percent annually for 25 years?

   The future value factor is 63.250. Hence the solution is $2000(63.250), or $126,500.

3. You are trying to decide between putting $3000 or $4000 annually for the next 20 years into an investment yielding 7 percent for retirement purposes. What is the difference in the value of investing the extra $1000 for 20 years?

   The future value factor is 41.0. Hence the solution is $1,000(41.0), or $41,000.

4. You will receive an annuity payment of $1200 at the end of each year for 6 years. What will be the total value of this stream of income invested at 7 percent by the time you receive the last payment?

   The appropriate future value factor for 6 years at 7 percent is 7.153. Hence the solution is $1200(7.153), or $8584.

5. You want to know how many years of investing $1200 annually at 9 percent it will take to reach a goal of $11,000.

   Divide the future value of $11,000 by the lump sum of $1200 to find a future value factor of 9.17 and look down the 9 percent column to find 9.200 (close enough). Read across the row to find that an investment period of 7 years is needed.

6. You want to know what percent of return is needed if you plan to invest $1200 annually for 9 years to reach a goal of $15,000.

   Divide the future value goal of $15,000 by $1200 to derive the future value factor 12.5 and look along the row for 9 years to locate the future value factor

12.49 (close enough). Read up the column to find that you need an 8 percent return.

An alternative approach is to use a calculator to determine the total future value, *FV*, of a stream of equal payments (an annuity). The equation is

$$FV = \frac{[(1.0) + i)^{n-1.0}] \times A}{i} \qquad\qquad (A.3)$$

where *FV* = the *Future Value*
         i = the *interest* rate per period
        n = the *number* or periods the *PV* is invested
       A = the *amount* of the annuity

Appendix A.3   Future Value of a Stream of Equal Payments—an Annuity—of $1 per Period   (Used to compute the future value of a stream of income payments)

n	1%	2%	3%	4%	5%	6%	7%	8%	9%	10%	11%	12%	13%	14%	15%	16%	17%	18%	19%	20%
1	1.0000	1.0000	1.0000	1.0000	1.0000	1.0000	1.0000	1.0000	1.0000	1.0000	1.0000	1.0000	1.0000	1.0000	1.0000	1.0000	1.0000	1.0000	1.0000	1.0000
2	2.0100	2.0200	2.0300	2.0400	2.0500	2.0600	2.0700	2.0800	2.0900	2.1000	2.1100	2.1200	2.1300	2.1400	2.1500	2.1600	2.1700	2.1800	2.1900	2.2000
3	3.0301	3.0604	3.0909	3.1216	3.1525	3.1836	3.2149	3.2464	3.2781	3.3100	3.3421	3.3744	3.4069	3.4396	3.4725	3.5056	3.5389	3.5724	3.6061	3.6400
4	4.0604	4.1216	4.1836	4.2465	4.3101	4.3746	4.4399	4.5061	4.5731	4.6410	4.7097	4.7793	4.8498	4.9211	4.9934	5.0665	5.1405	5.2154	5.2913	5.3680
5	5.1010	5.2040	5.3091	5.4163	5.5256	5.6371	5.7507	5.8666	5.9847	6.1051	6.2278	6.3528	6.4803	6.6101	6.7424	6.8771	7.0144	7.1542	7.2966	7.4416
6	6.1520	6.3081	6.4684	6.6330	6.8019	6.9753	7.1533	7.3359	7.5233	7.7156	7.9129	8.1152	8.3227	8.5355	8.7537	8.9775	9.2068	9.4420	9.6830	9.9299
7	7.2135	7.4343	7.6625	7.8983	8.1420	8.3938	8.6540	8.9228	9.2004	9.4872	9.7833	10.0890	10.4047	10.7305	11.0668	11.4139	11.7720	12.1415	12.5227	12.9159
8	8.2857	8.5830	8.8923	9.2142	9.5491	9.8975	10.2598	10.6366	11.0285	11.4359	11.8594	12.2997	12.7573	13.2328	13.7268	14.2401	14.7733	15.3270	15.9020	16.4991
9	9.3685	9.7546	10.1591	10.5828	11.0266	11.4913	11.9780	12.4876	13.0210	13.5795	14.1640	14.7757	15.4157	16.0853	16.7858	17.5185	18.2847	19.0859	19.9234	20.7989
10	10.4622	10.9497	11.4639	12.0061	12.5779	13.1808	13.8164	14.4866	15.1929	15.9374	16.7220	17.5487	18.4197	19.3373	20.3037	21.3215	22.3931	23.5213	24.7089	25.9587
11	11.5668	12.1687	12.8078	13.4864	14.2068	14.9716	15.7836	16.6455	17.5603	18.5312	19.5614	20.6546	21.8143	23.0445	24.3493	25.7329	27.1999	28.7551	30.4035	32.1504
12	12.6825	13.4121	14.1920	15.0258	15.9171	16.8699	17.8885	18.9771	20.1407	21.3843	22.7132	24.1331	25.6502	27.2707	29.0017	30.8502	32.8239	34.9311	37.1802	39.5805
13	13.8093	14.6803	15.6178	16.6268	17.7130	18.8821	20.1406	21.4953	22.9534	24.5227	26.2116	28.0291	29.9847	32.0887	34.3519	36.7862	39.4040	42.2187	45.2445	48.4966
14	14.9474	15.9739	17.0863	18.2919	19.5986	21.0151	22.5505	24.2149	26.0192	27.9750	30.0949	32.3926	34.8827	37.5811	40.5047	43.6720	47.1027	50.8180	54.8409	59.1959
15	16.0969	17.2934	18.5989	20.0236	21.5786	23.2760	25.1290	27.1521	29.3609	31.7725	34.4054	37.2797	40.4175	43.8424	47.5804	51.6595	56.1101	60.9653	66.2607	72.0351
16	17.2579	18.6393	20.1569	21.8245	23.6575	25.6725	27.8881	30.3243	33.0034	35.9497	39.1899	42.7533	46.6717	50.9804	55.7175	60.9250	66.6488	72.9390	79.8502	87.4421
17	18.4304	20.0121	21.7616	23.6975	25.8404	28.2129	30.8402	33.7502	36.9737	40.5447	44.5008	48.8837	53.7391	59.1176	65.0751	71.6730	78.9791	87.0680	96.0217	105.9306
18	19.6147	21.4123	23.4144	25.6454	28.1324	30.9057	33.9990	37.4502	41.3013	45.5992	50.3959	55.7497	61.7251	68.3941	75.8364	84.1407	93.4056	103.7403	115.2659	128.1167
19	20.8109	22.8406	25.1169	27.6712	30.5390	33.7600	37.3790	41.4463	46.0185	51.1591	56.9395	63.4397	70.7494	78.9692	88.2118	98.6032	110.2846	123.4135	138.1664	154.7400
20	22.0190	24.2974	26.8704	29.7781	33.0660	36.7856	40.9955	45.7620	51.1601	57.2750	64.2028	72.0524	80.9468	91.0249	102.4436	115.3797	130.0329	146.6280	165.4180	186.6880
21	23.2392	25.7833	28.6765	31.9692	35.7193	39.9927	44.8652	50.4229	56.7645	64.0025	72.2651	81.6987	92.4699	104.7684	118.8101	134.8405	153.1385	174.0210	197.8474	225.0256
22	24.4716	27.2990	30.5368	34.2480	38.5052	43.3923	49.0057	55.4568	62.8733	71.4027	81.2143	92.5026	105.4910	120.4360	137.6316	157.4150	180.1721	206.3448	236.4384	271.0307
23	25.7163	28.8450	32.4529	36.6179	41.4305	46.9958	53.4361	60.8933	69.5319	79.5430	91.1479	104.6029	120.2048	138.2970	159.2764	183.6014	211.8013	244.4868	282.3618	326.2368
24	26.9735	30.4219	34.4265	39.0826	44.5020	50.8156	58.1767	66.7648	76.7898	88.4973	102.1741	118.1552	136.8315	158.6586	184.1678	213.9776	248.8075	289.4945	337.0105	392.4842
25	28.2432	32.0303	36.4593	41.6459	47.7271	54.8645	63.2490	73.1059	84.7009	98.3471	114.4133	133.3339	155.6196	181.8708	212.7930	249.2140	292.1048	342.6035	402.0424	471.9811
26	29.5256	33.6709	38.5530	44.3117	51.1135	59.1564	68.6765	79.9544	93.3240	109.1818	127.9988	150.3339	176.8501	208.3327	245.7120	290.0883	342.7626	405.2721	479.4305	567.3773
27	30.8209	35.3443	40.7096	47.0842	54.6691	63.7058	74.4838	87.3508	102.7231	121.0999	143.0786	169.3740	200.8406	238.4993	283.5688	337.5024	402.0323	479.2211	571.5223	681.8527
28	32.1291	37.0512	42.9309	49.9676	58.4026	68.5281	80.6977	95.3388	112.9682	134.2099	159.8173	190.6989	227.9499	272.8892	327.1041	392.5027	471.3778	566.4808	681.1116	819.2233
29	33.4504	38.7922	45.2188	52.9663	62.3227	73.6398	87.3465	103.9659	124.1354	148.6309	178.3972	214.5827	258.5834	312.0937	377.1697	456.3032	552.5120	669.4474	811.5228	984.0679
30	34.7849	40.5681	47.5754	56.0849	66.4389	79.0582	94.4608	113.2832	136.3075	164.4940	199.0209	241.3327	293.1992	356.7868	434.7451	530.3117	647.4390	790.9479	966.7121	1181.8820
40	48.8864	60.4020	75.4013	95.0255	120.7998	154.7620	199.6351	259.0565	337.8824	442.5925	581.8260	767.0914	1013.704	1342.025	1779.090	2360.757	3134.522	4163.212	5529.829	7343.856
50	64.4632	84.5794	112.7969	152.6671	209.3480	290.3359	406.5289	573.7701	815.0834	1163.908	1668.771	2400.018	3459.507	4994.522	7217.714	10435.650	15089.500	21813.090	31515.330	45497.170

Illustrations Using Appendix A.4—Present Value of an Annuity of $1 per Period

To use this table, locate the present value factor for the time period and the interest rate.

1. You are entering a contract that will provide you an income of $1000 at the end of the year for the next 10 years. If the annual interest rate is 7 percent, what is the present value of that stream of payments?

   The present value factor is 7.024; hence the solution is $1000 x 7.024, or $7024.

2. You expect to have $250,000 available in a retirement plan upon retirement. If the amount invested yields 8 percent and you hope to live an additional 20 years, how much can you withdraw each year so that the fund will just be liquidated after 20 years?

   The present value factor for 20 years at 8 percent is 9.818. Hence the solution is $250,000 ÷ 9.818, or $25,463.

3. You have received an inheritance of $60,000 and invest that sum earning 9 percent. If you withdraw $8000 annually to supplement your income, in how many years will the fund run out?

   Solving for *n*, $60,000 ÷ $8000 = 7.5. Scan down the 9 percent column until you find the present value factor nearest 7.5, which is 7.487. This is on the row indicating 13 years; thus the fund will be depleted in approximately 13 years with $8000 annual withdrawals.

4. A seller offers to finance the sale of a building to you as an investment. The mortgage loan of $280,000 will be for 20 years and requires an annual mortgage payment of $24,000. Should you finance the purchase through the seller or borrow the funds from a financial institution at a current rate of 10 percent?

   $280,000 ÷ $24,000 = 11.667. Scan down the periods column to 20 years and then read across to locate the figure closest to 11.667, which is 11.470. This is in the column indicating 6 percent; thus, seller financing offers a lower interest rate.

5. You have the opportunity to purchase an office building for $750,000 with an expected life of 20 years. Looking over the financial details, you see that the before-tax net rental income is $90,000. Since you want a return of at least 15 percent, how much should you pay for the building?

   The present value factor for 20 years at 15 percent is 6.259, and $90,000 x 6.259 = $563,310. Thus, the price is too high for you to earn a return of 15 percent.

An alternative approach is to use a calculator to determine the present value, *PV*, of a stream of payments. The equation is

$$PV = \frac{1.0 - 1.0/(1.0 + i)^n] \times A}{i} \qquad\qquad (A.4)$$

where   *PV* = the *Present Value* of the investment
    i = the *interest* rate per period
    n = the *number* or periods the *PV* is invested
    A = the *amount* of the annuity

Appendix A.4 Present Value of a Stream of Equal payments—an Annuity—of $1 per Period (Used to compute the future value of a steam of income payments)

n	1%	2%	3%	4%	5%	6%	7%	8%	9%	10%	11%	12%	13%	14%	15%	16%	17%	18%	19%	20%
1	0.9901	0.9804	0.9709	0.9615	0.9524	0.9434	0.9346	0.9259	0.9174	0.9091	0.9009	0.8929	0.8850	0.8772	0.8696	0.8621	0.8547	0.8475	0.8403	0.8333
2	1.9704	1.9416	1.9135	1.8861	1.8594	1.8334	1.8080	1.7833	1.7591	1.7355	1.7125	1.6901	1.6681	1.6467	1.6257	1.6052	1.5852	1.5656	1.5465	1.5278
3	2.9410	2.8839	2.8286	2.7751	2.7232	2.6730	2.6243	2.5771	2.5313	2.4869	2.4437	2.4018	2.3612	2.3216	2.2832	2.2459	2.2096	2.1743	2.1399	2.1065
4	3.9020	3.8077	3.7171	3.6299	3.5460	3.4651	3.3872	3.3121	3.2397	3.1699	3.1024	3.0373	2.9745	2.9137	2.8550	2.7982	2.7432	2.6901	2.6386	2.5887
5	4.8534	4.7135	4.5797	4.4518	4.3295	4.2124	4.1002	3.9927	3.8897	3.7908	3.6959	3.6048	3.5172	3.4331	3.3522	3.2743	3.1993	3.1272	3.0576	2.9906
6	5.7955	5.6014	5.4172	5.2421	5.0757	4.9173	4.7665	4.6229	4.4859	4.3553	4.2305	4.1114	3.9975	3.8887	3.7845	3.6847	3.5892	3.4976	3.4098	3.3255
7	6.7282	6.4720	6.2303	6.0021	5.7864	5.5824	5.3893	5.2064	5.0330	4.8684	4.7122	4.5638	4.4226	4.2883	4.1604	4.0386	3.9224	3.8115	3.7057	3.6046
8	7.6517	7.3255	7.0197	6.7327	6.4632	6.2098	5.9713	5.7466	5.5348	5.3349	5.1461	4.9676	4.7988	4.6389	4.4873	4.3436	4.2072	4.0776	3.9544	3.8372
9	8.5660	8.1622	7.7861	7.4353	7.1078	6.8017	6.5152	6.2469	5.9952	5.7590	5.5370	5.3282	5.1317	4.9464	4.7716	4.6065	4.4506	4.3030	4.1633	4.0310
10	9.4713	8.9826	8.5302	8.1109	7.7217	7.3601	7.0236	6.7101	6.4177	6.1446	5.8892	5.6502	5.4262	5.2161	5.0188	4.8332	4.6586	4.4941	4.3389	4.1925
11	10.3676	9.7868	9.2526	8.7605	8.3064	7.8869	7.4987	7.1390	6.8052	6.4951	6.2065	5.9377	5.6869	5.4527	5.2337	5.0286	4.8364	4.6560	4.4865	4.3271
12	11.2551	10.5753	9.9540	9.3851	8.8633	8.3838	7.9427	7.5361	7.1607	6.8137	6.4924	6.1944	5.9176	5.6603	5.4206	5.1971	4.9884	4.7932	4.6105	4.4392
13	12.1337	11.3484	10.6350	9.9856	9.3936	8.8527	8.3577	7.9038	7.4869	7.1034	6.7499	6.4235	6.1218	5.8424	5.5831	5.3423	5.1183	4.9095	4.7147	4.5327
14	13.0037	12.1062	11.2961	10.5631	9.8986	9.2950	8.7455	8.2442	7.7862	7.3667	6.9819	6.6282	6.3025	6.0021	5.7245	5.4675	5.2293	5.0081	4.8023	4.6106
15	13.8651	12.8493	11.9379	11.1184	10.3797	9.7122	9.1079	8.5595	8.0607	7.6061	7.1909	6.8109	6.4624	6.1422	5.8474	5.5755	5.3242	5.0916	4.8759	4.6755
16	14.7179	13.5777	12.5611	11.6523	10.8378	10.1059	9.4466	8.8514	8.3126	7.8237	7.3792	6.9740	6.6039	6.2651	5.9542	5.6685	5.4053	5.1624	4.9377	4.7296
17	15.5623	14.2919	13.1661	12.1657	11.2741	10.4773	9.7632	9.1216	8.5436	8.0216	7.5488	7.1196	6.7291	6.3729	6.0472	5.7487	5.4746	5.2223	4.9897	4.7746
18	16.3983	14.9920	13.7535	12.6593	11.6896	10.8276	10.0591	9.3719	8.7556	8.2014	7.7016	7.2497	6.8399	6.4674	6.1280	5.8178	5.5339	5.2732	5.0333	4.8122
19	17.2260	15.6785	14.3238	13.1339	12.0853	11.1581	10.3356	9.6036	8.9501	8.3649	7.8393	7.3658	6.9380	6.5504	6.1982	5.8775	5.5845	5.3162	5.0700	4.8435
20	18.0456	16.3514	14.8775	13.5903	12.4622	11.4699	10.5940	9.8181	9.1285	8.5136	7.9633	7.4694	7.0248	6.6231	6.2593	5.9288	5.6278	5.3527	5.1009	4.8696
21	18.8570	17.0112	15.4150	14.0292	12.8212	11.7641	10.8355	10.0168	9.2922	8.6487	8.0751	7.5620	7.1016	6.6870	6.3125	5.9731	5.6648	5.3837	5.1268	4.8913
22	19.6604	17.6850	15.9369	14.4511	13.1630	12.0416	11.0612	10.2007	9.4424	8.7715	8.1757	7.6446	7.1695	6.7429	6.3587	6.0113	5.6964	5.4099	5.1486	4.9094
23	20.4558	18.2922	16.4436	14.8568	13.4886	12.3034	11.2722	10.3711	9.5802	8.8832	8.2664	7.7184	7.2297	6.7921	6.3988	6.0442	5.7234	5.4321	5.1668	4.9245
24	21.2434	18.9139	16.9355	15.2470	13.7986	12.5504	11.4693	10.5288	9.7066	8.9847	8.3481	7.7843	7.2829	6.8351	6.4338	6.0726	5.7465	5.4509	5.1822	4.9371
25	22.0232	19.5235	17.4131	15.6221	14.0939	12.7834	11.6536	10.6748	9.8226	9.0770	8.4217	7.8431	7.3300	6.8729	6.4641	6.0971	5.7662	5.4669	5.1951	4.9476
26	22.7952	20.1210	17.8768	15.9828	14.3752	13.0032	11.8258	10.8100	9.9290	9.1609	8.4881	7.8957	7.3717	6.9061	6.4906	6.1182	5.7831	5.4804	5.2060	4.9563
27	23.5596	20.7069	18.3270	16.3296	14.6430	13.2105	11.9867	10.9352	10.0266	9.2372	8.5478	7.9426	7.4086	6.9352	6.5135	6.1364	5.7975	5.4919	5.2151	4.9636
28	24.3164	21.2813	18.7641	16.6631	14.8981	13.4062	12.1371	11.0511	10.1161	9.3066	8.6016	7.9844	7.4412	6.9607	6.5335	6.1520	5.8099	5.5016	5.2228	4.9697
29	25.0658	21.8444	19.1885	16.9837	15.1411	13.5907	12.2777	11.1584	10.1983	9.3696	8.6501	8.0218	7.4701	6.9830	6.5509	6.1656	5.8204	5.5098	5.2292	4.9747
30	25.8077	22.3965	19.6004	17.2920	15.3725	13.7648	12.4090	11.2578	10.2737	9.4269	8.6938	8.0552	7.4957	7.0027	6.5660	6.1772	5.8294	5.5168	5.2347	4.9789
40	32.8347	27.3555	23.1148	19.7928	17.1591	15.0463	13.3317	11.9246	10.7574	9.7791	8.9511	8.2438	7.6344	7.1050	6.6418	6.2335	5.8713	5.5482	5.2582	4.9966
50	39.1961	31.4236	25.7298	21.4822	18.2559	15.7619	13.8007	12.2335	10.9617	9.9148	9.0417	8.3045	7.6752	7.1327	6.6605	6.2463	5.8801	5.5541	5.2623	4.9995

Appendix B
Estimating Social Security Benefits

The federal government's Social Security Administration (SSA) has a basic benefit credited to you for your retirement, for a period of disability, or for your survivors, provided you qualify based on the number of quarters of coverage you have earned. The level of benefits received from Social Security depends on your income in past years that was subject to Federal Insurance Contributions Act (FICA) taxes, commonly known as Social Security taxes, your age, and other criteria.

The tables that follow provide estimates of Social Security benefits for various ages, income levels, and benefit recipients. The tables are based on 1996 Social Security benefit levels, and you can estimate your own benefits by using your personal income data and age.

The figures found in the tables will be the amount of likely monthly benefits in today's dollars, assuming you have worked steadily and received pay raises equal to the U.S. average throughout your working career. To calculate a more specific figure, write to William M. Mercer, Inc., to obtain the booklet cited in the table or call the Social Security Administration for the pamphlet entitled "Estimating Your Social Security Retirement Check: Using the Indexing Method."

MONTHLY RETIREMENT BENEFITS AT AGE 65

Your Age in 1996	Who Receives Benefits	Your Present Annual Earnings				
		$12,000	$20,000	$30,000	$42,000	$57,600 and Up
65	You	$529	$728	$970	$1,066	$1,128
	Spouse* or child	$264	$364	$485	$1,533	$1,564
64	You	$522	$718	$956	$1,053	$1,118
	Spouse* or child	$261	$359	$478	$1,526	$1,559
63	You	$526	$723	$965	$1,066	$1,136
	Spouse* or child	$263	$361	$482	$1,533	$1,568
62	You	$529	$727	$970	$1,076	$1,152
	Spouse* or child	$264	$363	$485	$1,538	$1,576
61	You	$530	$729	$973	$1,082	$1,163
	Spouse* or child	$265	$364	$486	$1,541	$1,581
55	You	**$528	**$728	**$977	**$1,102	**$1,215
	Spouse*** or child	$267	$368	$494	$1,557	$1,614
50	You	**$502	**$692	**$930	**$1,062	**$1,195
	Spouse*** or child	$269	$371	$498	$1,569	$1,640
45	You	**$505	**$698	**$939	**$1,074	**$1,233
	Spouse*** or child	$271	$374	$503	$1,575	$1,660
40	You	**$509	**$703	**$943	**$1,080	**$1,255
	Spouse*** or child	$272	$377	$505	$1,578	$1,672
35	You	**$488	**$675	**$902	**$1,034	**$1,205
	Spouse*** or child	$274	$380	$507	$1,581	$1,678
30	You	**$478	**$663	**$883	**$1,013	**$1,182
	Spouse*** or child	$276	$382	$509	$1,584	$1,681

Source: Table reprinted with permission from *1996: Guide to Social Security and Medicare*, William M. Mercer, Inc., P.O. Box 35740, Louisville, Kentucky, 40202-9983.

*Benefit at age 65 or at any age with eligible child under age 16 in care.

**These amounts are reduced for retirement at age 65 because the Normal Retirement Age (NRA) is higher for these persons; the reduction factors are different for the worker and the spouse.

***The amount shown is for the spouse at NRA or caring for an eligible child (under age 16 or disabled), or for the child; the benefit for a spouse younger than NRA who does not care for an eligible child would be reduced for early retirement.

MONTHLY RETIREMENT BENEFITS AT DISABILITY

Your Age in 1996	Who Receives Benefits	Your Present Annual Earnings				
		$12,000	$20,000	$30,000	$42,000	$57,600 and Up
64	You	$521	$716	$951	$1,046	$1,105.00
	Child (or children & spouse)	$260	$358	$475	$1,523	$1,552.60
60	You	$527	$724	$962	$1,064	$1,126.00
	Child (or children & spouse)	$263	$362	$481	$1,532	$1,563.55
55	You	$527	$724	$968	$1,081	$1,154.00
	Child (or children & spouse)	$263	$362	$484	$1,540	$1,577.50
50	You	$527	$724	$970	$1,102	$1,191.00
	Child (or children & spouse)	$263	$362	$485	$1,551	$1,595.45
45	You	$527	$724	$971	$1,120	$1,228.00
	Child (or children & spouse)	$263	$362	$485	$1,560	$1,614.40
40	You	$527	$725	$971	$1,127	$1,264.00
	Child (or children & spouse)	$263	$362	$485	$1,563	$1,632.35
35	You	$528	$725	$972	$1,129	$1,293.00
	Child (or children & spouse)	$264	$362	$486	$1,564	$1,646.30
30	You	$528	$726	$973	$1,130	$1,305.00
	Child (or children & spouse)	$264	$363	$486	$1,565	$1,652.00

Source: Table reprinted with permission from *1996: Guide to Social Security and Medicare*, William M. Mercer, Inc., P.O. Box 35740, Louisville, Kentucky, 40202-9983.

MONTHLY SURVIVORS' BENEFITS IF YOU DIED IN 1996

Your Age in 1996	Who Receives Benefits	Your Present Annual Earnings				
		$12,000	$20,000	$30,000	$42,000	$57,600 and Up
65	Spouse, age 65	$529	$728	$970	$1,066	$1,128
	Spouse, age 60	$378	$1,521	$1,693	$1,762	$1,807
	Child; spouse caring for child	$397	$1,546	$1,727	$1,799	$1,846
	Maximum family benefit	$816	$1,357	$1,696	$1,865	$1,974
60	Spouse, age 65	$527	$1,724	$1,962	$1,064	$1,126
	Spouse, age 60	$377	$1,517	$1,687	$1,761	$1,805
	Child; spouse caring for child	$395	$1,543	$1,721	$1,798	$1,845
	Maximum family benefit	$809	$1,344	$1,684	$1,862	$1,971
55	Spouse, age 65	$527	$1,724	$1,968	$1,081	$1,154
	Spouse, age 60	$377	$1,517	$1,692	$1,773	$1,825
	Child; spouse caring for child	$395	$1,543	$1,726	$1,810	$1,866
	Maximum family benefit	$809	$1,344	$1,693	$1,891	$2,020
50	Spouse, age 65	$527	$1,724	$1,970	$1,102	$1,191
	Spouse, age 60	$377	$1,518	$1,694	$1,788	$1,852
	Child; spouse caring for child	$395	$1,543	$1,728	$1,826	$1,893
	Maximum family benefit	$809	$1,345	$1,698	$1,928	$2,084
45	Spouse, age 65	$527	$1,724	$1,971	$1,122	$1,236
	Spouse, age 60	$377	$1,518	$1,694	$1,802	$1,883
	Child; spouse caring for child	$395	$1,543	$1,728	$1,841	$1,927
	Maximum family benefit	$810	$1,345	$1,698	$1,962	$2,162
40	Spouse, age 65	$528	$1,725	$1,971	$1,129	$1,282
	Spouse, age 60	$377	$1,518	$1,694	$1,807	$1,916
	Child; spouse caring for child	$396	$1,543	$1,728	$1,846	$1,961
	Maximum family benefit	$810	$1,346	$1,699	$1,975	$2,243
35	Spouse, age 65	$528	$1,726	$1,973	$1,129	$1,302
	Spouse, age 60	$377	$1,519	$1,695	$1,800	$1,931
	Child; spouse caring for child	$396	$1,544	$1,729	$1,847	$1,976
	Maximum family benefit	$811	$1,349	$1,702	$1,976	$2,278
30	Spouse, age 65	$531	$1,730	$1,979	$1,134	$1,319
	Spouse, age 60	$379	$1,522	$1,700	$1,810	$1,943
	Child; spouse caring for child	$398	$1,547	$1,734	$1,850	$1,989
	Maximum family benefit	$818	$1,361	$1,713	$1,983	$2,308

Source: Table reprinted with permission from *1996: Guide to Social Security and Medicare*, William M. Mercer, Inc., P.O. Box 35740, Louisville, Kentucky, 40202-9983.